The Good Research Guide

The Good Research Guide

For small-scale social research projects

Sixth edition

Martyn Denscombe

Open University Press

Open University Press
McGraw-Hill Education
8th Floor, 338 Euston Road
London
England
NW1 3BH

email: enquiries@openup.co.uk
world wide web: www.openup.co.uk

and Two Penn Plaza, New York, NY 10121-2289, USA

First published 1998
Second edition published 2003
Third edition published 2007
Fourth edition published 2010
Fifth edition published 2014
First published in this sixth edition 2017

A catalogue record of this book is available from the British Library

ISBN-13: 978-0-335-22686-3
ISBN-10: 0-33-522686-8
eISBN: 978-0-335-22687-0

Library of Congress Cataloging-in-Publication Data
CIP data applied for

Typeset by Transforma Pvt. Ltd., Chennai, India

Printed and bound by CPI Group (UK) Ltd, Croydon, CR0 4YY

Praise page

"*Denscombe's* The Good Research Guide, *now in its 6th edition, continues to be one of the leading books in the field. It covers the topics a student or practitioner doing a research project needs to know from project design, theoretical underpinnings of research, data collection and analysis to writing up your research. Its accessible and practical approach means that it is an excellent resource for those new to undertaking independent research.*"

Liam Foster, Senior Lecturer in Social Policy and Social Work, Sheffield University, UK

"*Martyn Denscombe's text continues to remain core reading for those undertaking small pieces of research and those who need to gain a firm grounding in the principles of research theory and practice. From deciding on a research approach to the process of writing up, this finely balanced edition offers a comprehensive and detailed guide to the research cycle. Pragmatic, and with the needs of the researcher always in mind, it makes social science research accessible, undaunting, and, what's more, a completely possible, stimulating, and enjoyable endeavour.*"

Yunis Alam, Faculty of Social Sciences, University of Bradford, UK

"*The Good Research Guide* provides a comprehensive view of the complex strategies and approaches of conducting social research, explained in simple terms. Relevant examples and check lists provided in each section not only helps to gain better understanding but also reflect on one's own research.*

This book has tremendously helped me to gain knowledge and understanding of complex research strategies. It will provide clear guidance and direction for students and researchers in their research journey to achieve success."

Deborah Ebenezer, Research Student

"*I think the book has a very good précis of areas relevant to the title. It outlines very well in a logical order the elements pertinent to "social research". Each chapter is relatively comprehensive and deals with subject material that is important, in a language that is accessible throughout. It does what it says on the tin and provides practical information and guidance as a "how to" text for those needing help with this type of research project. In particular I think the checklists are an excellent chapter ending to help plan and bring into sharp focus what is needed for any particular approach. The within chapter examples are excellent and help to further inform the reader what the author is trying to convey. Chapter links help further embed concepts and show how the various research elements may be associated.*

Overall an excellent introductory text that embodies a no-nonsense approach to a subject that can be at times complex. By breaking down topic areas and giving simple examples the subject is eminently accessible to the reader. Well done!"

Stephen Pearson, Senior Lecturer in Human and
Applied Physiology, School of Health Sciences,
University of Salford, UK

"This new edition provides comprehensive guidance to those undertaking small-scale social research projects including dissertations in business and management and the social sciences and I would recommend its use for all those new to research and also to refresh the thinking of those with prior research experience. Part 1 addresses a range of strategies for social research including surveys, sampling, case studies, experiments, ethnography, the life course perspective, grounded theory, action research, phenomenology, systematic review and mixed methods. There are few texts which address research strategies in such a comprehensive manner. The text develops in Part 2 by providing clear guidance on the selection and use of appropriate methods of data collection such as questionnaires, interviews, observation and documentary analysis, taking into account the aims and objective of the research project. Part 4 considers both quantitative and qualitative data analysis with Part 4 providing essential information on research ethics, the reporting of research and on the conduct and presentation of the literature review essential to all research projects.

I have no hesitation in commending this text for use by undergraduate and post-graduate students as well as those undertaking research projects independent of an academic programme."

Dr. Bobby Mackie, Senior Lecturer, School of Business and Enterprise,
University of the West of Scotland, UK

Summary of contents

Contents

List of tables and figures

Acknowledgements

There are those close to home who contribute to the completion of a book by putting the author in a position to start, sustain and finish the book. For this reason, and many others, I would like to dedicate this book to my family.

Thanks especially to Viv – this book is for you.

Martyn Denscombe
Leicester
November 2016

Introduction

A book for 'project researchers'

Social research is no longer restricted to a small elite of professionals and full-time researchers. It has become the concern of a far greater number of people who are faced with the prospect of undertaking small-scale research projects as part of an academic course or as part of their professional development. Such people:

- need to complete the research within a relatively short time-span (perhaps within six months or less);
- do not have large sums of money available to fund the research;
- must be responsible for doing the work themselves, rather than being able to use others to help with data collection and analysis.

The aim of this book is to present these 'project researchers' with practical guidance and a vision of the key issues involved in social research. It attempts to provide them with vital information that is easily accessible and which gets to the heart of the matter quickly and concisely using straightforward language.

The book is pragmatic in its approach to social research. It does not present particular types of social research as being inherently better or worse than others but, instead, encourages project researchers to choose strategies and methods that are likely to work best in the context of the topic they are trying to investigate and the circumstances in which the research is being conducted.

Part 1

Strategies for social research

There is no single pathway to good research: there are always options and alternatives. At any stage of any enquiry researchers need to take decisions, make judgements and use discretion in order to successfully complete a project. One of the biggest decisions to be made concerns the choice of research *strategy*, and the first section of this book outlines a variety of strategies that can be used. These are not the full range of possibilities that exist because this would be beyond the scope of this book and would include strategies more appropriate for large-scale, long-term and very costly investigations. The focus, instead, is on the range of strategies that are well suited to the needs of project researchers engaged with small-scale, low-budget research being conducted over relatively short periods of time.

What are research strategies?

A strategy is a plan of action designed to achieve a specific goal. It entails a broad approach that has:

- a distinct research logic and rationale that shapes
- a plan of action (research design) to address
- a clearly identified research problem (a specific goal that can be achieved).

In the context of social research the terms 'approach' and 'methodology' are often used to mean the same thing as 'strategy'.

A research strategy is different from a research *method*. Research methods are the tools for data collection – things like questionnaires, interviews, observation and documents (which are outlined in Part 2 of this book). Methods are the equivalent of a microscope when used by a scientist, a thermometer when used by a medic, or a telescope when used by an astronomer. They do a job. They are types of equipment that allow relevant data to be collected and, reflecting this, they are often referred to as 'research tools' or 'research instruments'.

Which strategy to choose?

Is it ethical?

Research ethics are an overriding concern when it comes to the choice of strategy. It is hard to overstate the importance of research ethics in the context of contemporary social research and, for this reason, practical guidance on research ethics is provided in Chapter 18. These guidelines are based on some core principles of research ethics, the first of which is that no one should suffer harm as a result of participation in the research. The notion of 'harm' in this context is wide-ranging and it calls on the researcher to anticipate possible ways in which participants *might* suffer as a consequence of their involvement with the research. A strategy that carries too many potential ethical risks is a strategy to be avoided, and so there needs to be some form of risk assessment right at the beginning of the research when considering which strategy to use.

Is it feasible?

The choice of strategy needs to take into account certain practical aspects of conducting research. It is vital, for instance, that the researcher can get access to the kinds of people, contexts, events and documents that will be crucial for the success of the research. This might be a matter of getting the necessary authorization to contact people, enter locations or view documents. It might be a matter of getting agreement from people or organizations to collaborate with the research. Or, it might be a matter of having the resources for specialist equipment or travel to fieldwork locations. Whatever form it takes, the point is that *access to data sources* is crucial for the choice of research strategy.

Another practical consideration is the need to meet deadlines and to complete research within specified *time constraints*. Project researchers generally face deadlines for the completion of the research and it would be wrong to choose a strategy which could not possibly allow such deadlines to be met. Some strategies are relatively predictable in terms of their time span and lend themselves to fairly tight time-planning (e.g. surveys, case studies, experiments). Others are less predictable (e.g. grounded theory) or tend to take a relatively long time (e.g. ethnography). This must be taken into account in terms of the feasibility of using specific strategies.

Is it suitable?

In themselves, research strategies are neither 'good' nor 'bad', nor are they 'right' or 'wrong'. It is only in relation to how they are used that they take on the mantle of being good or bad, right or wrong. They can only be judged in relation to the purpose for which they are used and, reflecting this point, it is better to think of strategies in terms of how *useful* they are and how *appropriate* they are. Thought of in this pragmatic way, the justification for the choice of any specific strategy must depend on having a clear vision of the particular *purpose* for which it is being used. Unless we know what the research is trying to achieve, it is impossible to judge whether it is likely to be useful or appropriate. Table P1.1 indicates how the research strategies outlined in Part 1 can be valuable for different kinds of research purpose, and this should provide some initial guidance on the question of whether a particular strategy is suitable for the kind of research that is envisaged.

Table P1.1   Research strategies and research purpose: some links

Strategy	Purpose of research
Surveys and sampling	• measure some aspect of a social phenomenon or trend • gather facts in order to test a theory
Case studies	• understand the complex relationship between factors as they operate within a particular social setting
Experiments	• identify the cause of something • observe the influence of specific factors
Ethnography	• describe cultural practices and traditions • interpret social interaction within a culture
Life-course perspective	• focus on age and stages of life • look at periods of time in people's lives
Grounded theory	• clarify concepts or produce new theories • explore a new topic and provide new insights
Action research	• solve a practical problem • produce guidelines for best practice
Phenomenology	• describe the essence of specific types of personal experience • understand things through the eyes of someone else
Systematic reviews	• get an objective overview of evidence on a specific topic • evaluate the effectiveness of projects or interventions
Mixed methods	• evaluate a new policy and gauge its impact • compare alternative perspectives on a phenomenon • combine aspects of the other strategies

 Key point: The choice of strategy is a matter of 'horses for courses'

The researcher should choose a strategy that is likely to be successful in achieving the aims of the research, and be able to justify the choice of this strategy clearly and explicitly.

Quantitative research or qualitative research

As part of their decision about which strategy to use, project researchers need to consider whether to conduct quantitative research or qualitative research (or combine both, see Chapter 11). The terms 'quantitative research' and 'qualitative research' are widely used and commonly understood within social research communities, and they have come to represent contrasting alternatives that signify distinct, some would even say incompatible, approaches to research. Initially, the contrast concerns the *different kinds of data* that they use and the implications of this are explored in Chapters 16 and 17. In a nutshell, the distinction between the approaches centres on the fact that:

- quantitative research uses *numbers* as the unit of analysis;
- qualitative research uses *words or visual images* as the unit of analysis.

The terms are also associated with visions about the *size of the investigation* that is required. Quantitative research tends to favour larger-scale research with larger numbers and greater quantities. The larger the numbers involved, the more the results are likely to be generalizable and reliable, statistically speaking. By contrast, qualitative research tends to involve relatively few people or events. This reflects the preference for depth of study and detailed description which only becomes possible in relation to limited numbers. Qualitative researchers like to be 'close to the data' and like to have a detailed familiarity with the data in order to conduct the analysis. Their preference for small-scale studies also reflects the fact that words do not lend themselves to the kind of analysis that can utilize the power of computers in the same way that numbers do. For the qualitative researcher there *is* a vast difference in the time it takes to analyse results from larger amounts of data compared with smaller amounts. For these reasons:

- quantitative research tends to be associated with *large-scale* studies;
- qualitative research tends to be associated with *small-scale* studies.

The terms quantitative research and qualitative research also imply a distinction in terms of the *breadth of focus* of an investigation. In the case of quantitative research there is a tendency to focus on specific variables and to study them, if not in isolation, at least with reference to a limited range of other variables. Qualitative research, on the other hand, generally exhibits a preference for seeing things 'in context' and for stressing the importance of multiple interrelationships among a wide range of factors in operation at any one time in the setting. Qualitative research tends to operate on the assumption that '[social] realities are wholes that cannot be understood in isolation from their contexts, nor can they be fragmented for separate study of their parts' (Lincoln and Guba 1985: 39). As a generalization, then:

- quantitative research tends to be associated with analysing *specific variables*;
- qualitative research tends to be associated with a *holistic perspective*.

The notions of quantitative and qualitative research carry with them an image of contrasting approaches to *research design*. Quantitative research tends to be associated with precise research designs in which the process of analysis is clearly separated from the process of data collection. At the beginning the research questions or hypotheses are carefully formulated. After this comes the process of data collection which usually involves a predetermined sample to be collected or experimental procedure to be undertaken. Then there comes the data analysis stage in which the data that have been previously collected are subjected to statistical tests or other quantitative analysis. In contrast with this, qualitative research tends to be linked with the idea that research questions should not, and cannot, be specified precisely in advance of the data collection stage. Nor can data analysis be hived off to a period after the data collection has been completed. As exemplified by the grounded theory approach (see Chapter 7) this style of qualitative research sees the formulation of the research question, the collection of data and the analysis of data as an emerging and iterative process. In effect, the analysis commences at the earliest stage of research and continues throughout the whole time of the investigation. The distinction, then, revolves around the way that:

- quantitative research tends to be associated with data analysis *after* data collection;
- qualitative research tends to be associated with data analysis *during* data collection.

Finally, quantitative and qualitative research represent contrasting visions of the *role of the researcher*. Quantitative research is associated with the production of numerical data that are 'objective' in the sense that they exist independently of the researcher and are not the result of undue influence on the part of the researcher. Ideally, the numerical data are seen as the product of research instruments that have been tested for validity and reliability to ensure that the data accurately reflect the event itself, not the researcher's preferences. Qualitative research, by contrast, tends to place emphasis on the role of the researcher in the construction of the data. There is typically little use of standardized research instruments in qualitative research. Rather, it is recognized that the researcher is the crucial 'measurement device' and that the researcher's background, values, identity and beliefs might have a significant bearing on the nature of the data collected and the analysis of that data. In essence, this means that:

- quantitative research tends to be associated with researcher *detachment*;
- qualitative research tends to be associated with researcher *involvement*.

Paradigms of research

When choosing whether to use a quantitative or a qualitative approach (or combine both), project researchers might take some guidance from the particular *research community* within which they are working. Different subject areas and disciplines tend to operate within different *paradigms of research*, each having a different model of best practice when it comes to conducting research. Broadly speaking there are two such 'paradigms': these are commonly known as the *positivist* paradigm and the *interpretivist* paradigm. Quantitative research tends to be linked with positivism and qualitative research tends to be associated with interpretivism. This division is far from watertight but it continues to work as an initial assumption about the respective stances of quantitative and qualitative research.

Positivism

The positivist paradigm applies the natural science model of research to investigations of the social world. Social reality is treated in a similar way to physical reality as something that exists independently 'out there' with properties that can be studied scientifically. This allows the researcher to adopt an objective, detached approach to the study of social phenomena. The focus is generally on facts and figures relating to the causes and consequences of phenomena in the social world, and the approach tends to be associated with the use of quantitative data and statistics.

Interpretivism

The interpretivist paradigm, by contrast, is primarily concerned with developing insights into people's beliefs and their lived experiences through the use of qualitative data (text and images). The social world is regarded as a nuanced, multi-layered phenomenon whose complexity is best understood through a process of interpretation. The paradigm is generally sceptical about the prospects of achieving objectivity, arguing that researchers' thinking will inevitably be shaped to some extent by their own experiences and identities as members of the social world within which their research takes place.

In practice, of course, social research does not slot neatly into one or other paradigm and the two-paradigm depiction of research in the social sciences provides an over-simplified model of things. However, the distinction between positivist and interpretivist paradigms serves to capture broad notions about different styles of research and their underlying assumptions, and continues to be used widely in the context of discussions about the choice of research strategies. Project researchers need to be aware of this. In particular, those who need to conduct a small-scale piece of research as part of an academic qualification might be advised to make their choice of strategy bearing in mind the traditions of their own specific discipline and the predispositions of the people who are going to evaluate their research – their tutors and examiners.

Key point: Research communities can influence the choice of strategy

Different research communities have different traditions and preferences when it comes to the choice of research strategies.

Checklist for the choice of research strategy

When choosing a research strategy, you should feel confident about answering 'yes' to the following questions: ☑

Ethics
Will it allow me to be ethical in my dealings with participants?

- Can I avoid any harm to participants resulting from their involvement in the research? ☐
- Can I get informed consent from potential participants? ☐
- Will the strategy permit me to work within an appropriate code of research ethics? ☐
- Can I guarantee the confidentiality of the information given to me during the research? ☐

Feasibility
Can it be done?

- Is there sufficient time for the design of the research, collection of data and analysis of results? ☐
- Are sufficient resources available to cover the costs of the research (e.g. travel, printing)? ☐
- Is it possible and practical to gain access to necessary data (people, events, documents)? ☐

Suitability
Will it produce appropriate kinds of data?

- Has the purpose of the research been clearly identified? ☐
- Is there a clear link between the purpose of the research and the chosen strategy? ☐
- Will the strategy produce findings that can answer the research question(s)? ☐

Paradigm
Does it meet the expectations of my research community?

- Will the chosen strategy be favoured by those who will evaluate my research? ☐
- Will the choice of research approach (quantitative/qualitative/mixed methods) accord with the preferences of my research community? ☐

© M. Denscombe, *The Good Research Guide*. Open University Press.

1 Surveys

Surveys can take a number of forms. In social research the most common of these are the kind that attempt to ask people questions. Using the phone, the Internet, the postal service or face-to-face contact, their aim is to make contact with suitable respondents in order to obtain information from those people. Questionnaires and interviews are the data collection methods that are normally used.

Surveys can also involve the observation of behaviour and they can involve the analysis of documents. These type of survey, however, are less commonly used in small-scale social research and, for this reason, the focus of this chapter will be on those types of survey that *ask people questions*.

What is a survey?

When something is surveyed, it is 'viewed comprehensively'. This is clear in the case of geographical surveys, engineering surveys and ordnance surveys which map out the landscape or the built environment of roads and buildings. The principles, though, have been used to good effect on mapping out the social world as well and, indeed, surveys have emerged in recent times as one of the most popular approaches to social research. *Social* surveys tend to share with their physical counterparts three key characteristics. These are:

- *Empirical research.* Because 'to survey' carries with it the meaning 'to look', survey work inevitably brings with it the idea of empirical research. It involves the idea of purposefully seeking the necessary information from relevant people and relevant sites.

- *At a specific point in time.* Surveys are generally used to provide a snapshot of how things are rather than tracing events over a period of time. In most cases this is useful for 'bringing things up to date' and providing information about the current state of affairs. Although it is possible to use surveys as the basis for tracking changes over a period of time, this is relatively uncommon in the realms of small-scale research projects.
- *Wide and inclusive coverage.* In order to view things comprehensively surveys try to get a panoramic view of the situation and strive for wide and inclusive coverage of the people or things being investigated. The aim is to cast the net wide to include the whole range of relevant people (or things).

These characteristics of the survey approach include no mention of specific research methods. This is because *surveys are a research strategy* and, as such, they can be used with a variety of data collection methods – including questionnaires, interviews, documents and observation.

> **Social surveys can be used for research into things like:**
> - consumer preferences and customer satisfaction;
> - voting behaviour (opinion polls);
> - health-related behaviour, diet, smoking and alcohol consumption;
> - evaluation of innovations, programmes and educational courses;
> - television viewing and audience ratings.

Types of survey

Surveys differ in terms of the *techniques* they use to communicate with respondents: postal services, telephone networks, the Internet and face-to-face contact, each providing an alternative means for contacting people and obtaining data from them (see Table 1.1).

Postal surveys

Distributing a survey through the post used to be the most efficient and effective way of conducting a large-scale survey covering a wide geographical area. The postal network provided the researcher with the means for sending out self-completion questionnaires to a particular research population who could be identified through their names or addresses. Participants could then return the completed questionnaire, encouraged possibly by receiving a stamped envelope with the researcher's address on it. The process was fairly simple, straightforward and relatively cheap. It remains a viable and often used mode of distributing surveys today.

Table 1.1   Techniques of survey distribution

Type of survey	Technique used for distribution	Method of data collection
Postal	Mail	Questionnaire
Face to face	Personal	Interview
	Group	Questionnaire
Telephone	Landline	Interview
	Mobile	Questionnaire
Internet	Email	Interview
	Web based	Questionnaire
Social network	Facebook	Questionnaire
	Twitter	Questionnaire

However, three things need to be borne in mind when considering the use of a postal survey. First, there is the cost. The printing, packing and postage costs can quickly mount up, particularly with larger surveys. Providing stamped addressed envelopes for the return of questionnaires, for instance, can double the postage costs. Project researchers with limited resources need to think carefully about the costs involved. Second, there is the time delay. Planning and preparation take time, as they do with all research, but there are specific delays that stem from the turnround time involved with posting and returning questionnaires as part of a postal survey. In practice, the data collection is likely to take a number of weeks to complete even after the questionnaires have been posted out. Third, there is the response rate. The proportion of people who respond to postal surveys, as is often the case with surveys, tends to be quite low.

Face-to-face surveys

Face-to-face surveys involve direct contact between the researcher and individual respondents, and typically make use of questionnaires or interviews as the data collection method. The most easily recognized version of this kind of survey sees the researcher approaching people 'in the street' to ask if they will participate in the research. The sight of the market researcher with her clipboard and smile is familiar in town centres and shopping malls. Alternatively, the contact can be made by calling at people's homes. Sometimes this will be 'on spec' to see if the householder is willing and able to spare the time to help with the research. On other occasions, contact will be arranged in advance by letter or phone.

Either way, the face-to-face survey is a more expensive way of collecting data than the use of the post, Internet or telephone. Researcher time and travel costs are considerable. Weighed against this there is the prospect of probing beneath the surface to get a bit more depth to the information that is obtained. Plus, this kind of survey with its face-to-face contact offers some immediate means of validating the data. The researcher can sense if she is being given false information in the face-to-face context in a way that is not possible with questionnaires and less feasible with telephone surveys. And, with this kind of survey response rates pose less of a problem. Partly this is because the face-

Link up with
Quota
sampling,
p. 41.

to-face contact allows the researcher to use his/her interpersonal skills and powers of persuasion to encourage the potential respondent to take part in the survey. Partly it is because with face-to-face surveys the researcher can continue making contacts until he/she has accumulated the total number of responses that are required.

Group-administered surveys

Like individual face-to-face surveys, group-administered surveys are conducted in person. They rely on the researcher travelling to a specific site to distribute and collect the research instrument – normally a questionnaire. But, unlike face-to-face surveys, the data are collected from groups rather than individuals. Normally, these groups already exist. Rather than get a group of people together specifically for the purpose, it is easier from the researcher's point of view to use naturally occurring groups. For example, a survey of young people could involve the distribution of questionnaires in schools to whole classes – possibly 30 or more people at a time. The same approach could be taken with work groups, community meetings or any occasions where there will be a (naturally occurring) collection of people who are suitable for the purposes of the research.

This approach does not really lend itself to use with thousands of people at a time. For practical purposes the group-administered survey tends to work best with fairly small numbers. In this context it is relatively easy to organize and can often draw on the researcher's personal knowledge about the context of the research. In terms of turnround time this form of survey has advantages because the questionnaires are generally distributed, completed and returned

Link up with
Cluster
sampling,
p. 37.

in one process. Also, the personal, face-to-face contact means that response rates tend to be considerably higher than with postal, Internet or phone surveys. However, group-administered surveys are quite labour intensive and, depending on the locations for research, can incur significant travel costs.

Telephone surveys

Telephone surveys tend to be used mainly in conjunction with one-to-one interviews and they have become a well-established alternative to postal or face-to-face surveys. One reason for this is that the evidence would suggest people are as honest and open on the telephone as they are when answering postal questionnaires or being interviewed face to face. Another reason is that conducting surveys via the telephone can have particular benefits in terms of time and costs. Researchers do not have to travel to all parts of the country to conduct the interviews – they only have to pick up a telephone – and there are no significant delays with the return of data using a telephone survey because the responses are instantaneous. Local and national calls on landlines are not generally expensive, nor do calls to mobile phones need to incur significant costs. And the use of Skype, Facetime or similar software provides the survey researcher with a means for making international calls via the Internet virtually free of cost. They also enable the interviewer to have visual face-to-face contact on screen with the interviewee.

Telephone surveys, like postal surveys, can target particular geographical areas. Researchers can select the area they wish to survey and identify the relevant dialling code for that area. They can then contact telephone numbers at random within that area using *random-digit dialling*, where the final digits of the phone numbers are produced by computer technology which automatically generates numbers at random. Mobile phone numbers, however, are not allocated by geographical location (in the UK), which means that researchers cannot use prior knowledge about the geographical location of any mobile phone user as the basis for including them in a survey. As people come to use 'cell phones' instead of – not just in addition to – conventional landline telephones, this will pose something of a challenge for telephone surveys in terms of reaching a representative sample of the population.

Mobile phones, none the less, have introduced a new dimension to telephone surveys: they have enabled surveys to be conducted using Short Message Service (SMS) text questions and answers. In effect, they allow researchers to conduct questionnaire surveys (as distinct from the interview surveys associated with landline telephones). Such surveys need to keep things simple and short, and they are well suited to occasions when information is needed instantly by way of feedback from a situation. This could be an audience response to a performance, customer evaluation of a product or service, or some snap opinion poll on a matter 'of the moment'. Participants send their responses to a designated SMS text address – usually a short sequence of numbers.

Smartphones massively extend the range of possibilities for telephone surveys. Surveys designed for smartphones and tablets can include images and multimedia features that can make responding to a survey more interesting and more fun. Such surveys can also retrieve details about the location of respondents using the Global Positioning System (GPS).

Internet surveys

Internet surveys are an enticing for project researchers because they:

- *save time* – there are no delays involved in delivering questions or receiving answers;
- *save money* – online surveys eliminate the costs of printing, packaging and posting associated with postal surveys;

- *speed up data processing* – there is less burden in terms of data entry. Data can be downloaded directly without the need to transcribe text data or the manual entry of quantitative data into data files;
- *allow wide geographical coverage* – surveys are not restricted to particular localities. Online surveys can be national or international in scope with no additional burden in terms of the time or money needed to reach distant participants;
- *provide an environmentally friendly approach to conducting research* – online surveys reduce the need for paper and eliminate the need to travel. In these respects they save trees and avoid pollution.

Added to this, there is little evidence that respondents provide significantly different kinds of answer or supply different amounts of information as a consequence of the online data collection method (Denscombe 2006, 2008, 2009; Sue and Ritter 2012; Tourangeau et al. 2013).

There are three main ways in which surveys can be conducted using the Internet. The first of these involves direct contact through *emails*. Potential respondents can be contacted by email and, if they agree to cooperate with the research, they can be sent a set of questions. If the questions are all sent within one message then it constitutes an email questionnaire. If an initial question sets in train a dialogue between the researcher and the respondent contained in a series of messages then it becomes an email interview. There is not too much to go wrong using this approach. It is a simple, cheap and fast way to collect data.

A second possibility is to tap into online groups and social networks that already exist on the Internet, making use of instant messaging or forums that exist on the Internet, such as chat rooms or discussion groups.

A third option is to conduct a *web-based questionnaire survey*. This is the most widely used form of Internet survey. Its popularity stems from the availability of computer programs specifically designed for creating and distributing online questionnaires, and the fact that social researchers can gain access to this for little or no cost through online survey companies or computing facilities within their own organization.

Fears have been voiced about low response rates from Internet surveys, caused through people feeling ill at ease using computers or not having ready access to the Internet. As time progresses, though, the evidence would suggest that such anxieties are largely unfounded (Sue and Ritter 2012). Indeed, direct comparisons between different survey modes (postal, email, web-based) indicates that, generally speaking, there is now little difference in response rates between postal mail surveys and web-based surveys (Hoonakker and Carayon 2009).

Social network surveys

Social network sites (SNS) such as Facebook, Twitter, LinkedIn, Google+ and Instagram offer an alternative means of distributing social surveys (Wilson et al. 2012). They exploit new technologies to provide a fast and free method for researchers to make contact with potential participants. In particular, social network sites enable the researcher to make contact with people who have some *shared interest* or some shared identity via networks based on 'friends' or 'groups' or 'followers'.

Social network sites are very useful for researchers because they provide a way of targeting groups of people who have something in common – something of interest to the researcher. There is a ready-made 'research population' (see below) with whom it is relatively easy to make contact. It also helps when it comes to making contact with people who would normally be hard to identify and locate. Using their own personal networks, individuals can open up contact with other potential respondents who would not otherwise have been discovered by the researcher, rapidly expanding access to 'hard-to-find' research populations through a process of 'snowballing'.

Link up with Snowball sampling, p. 43.

 Key point

'Social networking sites and online questionnaires make it possible to do survey research faster, cheaper, and with less assistance than ever before. The methods are especially well-suited for snowball sampling of elusive sub-populations' (Brickman-Bhutta 2012: 57).

There are, however, two main limitations to the use of social network sites for surveys which are worth bearing in mind. The first is that it is difficult to get a cross-section of people using existing networks. This is because (1) the networks based on 'friends' or 'groups' or 'followers' are self-selecting (based on specific interests or identity) and (2) the main users of social network sites do not constitute a full cross-section of the population in terms of age and sex (Couper 2011; Smith 2013).

A second limitation stems from the *social* nature of such sites and the effect this might have on the honesty of answers that are given to any survey questions. This poses the question: 'Will respondents be more inclined to provide "socially acceptable" answers as they are conscious of the fact that the views they express might be visible to others on the network?' And, for the same reason, might they be more reluctant to divulge personal facts or attitudes that they worry will be regarded as 'bad' by friends or others using the SNS? The answer to this lies in ensuring that SNS users' responses are kept private and are never communicated via a public forum. Although the invitation to participate can legitimately make use of the public areas on the site, any subsequent contact needs to be done on a one-to-one basis as private messaging, and it is vital that potential respondents realize this.

The research population

When conducting any kind of survey, researchers need to be clear about the kind of people, events or items that will be relevant for the study and likely to provide valuable data in terms of the topic that is being investigated. It is worth noting that in this context the term 'population' has a specific meaning. Rather than meaning everyone who lives in a country, population refers to all the items in the category of things that are being researched. It means a *research* population. So, if a survey is used to study nurses in Scotland then the survey population refers to all nurses working in Scotland (not all the people who populate Scotland). Likewise, if the research involves a survey of trade union members in the transport industry in Wales then the term 'population' refers to all the transport workers in Wales who belong to a trade union.

Making contact with members of the research population

Whether the researcher wants to include all of the population in the survey or, as discussed in Chapter 2, a sample drawn from the population, the survey cannot begin without having planned some way of making contact with members of the research population. This shifts the emphasis from the question of 'who' to the matter of 'how', as it requires the researcher to think ahead about the practical task of establishing contact with potential participants in the survey or gaining access to suitable events or items. The survey researcher, in effect, needs 'contact points' for the research population. In practice, these tend to come in the form of lists of names, addresses, locations, membership numbers, job titles, schedules of events, inventories of items, etc. that allow the researcher to identify how members of the research population can be found. Examples of such information include:

- a list of *postal addresses* (e.g. for businesses in a particular industry);
- a list of *names* (e.g. of local residents based on an electoral register);
- *suitable locations* for finding particular kinds of people (e.g. shopping malls to find retail customers);
- a list of *email addresses* (e.g. for employees of a company, or clients for a service);
- *telephone numbers* from a directory (e.g. for people or companies in a specific area);
- *online groups* (e.g. for special interest groups or particular kinds of people).

Link up with
Sampling
frames, p. 35.

Participation by the research population

The willingness and ability of the research population to participate in the survey is something that can never be taken for granted. When planning a survey, careful thought needs to be given to the matter: what is the likelihood that those people identified as potential participants will agree to co-operate with the research? Much will depend on things like:

- the kind of people involved (e.g. busy or not busy);
- the capacity of the people invited to participate (language, literacy, age, vulnerable groups);
- the topic of the survey;
- the context in which the survey is delivered (when, where);
- the mode of delivery of the survey (face-to-face, Internet, post, telephone).

The *consequences* of participation also warrant consideration. At the planning stage for a survey it is essential that thought is given to the question of whether participation in the survey might in any way harm members of the research population, cause them stress or unduly inconvenience them. Researchers, in other words, must consider the ethics of inviting people to participate in their survey.

> **Link up with** Chapter 18, Research ethics.

Response rates

The extent to which a survey is successful in getting replies from those who were originally contacted is known as 'the response rate'. When planning a survey it is important to anticipate the likely response rate and take this into consideration when deciding on the numbers who will be contacted and asked to collaborate with the research. If you think you might get a 40 per cent response rate and you need 200 completed questionnaires on which to base your analysis, then clearly you will need to distribute 500 questionnaires – a considerably larger number.

There is no benchmark figure for judging what is an acceptable response rate and what is not. There is simply no hard and fast rule on the matter. It all depends on the circumstances. A large postal survey sent 'cold' without prior notification to households will get a low response rate – in all likelihood it would be far less than 10 per cent. A survey sent on behalf of a club or association to its members using a membership list is likely to achieve a far higher response rate – possibly over 70 per cent. A survey using face-to-face interviews arranged by personal contact between the researcher and the interviewees is likely to get a very high response rate – possibly up to 100 per cent. So much depends on who is contacted, how they are contacted and what they are contacted about.

Bearing these things in mind, rather than look for a universal benchmark figure for surveys above which response rates are acceptable and below which the results become suspect, it is more productive to gauge whether the response rate is acceptable by making a comparison with *similar* surveys. It is the response rates achieved by surveys that are similar in terms of their methods, their size, their target group, their topic of research, their use of prior contact and other relevant factors that provide an indication of what can be treated as an acceptable response rate.

> **Good practice**
> Look at the response rates achieved by similar types of survey. Use these as your target.

How to achieve good response rates

Survey researchers need to incorporate measures that will encourage people to participate in the survey and, just as importantly, avoid things that are likely to deter people from responding. There is no magic formula that will guarantee a good response rate, but the following factors have been found to have a significant bearing on response rates and they ought to be considered carefully when planning a small-scale survey.

Target appropriate people for the survey: respondent selection

A good response rate depends on using an accurate population list/sampling frame. A scatter-gun approach will cover a large number of potential respondents but many of these will not respond because the topic is not relevant to them. Also, if they do respond, the data from them might not be pertinent to the topic of the research. The more a survey can identify and locate relevant people (or items), the better the response rate is likely to be.

Follow up non-responses: reminders

The classic way to boost response rates is to 'follow up' non-responses and the standard advice for survey researchers is that they should build into the survey design some tactics for re-contacting anyone who does not respond on the first occasion. Measures should also be taken to repeat the reminder two or three times if needed. There is clear evidence that this boosts response rates in all kinds of surveys (Dillman et al. 2009).

Having said that, there are two issues linked with improving overall response rates through follow-ups which need to be borne in mind. First, there is the time delay caused by the process. When surveys are conducted under strict time constraints, as with much small-scale research, this can pose something of a dilemma. Second, there is the matter of anonymity. If questionnaire responses are completely anonymous and it is not possible to trace the questionnaires back to individual respondents, then it will not be possible to work out who has responded and who has not. Targeting individual non-respondents becomes impossible.

Give prior notification: invitations in advance

Consistently across the range of types of survey it has been found that prior notification is beneficial in terms of response rates. When potential respondents are made aware of the survey in advance there is more chance of them agreeing to participate in the survey. This applies whether the contact is made by post, email or in person. With online surveys, having access to a list of email addresses that can be used to pre-notify people in advance is beneficial in terms of boosting response rates.

Make the topic of interest to respondents: topic salience

Response rates are better when the topic has 'salience'. This means that the topic has to capture the attention of potential respondents. Literally, it has to stand out and be conspicuous. A survey of people belonging to a specific interest group, of course, should have no problem on this score since those involved will have been targeted exactly because of their (known) interest in the topic. In any surveys where such a matching of interests cannot be guaranteed, the onus is on researchers to do all they can to *make* the topic interesting. They need to present the topic in a way that is upbeat, enthusiastic and positive – doing all they can to *get* the respondent interested in the topic.

Show that participation will 'make a difference': response impact

People are more motivated to participate in a survey if they feel that their contribution can have some influence and might actually 'make a difference' – especially when there is some direct, personal benefit to be gained from agreeing to participate. Bearing this in mind, survey researchers should indicate (when it is possible) how taking part in the survey might be in the respondents' interests. If at all possible, they should let potential respondents know how their answers will be valuable, and how their contribution to the survey can have an effect on something in which they have a vested interest. So, for example, potential respondents could be encouraged to participate by knowing that the information they provide will be used to improve the quality of a particular service they receive or product they buy.

Establish the legitimacy of the survey: sponsorship

Response rates are likely to increase to the extent that the survey is regarded as legitimate research. Early in the contact with potential respondents the researcher needs to establish that the survey is for a worthy cause and that it is being conducted under the auspices of a credible organization. There needs to be a basis for *trust*. For small-scale research projects, especially those conducted as part of a university degree, this means that it is important to assure potential respondents that the survey is part of a genuine research project and that it will be properly conducted. The name of the university, assurances of confidentiality, and contact details for the researcher give the potential respondent some confidence that the survey is legitimate and, therefore, something that deserves attention.

Minimize the response burden: keep things simple and easy

Asking someone to take part in a survey involves asking for their time and effort. The amount of this 'response burden' can be a major deterrent to participating in a survey. If too much is asked of respondents then response rates will plummet as people fail to finish the questionnaire, put down the telephone or delete the message in frustration and annoyance. Recognizing this point, the task for the survey researcher is to *minimize the response burden* by including only those items that are absolutely essential and taking care to ask the questions in a way that keeps things as easy and straightforward as possible.

Provide information about progress towards completion

Many people who start an interview or questionnaire fail to complete it. They stop through frustration and exasperation at the amount of time and effort being asked of them. Such drop-outs obviously reduce the response rate and survey researchers need to do what they can to prevent this happening. One way of tackling the problem is to be clear and open at the outset about the amount of time that participation is likely to take. When considering whether to become involved in the research, people quite reasonably will want to know: how long will the interview take? How many pages are there in the questionnaire? It is good practice, therefore, to *let people know in advance how much of their time will be needed.*

During the process of completing the interview or questionnaire, people might also want to know: how much *more*? With a paper questionnaire people can see what needs to be done and can easily monitor their progress through the questionnaire. With online questionnaires, however, the 'finishing line' might not be so obvious and *using a 'progress bar' has been shown to be an effective way of improving response rates* – letting people know how far they have got, and how far they still have to go before completing the questionnaire. In the course of an interview, similarly, it might be wise to verbally reassure the respondent about how far they have progressed and how much is still left to do.

Provide incentives: rewards or feedback

Material incentives can increase response rates. Quite separate from any motivation stemming from the topic itself or the impact that the findings might have, the prospect of material rewards can serve to encourage people to take part in a survey. Market research companies using postal surveys might include a small amount of money as a 'token of thanks'. Online surveys can reward respondents with shopping tokens and vouchers of various kinds. Also, the promise of inclusion in a prize draw for a large cash prize or a free holiday can be effective with most kinds of survey, but such *material* incentives cost money – lots of it. Consequently, they tend to be used with large-scale commercial research projects where sponsors and clients pick up the bill. *Small-scale researchers cannot normally call on the funding necessary to use this as an effective method of increasing response rates.*

What small-scale, low-budget research *can* offer by way of incentives is *feedback*. Respondents can be motivated by offering them copies of the final report or summaries of the findings arising from the investigation. That is, they can be offered information rather than material rewards – information which stems directly from their participation in the project and which they may find useful and/or interesting. The offer of such feedback, whether it is taken up or not, is a nice gesture and one which signals that the researcher would like to offer something in return to the respondent.

Good practice: Plan ahead to minimize non-response rates

Remember, response rates are affected by:

- the amount of spare time people have;
- the extent to which the survey caters for respondents' abilities;
- social sensitivities around the topic being investigated;
- prejudices and preferences of potential respondents;
- the social climate and freedom to express views.

Non-response bias

Response rates are important because if a survey has a low response rate, then its findings will miss data from those who have chosen not to respond. At one level this will be disappointing for the survey researcher since fewer responses means less data. However, it is not simply the sheer *amount* of potential data that is lost which worries researchers; it is the fear that a (low) response rate can lead to something called *non-response bias*. This bias occurs when there is a pattern to the responses in which it becomes clear that those who have not completed the survey tend to be different from those who have. If this happens, the findings from the survey will systematically over-represent data collected from the people who are more likely to respond and, by the same token, systematically under-represent data for those who are less likely to respond. This is likely to have a direct bearing on how fair and objective the survey's findings will be.

There are two sources of non-response bias. The first of these is *non-contact* bias. If the survey is designed in such a way that it *systematically* favours the inclusion of some types of people (or items) at the expense of others, then a bias will result. An example of this would be if a survey involved researchers calling at home addresses to conduct interviews with residents, and the researchers made their visits between 9 a.m. and 5 p.m. This would tend to miss contact with households where everyone is at work during the day. To avoid this, they would need to make contact in the evenings as well as during the day.

A second cause of bias is *non-response through refusal*. In this case if the design of the survey serves to discourage people from responding and does so in a way that systematically deters certain types of people rather than others, then a non-response bias will occur. The social factors that affect response rates, identified above, are significant in this context because different types of people will be more likely to opt out of a survey depending on things like the nature of the topic, the burden of participating in the survey and the amount of time they have to spare.

Non-response bias and Internet surveys

Internet surveys can suffer three sources of non-response bias. First, they can systematically exclude those who cannot get access to the Internet either because of where they live or because they cannot afford it. In this instance poorer populations and disadvantaged groups are likely to be under-represented among survey respondents. Second, responses to Internet surveys are more likely to come from those who are regular users of the Internet, leaving infrequent and casual users of the Internet under-represented among survey respondents. Third, there is a potential for non-response bias arising through a process of self-selection among respondents. That is, those who participate in a survey might be representative not of the general public but just of those who are online and interested in a particular subject. This is particularly the case with web-based surveys that rely on responses from visitors to a specific website (where the link to the research questionnaire is located), but the point applies equally to surveys that use chat rooms, news groups or any other interest group.

Checking for non-response bias

When conducting a survey the researcher needs to ask an important question: *do the non-respondents differ in any systematic and relevant fashion from those who have responded?* Of course, to answer this question the researcher needs to have some information about those who have been targeted but not responded. This may prove difficult. None the less, it is good practice to endeavour to get some data about the non-respondents and to assess whether they are different from the respondents in any way that will have a bearing on the findings. For instance, are they different in terms of:

- who they are? (e.g. age, sex, gender, social class, religion, opinions)
- what they believe? (e.g. opinions, political views)
- what they do? (e.g. activities, lifestyles, purchasing behaviour)

> **Good practice**
> Researchers should take what practical measures are possible to find out if respondents are different from non-respondents in some way that is relevant to the survey and which might result in a non-response bias.

Weighting the findings

If it appears that the survey has an imbalance in terms of the type of people who have responded and those who have not responded, there is a solution; that is, to 'weight' the findings. It is worth stressing that this mathematical technique tends to be associated with large-scale surveys and is not normally a technique that should be applied to small-scale research. It is used where the researchers have firm evidence about the proportions of respondents they would *expect* to find included in their survey. So, for example, if an omnibus survey of consumer attitudes obtains 5,000 responses, of which 20 per cent come from the under-25 age range, and if national figures for the population indicate that this age group actually makes up 30 per cent of the population, researchers can mathematically boost this group's impact on the overall findings from 20 per cent to 30 per cent – reflecting what would have been the case had the survey been representative of the population. The other age ranges would also have their impact brought in line with the proportions known to exist in the wider population.

Which type of survey to choose?

When deciding which type of survey to use, researchers need to appreciate that each of the different types of survey brings with it certain possibilities and certain limitations. The choice should be based on what works best in relation to the particular research project, bearing in mind:

- the *objectives* of the research, and whether this is to get data from a representative cross-section of people or whether it is to focus on particular kinds of people who are likely to have a special knowledge about the topic of the research;
- the *resources* available to fund the survey, and the constraints this puts on decisions about the size of the research population, the size of any sample that might be used (see Chapter 2, Sampling), the number of weeks or months required to complete the survey, and the facilities (equipment, software) that can be used;
- the *geographical area* to be covered by the survey, and whether participants are dispersed across widely scattered locations;
- the *methods* of data collection to be used in the survey, and whether there is a preference for questionnaires or interviews;

- the *speed* of responses, and any urgency that surrounds the collection of responses from participants;
- the *response rate*, and the amount of pressure there is to minimize the time and effort it takes to respond to the survey – the 'response burden' – so that busy people are not deterred from participating;
- the *contact* with potential participants, and the extent to which it is necessary to have a ready-made list or directory that researchers can use to select potential participants for inclusion in the survey;
- the need for *face-to-face contact*, and the extent to which the research will benefit from the 'personal touch'. Direct contact can be important for engaging with participants, establishing rapport and gaining trust. It also helps the researcher to informally assess the validity of the responses being given and it allows the researcher to provide instant clarification on points if the participant is unsure;
- the need for *indirect contact*, and the way that remote and impersonal contact (e.g. using Internet surveys, postal surveys, self-completion questionnaires) can encourage people's willingness to answer openly and honestly when questions touch on things where there are particular social sensitivities (e.g. racism, sexism, homophobia, politics, religion);
- the *abilities/disabilities* of the respondents, and their capacity to complete the survey. If the type of survey includes forms some people cannot fill in, screens that some people cannot read or voices that some cannot hear, then obviously the survey will suffer. This is not just a practical matter of increasing response rates. There is a larger ethical issue here concerned with *social inclusion* and the need to ensure that certain groups are not disadvantaged through exclusion from participation in the survey;
- the *validity* of the answers, and the need to avoid the '*social desirability*' factor where the respondent might be more inclined to provide answers which he/she feels are the expected ones, the correct ones or ones which put him/her in a better light.

 Key point

'The major development of the twenty-first century, so far, is recognition that the use of all survey modes continues, and none seem likely to disappear. Each has strengths and weaknesses, allowing it to do things other modes cannot do' (Dillman et al. 2009: 495).

Web-based surveys: some practical guidelines

Which online survey package to use?

There are a number of online survey companies who cater for the needs of small-scale researchers by offering low-budget packages (e.g. SurveyMonkey). Entry-level packages (with restricted functionality) are generally offered for free. These are 'taster' packages that allow you to explore the software and get the feel for what is on offer. In practice, though, with the kind of surveys associated for instance with master's degrees and PhDs, it is likely that you will feel the need to upgrade to the next tariff. When comparing alternatives it is worth checking whether the particular tariff offers:

- a monthly sign-up period – you want to be able opt out as soon as the project is finished;
- reasonable measures to protect the security and privacy of data held on the server;
- a facility to download your survey data.

It is also advisable to check on any restrictions associated with the specific tariff with respect to:

- the number of respondents (e.g. 50, 100, 1,000);
- the number of questions allowed for each questionnaire;
- limits to the time span allowed for the survey (e.g. 1 week);
- limits on the number of times your data can be accessed or downloaded.

Many researchers will have access to the survey software they need because they are members of organizations (universities, health service organizations, local authorities, government agencies, charities and large commercial businesses) which either have their own software for conducting online surveys or have a licence to use the survey facilities offered by companies who specialize in providing online survey services. If this is the case, then it makes sense to use what is already available. The chances are that there will be no charges for using the survey software, and there is likely to be technical help on hand if it is needed.

Designing the questionnaire

The attraction of web-based questionnaires is that they can include a number of useful features that cannot be incorporated into paper questionnaires. They can also include images and background designs that make them visually attractive, and online survey companies usually provide templates and examples that help with the design of a good questionnaire. Particular features of online questionnaires that are worth incorporating include:

- prevention of multiple responses. You need to prevent the accidental duplication of responses from one person or the malicious 'ballot-box stuffing' from anyone determined to fix the results of the survey;
- inclusion of a progress bar to show respondents how far they are through the questionnaire;
- the use of drop-down menus and alternative question layouts;
- the forced completion of vital questions.

Distributing the questionnaire

Once the questionnaire has been designed the next stage is to start the survey by distributing the questionnaire. Online survey companies offer a variety of options including potentially expensive ways of attracting people to the survey through publicity and advertising – for example, paying for 'pop-ups' on a website or a link via a social networking site. They will also offer access to a 'survey panel' – a list of suitable people who volunteer to take part in such surveys and have been recruited on the basis of previous responses – but they will charge a fee for this.

With small-scale research, operating on a very limited budget, researchers generally prefer to do the work themselves rather than buying a ready-made distribution list from the online survey company. They identify potential participants and devise their own bespoke distribution list based on:

- a list of email addresses; or
- a list of mobile phone numbers; or
- social network friends and followers.

When the web survey is based on inviting specific people to participate, it is important to keep things simple and straightforward. To help with this the survey software provides a *unique web address* (a uniform resource locator, URL) giving direct access to the questionnaire. This is the web address that anyone answering the questionnaire will visit. When inviting people to participate in the survey it is good practice to put this web address in the message in the form of a hyperlink. All the person needs to do is click on the link to be taken directly to the questionnaire. Alternatively, it is possible to get a link to the survey via a QR code. Anyone with a smartphone or tablet (and with a suitable 'Quick Response' code application) will be able to access the survey by using their smartphone or tablet to read the 'Quick Response' (QR) barcode.

> **Good practice: Passwords**
> Restrict access to the survey by using a password. Ensure that only people who have been given the password can answer the questionnaire.

Retrieving the data

The answers from each questionnaire are automatically transferred into a data file and the *combined data* from all the completed questionnaires can be viewed online. The results can be viewed in the form of graphs, which is useful. It is also possible to look at the results for *each individual questionnaire*. As well as listing the answers to each question, it is possible to see additional information about each questionnaire – things like how long it took to complete and exactly when it was submitted. Depending on the tariff, there is the possibility of respondent tracking. This allows the researcher to see who needs to be contacted as a follow-up to remind them to complete the questionnaire.

Findings from the survey can be exported – and this is really useful. The benefits of being able to download the data directly into an Excel spreadsheet or statistics package are significant. It means that rather than the data being located on the remote server, the researcher can 'take possession' of it, have it on his/her own computer, to process and analyse as desired. However, this facility tends to come 'at a price', often requiring the researcher to upgrade from a free package to a subscription package.

Facebook surveys: an example

An example of how Facebook contacts can be used for surveys is provided by Brickman-Bhutta's (2012) research. Her aim was to make contact with Catholics who had ceased to actively practise their faith and who no longer attended church. This research population represented a classic 'hard-to-contact' group. But Facebook provided a means for getting the contact. She set up her own group, 'Please Help Me Find Baptized Catholics!'. The purpose of the group was explained on the group website and people were invited to sign up to the group. They were also asked to invite any of their 'friends' who were 'ex-Catholics' to join. After a month, when the group was established, she sent members of the group a link to her online questionnaire and, in this way, obtained a good number of responses from a research population for which there was no obvious list of contacts obtainable through other means. Next, she contacted the administrators of other Catholic groups on Facebook to try to enlist their help. Some administrators were helpful, others less so. The response rate from these groups was quite low, reflecting the fact that in many cases people sign up to a group on the spur of the moment and never, or hardly ever, return to the site at a later date. So, as a third measure she contacted her own network of 'friends' to cast the net as wide as possible. Overall, her approach worked well. In her words (Brickman-Bhutta 2012: 58):

> Within five days of releasing a 12-minute online survey to a Facebook group of potential volunteers, I harvested 2,788 completed questionnaires. Within a month, the total number of respondents increased to about 4,000. Total monetary costs averaged less than one cent (per questionnaire) – vastly less than the cost of surveys obtained through mail, phone, or even email.

Advantages of surveys

Costs and time

Surveys can be an efficient and relatively inexpensive means of collecting data. In the case of small-scale surveys the researcher's time might be the only significant cost involved and, although large-scale surveys can involve substantial costs, compared with strategies such as experiments and ethnography, they can produce a mountain of data in a short time for a relatively low cost. Results can be obtained over a fairly short period of time and the researcher can set a finite time span for this, which is very useful when it comes to planning the research and delivering the end product.

'Real-world' data

As an approach to social research, the emphasis tends to be on producing data based on real-world observations. The very notion of a survey suggests that the research has involved an active attempt by the researcher to go out and look and to search. Surveys are associated with getting information 'straight from the horse's mouth'.

Can collect both quantitative and qualitative data

The survey approach lends itself to being used with particular methods, such as the self-completion questionnaire, which can generate large volumes of quantitative data that can be subject to statistical analysis. However, surveys can just as easily produce qualitative data, particularly when used in conjunction with methods such as an interview.

Disadvantages of surveys

Tendency to focus on data accumulation and data description

With its emphasis on collecting empirical data there is a danger that the 'data are left to speak for themselves' without an adequate account of the implications of those data for relevant issues, problems or theories. There is nothing inevitable about this, however, and *good* survey research certainly does devote attention to the analysis of data.

Depth or detail

Data produced through surveys might lack depth and detail on the topic being investigated. Surveys tend to forfeit depth in favour of breadth when it comes to data that are produced, especially where quantitative data are used. This is not inevitable, though. Qualitative surveys using interview methods can produce data that are rich and detailed, although in this case the trade-off is that the number of people taking part in the survey will be much smaller.

Low response rates

Response rates from surveys are often quite low and getting a reasonable response rate can be quite a challenge for the researcher. This is particularly the case with large-scale surveys where potential participants are selected at random and where the researcher has no personal contact with the potential participants. It is easy to ignore a researcher's request for help that comes through the post or via email. Where selection to a survey involves personal contact the response rates tend to be higher. Low response rates can lead to non-response bias in the survey.

Contact with 'hard-to-reach' research populations

Surveys are easier to use when the research population can be identified and contacted through some pre-existing listing or directory. Where the research population cannot be located through such means – when they are 'hard-to-reach' – survey researchers need to use more time-consuming and possibly innovative means for contacting potential participants.

Further reading

Blair, J., Czaja, R.F. and Blair, E.A. (2014) *Designing Surveys: A Guide to Decisions and Procedures*, 3rd edn. Thousand Oaks, CA: Sage.

Callegaro, M., Lozar Manfreda, K. and Vehovar, V. (2015) *Web Survey Methodology*. London: Sage.

De Vaus, D. (2014) *Surveys in Social Research*, 6th edn. London: Routledge.

Dillman, D.A., Smyth, J.D. and Christian, L.M. (2014) *Internet, Phone, Mail, and Mixed-mode Surveys: The Tailored Design Method*, 4th edn. Hoboken, NJ: Wiley.

Schonlau, M., Fricker, R. and Elliot, M. (2002) *Conducting Research Surveys via E-mail and the Web*. Rand Monograph MR-1480-RC. Available at: http://www.rand.org/pubs/monograph_reports/MR1480.html.

Sue, V.M. and Ritter, L.A. (2012) *Conducting Online Surveys*. Thousand Oaks, CA: Sage.

Checklist for the use of surveys

When conducting a survey you should feel confident about answering 'yes' to the following questions: ☑

1 Has a specific research population been clearly identified? ☐

2 Is the type of survey being used suitable for making contact with the particular research population? ☐

3 Does a contact list of potential participants exist that can be used to distribute the survey (e.g. list of email addresses, list of employees' names)? ☐

4 Is the type of survey being used feasible in terms of time and costs involved? ☐

5 Will potential participants have the time and motivation to complete the survey? ☐

6 Are suitable measures in place to minimize non-responses and to achieve the best possible response rate? ☐

7 Will potential participants receive prior notification about the survey? ☐

8 Will follow-ups be used to bolster the response rate? ☐

9 Have efforts been made to avoid response bias and, where possible, have checks been made to see if there are significant differences between the respondents and the non-respondents? ☐

10 Will a pilot survey be conducted to check for potential problems? ☐

2 Sampling

The use of sampling involves a strategic decision by the researcher to focus on some, rather than all, of a research population. The basic principle of sampling is that it is possible to produce accurate findings without the need to collect data from each and every member of a research population. This can be an attractive proposition because it offers potential savings in terms of time and money. Sampling can be used in conjunction with other approaches to social research such as experiments, ethnography and grounded theory. In the context of small-scale social research, however, the use of sampling is most prominent in relation to surveys. For this reason, the principles and practices of sampling covered in this chapter are outlined in relation to social surveys, the premise being that these principles and practices can be adapted when necessary for use with other social research strategies.

> **Link up with**
> Research
> populations,
> p. 18.

Representative samples and exploratory samples

When a sample is selected from a research population it is done for one of two reasons. The aim will be to get either a *representative* sample or to get an *exploratory* sample. Each involves a different approach and they tend to be associated with different kinds of social research.

Representative samples tend to be associated with larger surveys and with the use of quantitative data. A representative sample involves a cross-section of the population. It matches the population in terms of its mix of ingredients, and relies on using a selection procedure that:

- includes all relevant factors/variables/events;
- matches the proportions in the overall population.

Information gathered from a representative sample allows the researcher to draw valid conclusions about how things are in the overall research population.

Exploratory samples are often used in small-scale research and tend to lend themselves to the use of qualitative data. An exploratory sample is used as a way of probing relatively unexplored topics and as a route to the discovery of new ideas or theories. The point of the sample is to provide the researcher with a means for generating insights and information. For this purpose it is not always necessary to get an accurate cross-section of the population. There are times when this might be the case, but selection to an exploratory sample is more likely to include interesting, extreme and unusual examples that can illuminate the thing being studied.

Good practice

Researchers need to be very clear and explicit about whether their intention is to use a *representative* sample or an *exploratory* sample.

Sample selection: probability and non-probability sampling

Echoing in many respects the alternative purposes for which social researchers might use sampling, there are two distinct approaches which can be used for the *selection* of samples. Researchers can either choose *probability sampling* as the basis for selecting their sample from the research population, or they can use *non-probability sampling*.

Probability sampling relies on the use of random selection from the research population. It is known as probability sampling because it is based on statistical theory relating to the 'normal distribution' of events. The theory behind its use is that the best way to get a *representative sample* is to ensure that the researcher has absolutely no influence on the selection of people/ items to be included in the sample. The sample, instead, should be based on completely *random* selection from among the population being studied. Probability sampling works best with large numbers, where there is a known population (number, characteristics) and it tends to be associated with large-scale surveys using quantitative data.

Non-probability sampling involves an element of discretion or choice on the part of the researcher at some point in the selection process and it is used when researchers find it difficult or undesirable to rely on random selection to the sample. The reasons for this are varied but, in the main, they will be because:

- The researcher feels it is not feasible to include a sufficiently large number of examples in the study.
- The researcher does not have sufficient information about the *research population* to undertake probability sampling. The researcher may not know who, or how many people or events, make up the research population.
- It may prove exceedingly difficult to contact a sample selected through conventional probability sampling techniques. For example, research on drug addicts or the homeless would not lend itself to normal forms of probability sampling.

Non-probability sampling can still retain the aim of generating a *representative sample*. In the interests of saving costs, however, the selection of the sample involves an element of expediency and established good practice rather than strict adherence to the principles of random selection. Equally, non-probability sampling can be used where the aim is to produce *an exploratory sample* rather than a representative cross-section of the population. Such approaches involve non-probability sampling because people or items are selected for the sample on the basis of things like their expertise, their experience or the fact that they might be unusual or different from the norm (Table 2.1).

Table 2.1 Approaches to sampling

Probability	Random selection	Representative sample	larger numbers
Non-probability	Researcher-influenced selection	Representative sample or exploratory sample	↑ ↓ smaller numbers

Sampling frames

A sampling frame provides a basis for selecting potential participants from within a larger research population. It is particularly important when researchers intend to use probability sampling, but can also be valuable for non-probability sampling as well. A sampling frame contains information about the *research population*. Generally it takes the form of a list of names or addresses that includes all of the members of the population from which the sample is to be selected. Sometimes a suitable sampling frame can be easy to find. Research that involves formal organizations can often draw on things like membership lists, email addresses and employee records to provide a suitable sampling frame that includes all members of the population to be researched. The information is already kept for other administrative purposes. Research involving particular industries and occupations can find that things like trade directories, commercial

Link up with
Research
populations,
p. 18.

listings and memberships of professional associations provide suitable sampling frames. And, surveys targeting the
general public might be able to use electoral registers or the
Postcode Address File (PAF) – a list of postcodes and postal
addresses produced by the Post Office which contains about
99 per cent of all private residential addresses.

 Key point

A good sampling frame should be:

- *relevant:* it should contain things directly linked to the research topic;
- *complete:* it should cover all relevant items;
- *precise:* it should exclude all the items that are not relevant;
- *up to date:* it should incorporate recent additions and changes, and
  have redundant items cleansed from the list.

Probability sampling techniques

Random sampling: each person has an equal chance of being selected

Random sampling is often portrayed as the ideal basis for generating a representative sample. This is because with random sampling the inclusion of a
person in the sample is based entirely on chance. Random selection ensures
that there is no scope for the researcher to influence the sample in some way
that will introduce bias.

It is important to appreciate that the term 'random', as used in this context,
does not mean that selection can be haphazard or based on an 'any one will do'
approach. Also, it is a dangerous mistake for the project researcher to use
the term 'random' in a loose or colloquial way when dealing with sampling
techniques. For research purposes the term 'random' actually involves quite
specific constraints on the way that persons get selected. From a statistical
point of view randomness means that 'each unit should have an equal and
known probability of inclusion in the sample'.

To get a random sample there needs to be:

1 A *known population* from which the sample is to be taken. The researcher
   needs to know something about the make-up of the overall population from
   which the sample is to be extracted (such as the total number, who they are
   or where they exist).
2 A *sampling frame* that provides a list of all the items in the population and
   which allows them to be picked via some unique identifier (such as a name,
   an address, an employee number or a birth date).
3 A process of random selection which provides the basis for including specific units in the sample.

For research purposes this can involve the use of a *random number generator* – a utility available free online or through appropriate computer software packages.

Key point
A random sample is like a lottery draw. The underlying principle is that no person can influence which items get picked. The selection is based on just one factor - *pure chance.*

Systematic sampling: every *n*th case is included

Systematic sampling adheres closely to the principle of random selection but, in this case, the researcher selects items in a systematic way – picking every *n*th item from an appropriate list. For a sample of 50 from a population of 250 it will be every 5th item, for a sample of 70 from a population of 490 it will be every 7th item – *n*th depending on the size of the required sample relative to the number in the research population. It should not matter where on the list the selection starts. The researcher, however, will want to feel sure that there is no order or pattern in the list that might be related to the topic being investigated because this could undermine the principle of random selection and cause some bias to creep into the sample as a result of the system of selection.

Cluster sampling: clusters within the population

Rather than using random sampling to select individual people or items, cluster sampling uses random sampling to select specific clusters or groups. Within each of the clusters all people/items are included in the sample. The advantage of this sampling technique is that the clusters, as the name suggests, contain items that are closely grouped together – normally in one location or in one geographical area. By focusing on such clusters, the researcher can save a great deal of time and money that would otherwise have been spent on travelling to and fro visiting research sites scattered throughout the length and breadth of the land. For this reason cluster sampling is often used by market researchers and others who need to conduct surveys on a limited budget.

There are, however, two important conditions that need to be met for the use of cluster sampling. First, the clusters must be pre-existing, naturally occurring groups. Second, each cluster should reflect the heterogeneity of the total population. The idea is that within each cluster the researcher might expect to find a mini-version of the total population and that by including all members of the cluster within the sample, the researcher will be able to get a representative sample that will produce findings that accurately match the situation in the total research population.

Multi-stage sampling: samples drawn from samples

Multi-stage sampling involves selecting samples in a sequence of stages, each sample being drawn from within the previously selected sample. The underlying principle is still one of random selection, only in this case it involves sampling at multiple stages rather than all at once. In principle, multi-stage sampling can go on through any number of levels, each level involving a sample drawn from the previous level.

The distinction between multi-stage sampling and cluster sampling is that cluster sampling uses all the items or people that exist within each cluster whereas multi-stage sampling selects a sample from within the selected group. This is particularly useful if: (1) the researcher suspects that the population within the chosen clusters will not provide a cross-section of the wider population or (2) if resources dictate that it is too expensive to include everyone in the cluster.

Stratified sampling: sampling based on subgroups in the population

Stratified sampling continues to adhere to the underlying principle of random selection. However, it introduces some element of researcher influence into the selection process and, to this extent, moves away slightly from pure random sampling. Stratified sampling subdivides the research population into different subgroups (strata) and then chooses the required number of items or people from within each subgroup using random sampling techniques. The reason for introducing stratification into the selection process is to ensure that crucial parts of the population are appropriately represented in the overall sample. It allows the researcher to select a sample which he/she knows will include, for instance, equal numbers of men and women, or perhaps an appropriate balance of different age groups within the sample. There are two important conditions that apply to the use of stratified sampling. First, the subgroups must be fairly homogeneous in the sense that they share something in common which can be used to separate them into clearly identifiable subgroups. Second, this factor must be relevant and significant in terms of what is already known about the topic.

Example 2.1

Probability sampling techniques

Table 2.2 illustrates how different probability sampling techniques can operate. The numbers involved are small which, for the purposes of an illustration, is actually quite useful because it highlights some of the problems that can arise when probability sampling is used with small sample sizes. In practice, however, the size of the samples would need to be considerably larger to allow the probability samples to produce sufficiently accurate results.

In this illustration the research population consists of 27 people. Let us presume that they are members of a football supporters' club and that we wish to select a sample of 9 people to take part in our research (and bear

Table 2.2 Illustration of four probability sampling techniques

Sampling frame								Segregated sampling frame		
List no.	Name	Location	Sex	Random	Systematic	Cluster	Stratified	List no.	Sex	Name
001	Ahmed	A	M	•			•	001	M	Ahmed
002	Ashton	F	M	•				002	M	Ashton
003	Bernbaum	C	M		•			003	M	Bernbaum
004	Bradford	E	F	•				005	M	Chang
005	Chang	B	M					006	M	Davies
006	Davies	A	M		•	•		009	M	Ewusie
007	Diego	H	F			•		012	M	Goldberg
008	Duval	E	F			•		013	M	Gupta
009	Ewusie	I	M		•		•	015	M	Jones
010	Fleur	A	F					017	M	Mars
011	Gerhardt	I	F				•	018	M	Merton
012	Goldberg	D	M		•		•	019	M	O'Reilly
013	Gupta	B	M			•	•	020	M	Overton
014	Johnson	G	F	•		•		021	M	Rahman
015	Jones	B	M	•	•	•		023	M	Silva
016	Kheidr	I	F			•		024	M	Tunstall
017	Marsh	D	M					026	M	Webber
018	Merton	G	M		•			027	M	Williams
019	O'Reilly	H	M	•				004	F	Bradford
020	Overton	C	M	•				007	F	Diego
021	Rahman	G	M		•	•		008	F	Duval
022	Robinson	C	F					010	F	Fleur
023	Silva	E	M	•			•	011	F	Gerhardt
024	Tunstall	F	M		•		•	014	F	Johnson
025	Waterman	F	F			•	•	016	F	Kheidr
026	Webber	H	M					022	F	Robinson
027	Williams	D	M		•			025	F	Waterman

in mind that, in reality, the numbers might be one hundred times greater than this miniature illustration). The *sampling frame* consists of a list of members' names. These are ordered alphabetically, and each name has been assigned a number. In principle, this is sufficient for us to produce either a pure random sample or a systematic random sample. The sampling frame contains two further bits of information about the members – location and sex. These permit the use of cluster sampling and stratified sampling.

A *random sample* can be selected using random number generating software. Simple utilities for this can be found on the Internet, or they come as part of standard data analysis software. Such software can be used to generate a list of 9 numbers between values 1 and 27. Those whose names are matched with these numbers on the list are then selected to form the random sample. Note that in the example shown in Table 2.2 the randomly selected sample consists of 7 males and 2 females (the ratio in the research population is 18:9). Running the random number generator again will produce a different sample and, in all probability, a different balance of males to females. This effect is exaggerated by the very small numbers involved but as the sample size increases towards 1,000 or more the difference caused by using different random numbers would vastly diminish.

A *systematic sample* can be produced simply by selecting every third person on the list. This will provide the researcher with 9 people who have been selected simply by chance in terms of where they happen to appear on the list. This presumes, of course, that there is nothing in the order of the list that could bias the sample. Note that in this particular systematic sample there are 9 males and 0 females. However, if the start point is changed the proportions change dramatically. Check how the balance changes when we start the systematic selection at number 001 (3 males, 6 females) or number 002 (6 males, 3 females) instead.

For a *cluster sample* the selection is based on the random selection of 3 clusters and the inclusion of all those within the cluster as part of the sample. In this illustration the cluster is based on location. If locations B, H and I happen to be randomly selected, the sample will incorporate the 9 people who exist in these locations. The assumption here is that location itself is not a significant factor that could bias the sample.

A *stratified sample* is designed to ensure that there is an appropriate representation of the population within the overall sample. In this illustration a stratified sample could be used to ensure that males and females are represented proportionately in the sample. We know from our sampling frame that there is a ratio of 2:1 of males to females in our population (the football supporters' club members). To get a stratified sample we need to segregate the membership list according to sex. This is how the sampling frame is reorganized on the right of the table – males separated from females. Then, 6 random numbers can be generated for selecting from the list of males and 3 random numbers likewise for selecting from the list of females. In this way the researcher guarantees to get a sample where appropriate proportions have been randomly selected from within specific strata of the membership of the football supporters' club.

Non-probability sampling techniques

Quota sampling: selected to meet specific criteria

Quota sampling is widely used in market research. It operates on very similar principles to stratified sampling. It establishes certain categories (or strata) which are considered to be vital for inclusion in the sample, and also seeks to fill these categories in proportion to their existence in the population. There is, though, one distinctive difference between stratified and quota sampling. With quota sampling, the method of choosing the people or events that make up the required number within each category is not a matter of strict random selection. In effect, it is left up to the researcher to choose who fills the quota. It might be on a 'first to hand' basis – as when market researchers stop people in the street. The people might be appropriate but were chosen because they just happened to be there, not as part of a random selection from a known population. The technical difference here excites statisticians but need not trouble the project researcher too much. The crucial point is that, like stratified sampling, it has the advantage of ensuring the representation of all crucial categories in the sample in proportion to their existence in the wider population. It does so without waste. Because the quotas are set in advance, no people or events that subsequently become 'surplus to requirements' are incorporated into the research. Quota sampling, then, has particular advantages when it comes to costs – especially when used with face-to-face interviewing.

Example 2.2

Quota sampling

Stores in a shopping mall might want to know what their customers think about the facilities that are available (e.g. parking, toilets, restaurants) and whether there are any particular features of the mall that attract them to visit it. A quota sample for face-to-face interviews in the mall could be devised on the basis of including 200 males and 200 females, and within each group there could be a quota of 40 in each of five age categories 12–18, 19–30, 31–45, 46–64, 65+. The quotas for interview, then, would be 40 males aged 12–18, 40 females aged 12–18, 40 males aged 19–30, 40 females aged 19–30, and so on. Interviewers would approach appropriate shoppers and continue to conduct interviews until they had filled the quota for each subgroup.

Purposive sampling: hand-picked for the topic

Purposive sampling operates on the principle that we can get the best information through focusing on a relatively small number of instances deliberately selected on the basis of their known attributes (i.e. not through random selection). With purposive sampling the sample is 'hand-picked' for the research on the basis of:

- *relevance:* to the issue/theory being investigated;
- *knowledge:* privileged knowledge or experience about the topic.

Purposive sampling works where the researcher already knows something about the specific people or events and deliberately selects particular ones because they are seen as instances that are likely to produce the most valuable data. They are selected with a specific purpose in mind, and that purpose reflects the particular qualities of the people or events chosen and their relevance to the topic of the investigation.

A purposive sample can be used in order to ensure that a wide cross-section of items or people are included in the sample. When used in this way purposive sampling is, to a degree, emulating a 'representative sample'. Based on prior knowledge, the researcher can deliberately select the sample in order to ensure that the full range of items or people is included (e.g. all age groups, all ethnic groups). This can be useful with small-scale surveys where random sampling of itself might not be likely enough to include groups that occur in relatively small numbers in the population.

Purposive sampling, however, is particularly well suited for creating an 'exploratory sample'. It provides a way of getting the best information by selecting people most likely to have the experience or expertise to provide quality information and valuable insights on the research topic. It allows the researcher to home in on people or events which there are good grounds for believing will be critical for the research. These might be extreme cases, rare cases or critical cases rather than ordinary ones. Miles et al. (2014) call such special instances 'outliers', and commend their inclusion in the process of discovery as a check which explores rival possible explanations and tests any explanation based on mainstream findings, by seeing if they can work with instances which are distinctly *not* mainstream.

Example 2.3

Purposive sampling for key informants
A study of online banking fraud might start by identifying some individuals who play key roles in the detection and prevention of such fraud. Major high street banks have specialist teams dedicated to online security and the researcher could make contact with these teams to arrange interviews. Victims of online banking fraud could be sought to provide their particular perspective, and the researcher might even try to include fraudsters themselves to get even more insight to the topic.

Theoretical sampling: selected to help generate theories

With theoretical sampling the selection of participants follows a route of discovery based on the development of a theory which is 'grounded' in evidence. At each stage, new evidence is used to modify or confirm a 'theory', which then points to an appropriate choice of instances for research in the next phase. The sample evolves, and it continues to grow until such time as the researcher has sufficient information in relation to the theory that is being developed.

Link up with Chapter 7, Grounded theory.

> **Example 2.4**
>
> **Theoretical sampling**
>
> A study of teachers' control of classrooms in secondary schools might involve observation in classrooms and in-depth interviews with teachers. From early fieldwork the researcher could be alerted to the particular significance of noise emanating from classrooms as an indicator of (lack of) control. Building on this, theoretical sampling would involve choosing further observations and interviews deliberately to make comparisons and to check the initial 'theory' – perhaps looking for instances where noise might not be likely to signify a lack of control (e.g. music lessons or PE lessons).

Snowball sampling: participants refer the researcher on to other potential participants

With snowball sampling the sample emerges through a process of reference from one person to the next. At the start, the research is likely to involve just one or a few people. Each can be asked to nominate some other people who would be relevant for the purposes of the research. These nominations are then contacted and, it is hoped, included in the sample. The sample thus snowballs in size as each of the nominees is asked, in turn, to nominate further persons who might be included in the sample.

Snowball sampling is an effective technique for building up a reasonable-sized sample, especially when used as part of a small-scale research project. One advantage is that the accumulation of numbers is quite quick, using the multiplier effect of one person nominating two or more others. Added to this, the researcher can approach each new person, having been, in a sense, sponsored by the person who had named him/her. The researcher can use the nominator as some kind of reference to enhance his/her bona fides and credibility, rather than approach the new person cold. Snowball sampling is particularly useful where there is no sampling frame of any kind which can allow the researcher to identify and make contact with appropriate participants. For this reason, it is often used in conjunction with qualitative research based on small-scale exploratory samples, and its use is perfectly compatible with purposive sampling and theoretical sampling. People can be asked to nominate others who meet certain criteria for choice, certain conditions related to the research project and certain characteristics such as age, sex, ethnicity, qualifications, residence, state of health or leisure pursuits.

> **Link up with**
> Facebook
> surveys,
> p. 29.

> **Example 2.5**
>
> **Snowball sampling**
>
> A study of smoking cessation among 'under-age' smokers could use snowball sampling to good advantage. There is no sampling frame for such people and there is no obvious or simple way to identify such people. So, the

researcher could make enquiries until one such person is found. This person is likely to know of others his/her age who have started smoking and subsequently quit before they reached the age of 16. Assuming the young person is willing to cooperate, he/she could be asked to identify two others who have quit smoking. In turn, these two could be asked to identify others who fit the needs of the sample, and so on. This process builds a sample that snowballs in size.

Convenience sampling: first to hand

Convenience sampling is built upon selections which suit the convenience of the researcher and which are 'first to hand'. An element of convenience is likely to enter into sampling procedures of most research. Because researchers have limited money and limited time at their disposal, it is quite reasonable that where there is scope for choice between two or more equally valid possibilities for inclusion in the sample, the researcher should choose the most convenient. If, for example, two or more clusters are equally suitable as research sites, it would be crazy to opt for ones that were the furthest away without some good reason to do so. Convenience sampling, however, takes this to an extreme by using convenience as the main basis for selecting the sample, not a subsidiary one. The criterion for selection to the sample is that items are convenient and the key advantage of convenience sampling is that it is quick, cheap and easy.

Example 2.6

Convenience sampling

A student who wishes to conduct a survey into consumer preferences in relation to soft drinks might choose all the fellow students on the course to be the 'sample'. They are easy to find and can probably be persuaded fairly easily to complete a questionnaire on the subject. Alternatively, using face-to-face interviews, the student could collect data from students using the canteen. Those who are interviewed will constitute a 'convenience sample'.

 Caution

Convenience itself offers nothing by way of justification for the inclusion of people or events in a sample. It might be a reasonable practical criterion to apply when faced with equally viable alternatives but, in its own right, is not a factor that should be used by researchers to select the sample. Choosing things on the basis of convenience runs counter to the rigour of scientific research. It suggests a lazy approach to the work. Good research selects its items for study not on the basis that they are the *easiest* to obtain but for specific reasons linked to the subject matter of the research and the requirements of the investigation. For this reason, *the practice of convenience sampling is hard to equate with good research.*

Size of the sample

There are basically three approaches to the calculation of the sample size: statistical, pragmatic and cumulative. The statistical approach is usually presented as the 'proper' approach. As we shall see, however, it is best suited to large-scale surveys and probability sampling techniques. It is the kind of approach that works well for things like opinion polls and government surveys which involve very large populations and which cost a lot of money. Smaller-scale surveys tend to use a more pragmatic approach. This is partly to do with the costs and partly to do with the difficulties in meeting all the conditions needed for the statistical approach to sample-size calculation. Market researchers often use a pragmatic approach, estimating the sample size on the basis of years of practical experience and on what works well enough within given resource constraints. The third approach is normally associated with small-scale, qualitative research. The cumulative approach is one in which the researcher continues to add to the size of the sample until a point is reached where there is sufficient information and where no benefit is derived from adding any more to the sample.

The statistical approach: large-scale surveys using probability sampling for a representative sample

If the survey is large-scale and it uses probability sampling there is a precise way of calculating the required sample size. This is based on statistical theory and the *normal curve* distribution of events. Without getting involved too heavily in statistical theory the calculation of an appropriate sample size will depend on four things:

- The *size* of the research population. It is important to appreciate, though, that population size is significant where smaller numbers are concerned but, as Table 2.3 indicates, when the population moves beyond 5,000, changes in the size of the population cease to have much impact on the sample size.
- The *accuracy* of the estimates. Social researchers need to feel confident that their estimates lie close to the real (i.e. population) figure and they will normally tolerate a margin of error of 3 per cent or 5 per cent. The margin of error that is deemed acceptable for a specific project is known as the *confidence interval*.
- *Confidence* that the sample will produce results that are representative of the population. This is the *level of confidence*. Social researchers know that there is always a chance that the sample might be extreme and unusual, and

they want to feel very confident that their findings are not the product of any such extreme or unusual sample. In practice, they tend to want a 95 per cent confidence level. They want to know that there would be a less than one in twenty chance of the findings being a fluke.

- *Variation* in the population: less variation requires a bigger sample size. In terms of the particular attribute being measured (e.g. voting intention) it matters whether the population is evenly matched (nearing a 50:50 split) or is widely divided (e.g. 70:30 split). Researchers can get some idea of this in advance (i.e. before they actually conduct their survey) either from a review of existing research or by using a pilot survey. If this factor cannot be estimated it should be assumed that the population is evenly matched because this is a 'worst case scenario' as far as things are concerned when it comes to the size of the required sample. By default, the software plays on the safe side.

Taking these four factors into consideration it is possible to calculate the required sample size. There is a formula for this calculation but the maths do not need to concern the project researcher because there are plenty of software utilities freely available on the Internet that do the calculations at the press of a button. A web search on 'sample size calculator' will identify plenty of these. Some of these ask for variation (or 'response distribution') figures while others do not. If in doubt, enter '50%' in this box.

Accuracy and sample size

There is an interesting point that springs from statistical estimates and sample size. It is that there is relatively little advantage to be gained in terms of accuracy once a sample has reached a given size. There are diminishing returns to increases in the size of samples. This runs contrary to common sense, which would probably say to us that the degree of accuracy of results would depend on what proportion of the population is included in the sample. Common sense might say that a sample of 25 per cent of cases will produce better results than a sample of 10 per cent. Statistics would say that where the population size is large, there is hardly any increase in accuracy to be obtained by incorporating another 15 per cent (see Table 2.3).

 Caution: The anticipated response rate

There is an important distinction to be made between sample size in the sense of the number of people initially contacted and sample size in the sense of the eventual number who respond. It is the eventual sample size that is crucial for the research. The researcher needs to predict the kind of response rate he/she is likely to achieve and build in an allowance for non-responses. If data are needed from a sample of 100 people and a response rate of 30 per cent is anticipated, the size of the sample that needs to be initially contacted will be 334.

Table 2.3 Sample size and population size (probability sampling)

Number in the population	Required sample size[1] (at 95% confidence level)		
	5% margin of error	3% margin of error	1% margin of error
50	44	48	50
100	80	92	99
250	152	203	244
500	217	341	475
1,000	278	516	906
5,000	357	879	3,288
10,0000	370	964	4,899
100,000	383	1,056	8,763
1 million	384	1,066	9,513
10 million	384	1,067	9,595

Note: [1] Refers to final usable responses.

The pragmatic approach: smaller-scale surveys using non-probability sampling for a representative sample

In practice, social research frequently involves surveys with relatively small numbers – *between 30 and 250* – and when estimating the required sample size such surveys tend to depend on non-probability sampling techniques. There are three pragmatic reasons for this. First, there is the matter of resources. In the real world of research the availability of resources is one factor that always affects the researcher's decision on sample size. The fact is that research does not take place with infinite time and money. In practice, it has to be tailored to meet the constraints imposed by the amount of time and money which can be spent on the investigation, and there are not too many individuals or organizations who can actually afford the scale of investigation that involves samples of 1,000 or more. Project researchers such as those conducting a survey as part of an academic degree are very unlikely to have the time or money to work with large populations and large samples.

Second, there is the nature of research populations and the fact that many of the populations that social researchers might like to investigate are relatively small. Work organizations in the UK, for example, are predominantly small and medium-sized enterprises involving workforces of less than 250 people and any survey of individual workplaces might well be obliged to operate with relatively small numbers. This is true of so many of the groups, events and locations the social researcher might want to study. Project researchers, in particular, are likely to want to focus on localized units involving smallish numbers of people or items.

Third, the pragmatic approach subscribes to the argument that, used properly, non-probability sampling techniques can produce data that is *sufficiently* accurate for the purposes of research. Within the statistical approach, it should be noted, there are ways of accommodating the need for small samples and coping with the likely impact of such small samples on the accuracy of the data they produce. The pragmatic approach, however, tends to rely on non-probability sampling instead. This is because it is less expensive to undertake research using things like quota sampling techniques rather than random sampling techniques. There is, however, an ongoing debate about whether the use of non-random sampling techniques with smaller sample sizes jeopardizes the accuracy of the data. The pragmatic approach takes the position that the level of accuracy needs to be weighed against the additional costs involved and that *the aim is to get accuracy that is good enough for the purposes of research within the resources available for research.* Commercial research companies actually advise potential customers that for a given sum of money they can be supplied with results within a given level of accuracy; a greater level of accuracy will cost more. As a consequence, the customer and the commercial research company need to agree about whether results will be accurate *enough* in relation to the resources available.

 Key point: A pragmatic approach to sample size

'In practice, the complexity of the competing factors of resources and accuracy means that the decision on sample size tends to be based on experience and good judgement rather than relying on a strict mathematical formula' (Hoinville et al. 1985: 73).

The good judgement behind the pragmatic approach to sample size is based on four important factors. These do not provide the exact figure as would be the case with the statistical approach, but they do provide guidelines that can help the researcher decide what sample size might be appropriate and acceptable.

- *Comparison with other similar surveys.* The researcher's literature review should identify instances where other researchers have conducted surveys under comparable conditions, and the sample sizes used in such surveys can provide some starting point for deciding what numbers to include in the sample.
- *Samples should not involve fewer than 30 people or items.* Certainly, it is a mistake to use statistical analyses on samples of fewer than 30 without using great care about the procedures involved.
- *Allowance for the number of subdivisions likely to be made within the data.* A sample size which initially looks quite large might produce only very small

returns in relation to specific sub-categories that will be used for analysis of the data. So, for example, a sample of 100 people used to investigate earnings and occupational status might need to be subdivided according to the age, sex, ethnicity, marital status and qualifications of the people, and according to whether they are full-time, part-time, unemployed, child-rearing or retired. This simple investigation would need a cross-tabulation of five personal factors by five occupational factors, i.e. 25 subdivisions of the data. If the data were equally distributed, this means that there would be only four cases in each of the subdivisions, which is hardly an adequate basis for making generalizations. In practice, of course, we know that the data would not be evenly distributed and that many of the subdivisions would end up with no cases in them at all. The researcher therefore needs to think ahead when planning the size of the sample to ensure that the subdivisions entailed in the analysis are adequately catered for. The smaller the sample, the simpler the analysis should be, in the sense that the data should be subjected to fewer subdivisions.

- *Awareness of the limitations.* Special caution is needed about the extent to which generalizations can be made on the basis of the research findings. Provided that the limitations are acknowledged and taken into account, the limited size of the sample need not invalidate the findings.

The cumulative approach: small-scale surveys using non-probability sampling for an exploratory sample

There are some approaches to social research where the size of the sample cannot be estimated with certainty at the start of the investigation. The sample size grows during the course of the research and continues to grow until the researcher has accumulated sufficient information for the purposes of the research. This cumulative approach relies on non-probability techniques such as purposive, theoretical or snowball sampling and is normally associated with research that:

- is relatively small-scale (with sample sizes in the region of 5–30);
- uses qualitative data;
- cannot identify the research population in advance;
- aims to produce an exploratory sample, not a representative one.

The cumulative approach to sample size is illustrated perhaps most neatly in the grounded theory approach and its use of theoretical sampling. Here the process is one of 'discovery'. Almost like a detective, the researcher follows a trail of clues. As each clue is followed up, it points the researcher in a particular direction and throws up new questions that need to be answered. Sometimes the clues can lead the researcher up blind alleys. Ultimately, though, the researcher needs to pursue his/her investigation until the questions have been answered and things can be explained.

> **Link up with Chapter 7, Grounded theory.**

A consequence of this is that *the size and composition of the sample are not completely predictable at the outset.*

Good practice: The cumulative approach and sample size estimates

The fact that the exact size of the sample cannot be stated with certainty at the start of research does not mean that the researcher should start with no idea of the final numbers to be included in the sample. Indeed, it makes good practical sense for researchers using a cumulative approach to have some broad idea of the likely size of their accumulated sample despite their desire to pursue threads of inquiry through to a point where they are satisfied they have enough information. A shrewd look at the time and resources available, and some reading of similar studies, will help to give a reasonable indication before the research starts.

Sampling error and sampling bias

There are two kinds of sampling error. The first of these are 'random' errors which occur as an inevitable consequence of using data from a subset of the overall research population. Those included in the sample are unlikely to be a perfect match with the profile of the overall research population and the data they supply are not going to be exactly the same as they would have been for the whole research population. If a second sample was chosen (using the same method of selection) it would almost certainly produce data that would be slightly different again. The same would be true of all subsequent samples.

When the aim of the research is to get a representative sample and to generalize from the sample data to the research population as a whole, this might seem to be a problem. When using probability sampling techniques, however, the consequences of random error can be overcome because:

- if the samples are sufficiently large the random errors serve to cancel each other out;
- the science of statistics takes random error into account and statistical analyses based on probability allow researchers to predict the amount of the error and the chances of it occurring.

In a statistical sense, then, random error is not a 'mistake': it is an inbuilt feature of sampling whose effect can be predicted and controlled for.

The second kind of sampling error is 'systematic' error. In this case a disparity between the sample and the population stems from a pattern of errors that occur in a systematic way to distort the findings. This is a 'mistake' that researchers need to avoid. A prime source of such systematic error is sampling bias resulting from the use of a sampling frame that is incomplete or not up to date.

A particular danger is that the frame might miss out particular types of people. For example, a list of private addresses will not lead the researcher to those who are homeless and live on the streets. An electoral register will not include those under 18 years of age or those who, for whatever reason, have not registered to vote. Those who are omitted might well be different in some important respects from those who actually exist on the list, and overlooking them as part of the research can lead to a biased sample. Just as damaging for the purposes of research, registers can include certain items that should not be there. They can contain names of people who have passed on – in either a geographical or a mortal sense. People move home, people die, and unless the register is regularly and carefully updated on a routine basis there is the likelihood that it will be out of date and include items it should not. Either way, the impact can be significant. If the sampling frame systematically excludes things that should be in, or systematically includes things which should be out, the sample will almost inevitably be biased.

> **Link up with** Non-response bias, p. 23.

Internet surveys and sampling frames

In general, the nature of the Internet makes good sampling frames relatively more difficult to find. This is because addresses, identities and contact points on the Internet are very different from postal addresses and phone numbers in the 'real' world. In cyberspace, an address and an identity can be very temporary and provide no background information of value to the researcher. People often have more than one email address, use more than one Internet service provider (ISP) and there is no guarantee that any address will be used by just one individual. Having said this, there are certain types of email lists that are well suited to being used as a sampling frame when conducting Internet surveys. Primarily, this is when the research is focused on populations who exist in some sort of formal organization because the administration of organizations almost invariably requires the maintenance of good records of the membership, e.g. employees at work, pupils in schools, members of clubs, volunteers with charities. Such email lists tend to serve known populations and can therefore prove to be a valuable basis for a sampling frame.

> **Link up with** Internet surveys, p. 15.

Which sampling technique should be used?

From the outline of sampling techniques above we can see that the survey researcher has 10 basic options from which to choose, each characterized by a different method of selecting the people or items to be included in the sample. As Figure 2.1 shows, the sampling techniques sit somewhere on a continuum with, at one extreme, a selection technique which eliminates altogether the influence of the researcher (random selection) and at the other extreme a

Figure 2.1 Sampling strategies

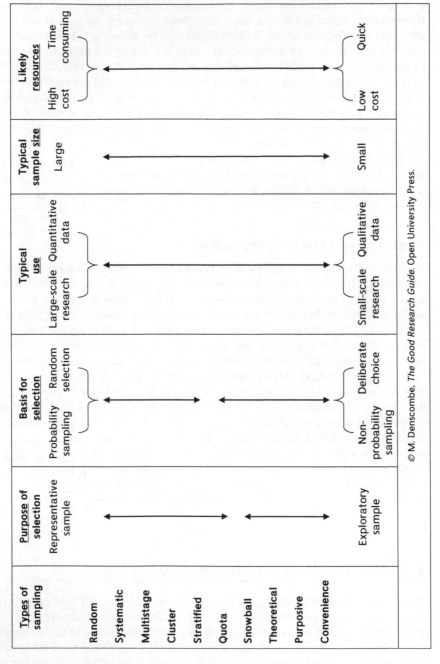

selection technique where selection of the sample is left entirely to the discretion of the researcher (convenience sampling). In between, there are a range of techniques which differ in the extent to which they adhere to the principle of random selection. However, not only do the techniques sit on a sliding scale in terms of the basis for selecting the sample, they also have corresponding positions in terms of the purpose of the sample, the kind of data to be collected, the size of the sample and the amount of resources they are liable to consume. The choice of sampling technique depends, therefore, on how the various techniques fit the needs of the researcher and the kind of research he/she proposes to undertake. When deciding which technique to use the researcher needs to consider five core questions:

1 Is my purpose to produce a representative sample or an exploratory sample?
2 To what extent is this purpose better served by selecting the sample on the basis of random selection or deliberate choice?
3 Will qualitative data or quantitative data be more appropriate for addressing my research questions?
4 Does a suitable sampling frame exist and can I gain access to it?
5 In terms of the resources available for the research (time and money), which sampling technique is both feasible and likely to produce relevant information?

Advantages of sampling

Savings in time and costs

The principal advantage of sampling is that it reduces the time and costs of collecting data when compared with a strategy of including all people or items within the research population.

Provides sufficient accuracy

Sampling need not involve a significant loss of accuracy in terms of its findings. Although there might need to be some compromise in terms of the level of accuracy and level of confidence in the findings, this should be within the bounds of tolerance for most social research projects.

Different techniques for different purposes

There is a range of sampling techniques which covers the requirements of most social researchers. While certain techniques will suit the needs of positivistic styles of research with a focus on quantitative data, other sampling techniques have evolved to suit the needs of interpretive styles of research with a preference for qualitative data. Some techniques are good for getting representative samples, others are good for getting exploratory samples.

Disadvantages of sampling

Sampling error

There is always the possibility of sampling error which needs to be taken into account. Reliance on findings from a subsection of the total research population inevitably opens up the prospect that another sample from that same research population might produce slightly different findings. Statistically, it is possible to accommodate this fact, but the underlying point is that the use of sampling brings with it a level of uncertainty. It always becomes a matter of how *likely* it is that the findings are correct, and within what margins of error.

Sample bias

Sample bias is a constant source of concern. Researchers need to be vigilant to avoid bias stemming from the choice of people to include (the sampling frame) or the kind of people who participate (non-response bias).

Availability of sampling frames

Finding suitable sampling frames can pose a challenge, especially for the use of probability sampling.

Further reading

Barnett, V. (2009) *Sample Survey Principles and Methods*, 3rd edn. Chichester: Wiley.

Daniel, J. (2012) *Sampling Essentials: Practical Guidelines for Making Sampling Choices*. Thousand Oaks, CA: Sage.

Emmel, N. (2013) *Sampling and Choosing Cases in Qualitative Research: A Realist Approach*. London: Sage.

Fowler, F.J. (2014) *Survey Research Methods*, 5th edn. Thousand Oaks, CA: Sage.

Checklist for the use of sampling

When undertaking sampling you should feel confident about answering 'yes' to the following questions: ☑

1 Does the selected sampling technique fit comfortably with the *purpose* for which the sample is being used (representative sample or exploratory sample)? ☐

2 Has a specific sampling *technique* been chosen for use in the research, and has it been explicitly named in any account of the research methodology? ☐

3 Does the approach to sampling distinguish clearly between random selection (based on probability sampling) and purposive selection (based on non-probability sampling)? ☐

4 If a *sampling frame* is available, is it relevant, complete, precise and up to date? ☐

5 Can the *sample size* be justified on the basis of criteria relevant to the type of sampling technique being used? ☐

6 Have appropriate measures been taken to avoid *sampling bias*? ☐

7 If the sample size is less than 30, have the implications of this for *statistical analysis* been recognized in the research? ☐

© M. Denscombe, *The Good Research Guide*. Open University Press.

3   Case studies

Case studies focus on one (or just a few) instances of a particular phenomenon with a view to providing an in-depth account of events, relationships, experiences or processes occurring in that particular instance. *The aim is to illuminate the general by looking at the particular.* The case study approach is widely used in social research, particularly with small-scale projects, and in practice it has become aligned with qualitative research rather than quantitative research.

The decision to use a case study approach is a *strategic* decision that relates to the scale and scope of an investigation, and it does not dictate which method(s) must be used. Indeed, one strength of the case study approach is that it allows the use of a variety of methods depending on the circumstances and the specific needs of the situation.

What is a 'case'?

Natural setting

'The case' that forms the basis of the investigation is normally something that already exists. It is not a situation that is artificially generated specifically for the purposes of the research. The case is a *naturally occurring* phenomenon. It exists prior to the research project and continues to exist once the research has finished.

Boundaries

To qualify as something suitable for case study research it is crucial that the thing to be studied has some distinctive identity that allows it to be studied in isolation from its context. Basically, a case needs to be a *self-contained entity* and have fairly *distinct boundaries*.

Key features

Cases are a particular instance of a broader category of thing and a case has specific features in common with other things 'of its type'. It is the presence of these features which determines the extent to which the case can provide data that are relevant to the practical problem or theoretical issue that the researcher wants to investigate.

As Table 3.1 shows, there are a wide range of social phenomena that can meet these three criteria and which can be studied using the case study approach.

Table 3.1   Types of cases

Type	Examples
Event	Strike, street riot, ceremony, music festival
Organization	Commercial business, hospital, school
Policy	New health intervention, change to pension schemes
Location	Shopping mall, nightclub, accident hotspot
Process	In-service training, recruitment procedure

The case study approach

As s strategy for research the case study approach has certain defining characteristics. These are summarized in Table 3.2. These characteristics indicate quite clearly how the case study approach contrasts with approaches to social research based on surveys or experiments.

Table 3.2   Characteristics of the case study approach

One setting	rather than	Many instances
Depth of study	rather than	Breadth of study
The particular	rather than	The general
Relationships/processes	rather than	Outcomes and end-products
Holistic view	rather than	Isolated factors
Multiple sources of data	rather than	One research method

Spotlight on one instance or a few instances

The main characteristic of the case study approach is its *focus on just one instance of the thing that is to be investigated*. Occasionally, researchers use two or more instances but, in principle, the idea of a case study is that the spotlight is focused very narrowly. The case study approach, then, is quite the opposite of any mass study. The logic behind concentrating efforts on one case rather than many is that there may be insights to be gained from looking at the individual case that can have wider implications and, importantly, that would not have come to light through the use of a research strategy that tried to cover a large number of instances.

In-depth study

The prospect of getting some valuable insight depends on being able to investigate things in depth. When a researcher takes the strategic decision to devote all his/her efforts to researching just one instance, there is obviously far greater opportunity to delve into things in more detail and discover things that might not have become apparent through more superficial research.

Focus on relationships and processes

Case studies pay attention to the detailed workings of the relationships and social processes within social settings. They do so because they are not only interested in *what* goes on in the setting, they are also interested in explaining *why* those things occur. End-products, outcomes and results all remain of interest, but the real value of a case study is that it offers the opportunity to go into sufficient detail to unravel the complexities of a given situation. A case study conducted in Company A, for example, might reveal that it has a high turnover of labour. To an extent this fact is interesting in its own right, but the strength of a case study approach is that it allows the researcher to investigate the relationships and processes that *explain* the actual level of turnover – the interplay between things like the recruitment policy, staff development programme, nature of the work, levels of pay and the social background of the workforce.

A holistic view

Relationships and processes within social settings are interconnected, and to explain why things happen as they do within a particular case study setting it is necessary to understand how the various facets of the setting are linked together. The case study approach works well here because, rather than deal with 'isolated factors', it takes a 'holistic' view of what is going on. It views the case as a whole, in its entirety, and is thus able to discover how the many parts affect one another.

Multiple methods

The case study approach allows the researcher to use a variety of types of data (qualitative or quantitative) and a combination of research methods (observation, interviews, documents, questionnaires) as part of the investigation. It not only allows this, it actually invites and encourages the researcher to do so in order to get a holistic view. Whatever methods are appropriate can be used for investigating the relationships and processes that are of interest.

> **Link up with Chapter 11, Mixed methods.**

The purpose of a case study

Case studies can be used for a number of purposes. Predominantly, they have been used in relation to the discovery of information (following an inductive logic). The case study approach enables the researcher to delve deep into the intricacies of the situation in order to describe things in detail, compare alternatives or, perhaps, provide an account that explores particular aspects of the situation.

The information can also be used to understand the underlying causes of the things that have been observed to occur in the case study setting. Used in such ways, case studies provide new information which is valuable: (1) in its own right for what it *says*; (2) for what it *suggests* by way of new avenues to explore; or (3) for what it *explains* in terms of how aspects of the case are interlinked.

Case studies have been used, though less commonly, in relation to the testing of theory (following a deductive logic). The purpose of the case, here, is to allow the researcher to see whether things that a theory predicts will take place will actually be found in practice in real-world settings. Used in this way, the case study either: (1) tries to reinforce the value of a theory by demonstrating how it works in reality; or (2) sets out to test whether a particular theory might work under the specific conditions to be found in the case setting.

It is quite possible for case studies to have more than one purpose. Table 3.3 outlines the possible ways in which case studies might be used, but should not be seen as implying that any particular case study must be restricted to just one type of purpose.

Table 3.3   The purpose of a case study: six possibilities

Discovery-led	
Description	Describes what is happening in a case study setting (e.g. events, processes and relationships)
Exploration	Explores the key issues affecting those in a case study setting (e.g. problems or opportunities)
Comparison	Compares settings to learn from the similarities and differences between them
Explanation	Explains the causes of events, processes or relationships within a setting
Theory-led	
Illustration	Uses a case study as an illustration of how a particular theory applies in a real-life setting
Experiment	Uses a case study as a test-bed for experimenting with changes to specific factors (or variables)

Selecting a case

The case study approach generally calls for the researcher to make choices from among a number of possible events, people, organizations, etc. The researcher needs to pick out one example (or just a few) from a wider range of examples of the class of thing that is being investigated: the choice of one school for a case study from among the thousands that could have been chosen; the choice of one eye injury clinic from among the many in hospitals across the country; the focus on one bus company from among the hundreds throughout the nation which provide local public transport services. Whatever the subject matter, the case study normally depends on a conscious and deliberate choice about which case to select from among a large number of possibilities.

An important point to realize about this is that cases are not randomly selected: they are selected on the basis of known attributes. As a distinct alternative to the randomization principle associated with classic experiments and large-scale surveys, instances selected for a case study are deliberately chosen on the basis of their distinctive features.

Relevance to the topic

A suitable case will be one with features that are relevant in terms of the practical problem or theoretical issue that the researcher wants to investigate. This criterion for selection is crucial for the success of the case study and the researcher's decisions on this point need to be explicit and justified as an essential part of the case study methodology. For example, if the area of interest is 'small firms in the automotive industry', the criterion for the selection of any particular organization as the basis for a case study would be 'size'. If size is defined in terms of the number of employees, then details would need to be given about the number of employees in the selected firm and how this compares with (1) definitions of small firms (the theory), and (2) a profile of the size of other firms throughout the automotive industry. Such details are vital because they justify the choice of the particular firm as a suitable example of the broader category of the thing being studied (small firms) and they form the basis for any generalizations that can be made from the case study findings.

Type of case study

Typical instance

The selection of a particular case can be based on the argument that it is typical. The logic being invoked here is that the particular case is similar to others that might have been chosen, and that the findings from the case study are therefore likely to apply elsewhere. Because the case study is like most of the rest, the findings can be generalized to the whole class of thing.

Extreme instance

A case might be selected on the grounds that, far from being typical, it provides a contrast with the norm. An illustration of this would be the selection of an organization which is notably smaller or notably larger than usual. Among local authorities in the country, a very small authority might be chosen for a case study, and the logic for doing so would be that this would allow the influence of the factor (size) to be more easily seen than it would be in the average size authority. In an extreme instance, a specified factor is seen in relief – highlighted in its effect.

Test-site for theory

The logic for the selection of a particular case can be based on the relevance of the case for previous theory. This is a point Yin (2014) stresses. Case studies can be used for the purposes of 'theory-testing' as well as 'theory-building'. The rationale for choosing a specific case, then, can be that it contains crucial elements that are especially significant, and that the researcher should be able to predict certain outcomes if the theory holds true.

Least likely instance

Following the idea of test-sites for theory, a case might be selected to test the validity of 'theory' by seeing if it occurs in an instance where it might be least expected. So, for example, a researcher who wants to test the 'theory' that school teachers place a high value on their autonomy could deliberately select a situation where such autonomy would seem to be least valued: a school with team teaching in open plan classrooms. If there is evidence supporting the 'theory' even under such 'least likely' conditions, then the 'theory' has all the more credibility.

Practical considerations

Although researchers should never rely on practical reasons as the principal or the sole criterion for selecting a case, it would be naive to ignore the fact that, in the real world of research, such factors do have a bearing on the selection of cases.

A matter of convenience

In the practical world of research, with its limits to time and resources, the selection of cases is likely to include a consideration of convenience. Faced with alternatives which are equally suitable, it is reasonable for the researcher to select the case which involves the least travel, the least expense and the least difficulty when it comes to gaining access. The crucial point here, though, is that convenience should only come into play when deciding between equally suitable alternatives. Selection on the basis of 'the first to hand', 'the easiest' or 'the cheapest' is not a criterion in its own right which can be used to justify the selection of cases. If used on its own, in fact, it would almost certainly be a symptom of poor social research. Used properly, it is subordinate to the other criteria.

Intrinsically interesting

If a case is intrinsically interesting, then it can prove an attractive proposition. The findings are likely to reach a wider audience and the research itself is likely to be a more exciting experience. There are even some experts in the field who would go as far as to argue that selection on the basis of being intrinsically interesting is a sufficient justification in its own right (Stake 1995). This goes to the heart of the debate about whether cases are studied 'in their own right', as Stake would maintain, or for what they reveal about others of the kind, and, in light of its controversial nature, it would be rather foolhardy for the newcomer or project researcher to use this as the sole criterion for selecting a case. The vast majority of social researchers would not see it as a justification for selection in its own right. It might work for journalism, but social research by most definitions calls for more than just this (Ragin and Amoroso 2011). It is far wiser, therefore, to regard any intrinsic interest of the case as a criterion to be used when deciding between instances that in all other crucial respects are equally suitable, and as a bonus.

No real choice

On some occasions, researchers do not really have a great deal of choice when it comes to the selection of suitable cases for inclusion in the investigation. The choice is more or less dictated by circumstances beyond their control. This happens in the following two circumstances.

The study is part of commissioned research

Commissioned research might leave the researcher with little leeway in the selection of cases. The funder will likely stipulate that the research must be linked to a specified organization or activity, leaving no discretion on the matter to the researchers themselves. Under such circumstances, there is no real choice in the selection of cases.

There are unique opportunities

There are times when events occur which provide the researcher with unique opportunities. The events themselves, of course, will not be unique; they will be instances of a class of such events. The opportunity to study such events, however, may be unique. Situations which could not be planned or created present themselves as 'one-off chances'. At one level, this could take the form of social catastrophes, such as war, famine or natural disaster. At a more mundane level, the unique opportunities could reflect the unpredictable or rare nature of the events. Strikes, for example, might be the kind of class of events that could be illuminated through the depth study of individual cases. Researchers, though, will have little choice over which instances they select as their cases and will necessarily find themselves homing in on such events as and when they occur. As a consequence, there is no real element of choice in the selection of the cases.

Can you generalize from a case study?

When opting for a case study approach researchers are likely to confront scepticism about how far it is reasonable to generalize from the findings of one case. The researcher will probably find people asking questions such as:

- How *representative* is the case?
- Isn't it possible that the findings, though interesting, are *unique* to the particular circumstances of the case?
- How can you *generalize* on the basis of research into one instance?

These are reasonable questions. They reflect the key issue of generalization in social research (Denscombe 2010) and should not be ignored in the hope that readers of the research report will overlook the point. Indeed, it is good practice for any researcher who decides to choose a case study approach to pre-empt possible criticism by addressing the issue head-on.

Analytic generalizations

One way to address the matter is to emphasize the point that individual case studies should not be regarded as though they form part of a survey sample. They are not a 'slice of the cake' whose function is to reveal the contents of the whole cake. Instead, the findings from a case study are used for the *development of theory*. The point of a case study is to analyse the situation and to arrive at certain concepts, propositions or hypotheses that might explain what is happening, and why, in the particular setting that has been investigated. Viewed in this way, each case study is like an individual experiment and, as Yin (2009: 15) argues:

> Case studies, like experiments, are generalizable to theoretical propositions and not to populations or universes. In this sense, the case study, like the experiment, does not represent a 'sample', and in doing a case study, your goal will be to expand and generalize theories (analytic generalization) and not to enumerate frequencies (statistical generalization).

From this perspective, the findings from case studies are not to be regarded as final or absolute. As with experiments, the findings should be understood as being provisional and in need of corroboration through other research which can check their validity. Or, looked at another way, the findings might be regarded as part of an ongoing process in which initial findings are not only checked for accuracy, they are used to refine the ideas and theories developed in the earlier pieces of research. Either way, though, case studies tend to be seen as a *starting point* for research, serving as a descriptive or exploratory foundation that helps with the development of theory, and it is in this *analytic* respect that the findings from case studies can be generalized.

Transferable findings

Analytic generalizations implicitly treat case studies as part of a broader research programme where the value of any individual case study depends on its link with alternative types of research or further case studies. Within small-scale research projects, however, case studies do not normally occur as part of an ongoing programme of research. In all probability they take place as 'one-offs'. This calls for a slightly different kind of rationale when it comes to generalizing from case study findings. Rather than treating case studies as a starting point for research, they need to be regarded as ends in themselves, finished products whose findings have some value in their own right.

The rationale for generalizing, in this instance, depends on *how far the findings are 'transferable' to other settings*. What is crucial is the extent to which those who read the case study findings are able to infer things from them that apply to other settings.

> **Link up with Transferability of findings, p. 328.**

The possibility of transferable findings stems from the fact that although each case is in some respects unique, it is also a single example of a broader class of things. It is one of a type (Hammersley 1992; Ragin and Becker 1992), and the extent to which findings from the case study can be generalized to other examples in the class depends on how far the case study example compares with others of its type. To make some assessment of how far the findings have implications across the board for all others of the type, or how far they are restricted to just the case study example, readers must be provided with the necessary information on which to make an informed judgement on this matter. It is vital, therefore, that reports based on the case study include sufficient detail about how the case compares with others in the class for the reader to make an informed judgement about how far the findings have relevance to other instances. Details should be given about:

- the type of thing (organization, event, process);
- the case (detailed facts and figures);
- how it compares with others of its type (e.g. factors like size, location, frequency).

Comparison might call for the inclusion of details on factors such as:

- physical location – geographical area, town, building, room, furniture, décor;
- historical location – developments and changes;

- social location – catchment area, ethnic grouping, social class, age, sex and other background information about the participants;
- institutional location – type of organization, size of organization, official policies and procedures.

Example 3.1

Transferable findings

In a case study involving a small primary school the 'case' is one of a broader type of other schools which are small and which are in the primary sector. The transferability of the findings from the case study to other small primary schools will depend on how far the case study example shares with other schools of the type (small size, primary sector) features which are significant with respect to the findings. This could include things like its catchment area, the ethnic origins of the pupils and the rate of staff turnover. The transferability of the findings from the particular case study school to other small primary schools will depend on the extent to which its profile on these factors is to be found in other examples of this type of school. This means that the researcher must obtain data on the significant features (catchment area, the ethnic origins of the pupils and the rate of staff turnover) for primary schools in general (likely to be based on regional or national figures), and then demonstrate where the case study example fits in relation to the broader picture.

Advantages of the case study approach

Suitable for small-scale research

The case study approach can fit in well with the needs of small-scale research through concentrating effort on one research site (or just a few sites).

Makes use of naturally occurring settings

The case study approach is particularly suitable in circumstances where it is not possible to manipulate features of the setting for the purposes of the research. Because the approach is concerned with investigating phenomena as they naturally occur, there is no necessity for the researcher to impose controls or implement changes to key factors or variables.

Flexible approach

Theory-building and theory-testing research can both use the case study approach to good effect.

Facilitates the use of multiple methods

The case study approach allows the use of a variety of research methods. More than this, it more or less encourages the use of multiple methods and multiple sources of data in order to capture the complex reality under scrutiny.

Takes a holistic view

The focus on particular instances allows the researcher to take a holistic view (rather than a view based on isolated factors) and to look in depth at the subtleties and intricacies of complex social phenomena.

Disadvantages of the case study approach

Producing generalizable findings

The point at which the case study approach is most vulnerable to criticism is in relation to the *credibility of generalizations* made from its findings. The case study researcher needs to be particularly careful to allay suspicions and to demonstrate the extent to which the case is similar to, or contrasts with, others of its type.

Gaining access to case study settings

Negotiating access to case study settings can be a demanding part of the research process. Research can flounder if permission is withheld or withdrawn. In case studies, access to documents, people and settings can generate ethical problems in terms of things like confidentiality.

Focus on process rather than outcomes

Case study research tends to focus on processes rather than measurable end-products. To this extent the approach is sometimes seen as producing 'soft' data because it uses qualitative data and interpretive methods rather than quantitative data and statistical procedures. In line with this, case studies are sometimes regarded as acceptable in terms of providing descriptive accounts of the situation but rather ill-suited to analyses or evaluations. None of this is necessarily justified, but it is a preconception which the case study researcher needs to be aware of, and one which needs to be challenged by careful attention to detail and rigour in the use of the approach.

Defining boundaries to the case

On the technical side, the *boundaries* of the case can prove difficult to define in an absolute and clear-cut fashion. This poses difficulties in terms of deciding which sources of data to incorporate in the case study and which to exclude.

Further reading

Simons, H. (2009) *Case Study Research in Practice*. London: Sage.

Stake, R. (1995) *The Art of Case Study Research*. Thousand Oaks, CA: Sage.

Swanborn, P. (2010) *Case Study Research: What, Why and How?* London: Sage.

Thomas, G. (2016) *How to Do Your Case Study: A Guide for Students and Researchers*, 2nd edn. London: Sage.

Yin, R. (2014) *Case Study Research: Design and Methods*, 5th edn. Thousand Oaks, CA: Sage.

Checklist for the use of case studies

When undertaking research which involves the case study approach you should feel confident about answering 'yes' to the following questions: ☑

1 Is the research based on a 'naturally occurring' situation? ☐

2 Have the criteria for selection of the case (or cases) been described and justified? ☐

3 Has the case been identified as a particular instance of a type of social phenomenon (e.g. kind of event, type of organization)? ☐

4 Have the significant features of the case been described and have they been compared with those to be found elsewhere among the type of thing being studied? ☐

5 Is the case a fairly self-contained entity? ☐

6 Have the boundaries to the case been described and their implications considered? ☐

7 Has careful consideration been given to the issue of generalizations stemming from research? ☐

8 Does the research make suitable use of multiple methods and multiple sources of data? ☐

9 Does the research give due attention to relationships and processes, and provide a 'holistic' perspective? ☐

4　Experiments

What is an experiment?

An experiment is an empirical investigation under controlled conditions designed to examine the relationship between specific factors. The point of conducting an experiment is to isolate individual variables and observe their effect in detail. The purpose is to discover new relationships or properties associated with the thing that is being investigated, or to test existing theories.

This definition draws on a rather idealized image of the way experiments are conducted but it captures the essence of the notion and incorporates the three things that lie at the heart of conducting experiments in social research:

* *Controls.* Experiments involve the manipulation of variables. The researcher needs to identify factors that are significant and then introduce them to, or exclude them from, the situation so that their effect can be observed.
* *Empirical observation and measurement.* Experiments rely on detailed empirical observation of changes that occur following the introduction of potentially relevant factors. They also involve the precise measurement of the changes that are observed.
* *The identification of causal factors.* The introduction (or exclusion) of factors from the situation enables the researcher to pinpoint which factor actually causes the observed outcome to occur.

When to use an experiment

There are five conditions that need to be met in order for experiments to be selected as a suitable research approach. The first of these is that they should be used as part of explanatory research rather than exploratory research. This means that the focus should be on questions about 'why' things happen and 'how' they are linked, with the research being designed to explain the link between two or more factors.

Second, the research should be able to draw on a fairly well-established body of knowledge about the topic to be investigated. The factors that are looked at must not be plucked out of thin air but chosen, instead, on the basis of existing knowledge about the topic. They should be selected deliberately because they are known to be relevant and significant. As a corollary to this, experiments are not so well suited to descriptive research or to exploratory research where the point of the research is to discover which factors are significant.

Third, and following on from the previous point, existing knowledge about the topic for the research should allow research questions to take the form of hypotheses. Hypotheses are 'testable propositions' which state that, under certain conditions, a specific outcome might be expected to occur. They are useful because they entail a predicted outcome that can be verified or refuted through the experiment.

Fourth, the kinds of observations and measurement techniques used in experiments mean that they are usually associated with quantitative data rather than qualitative data. Because experiments depend on controlling variables and upon the careful measurement of changes that occur during the experiment, they produce data that are numerical and which lend themselves to statistical analysis.

Fifth, the design of experiments requires the ability to implement controls over factors that are to be studied in the experiment. In 'natural experiments' (described below) this is *not* the case but in other kinds of experiments the researcher needs to have the capability, authority and resources to manipulate relevant variables.

 Key point

Experiments are suitable for explanatory research that draws on well-established theory in order to identify the relevant variables that need to be studied.

Types of experiment

Laboratory experiments

Laboratories are purpose-built contexts for the research. They are normally enclosed spaces (buildings or locations) which are set out purposefully to aid the collection of data on specific factors linked to the experiment. They often make use of specialized equipment or facilities to help the researchers obtain detailed data about the phenomenon they are studying.

Laboratory experiments, by their nature, are located *on site* rather than 'in the field'. People or items come to the laboratory in order for the research to take place, rather than things being studied *in situ*. This is necessary, of course, in order to take advantage of the purpose-built nature of the setting and the benefits this has for: (1) *close control* of variables to isolate causal factors; and (2) *precision and consistency of the observations* and measurements that are made.

 Caution: Ecological validity

A crucial question for laboratory experiments is whether they allow the researcher to draw conclusions that apply to people's behaviour in normal, everyday life. The advantages of laboratory experiments in terms of precision and consistency need to be weighed against the fact that they are conducted under conditions that are artificially created. This can affect the way people react. Laboratory experiments, therefore, need to be judged in terms of their *ecological validity* – how well they replicate conditions that would naturally occur outside the laboratory in 'real' life.

Field experiments

Field experiments are experiments that take place outside the laboratory. They are conducted 'in the field' in places such as factories, offices, schools and hospitals. Such settings are not artificially created for the purposes of the research, but they do allow researchers to manipulate certain key variables and focus on measuring the impact of a specific new factor that is introduced into the setting. This new factor often takes the form of a new procedure, a new rule or some other kind of specific new initiative that has been introduced to the setting. The field experiment involves a systematic evaluation of the new factor with the purpose of finding out whether the introduction of the new variable has caused changes to occur as had been anticipated. A classic example of such a field experiment is the Hawthorne experiments where changes to the working environment were introduced in a factory setting in order to find out if things like changes to the level of lighting caused changes in the level of productivity.

Link up with Hawthorne studies, p. 174.

Randomized controlled trials

Randomized controlled trials (RCTs) are a type of field experiment in which the effect of specific 'treatments' is measured in trials involving comparisons between experimental groups and control groups. Random allocation to the groups is used to ensure that there is no difference between the groups.

Randomized controlled trials are regarded as the gold standard for research design in the realms of medical and health research concerned with clinical trials of drugs and other health interventions, and are the preferred approach of the 'evidence-based movement' for whom it represents the most scientific way of conducting research (Higgins and Green 2011).

Natural experiments

Natural experiments make use of events and circumstances that occur naturally in everyday life which provide researchers with the opportunity to observe the effects of particular variables and explain the causes of particular phenomena.

When researchers move outside the laboratory in order to gather data in more natural settings, they are likely to pay a high price in terms of their ability to control the variables. They rely on observing events which occur in circumstances over which they have no control. Sociologists cannot control levels of incomes in order to conduct experiments on things such as poverty. Nor can health educators manipulate levels of smoking among adolescent girls in order to study them. Economists cannot generate a recession in order to investigate its consequences. It is simply not possible to manipulate circumstances like these. So, rather than trying to manipulate the situation, researchers take advantage of 'naturally occurring' experiments – situations in which they can see the possibility of observing and measuring the impact of isolated variables through circumstances as they happen, without creating artificial environments or imposing artificial controls.

Retrospective experiments

Retrospective experiments begin with the 'effect' and the researcher sets out to deduce what factor(s) could possibly be the cause of this outcome. The idea is to work backwards from the effect to find the cause. For example, the researcher might ask, 'Does imprisonment affect earnings after release from detention?' The research design here would be to identify a number of people who had been to prison. This independent variable – imprisonment – is not something the research can or should manipulate. It is a *fait accompli*, existing prior to and quite separate from the research. However, by comparing ex-prisoners with people who in most other respects match them, it is possible to deduce whether or not that factor has had a direct causal effect on the earnings.

Experiments involving people – the observer effect

When experiments involve people there are three issues that arise which would not apply if the experiment was conducted on plants, chemicals or natural materials. When humans are the thing that is being studied, the nature of the experiment needs to take into account the fact that:

- people react to the knowledge that they are being observed;
- participation in experiments can potentially harm people;
- experiments might involve artificial settings that are different from the real world.

Humans have self-awareness and this makes them very different from plants, chemicals or natural materials. When humans become aware that they are the focus of attention for research, there is the very real possibility that they will act differently from normal. They might become self-conscious or anxious about having their behaviour scrutinized by the researcher and consequently alter their behaviour in some way. This is known as the *observer effect*. They might, on the other hand, enjoy being in the limelight and respond accordingly with enthusiasm and motivation that would not have existed if they had not realized they were the subject of special attention. This is known as the *halo effect*. If the participants know the true purpose of the research there is, in addition, the prospect that they will alter their behaviour directly to take this into account. They might try to help the researcher by doing what they think is expected of them, or they might try to do the opposite. These are *self-fulfilling prophecies* that can result from the knowledge which participants have (or believe they have) about what the experiment is trying to achieve.

 Key point: The observer effect

People are likely to alter their behaviour when they become aware that they are being observed. Unlike atoms, people can become aware of being studied – conscious of it – and then react in a way that is not usual.

Experimenters can take steps to overcome the observer effect. They can, for instance, make hidden observations from behind a one-way mirror. If people do not realize they are being observed, then their behaviour should not be affected. Or researchers can disguise the real purpose of the research to avoid altering behaviour in relation to the factor being investigated. They can deceive participants into thinking that the research is about one thing when it is actually about another quite separate topic. But both solutions to the observer effect – secret observations and disguised purpose – raise ethical problems and need very careful consideration before being used.

Example 4.1

Experiments, observation and ethics

A series of experiments conducted by Stanley Milgram at Yale University between 1961 and 1962 highlight the ethical issues that can arise from experiments involving people (Milgram 1974). These experiments were cleverly designed to make participants believe they were administering progressively stronger electric shocks to a fellow participant as part of an experiment which they were told was about 'learning'. In fact, the person apparently receiving the electric shocks was part of the research team and actually received no shocks at all – but the research 'subjects' did not know this. During the experiment the subjects were led to believe that, as part of the experiment on learning, they needed to administer progressively higher voltage electric shocks to the other participant. The experiments involved deception about the nature of what was being studied – it was actually about obedience to authority – and involved the subjects being covertly observed from behind a one-way mirror. These alone raise ethical questions. What made the experiments notorious, however, was their impact on the participants. For some people the experience of taking part in the research turned out to be very stressful and perturbing – they believed they had been cajoled into giving potentially fatal electric shocks to the other person (Perry 2013).

| Link up with Chapter 18, Research ethics. | The point these experiments highlight is that research involving humans must never lose sight of the fact that it is dealing with real people who have emotions and feelings, and that the well-being of participants must never be sacrificed in the pursuit of findings, no matter how 'useful' those findings might be. |

 Key point

A researcher can do things to chemicals and plants that cannot be contemplated with fellow human beings. People have feelings, people have rights.

Causal relationships and variables

Experiments are generally concerned with determining the *cause* of any changes that occur to the thing being studied. It is not normally enough to show that two things that occur are linked; that they always occur at the same time or they always happen in sequence. Useful though it is to know about such a relationship, experiments usually aim to discover which of the factors is the cause. This requires a distinction to be made between *dependent* and *independent variables*. It is vital that the researcher has a clear idea of which is which, and sets up the experiment in a way which produces results that show the distinction between the two:

- The *independent variable* is the one that has the impact on the dependent variable. Its size, number, structure, volume or whatever exist autonomously, owing nothing to the other variable. A change in the independent variable affects the dependent variable.

- The *dependent variable* is the factor that alters as a result of changes to the independent variable. It literally 'depends' on the independent variable. Any change in the dependent variable does not affect the independent variable.

Example 4.2

Causal relationships with respect to tobacco smoking

Tobacco smoking is related to the incidence of lung cancer. Both are variables and both appear to be linked to each other: more smoking, higher incidence of lung cancer; less smoking, lower incidence. Smoking increases the likelihood of lung cancer. Lung cancer does not increase the likelihood of smoking. In this example, there is clearly a dependent variable and an independent variable. Smoking tobacco is the independent variable, and lung cancer is the dependent variable.

The use of controls

When conducting an experiment the aim is to show that the dependent factor (for example, the incidence of lung cancer in the population) responds to changes in the independent factor (prevalence of smoking in the society). To do this, the researcher needs to be sure it was definitely the prevalence of smoking that was responsible for the observed levels of lung cancer and not some other factor (e.g. diet or amount of exercise) that actually caused it. This requires the experimenter to control variables such as smoking, diet, exercise and other factors that could perhaps affect the incidence of lung cancer to ensure that, of all of them, it is only the one factor, smoking, that could possibly be linked to the level of lung cancer in the population. There are a number of ways in which experiments can be designed to achieve this, each of which involves the use of controls.

Introduce a new factor

The most straightforward way to isolate the impact of a variable is to introduce it while keeping all other relevant factors unchanged. Under these circumstances – 'all things being equal' – it is possible to pinpoint the impact of the new factor and to deduce that any observed changes that occur can be attributed to the new factor. Since the introduction of the new factor is the only thing that has changed, it alone can be held responsible for any subsequent changes that occur. In practice, however, social researchers face two particular difficulties in this regard. First, it can be extremely difficult to ensure that none of the other variables change. Second, variables are often linked so that a change in one variable might cause changes across a range of other variables.

Eliminate the factor from the experiment

Rather than introduce a new factor to the situation, the researcher might find it easier to eliminate one factor. So, for instance, a study of the link between hyperactivity and diet in children might see the researcher deliberately excluding all artificial colourings from the subjects' diets and then observing any change in behaviour. If other factors remain unaltered, it would be logical to deduce that any observed change was due to the absence of this factor.

Hold the factor constant

In social science, a large number of the key relevant variables come in the form of attributes that cannot be written out of the equation through eliminating them from the situation altogether. Things like income, weight and age are attributes that cannot be eliminated. However, they can be controlled for by 'holding the factor constant'. To prevent the factor from having an unwanted intrusion on the outcome of the experiment, the researcher can devise a situation in which the participants are all of the same income or of the same weight. Observed outcomes from the experiment, as a result, can be deduced to stem from some factor other than income or weight.

Control groups

A standard method of introducing controls involves the use of control groups. In principle, control groups are identical to experimental groups. In practice, the aim is to ensure, as far as is possible, that there is no significant difference between the two groups. This is achieved by *random allocation* to the groups so that membership is based on pure chance and no other factor. Alternatively, the experimenter might use *matched groups* where selection is based on key factors which are known to be significant in relation to the outcome of the experiment (e.g. age, sex, etc.).

The use of control groups follows a fairly straightforward logic. Control groups provide a baseline for measuring the changes observed during an experiment. If the control group and the experimental group are identical at the start of the experiment, and a specific variable is introduced to the experimental group but not to the control group, then at the end of the experiment any difference between the experimental group and the control group must have been caused by the variable that was introduced. This was, after all, the only factor that differentiated between the groups.

The experiment involves introducing a factor to the experimental group and leaving the other group with no artificially induced changes. Having added the new factor, the experimenter can then look at the two groups again with the belief that any *difference* between the groups can be attributed to the factor which was artificially induced. Note here that it is not the *change* in the experimental group as such which is important. Certain changes over time are likely to happen, irrespective of whether an experiment had taken place. Time moves on for all of us. But, if the two groups were as identical as possible at the outset, any change of this kind in one group will also occur in the other group. So, instead of measuring the change from time 1 to time 2, we measure the difference between the control group and the experimental group at the end of the experiment at time 2. Any differences we observe can be logically deduced

Figure 4.1 Experiments and the use of control groups

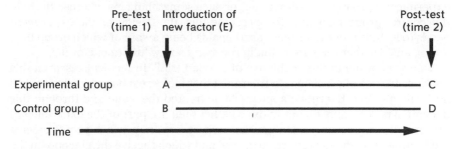

Experimental group and control group are matched groups or samples.
Factor E causes a change in the experimental group of (C – A) – (D – B).

to come from the factor which was artificially induced in the experiment
(see Figure 4.1).

Allocation to groups

The use of control groups eliminates alternative possible explanations for any
observed differences between groups after the treatment. However, this is only
true if we can be sure that there is no difference between those who are allocated to the control group and those allocated to the experimental group; that at
the start of the experiment the groups are the same. One way to ensure this is on
the basis of *random allocation to groups*. If the research subjects are chosen on
a random basis, there should be a tendency for those factors which are not crucial to cancel themselves out. The principle here is that by
the choice of a large enough group of participants on a random basis, any interference with the results through 'con-
founding' factors would cancel themselves out in terms of
the results for the whole research group.

> **Link up with**
> Random
> sampling, p. 36.

An alternative way of making sure that control groups and experimental
groups are the same is by *matching the groups* in terms of factors that are
known to be relevant. A social researcher, in this respect, might want to ensure
that groups are balanced in terms of things such as age, sex, occupation and
ethnicity in an effort to establish equivalent groups. Of course, this would
involve allocation on the basis of quotas rather than random allocation, but it is
likely to prove a method better suited to small-scale research. Whatever way it
is achieved, though, the crucial thing is that the researcher creates groups that
have no difference on anything relating to the variable that will be introduced.

Blind trials

A factor that is not eliminated by the use of control groups is the participants'
knowledge that they have been allocated to one group or the other. The *observer*

effect comes into play, raising the prospect that those who know they are in the experimental group will *expect* to experience something new whereas those in the control group may not. To overcome this, the design of the experiment needs to include ploys to prevent participants being aware of which group they are in, and whether they are actually receiving a new 'treatment' or not.

One way of doing this is the use of a 'blind trial'. In medical research this involves the use of placebos – a treatment that looks real but which in fact has no healing effect. Everyone appears to be treated the same and through this deception participants do not know whether they are part of the experimental group or the control group. Only the experimenters know which people receive the treatment (in the experimental group) and which receive the placebo (in the control group). This effectively eliminates any possibility that participants' *expectations* could account for any observed changes following the introduction of the treatment.

Design: true experiments and quasi-experiments

To qualify as a 'true' experiment the research design needs to allow the researcher to identify the cause of changes that are observed during the experiment and, crucially, to do so in a way that eliminates any alternative possible explanations for the results. It needs to be able to rule out all other factors that might possibly explain what caused the event or the changes that were observed. A true experiment achieves this through a combination of four things. The design should include:

1 both a *pre-test* and a *post-test* to get measurements before and after the introduction of the variable being investigated;
2 the use of a *control group* for comparisons;
3 the *random allocation* of people or items to the 'control' group and the 'experimental' group;
4 the *introduction (or control) of a variable* whose impact the experiment wishes to observe.

This basic experimental design is known as a *pre-test-post-test control group design* and is often portrayed in the following way:

Group A R--------O_1--------X--------O_2
Group B R--------O_1--------------------O_2

Notation:
  R stands for random allocation to groups;
  X stands for introduction of new factor or treatment;
  O stands for observation;
  Subscripts 1 and 2 refer to the sequential observations.

There are a multitude of experimental research designs that build upon these basic building blocks. Essentially they consist of various combinations of five basic ingredients:

- the times when measurements/observations are made (pre-test/post-test);
- the number of comparison groups used (two-group designs, multiple-group designs);
- whether the control group receives no 'treatment' or it receives an alternative treatment to that received by the 'experimental' group;
- the allocation to groups and whether this is random or not;
- the number of new factors introduced.

The use of pre- and post-test observations acts as a baseline against which to measure any changes that occur, and the use of control groups similarly provides a basis on which the researcher can make comparisons between the experimental group and the control group. Coupled with the allocation to groups on a purely random basis, these allow the researcher to eliminate a host of potential alternative explanations and logically deduce the specific cause of the changes that are observed.

'Quasi-experiment' is a term used to describe a research design that follows the spirit of the experimental approach but which, for practical reasons, cannot meet one or more of the essential conditions. This situation is most likely to occur when experiments are conducted outside the laboratory 'in the field' where circumstances dictate that it is not possible to implement controls on all the relevant variables. Outside the laboratory researchers might find that:

- they cannot allocate people to groups on a random basis. This will necessitate conducting the experiment using 'non-equivalent' groups; or
- they cannot use a control group for comparisons; or
- they cannot conduct both a pre-test and a post-test to get measurements before and after the introduction of the variable being investigated.

Cook and Campbell (1979) argue that a quasi-experimental design should include no more than one of these three shortcomings. It can use non-equivalent groups *or* it can lack a control group *or* it can lack pre-test measurements – but it cannot incorporate more than one of these without severely jeopardizing its power to identify causal factors. Provided it lacks no more than one of these conditions, however, a quasi-experiment can still be useful. It is an option that can be used prudently as a fall-back position if it proves impossible to meet all the conditions for a true experiment. Its limitations should always be acknowledged and it should be used cautiously when it comes to identifying causal factors. Cook and Campbell specifically warn against the dangers of making unwarranted causal inferences on the basis of quasi-experimental research designs, especially those where assignment to groups is not based on random selection: 'While they are often useful for suggesting new ideas, they are normally not sufficient for permitting strong tests of causal hypotheses because they fail to rule out a number of plausible alternative interpretations' (1979: 95).

Advantages of experiments

Credibility

The use of experiments is regarded by many people, including some social scientists, as the most scientific and, therefore, the most credible approach to research. It has a status that trades off an association with 'hard' science, and carries with it a sense of objectivity and impartiality in terms of its findings.

Repeatable

In the case of laboratory experiments, randomized controlled trials and retrospective experiments, the research should lend itself to being checked by other researchers by being repeated using identical procedures. With field experiments and natural experiments, however, there is only a limited possibility of repeating the experiment.

Precision

The nature of experimental research permits a high level of precision and consistency when it comes to the measurements that form the basis of the data.

Causes and explanations

Experiments take place under conditions which involve controls on relevant variables and which allow the researcher to identify the exact cause of things that are observed.

Disadvantages of experiments

Artificial settings

With laboratory experiments there are questions about whether the experimental situation creates conditions comparable with the 'real-world' situations in which the behaviour/decisions would be made, or whether it encourages artificial responses in line with the artificial setting.

Deception and ethics

There are two ethical considerations that need to be borne in mind when considering the use of experiments. First, will the experiment's success depend on keeping its true purpose secret from the research subjects? If so, this raises a question about the ethics of deception when used in social research. Second, if the research design employs the use of control groups, which is likely, will there be any advantage or disadvantage experienced by those in the respective groups? Is it possible that adverse comparisons might result through different treatments of experimental and control groups? If there is a significant difference, this could pose both ethical and practical/political problems for the researcher.

Control of the relevant variables

Being able to control the relevant variables lies at the heart of the experimental method. However, this can be hard to accomplish. Even when it is possible in a practical sense, there can be ethical issues that arise which need to be taken into account.

Cause and effect

The experimental approach tends to focus on observable effects and works better with relatively straightforward matters. It can miss indirect causes (de Vaus 2001) and is not really well suited to dealing with the more complex underlying causes of many social phenomena (Pawson and Tilley 1997).

Random allocation to groups

When random allocation to the experimental group and the control group is not possible questions will arise about whether the groups genuinely constitute a 'matched pair'. Researchers need to be sure that there is no element of self-selection to the groups and that the groups are 'equivalent'.

Further reading

de Vaus, D. (2001) *Research Design in Social Research*. London: Sage, chs 4–6.

Dunning, T. (2012) *Natural Experiments in the Social Sciences: A Design-Based Approach*. Cambridge: Cambridge University Press.

Milgram, S. (1974) *Obedience to Authority: An Experimental View*. New York: Harper & Row.

Thyer, B.A. (2012) *Quasi-Experimental Research Designs*. New York: Oxford University Press.

Webster, M. and Sell, J. (2014) *Laboratory Experiments in the Social Sciences*, 2nd edn. Burlington, MA: Amsterdam Press.

Checklist for the use of experiments

When undertaking research which involves experiments you should feel confident about answering 'yes' to the following questions: ☑

1 Have the key variables been clearly identified? ☐

2 Has a clear distinction been drawn between dependent and independent variables? ☐

3 Can the relevant variables be controlled for the purposes of designing the experiment? ☐

4 Is there a clear hypothesis or proposition that can be tested? ☐

5 Have detailed records been kept of the procedures and the results (in order to evaluate the design and replicate the experiment)? ☐

6 If a control group is used, is it closely matched in all key respects with the experimental group? ☐

7 If the research subjects are fully aware of the nature of the experiment in which they are taking part, has 'the observer' effect been taken into account? ☐

8 If the research subjects are not fully aware of the nature of the experiment in which they are participating, will they be fully informed after the experiment has taken place? ☐

9 Does the experimental situation create conditions comparable to the 'real-world' situations in which the behaviour/decisions would be made? ☐

10 Is the research ethical in terms of its treatment of those involved in the experiment? ☐

5　Ethnography

What is ethnography?

The term *ethnography* literally means a description of peoples or cultures. It
has its origins as a research strategy in the works of the early social anthropologists whose aim was to provide a detailed account of the cultures and lives of
small, isolated tribes. Such tribes were seen, with some justification, as 'endan-
gered species', and the social anthropologists saw the need to map out those
cultures before they became contaminated by contact with the industrial world
or withered away to extinction.

The image of the pith-helmeted outsider dressed in khaki shorts arriving on
the shores of some remote and exotic palm tree island to set up camp and study
the lives of the 'native' has become legendary – largely through the works of
people like Bronislaw Malinowski (1922) and Margaret Mead (1943). The concerns of such social anthropologists and the research strategy they employed
set the scene for much of what is undertaken as 'ethnography' today:

- It requires the researcher to spend considerable *time in the field* among the
  people whose lives and culture are being studied. The ethnographer needs to
  share in the lives rather than observe from a position of detachment.
  Extended fieldwork allows for a *journey of discovery* in which the explanations for what is being witnessed emerge over a period of time.
- Routine and normal aspects of *everyday life* are regarded as worthy of consideration as research data. The mundane and the ordinary parts of social
  life are just as valid as the special events and ceremonies which can all too
  easily capture our attention.

- There is special attention given to the way the people being studied see their world. Quite distinct from the researcher's analysis of the situation, the ethnographer is generally concerned to find out *how the members of the group/culture being studied understand things*, the meanings *they* attach to happenings, the way *they* perceive their reality.
- There is an emphasis on the need to look at the interlinkages between the various features of the culture and to avoid isolating facets of the culture from the wider context within which they exist. Ethnography generally prefers a *holistic approach* which stresses processes, relationships, connections and interdependency among the component parts.
- There is some acknowledgement that the ethnographer's final account of the culture or group being studied is more than just a description – it is a *construction*. It is not a direct 'reproduction', a literal photograph of the situation. It is, rather, a crafted construction which employs particular writing skills (rhetoric) and which inevitably owes something to the ethnographer's own experiences.

Types of ethnography

The alien and the exotic

Early anthropologists studied groups in societies that were *different* from their own. Their aim was to explain the culture and lifestyles they found in the 'primitive' society where their fieldwork was based and, through a process of *comparison and contrast*, to cast fresh light on aspects of their own society as well. Ethnography, in this respect, resembles an anthropological approach. However, it does not restrict its attention to remote tribes in distant lands. Indeed, the most popular development of ethnography has been its application to lifestyles, understandings and beliefs within 'our own' society.

In its early days, ethnography 'within our own society' tended to focus on groups who were relatively small in number and who tended to be somewhat alien to the mainstream of society. The 'anthropological stance' was applied to oddball cultures that stood out as different from the norm. And, just as with the study of 'natives' in far-off lands, there was an immediate attraction for studying such groups. They offered something intrinsically interesting in the way their lifestyles seemed quaint, crazy, even exotic, compared with the everyday experience of those who studied the groups and those who read the resulting books. The focus was on 'deviant' groups, such as hobos, alcoholics, drug users, hells angels, religious sects, street gangs, and the like, and ethnography retains today an interest in the exotic and the special, with ceremonies and the unusual features of social life. A recent ethnography, for example, focused on 'urban explorers' (Garrett 2013). These are groups of people who put themselves on the margins of society by taking risks (both physical and legal) that most people would not dare to contemplate in order to explore architectural sites normally 'off-bounds' to the public; from the heights of skyscrapers and construction site cranes to the depths of sewers, drains and underground bunkers. Garrett spent a period of four years embedding himself 'in the community to see how the people within it work and play, the rules they give themselves and the stories they tell (Garrett 2013: 1).

Routine life

The ethnographic approach can be applied to routine features of social life and is not something that is exclusively reserved for the study of alien or exotic cultures. There is a kind of ethnography, indeed, that focuses on cultures and lifestyles that might be regarded as routine, mundane, normal and fairly unspectacular. This is illustrated in the case of ethnographies of occupations; for example, life in classrooms (Woods 2012), the work of taxi drivers (Gambetta and Hamill 2005) or life on a building site (Riemer 1979). Attention has even been given to Wall Street investment bankers, with an insider's account of the customs, lifestyles and experiences that make up the everyday lives of financial high-flyers (Ho 2009). The point to recognize is that routine, everyday lifestyles closer to the mainstream of normal social life can be treated as valid topics for ethnographic enquiry.

Life on the Internet

In recent decades the Internet has emerged as a feature of everyday life that has attracted the attention of ethnographers. This is because the Internet has developed forms of culture and customs that are new and distinct to the cyberworld. The Internet is inhabited by various groups of people who share specific interests, beliefs and understandings, who have cultures that can be investigated using an ethnographic approach (Boellstorff et al. 2012). The interest in 'online cultures' and 'online communities' has given rise to what Hine (2000) has called 'virtual ethnography' and Kozinets (2015) has termed 'netnography'.

Life history as a 'personal ethnography'

Ethnography focuses on the customs and practices of *groups* of people. There is, though, an approach that is in many ways similar to ethnography but which focuses instead on the individual: this is the 'life history' approach. The aim of the approach is to portray the lives of specific people, to map how their experiences change over time, and to link these experiences with the cultural, social or historical context in which they occur. Like biographies, life histories can be based on the whole of a person's lifespan from beginning to end, but can also be used to cover portions of lives – extended and substantial parts of people's lives but not the whole of the life.

There are two themes running through most life history research, both of which fit closely with ethnography. The first is that the research provides a 'thick' description of the life of the person. It includes the kind of fine detail that allows the reader to see the complex and multi-layered facets of the person's

> **Link up with Chapter 6, The life course perspective.**

life. The second is that the individual's understanding of things is treated as a crucial part of the life history. As Marshall and Rossman (2011: 151) put it, the life history approach 'understands a culture through the history of one person's development of life within it, told in ways that capture the person's own feelings, views, and perspectives'.

Data collection in fieldwork settings

Naturalism

Going 'into the field' to witness events at first hand in their natural habitat lies at the very heart of what it means to do ethnography. Ethnographers generally wish to preserve the natural state of affairs. To do this they want to avoid disrupting the situation by their very presence as observers in the field. This is why *naturalism* is a key concern of ethnography. The ethnographer's concern with naturalism derives from the wish to study things in their natural state – undisturbed by the intrusion of research tools or the disruption of experimental designs.

Covert research

One method of conducting ethnographic research with minimal effect on the natural state of affairs is to disguise the researcher's role and to 'go undercover'. In this way it might be possible for an ethnographer to conduct fieldwork without people knowing that they have a researcher in their midst. The researcher can blend into the background by adopting a role that fits in with the normal situation. This has benefits as far as ethnography is concerned because: (1) it preserves the naturalness of the setting; and (2) it generally sidesteps any need to get authorization to conduct the research. However, it gives rise to a different type of problem. The decision to undertake covert research means that the researcher cannot also have 'informed consent' on the part of the subjects of his/her research, and this raises substantial ethical problems.

> **Link up with Chapter 18, Research ethics.**

Overt research and 'gatekeepers'

Ethnographers do not always work in a covert manner. Indeed, it is fair to say that most ethnographies actually involve some degree of openness about the role of the researcher. When this is the case, the ethical problems are less likely to be an impediment to the research.

The opportunity to conduct overt ethnographic research generally requires the researcher to make contact with 'gatekeepers' who can help with the vital business of gaining access to the fieldwork settings. Gatekeepers' authority to grant or withhold access varies, of course, depending on the degree to which the people, places and events being studied are part of a formal environment. In formal settings, such as work organizations, hospitals or schools, the assistance of people in key positions of authority is pretty much a prerequisite. For example, in the educational context headteachers have formal jurisdiction over entry to school premises and can withhold or grant access to teachers and pupils.

In less formal settings the role of the gatekeeper is different. As Whyte illustrated so graphically in his research (Whyte [1943] 1993), the role of gatekeeper can become more akin to a guarantor for the *bona fide* status of the researcher. Whyte's gatekeeper, 'Doc', had no formal authority to grant or deny access; he used his status with the group to open up the possibility of Whyte making contact with potential participants, and acted as a sponsor/guarantor to enable some trust relationship to develop.

 Caution

An 'overt' researcher role increases the chances of disrupting the naturalness of the situation. If people realize that they are the subject of research then there is a real prospect that they might act differently than they would under normal circumstances.

Link up with Observer effect, p. 72.

The influence of gatekeepers, as Burgess (1984) argues, goes beyond a simple granting or denial of contact with research subjects: it is a continual *process* in fieldwork research. It is a process because fieldwork is generally conducted over a period of time and it is a process, perhaps more importantly, because access needs to be sought to new people, places and events as new lines of enquiry become incorporated in the research. Permission from a gatekeeper, therefore, is necessarily renewable and renegotiable, and should be viewed as an 'access *relationship*' rather than a one-off event.

Description and theory

Thick description

Ethnography involves the description of things witnessed first-hand in the field by the researcher. Such descriptions, however, if they are to prove useful from an ethnographic perspective, must go beyond a superficial glance. It is vital that they contain sufficient depth and detail to allow real insights into the situation being studied. The term 'thick description' is often referred to in this context. A 'thick description' (Geertz 1973) aims to describe particular acts or events in relation to their cultural context. The emphasis is not just on describing what 'is' but on explaining how the nature of this phenomenon is closely linked to other aspects of its social context. To illustrate what this means, Geertz himself draws on the example of 'winking'. Simply describing the action itself is 'thin description'. It is important to include as part of the description, but if we want to understand the meaning of the action we need a 'thick description' which supplies information about the intentions of the person doing the winking and the symbolic significance of the gesture in different settings. Only then can we understand whether the action is to be construed as a twitch, as a friendly gesture, as flirting, as a subtle conspiracy or whatever.

Idiographic and nomothetic approaches

Detailed descriptions can stand in their own right as a valuable contribution to knowledge or, alternatively, they can be treated as building blocks towards the creation of more general theories about the kind of culture, lifestyle, beliefs or events being researched. An *idiographic* approach aligns with the first of these two positions. It sees the purpose of ethnographic research as being to produce detailed pictures of events or cultures – descriptions which stand in their own right. From this standpoint there is no need to worry about how representative the situation is or what the broader implications might be in terms of other events or cultures of the type, or of contributing to wider theories. Any ethnographic description is to be regarded as a stand-alone 'one-off' that is to be judged by the depth of its portrayal and the intricacy of its description. There is no attempt to derive something from the description that goes beyond the specifics of the situation and which can, in some way or other, link to broader issues.

Link up with Chapter 9, Phenomenology.

A *nomothetic* approach, however, challenges the value of producing numerous stand-alone descriptions. It argues that if each ethnographic study produces a one-off, isolated piece of information, then there is little prospect of building up any generalized knowledge about human societies. The nomothetic approach takes the position that ethnographic research should be undertaken quite deliberately to develop more generalized and 'theoretical' conclusions that will apply outside the confines of the individual ethnographic study: it should help to generate theories. Or it might even be used to test theories. Porter (1993), for example, argues that ethnographic research should be used as a way of checking whether a theory really does hold true in 'real life'.

So, at one end of the spectrum there are those who regard the main purpose of ethnography as providing rich and detailed descriptions of real-life situations as they really are. At the other end of the spectrum there are those who see the role of ethnographic fieldwork as a means of developing theories by checking them out in small-scale scenarios. Somewhere towards the middle of the spectrum lies the pragmatic view 'that "idiographic" and "nomothetic" approaches are not mutually exclusive, and that we can have both rich and intensive description *and* generalizability' (Woods 2012: 268). Advocates of the middle position are keen to hold on to the idiographic aspect of ethnographic research in as much as it provides a valuable and distinct kind of data – the detailed descriptions of specifics based on first-hand observation in naturally occurring situations. But they also recognize the need for conclusions to be drawn from the research which have implications beyond the bounds of the particular events, customs or people studied. In the words of Hammersley (1990: 598), the 'descriptions must remain close to the concrete reality of particular events but at the same time reveal general features of human social life'.

Good practice: Generalizing from ethnographies

To accommodate the need for ethnographies to combine detailed description of particular settings with the need to produce findings that have some general implications beyond the specifics of the situation studied, ethnographies should:

- compare their findings with those of other similar ethnographies;
- consider how their findings tie in with, or contradict, existing relevant theories and understanding about human social behaviour;
- explain the significance of the topic in relation to the beliefs and priorities of the researcher's own culture.

Reflexivity: ethnographers as part of the world they seek to describe

Ethnographers tend to be very sensitive to the matter of reflexivity and the way it affects their perception of the culture or events they wish to describe. What concerns them is that the conceptual tools they use to understand the cultures or events being studied are not, and can never be, neutral and passive instruments of discovery.

As researchers, the meanings we attach to things that happen and the language we use to describe them are the product of our own culture, social background and personal experiences. Making sense of what is observed during fieldwork observation is a process that relies on what the researcher already knows and already believes, and it is not a voyage of discovery which starts with a clean sheet. We can only make sense of the world in a way that we have learnt to do using conceptual tools which are based on our own culture and our own experiences. We have no way of standing outside these to reach some objective and neutral vantage point from which to view things 'as they really are'. To an extent, we can describe them only 'as we see them', and this is shaped by *our* culture, not theirs.

The question that taxes ethnographers is this: 'How far can my description of the culture or event depict things from the point of view of those involved when I can only use my own way of seeing things, my own conceptual tools, to make sense of what is happening?' Broadly, ethnographers are conscious of the way in which their account of any particular lifestyle or beliefs is a construction based upon the researcher's interpretation of events. Even when it comes to writing up the ethnography, there are deep-rooted doubts about claims to objectivity. The outcome of ethnographic research is generally recognized by those who write it as being a creative work in its own right – the outcome of interpretation, editing and skilful writing techniques as well as a reflection of the reality of the situation they set out to study (Woods 2006). Inescapably, the account is partial – an edited and abridged version – which owes something to the ethnographer as well as the culture or events observed. There is nothing new to this. Malinowski appreciated the point many years ago:

| Link up with Producing accounts of research, p. 367. |

In ethnography, the distance is often enormous between the brute material of information – as it is presented to the student in his own observations, in native statement, in the kaleidoscope of tribal life – and the final authoritative presentations of the results. The ethnographer has to traverse this distance in the laborious years between the moment when he sets foot upon a native beach, and makes his first attempts to get into touch with the natives, and the time when he writes down the final version of his results. (Malinowski 1922: 4)

Putting the researcher's 'self' into ethnographic research

One of the characteristic features of ethnography is the significance it attaches to the role of the researcher's 'self' in the process of research. The researcher's identity, values and beliefs become part of the equation – a built-in component that cannot be eliminated as an influence on the end-product findings of the project.

Ethnographic research, therefore, calls for a certain degree of introspection on the part of the researcher. He/she needs to reflect upon the way that background factors associated with personal experiences, personal beliefs and social values may have shaped the way that events and cultures were interpreted.

However, the ethnographic researcher needs to go beyond mere reflection. This is, in a sense, a private activity. Necessary though it is, it needs to be portrayed more publicly if it is to support the research outcomes. Researchers need to supply their readers with some insights into the possible influence of the researcher's self on the interpretation of events or cultures. There needs to be a public account of the self which explores the role of the researcher's self. This account of the self will vary in the amount of detail it provides, depending on the nature of the research topic, the kind of methods used and the audience for whom the ethnography is written. It is obviously a matter of judgement here about the extent to which the account should delve to the depths of detail about researchers' personal matters, and the amount of detail that the readership needs to know in order to arrive at a reasonable evaluation of the likely impact of the 'self' on the research.

Good practice: Reflecting on the researcher's 'self'

Ethnographies require some reflection by the researcher on how his/ her biography, values and experiences might have a bearing on the nature of the study. This 'public account of the role of the self' can be included in the methodology section and possibly in the Preface or Introduction to reports of the findings. As a broad guideline, the following factors might be considered:

- personal beliefs relating to the topic (politics, values, standpoint);
- personal interests in the area of investigation (vested interest, history of events);
- personal experiences linked to the research topic;
- personal expertise in relation to the topic (qualification, experience).

To give an account of the way personal beliefs, interests, experience and expertise might have a bearing on findings, the researcher is likely to need to draw upon personal details about his/her:

- age;
- sex;
- ethnicity;
- social background (class, family, environment);
- education and qualifications;
- work experience and skills.

Advantages of ethnography

Detailed data based on direct observation

As a research strategy ethnography is based on direct observation via fieldwork, rather than relying extensively on second-hand data or statements made by research subjects. It is grounded in empirical research involving direct contact with relevant people and places, and it provides data rich in depth and detail. Potentially, it can deal with intricate and subtle realities.

Holistic

Ethnography aspires to holistic explanations which focus on processes and relationships that lie behind the surface events. It puts things in context rather than abstracting specific aspects in isolation.

A fresh view on things

There is an element of contrast and comparison built into ethnographic research which encourages the researcher to look beyond 'the obvious' and to see things relative to other cultures and lifestyles. Cultures and lifestyles are viewed as 'anthropologically strange'.

Actors' perceptions

Ethnographic research is particularly well suited to dealing with the way members of a culture see events – as seen through their eyes. It describes and explores the 'actors' perceptions'.

Self-awareness

It has an open and explicit awareness of the role of the researcher's *self* in the choice of topic, process of research and construction of the findings/ conclusions. It acknowledges the inherent reflexivity of social knowledge.

Disadvantages of ethnography

Access

Gaining access to relevant people and situations can pose a particular challenge for ethnographic research. With covert research there are ethical issues that need to be addressed with care, and with overt research the success of the research generally depends on assistance from suitable gatekeepers. With both covert and overt research there might need to be a trade-off between the desire to retain the naturalness of the setting and the desire to respect the rights of the people being studied.

Ethics

The close involvement of ethnographic researchers with the people and cultures being studied, combined with the depth and detail of the information collected, means that special attention needs to be paid to ethical problems associated with intrusions upon privacy, disclosure of identities and with gaining informed consent from research subjects.

Reliability

Ethnographic studies, because of their nature, are hard to replicate in order to check the findings. Accounts of the situation often depend on records kept by a single researcher and they tend to rely heavily on the researcher's interpretation of events.

Tensions within the approach

There is a tension within the realms of ethnography stemming from its twin concerns with naturalism and reflexivity. Ethnographies generally attempt to accommodate an internal contradiction between (1) 'realist' aspirations to provide full and detailed *descriptions* of events or cultures as they naturally exist, and (2) a 'relativist' awareness of the reflexive nature of social knowledge and the inevitable influence of the researcher's 'self' on the whole research endeavour.

Stand-alone descriptions

Ethnographic research has the potential to produce an array of 'pictures' which coexist, but which tend to remain as separate, isolated stories. There is arguably an in-built tendency to scatter these building-block pictures at random, rather than erecting a structure where each is a brick which serves as a base for further bricks to be laid upon, moving it ever upwards. To avoid this, ethnographies need to be guided by (or towards) a coherent theoretical framework.

Further reading

Boellstorff, T., Nardi, B., Pearce, C. and Taylor, T. (2012) *Ethnography and Virtual Worlds: A Handbook of Method*. Princeton, NJ: Princeton University Press.

Brewer, J. (2000) *Ethnography*. Buckingham: Open University Press.

Hammersley, M. and Atkinson, P. (2007) *Ethnography: Principles in Practice*, 3rd edn. London: Tavistock.

Kozinets, R. (2015) *Netnography: Redefined*. London: Sage.

Murchison, J. (2010) *Ethnography Essentials: Designing, Conducting, and Presenting Your Research*. San Francisco, CA: Jossey-Bass.

O'Reilly, K. (2012) *Ethnographic Methods*, 2nd edn. London: Routledge.

Checklist for ethnographic research

When undertaking ethnographic research you should feel confident about answering 'yes' to the following questions: ☑

1 Have cultures, lifestyles, customs and beliefs been identified as the main interest of the research? ☐

2 Does the research involve a substantial time 'in the field' collecting empirical data? ☐

3 Has due consideration been given to the impact of conducting the research and the extent to which it disrupts the naturalness of the setting? ☐

4 If a covert role is adopted have the ethical implications been explored? ☐

5 If an overt role is adopted has access to the fieldwork settings been authorized through relevant 'gatekeepers'? ☐

6 Does the research adopt a holistic approach, linking all significant contributing factors? ☐

7 Does the research include an account of the role of the researcher's 'self'? ☐

8 Is there a description of how the ethnography builds on (or contradicts) existing explanations of the phenomenon? ☐

9 Are the findings compared and contrasted with other ethnographies on similar topics? ☐

10 Is there due recognition of the fact that the ethnography is a researcher's construction rather than a literal description of the situation? ☐

© M. Denscombe, *The Good Research Guide*. Open University Press.

6 | The life course perspective

What is the life course perspective?

The 'life course' refers to people's journey through life from birth to death, and the life course perspective is an approach to the study of people's lives which analyses things in relation to that journey. The term 'life cycle' has a similar meaning. However, because it tends to be associated with the biology of plant life and animals, social researchers generally prefer to use the term 'life course' which better reflects the social, cultural and historical aspects of going through human life.

Age has a particular significance in relation to the life course, and the life course perspective highlights this fact. In doing so, it offers an alternative to approaches that focus on social class, gender or ethnicity (Settersten 1997; Hunt 2005). Life course researchers, however, do not focus on age to the exclusion of other factors. They tend to prefer *multi-causal* explanations that look at age in conjunction with other factors. Just as feminist studies take gender as the key issue, and then note how other social factors such as class and ethnicity play out in connection with gender, the life course approach acknowledges the influence of class, gender and ethnicity but is interested *primarily* in age.

Types of life course perspective

There are four strands to the life course perspective. These focus on:

* the characteristics of particular *stages in life*, looking at the social, psychological or biological traits associated with different age groups;

- the effects of social change or significant *life events* on the life of cohorts of people (i.e. people born at a particular time or who have shared a particular experience);
- the lives of people in the context of their *journeys through life*, looking at the impact of personal experiences and decisions on the direction their lives have taken;
- the development of people's bodies and minds through *the ageing process*, and the eventual decline in their mental and physical capabilities.

These strands share the view that human lives need to be understood in relation to where people are on the continuum from birth to death and, in large part, they also agree that experiences and decisions earlier in the life course can have a significant impact on subsequent developments. Where they differ is that they look at the life course through the lens of different disciplines. The life course perspective has captured the interest of researchers across a range of behavioural science disciplines, including sociology, social history, psychology, biology and health-related studies, and as Figure 6.1 indicates, these four strands tend to reflect the primary interests of these distinct disciplines.

Figure 6.1 Four types of life course perspective

Perspective	Discipline	Focus on ...
Stages of life	Sociology	Age-related norms of behaviour and social roles
Life events	Cultural studies	Transitions between stages
		Economic and political upheavals
Journeys through life	Social history	Social context and social change
	Health	Childhood, old age
Ageing*	Biology	Physical development and age-related health issues
	Psychology	Mental and cognitive development

Note:*Because this book is concerned with *social* research, this chapter concentrates on the social, cultural and historical approaches rather than *biological* approaches that focus on how the body grows, matures and declines over the passage of time, or *psychological* approaches that focus on how the mind develops over time in terms of cognitive abilities, emotions and personality development.

Stages of life

The stages of life strand operates on the premise that the life course can be divided into a number of sections each of which is distinctive in terms of the age of the people involved and the social norms relating to it. Those who focus on stages of life want to understand how lives are structured in terms of these stages.

They are interested in the way that societies and cultures organize the passage through life, and they want to know about social norms and what roles people might be expected to play at different times throughout their life. Figure 6.2 shows (1) how stages of life can be loosely associated with a person's chronological age, (2) how they can be divided into sub-stages (which can be useful because they narrow the age-range being investigated) and (3) how they tend to be associated with some general issues of interest to life-course researchers.

Sometimes researchers will cover *all stages of the life course* in order to provide a picture of the life 'as a whole' from birth to death. The aim is to provide an overview of core features of each stage of life and to build a picture of the progression through life which characterizes the people being studied. On occasion the stages of life are compared with earlier times or with other cultures, but not always. For practical reasons these studies tend to rely heavily on demographic data and secondary source data to be found in official statistics and historical records.

Sometimes, *a single stage of life* is treated as the main point of interest (e.g. youth, middle age, 60–75 year olds). When the research looks at life stages as they exist today this kind of life course research lends itself to empirical investigation because it is feasible to collect data directly from members of the age group being studied using interviews, questionnaires, etc. This is a kind of life course research, therefore, that can fit nicely with the remit for small-scale empirical research projects.

Sometimes the life course research *compares stages of life*, looking at how things have changed over time. This perspective looks at the situation of those in a specific stage of life usually as it is today, and compares it with the situation for those in the same stage of life when living in some earlier historical time. This might be, for example, a comparison of the lives of 'youth' today with those of 'youth' in the 1950s. Such research tends to combine the use of primary source data (from interviews or questionnaires) with secondary source data (from archives and historical records).

Example 6.1

Stages of life

Two classic examples of the life course perspective that are based on stages of life are Erik Erikson's *Identity and the Life Cycle* (first published in 1959) and Daniel Levinson's *Seasons of a Man's Life* (published in 1978). Both see life as developing through a sequence of stages, each stage characterized by a distinct set of social and psychological traits. Another example is provided by Laslett (1996) who identifies four stages of life, and argues provocatively that the 'Third Stage' is the best. 'First comes an era of dependence, socialization, immaturity and education; second an era of independence, maturity and responsibility, of earning and of saving; third an era of personal fulfilment; and fourth an era of final dependence, decrepitude and death'.

(Laslett 1996: 4)

Figure 6.2 Stages of life

Age	Stage of life	Sub-stages	Some alternative definitions	Some key themes and issues
Birth	Childhood	infancy	Child 0–18 (UN definition)	Socialization within family
		toddler	Age of criminal responsibility (10 England, 8 Scotland)	Cognitive development
		childhood		Physical growth
				Early learning & education
12				Dependence
13	Adolescence		Adolescence 10–19 (UN and UNICEF definition)	Peer influence
				Emotional development
			Youth 14–24 (UN definition)	Relationships within family
			Age of consent 16 (UK)	Physical maturity
17				Dependence
18	Adulthood	young adult	Young people 10–24 (UNICEF/WHO definition)	Employment
				Self-sufficiency
				Love and relationships
				Independence
29				
30		prime adulthood	Early middle years 29–39	Work and careers
				Child-rearing
				Own family
39				Caring and responsibility
40		middle age	Mid-life 40–50	Independence
				Work and careers
49				Empty nester – children left home
50		late adult	Later middle years 50–64	Independence
64				Retirement
65+	Old age	young old-age 65–75	Third age	Caring for own parents
				Adaption to aging
				Independence
		elderly 75+	Fourth age	Single-person household
				Needing health care and support
				Dependence
Death				Dying, death and grief

There is some debate about how many distinct stages there are, how they can be defined and at what times they occur in people's lives. Most life-perspective researchers warn against the idea that life stages can be mapped directly onto specific 'years since birth'. People develop and mature at different rates, survive for different lengths of time and experience different events during their life course. There are variations between countries in terms of *legal definitions* of what constitutes 'childhood' and 'adolescence'. And there are *variations between cultures* in the way stages of life are perceived and treated. Adolescence, for instance, is a life stage that did not exist in the past and does necessarily exist in other cultures today.

There is also the point that people can sometimes move back and forth between particular life stages and that things do not always operate in a nice, neat sequential flow from one life stage to a subsequent life stage. There is the possibility of what has been termed 'yo-yoization' with individuals going back and forth between phases that, in the past, were part of a one-way journey from childhood to old age. It is not unusual, for example, to find adults moving back to live 'at home' with their parents following the break-up of a marriage, or because their work situation means they can no longer afford to live in a home of their own. They move back from an independent stage of life to one of dependency.

For such reasons it is not possible to identify universal and objective stages of life that will apply to all people in all circumstances. Which means that those who adopt a stages of life approach have to acknowledge that:

- the stages are relevant for a particular culture at a particular point in time;
- chronological age needs to be seen as a rather rough and ready guideline for life stages;
- the stages of life are not necessarily sequential or mutually exclusive.

 Key point
The life course perspective focuses attention on *culturally defined*, age-related phases through which people tend to pass during their lifetime.

Life events

Historical events and the study of cohorts

This strand of the life course perspective looks at how people's lives have been shaped by the particular era in which they were born and the way that historical events have given a direction to their later lives. It looks at the way events such as wars, political upheaval and economic disasters can have a profound effect on the lives of those who live through them, and it can look at how people's experience of things like poverty or illness can affect their later life.

When researchers want to investigate the impact of some significant historical event they generally look at the lives of different *cohorts* of people. Cohorts are normally comprised of people born around the same time or people who have all experienced a similar and significant event in their lives. Sometimes the focus is *on similarities that exist among members* of a cohort. The quest is to find out how this common characteristic has affected their subsequent lives. It can be termed the *within cohorts approach*. Other times, researchers use a *between cohorts approach*. This can either look at the same stage of life at different historical times, for instance, the analysis could compare the situation of 18–25 year olds in the 1950s with that for the same age group today, or, the analysis can look at *different stages of life at the same historical time*. In this case the analysis could compare, for example, the situation of 18–25 year olds with that of 26–40 year olds.

Personal events and transitions

There are events that happen during the life course which, though they are significant, are not the result of a particular era or historical event. These life events are more personal. They include things like getting married, setting up home with someone, the birth of a child, divorce, changes in employment, the onset of a serious illness or the death of a loved one. Such events can be literally 'life changing', serving to move people from one life situation to another. They can act as markers for a *transition* from one stage of life to the next. A transition involves a significant change in status and role, and it is often accompanied by a symbolic ceremony (e.g. wedding or graduation event). The timing of such transitions is significant, and researchers are interested in the conventions that exist which specify when it is right and proper for transitions to occur from one kind of role to the next.

Trajectories

Significant life events, whether historical or personal, produce a distinct pathway through life. These pathways are known as *trajectories*. A trajectory captures the notion of a *direction* in the life course and, in particular, the way that earlier events and experiences set the route for the subsequent life course.

 Key point

The life-events approach draws attention to the importance of change and changing life circumstances for the way people perceive things, the way they experience things and for the decisions they make in relation to things that shape their lives.

Journeys through life

The life course can be viewed in terms of a *journey through life*. This perspective has proved particularly valuable for social workers, welfare workers, health-care workers, teachers and others who are concerned with the life trajectories of their clients and who appreciate that the circumstances people find themselves in need to be understood in the context of:

- where they are in the life course;
- the key events and experiences in their lives that have shaped their life so far;
- the key decisions they have taken with respect to their life.

To build up a picture of a person's journey through life, researchers can make use of a *life review* in which an individual reflects on his/her life and considers the implications of past events for current circumstances, who they are and what they stand for. In this approach the individual is invited to think back on their life and to construct a personal biography. This provides an account of life experiences which, although subjective, can reveal the sense which people make of their life, the meaning they attach to the phases of life and the decisions that have had significant consequences for their life trajectory.

Key point

Life course research can look at the stories people have to tell about their own history – their own lives in their own words.

Link up with
Life history,
p. 85.

Personal accounts

Where the cohort or the individuals involved in the research are still alive, there is the prospect of getting primary source data through methods such as *interviews* or *questionnaires*. These can be used to ask people about their recollection of events and the reasons they took particular decisions. *Focus groups* can also provide a useful source of data. As Chatrakul Na Ayudhya et al. (2014: 159) suggest, 'Focus groups may provide a link between the individual story accessed via individual biographical interviews and the cohort-wide experience of being of that age and social group at that point in time and place'.

When listening to people's accounts of events in the past, however, we need to be wary of 'retrospective bias'. As Clausen (1986: 14) warns, 'It is dangerous to accept retrospective accounts as gospel, and well-meaning persons may be quite unable to reconstruct the past in an unbiased manner, or even to remember it accurately'. Sometimes people's memories are subconsciously based on what they have been told about the past, rather than a genuine first-hand recollection of what happened, and, almost inevitably, past events are remembered from the position of where the person is today – their current personality, ambitions, identity and self-interest. So, although people's accounts of the past can provide valuable knowledge and insights, the researcher should always be aware that they are reconstructions of how things were in the past viewed from how things are in the present.

Link up with Chapter 13, Interviews.

Historical data

When the cohort or individuals are no longer alive, of course, there is little alternative than to build up a picture of key events and place them in their social context by making use of evidence drawn from historical sources. It is the only way of piecing together a picture of how things were when there is no one left to ask. For this reason, life perspective researchers might need to rely on:

Link up with Chapter 15, Documents.

- archive records;
- biographies and personal diaries;
- newspaper reports.

Longitudinal studies

Some life course researchers see longitudinal studies as providing the best method for collecting data. Their argument is that data ought to be based on tracking people over time and that the use of cross-sectional surveys has limitations when it comes to looking at similarities or differences between cohorts of people. This limitation would become evident if we used a cross-sectional survey to look at the political attitudes of 60 year olds and 40 year olds. The survey might find that the 60 year olds are more conservative than the 40 year olds. It might be tempting to conclude from this that *age* is the causal factor and that as we grow older we become more inclined towards conservatism. However, if those very same 60 year olds had been surveyed 20 years ago – when they themselves were 40 – the data might have revealed that their attitudes were conservative even at that time. Were this to be the case, it would be false to attribute the more conservative attitudes of the 60 year olds to the ageing process. It could, instead, be attributed to the cohort effect and the impact of historical time – the time in which they were born and the eras through which they have lived.

The use of longitudinal studies allows life course researchers to overcome this uncertainty. Longitudinal studies collect data covering an extended period of time. They track people's progress over time, generally through a regular series of survey points. This allows the researchers to build up a picture of how the age cohort or individual people develop over time. It allows them to monitor changes in circumstances and attitudes, and to analyse the impact of events that affect the people being studied.

There are numerous examples of longitudinal studies that lend themselves to life course research. In the UK, the National Child Development Study has tracked the lives of 17,000 people born in a single week of 1958, focusing upon things like their progress through education and work, and looking at aspects of their family life, their well-being and their social attitudes. The Millennium Cohort Study similarly has followed the lives of around 19,000 children born in the UK in 2000–01. In the USA, the National Longitudinal Study of Youth traced the progress of 12,686 young people born in the late 1950s and early 1960s, looking at their experiences in relation to things like family life, education, work and health.

 Caution

Longitudinal studies tend to be large-scale, national surveys that require funding and resources beyond the scope of small-scale research projects.

Secondary sources

It is sometimes possible for life course researchers to use data from pre-existing longitudinal studies. Such secondary source data, provided that it is publicly available and based on a suitable sample of people, can provide the project researcher with a way to use longitudinal data without the costs of setting up such a study or the need to spend years waiting to collect the data.

An example of the use of secondary source data from longitudinal studies is provided by Britton et al.'s (2015) study of alcohol consumption in the UK. They used data from nine longitudinal studies each of which tracked the alcohol consumption of individuals over an extended period of time. Combining the data from these nine separate studies gave them an impressively large sample size of nearly 60,000 people. However, the main point of using the longitudinal studies was not just to do with the size of the sample. Primarily it was because these studies provided a picture of alcohol consumption by individuals as they aged. Using data from the longitudinal studies allowed them to see alcohol consumption *trajectories*. In their words:

> Cross-sectional surveys are limited as they are fixed in one specific historical moment. Alcohol consumption fluctuates across life and only analysis of longitudinal data, with repeat alcohol measures, is able to reveal changes in consumption within the same individuals as they age. Estimating alcohol consumption trajectories as people age and mature through the life course can ultimately be used to identify associated harm.
>
> (Britton et al. 2015: 2)

Multiple sources of data

As a research strategy, the life course perspective does not dictate which methods of data collection can be used. To the extent that the life perspective approach is multidisciplinary, there is inevitably a range of preferred options available to the researcher and, as with all strategies, the choice of methods depends on the question that is being addressed and the practical opportunities that exist for accessing relevant data. Life course researchers, however, generally exhibit a preference for using multiple sources of data. They combine, for instance, first-hand accounts and eye-witness reports with documented sources as part of a multi-method approach. The reason for this is that personal evidence, whether collected through interviews or through historical sources, can provide a subjective account of the situation influenced by emotions, personal interests and the limits of memory. There are benefits, therefore, to combining such accounts with other sources of data that can add a more objective view of things. This is where the use of documentary sources comes into play to corroborate the story and provide a fuller picture of the events in question.

Link up with Chapter 11, Mixed methods.

 Key point

Life course researchers can use one or more sources of data. They can:

- collect data directly from people about their current situation and past events in their lives;
- use archive data about earlier generations and past events;
- use official statistics and reports to provide contextual information;
- conduct a longitudinal study, or use data from existing longitudinal studies.

Choice and constraint

The life course perspective recognizes that there are circumstances beyond the control of individuals which shape the trajectory of their lives. First, *events 'happen to' people* and a characteristic of the life course perspective, as we have seen, is its interest in understanding how specific social, cultural and historical events shape people's subsequent progress through life. Second, pathways through life are constrained by the way society uses *chronological age* to define, in law, what people of particular ages are allowed to do. This is especially the case in younger years during 'childhood' and 'adolescence'. In the UK the ages of 10, 16, 18 and 21 are used in law to specify when young people can be deemed responsible in terms of criminal acts, sexual activity, voting, marriage, joining the military, and purchasing alcohol and tobacco. Third, the opportunities open to people during their lives are strongly influenced by *structured inequalities* that exist in society based on social class, gender and ethnic group. Such structured inequalities are not things over which people can exercise much choice. They are part of the social structure – the fabric of the society in which the life course develops.

Equally, however, the life course perspective can be interested in the personal decisions which people make and the possibility that individuals can shape their own destiny. It recognizes that people's lives are not necessarily *determined* by events and constraints beyond their power to control and that there is scope for some people to 'escape' the predicted path and to exercise some free choice in relation to the social roles they occupy. At crucial times people can be faced with alternatives and take decisions that have a profound effect on their future lives, and life course researchers generally have a keen interest in when those decisions are taken and what the reasoning is behind them.

Example of life course research

Children of the Great Depression (Elder 1974) is widely regarded as the book that established 'the life course' as a recognized and distinctive approach. Elder's research involved a *longitudinal study* that, in his words, 'followed a group of children from their pre-adolescent years early in the Depression to their middle-age years, tracing step by step the ways in which deprivation left its mark on relationships and careers, life-styles and personalities' (Elder 1974: 271). The *life course* of the young people, then, was analysed in relation to a specific historical/economic *event* – the Great Depression, which started in 1929 and ravaged the US economy through the 1930s.

The *cohort* for this study consisted of people who were all born in 1920–21. The impact of the Great Depression on their life course was analysed using the main *life stages* of pre-adolescence, high school years, young adulthood and early adult years.

Elder's study made use of *secondary source material*. This was unavoidable because he needed information dating back four decades. His principal source was the Oakland Growth Study which was undertaken by the Institute of Child Welfare (part of the University of California). This study was primarily interested in the physical growth and psychological development of young people. However, the research coincided with the Great Depression and Elder was able to re-analyse the data (and that from the subsequent follow-ups) to look at the link between the economic hardship endured during the Great Depression and the cohort's subsequent life course from age 11–12 to age 42–43.

The Oakland Growth Study started in 1931. The *sample* consisted of 167 young people who were all born in 1920–21 and lived in the vicinity of San Francisco. The 'cohort' of 84 boys and 83 girls were 'fifth-graders' aged 11–12 years who came from five elementary schools in Oakland. The sample was considered to include a reasonable cross-section of the local population although, as Elder points out, it was not a representative sample of the wider (US) population.

The Oakland Growth Study monitored these young people continuously from 1932 to 1939 when they finished high school. It did so using *multiple methods* for collecting data:

- a series of *questionnaires* that asked about occupational aspirations, emotional climate at home, relations with parents and friends, and feelings about themselves;
- *interviews* conducted with mothers at their homes on three separate occasions (1932, 1934 and 1936) covering topics such as child-rearing practices, family relationships and social activities. The visits also allowed researchers to collect data on occupations, income and the personal demeanour of the mothers (as Elder 1974: 21 notes, fathers were not included because 'they were not regarded by behavioral scientists in the 30s as a key figure in socialization');
- *systematic observation* of the social behaviour and personal attributes of the young people during 'free play' sessions during visits to the Institute of Child Welfare.

After the Oakland study a series of *follow-up studies* was conducted during the 1940s to 1960s. Of the original 167 young people in the study, 69 men and 76 women took part in at least one of the follow-ups and these were found to be a representative cross-section of the original group. The follow-ups involved:

- a short questionnaire on occupational interests and activities (1941);
- contact through phone calls or letters (1948);
- extensive interviews supplemented with physical and psychiatric assessments of the participants (1953–54 and 1957–58);
- a mailed questionnaire (1964).

Elder's approach not only traced the life course of those involved; it located this within the *social context* of the time. Using *documented sources* his analysis was linked to the social values of the time, particularly those relating to family roles, and made use of published records about the extent of economic decline during the Depression years.

His findings focus on the *transition* from times of relative economic prosperity to times of economic hardship and the way that the changing economic circumstances led to changing *roles* within the family.

Severe economic loss increased the perceived power of mother in family matters within the middle and working class, and diminished father's social prestige, attractiveness, and emotional significance, as perceived by sons and daughters. These conditions weakened father's role as a control figure for the children and the effectiveness of parental control in general, though especially in relation to sons; and encouraged dependence on persons outside the family.

(Elder 1974: 278)

The experience of living through the Great Depression was also found to have a marked impact on the *trajectory* of the cohort of boys and girls. The longitudinal study showed how, in various ways, family values, personalities and attitudes to work had been affected by the time the cohort had reached their forties. For example, those men who had lived in families particularly hard hit by the recession tended to prefer job security and a moderate income rather than striving for better paid but less secure jobs. Women who had experienced hardship during the 1930s tended to attach particular importance to the stability of family life, and valued their role as homemaker and mother to their children above other aspects of life.

Advantages of the life course perspective

A focus on age-related issues

The life course perspective provides a way of understanding things which puts age at the centre of things. This tallies nicely with the increasing sensitivity to age and time in contemporary western society, and offers an alternative to analyses based on social class, gender or ethnicity.

A more complete picture

By looking at things in the context of *periods of time* the approach provides an understanding of people's experiences and their attitudes to life, which is arguably more rounded and more complete than approaches that focus primarily on how things are at the moment.

Suitable for small-scale enquiries

There are aspects of the approach that are viable for researchers undertaking low-budget projects with a short-term deadline. Access to relevant documentary sources need not cost a great deal, and empirical research does not always need to be based on large samples. This is particularly true when using interviews for 'life reviews' or similar individual life course research. And if the research is looking at cohorts, it is still possible to use purposively selected samples and relatively small-scale surveys.

Multidisciplinary

The life course perspective is a multidisciplinary, multi-causal approach that encourages the use of mixed methods of research.

Disadvantages of the life course perspective

Alternative types

There are four strands to the life course perspective and it can be approached from a variety of disciplines and perspectives. As a consequence, there is not a single life course 'theory' as such (Mayer 2003).

Resources

Where the life course perspective uses a longitudinal study, the benefits in terms of tracking people through their life need to be weighed against the time and costs involved. Longitudinal studies tend to use large samples of people, and are therefore expensive. And they take place over a number of years. In these respects longitudinal studies are not well suited to small-scale research projects.

Stages of life

For practical purposes the stages of life are often mapped quite closely on to chronological age. Ultimately, however, the link is one of convention and convenience, and there is increasing variability about the age at which people move between roles. When using a life course perspective, then, researchers need to avoid the dangers of taking chronological age as a definitive marker in relation to the life course or linking phases in the life course too rigidly to chronological age.

Further reading

Clausen, J.A. (1986) *The Life Course: A Sociological Perspective*. Englewood Cliffs, NJ: Prentice-Hall.

Elder, G.H. Jr (1974) *Children of the Great Depression: Social Change in Life Experience*. Chicago, IL: University of Chicago Press.

Giele, J.Z. and Elder, G.H. Jr (1998) *Methods of Life Course Research: Qualitative and Quantitative Approaches*. Thousand Oaks, CA: Sage.

Green, L. (2010) *Understanding the Life Course: Sociological and Psychological Perspectives*. Cambridge: Polity.

Hunt, S.J. (2005) *The Life Course: A Sociological Introduction*. Basingstoke: Palgrave Macmillan.

Hutchison, E.D. (2015) *Dimensions of Human Behavior: The Changing Life Course*, 5th edn. Thousand Oaks, CA: Sage.

Nilsen, A., Brannen, J. and Lewis, S. (eds) (2013) *Transitions to Parenthood in Europe: A Comparative Life Course Perspective*. Bristol: Policy Press.

Checklist for using the life course perspective

When undertaking life course research you should feel
confident about answering 'yes' to the following questions: ☑

1 Does the research strategy involve an understanding of human
   behaviour based on one or more of the following?   ☐

   • The characteristics of particular *stages in life*.
   • The effects of *significant events* on the life of people.
   • The impact of personal experiences and decision.
     on the direction of people's *journey through life*.

2 When stages of life are used in the research:

   • have the stages been clearly defined?   ☐
   • are they used for one or more of the following purposes:
     ◦ describing its characteristic features?   ☐
     ◦ comparison with other stages?   ☐
     ◦ comparison with other times or cultures?   ☐
   • are the stages acknowledged as existing within a
     specific cultural and historical context?   ☐

3 When cohorts are used in the research have they been explicitly
   linked to a particular time, age, date or significant event?   ☐

4 Has the decision to use, or not to use, longitudinal studies in the
   research been explained and justified?   ☐

5 When considering trajectories in the life course, does the research
   identify:

   • the influence of social, cultural and institutional
     constraints (i.e. structure)?   ☐
   • the role of personal decisions and free choice
     (i.e. agency)?   ☐

6 Has due recognition been given to factors other than age/time
   (e.g. gender, ethnicity, culture) which might contribute to a
   multi-casual explanation?   ☐

7 Does the research make use of multiple sources of data?   ☐

8 Have any culturally specific findings been acknowledged as
   limitations of the research?   ☐

© M. Denscombe, *The Good Research Guide*. Open University Press.

7 Grounded theory

What is the grounded theory approach? • When is the grounded theory approach useful? • Starting grounded theory research • Theoretical sampling • Completing the research (theoretical saturation) • Methods of data collection • Analysing the data • Displaying the process of analysis • Theories and grounded research • Developments in grounded theory • Advantages of the grounded theory approach • Disadvantages of the grounded theory approach • Further reading • Checklist for using the grounded theory approach

The grounded theory approach has become a popular choice of methodology among social researchers in recent times. In particular, it has been adopted by those engaged in small-scale projects using qualitative data for the study of human interaction, and by those whose research is exploratory and focused on particular settings.

What is the grounded theory approach?

The approach originated with the work of Barney Glaser and Anselm Strauss and, in particular, their book, *The Discovery of Grounded Theory*, which was published in 1967. Since that time the notion of grounded theory has come to mean slightly different things to different people. There has been a tendency for researchers to 'adopt and adapt' grounded theory and to use it selectively for their own purposes. There are, though, two basic points upon which most grounded theory researchers agree:

Theory:	Grounded theory is an approach dedicated to generating theories. In this sense it contrasts with approaches that are primarily concerned with testing theories (e.g. experiments), and it is different from research whose main purpose is to provide descriptive accounts of the subject matter (e.g. ethnography).
Grounded:	Grounded theory is an approach that emphasizes the importance of empirical fieldwork and the collection of data that are 'grounded' in 'real world' situations. It is different, here, from approaches based on 'armchair theorizing' or explanations that start at a high level of abstraction and then, subsequently, deduce ways of checking if the theory actually works. Grounded theory starts with empirical research and lets the theory emerge from the data. The emergence of the theory is a process, and this means that grounded theory researchers need to continue to collect data on site throughout the course of their research.

Building on these two pillars there are four other characteristic features of the grounded theory approach which define it as a distinct strategy for social research.

Theories should be generated by a systematic analysis of the data

The emphasis on collecting data in the field does not mean that the researcher should simply amass as much detail as possible about particular situations and then 'let the data speak for themselves'. Always high on the agenda for grounded theory research is a concerted effort to *analyse* the data and to generate theories from the data. Also, grounded theory is characterized by the specific way in which it approaches the business of analysing the data. Concepts and theories are developed out of the data through a persistent process of comparing the ideas with existing data, and improving the emerging concepts and theories by checking them against new data collected specifically for the purpose – the 'constant comparative method'.

The selection of items to be included in the research reflects the developing nature of the theory

The items to be included follow a trail of discovery – like a detective follows a 'lead'. Each new phase of the investigation reflects what has been discovered so far, with new angles of investigation and new avenues of enquiry to be explored. So, in the spirit of 'grounded theory' it is neither feasible nor desirable for the researcher to identify prior to the start exactly who or what will be included in the sample. This runs right against the grain as far as conventional social research practice is concerned. Normally, the social researcher would be expected to have a very clear vision of the intended sample, chosen on the basis of criteria linked to the ideas and theories being tested by the research.

Researchers should start out with an 'open mind'

In marked contrast to the researcher who sets out to *test* a theory, the researcher who follows the principles of grounded theory needs to approach the topic *without a rigid set of ideas* that shape what they focus upon during the investigation. Rather than basing an investigation upon whether certain theories do or do not work, the researcher embarks on a voyage of discovery.

This should not be seen to imply that a good social researcher starts out with a 'blank' mind.

> To be sure, one goes out and studies an area with a particular ... perspective, and with a focus, a general question or a problem in mind. But the researcher can (and we believe should) also study an area without any preconceived theory that dictates, prior to the research, 'relevancies' in concepts and hypotheses.
>
> (Glaser and Strauss 1967: 33)

Theories should be meaningful to those 'on the ground'

The grounded theory approach has its roots in *pragmatism* whose guiding philosophy is clearly acknowledged by Glaser and Strauss. Pragmatism places great emphasis on the 'practical' rather than the 'abstract' when it comes to issues of knowledge and truth, and it operates on the premise that the value of any theory can only be gauged by how well it works in practice. For grounded theory this means that the theories produced should *make sense to those whose actions it explains*.

When is the grounded theory approach useful?

The grounded theory approach does not purport to be the only proper way of conducting social research. It is but one approach among many. What it does claim, however, is that it offers an approach that is well suited to the needs of the following four kinds of research.

Qualitative research

Although in their original exposition of grounded theory Glaser and Strauss claimed that the approach could be applied to quantitative data as well as qualitative data, and despite subsequent claims that 'It transcends specific data collection methods' (Glaser 1978: 6), the grounded theory approach has become firmly associated over time with qualitative research. The nature of Glaser and Strauss's own research effectively set the tenor for the kind of research that has come to be associated with the grounded theory approach and by far the most common use of the grounded theory approach by other researchers has been with studies using qualitative data.

Exploratory research

Because there is an emphasis on discovery and because there is a stress on the need to approach investigations without being blinkered by the concepts and theories of previous research, the grounded theory approach fits neatly with the needs of researchers who are setting out to explore new territory in terms of either the subject matter of their investigation or the extent to which relevant theories have already been developed.

Studies of human interaction

The grounded theory approach is appropriate for social research that focuses on human interaction, particularly where the researcher wishes to investigate:

- practical activity and routine situations;
- the participants' points of view.

This reflects the roots of grounded theory within an approach called *symbolic interactionism*. This is a form of social research that focuses on the way that participants in social settings make sense of situations and events through the use of symbolic actions.

Small-scale research

Grounded theory's affinity with qualitative research, its desire to generate explanations from the study of particular instances, its need for detailed data about activities and practice and its value for exploratory research, combine to make it an approach that is well suited to small-scale research conducted by individual researchers operating within the constraints of a tight budget.

Starting grounded theory research

Initial ideas and concepts

The grounded theory approach expects the researcher to start research without any *fixed* ideas about the nature of the setting that is about to be investigated. As we have seen, the aim is to approach things with an open mind. Essentially, this requires grounded theory researchers to treat any existing ideas they might have about the topic of enquiry as 'provisional' and open to question. Anything they already 'know' can only act as a tentative starting point from which to launch the investigation.

Initial sites for fieldwork

Researchers who adopt the grounded theory approach need to start their investigation by concentrating on a particular situation, event or group. At the beginning, all that is required is that this site is 'relevant'. The criterion for its selection need only be that it might reasonably be expected to provide relevant information on the situation, event or group the researcher is interested in investigating.

Theoretical sampling: the selection of sites for fieldwork

After having selected the initial site for research, subsequent sites are selected according to a process of *theoretical sampling*. This form of sampling is a distinctive feature of the grounded theory approach and it involves five key features:

1 Sites to be included in the research are *deliberately selected by the researcher* for what they can contribute to the research. This means that, unlike random sampling, theoretical sampling is a form of non-probability sampling in which the new sites are consciously selected by the researcher because of their particular characteristics. Sites are selected because of their *relevance to emerging categories and concepts*. They are deliberately chosen to allow comparisons and contrasts with previous sites and they allow the researcher to test out emerging concepts and verify the developing theory as the research goes along.

> **Link up with**
> Purposive
> sampling,
> p. 41.

2 Theoretical sampling is *cumulative*. There is a sense of building on the previous instances that have been sampled to date, and on building up a strong foundation for the concepts and categories that are being refined through the grounded research approach. Events, instances or people sampled early in the research should be considered as an integral part of the overall sample – a vital component in the path of discovery – and not jettisoned as being obsolete, irrelevant or wrong.

> **Link up with**
> Cumulative
> sampling,
> p. 49.

3 Theoretical sampling involves an increased *depth of focus*. Initially, the researcher's aim is to keep things as 'open' as possible early on. As things move on, though, the researcher will be able to concentrate on a smaller number of themes – those that emerge as being more crucial to the analysis – and, because these are more central to the analysis and are fewer in number, they can be investigated in more depth.

4 Theoretical sampling needs to retain some element of *flexibility*. Partly this is necessary to allow the researcher to respond to opportunities that arise during the course of fieldwork. Equally it is vital to permit the exploration of new avenues of investigation that the researcher could not have anticipated as being relevant.

5   Researchers following the principles of grounded theory will not want to, or be able to, specify at the outset exactly what the sample will include. They will not be able to state exactly how large the sample will be or exactly what sites (events or whatever) will be included because the sample *emerges*, reflecting the pursuit of generating theory. The process of research will involve the continued selection of units until the research arrives at the point of *theoretical saturation* (see below). It is only when the new data seem to confirm the analysis rather than add anything new that the sampling ceases and the sample size is 'enough'.

Example 7.1

Theoretical sampling

A researcher wishing to investigate 'classroom control' could initiate research by observing a small number of lessons in one school. In the first instance the selection of the particular lessons and the specific school only requires that the sites are relevant for the broad purposes of the research. When some lessons have been observed and various participants interviewed, however, the subsequent sites for research will be selected to follow up ideas prompted by an early review of the data. Schools might be selected as instances where control problems are acknowledged to be rife, and lessons might be selected for observation that offer a relevant contrast in terms of the way they are routinely organized. History and English lessons in a normal classroom might be compared with art lessons, sports classes and chemistry laboratory sessions. The relevance of such different contexts might not have been realized at the beginning, but their significance is something that emerges as the research progresses and new paths of enquiry emerge.

Completing the research (theoretical saturation)

Grounded theory research ought to continue until the research arrives at the point of 'theoretical saturation'. It is only when the new data seem to confirm the analysis rather than add anything new that the sampling ceases and the sample size is 'enough'. This stands in stark contrast to the conventions that expect researchers to be clear at the outset about the size and nature of their intended sample.

   Key point: Theoretical saturation

Theoretical saturation occurs 'when additional analysis no longer contributes to discovering anything new about a category' (Strauss 1987: 21).

Methods of data collection

The grounded theory approach is not restricted to any particular method of data collection. There are, however, certain methods that lend themselves better than others to use within a grounded theory approach. These are methods that allow the collection of data in a relatively 'raw' state, not unduly shaped by prior concepts or theories. In practice this means there is a preference for methods that produce qualitative data which are relatively *unstructured*, and grounded theory researchers tend to use:

- unstructured or semi-structured interviews rather than structured interviews;
- open-ended questions in a questionnaire rather than fixed-choice questions that only offer a small number of preset options;
- field notes rather than observations based on a tick-box schedule.

Analysing the data

Codes, categories and concepts

The first stage of analysis involves the coding and categorizing of the data. This means that the researcher begins to assign bits of the 'raw data' to particular categories. Careful scrutiny of the data (for example, an interview transcript) will allow the researcher to see that certain bits of the data have something in common. Possibly they will refer to the same issue. Possibly they will involve statements about the same emotion. Possibly they will share the use of a similar word or phrase in relation to a specific topic. Whatever it is, the chunks of raw data have something in common that the researcher can identify and that allows those chunks of data to be coded (tagged) as belonging to a broader category.

Link up with Chapter 17, Qualitative data.

Unlike codes used with quantitative data, in grounded theory the codes are open to change and refinement as research progresses. Initially, the codes will be fairly descriptive and are likely to involve labelling chunks of data in terms of their content. This is referred to as *open coding*. As the codes take shape, the researcher will look for relationships between the codes – links and associations that allow certain codes to be subsumed under broader headings and certain codes to be seen as more crucial than others. This is referred to as *axial coding* since it shifts the analysis towards the identification of key (axial) components. Eventually, the researcher should be in a position to focus attention on just the key components, the most significant categories, and concentrate his/her efforts on these. This *selective coding* focuses attention on just the core codes, those that have emerged from open and axial coding as being vital to any explanation of the complex social phenomenon.

The aim of this process is to arrive at *concepts* that help to explain the phenomenon – basic ideas that encapsulate the way that the categories relate to each other in a single notion. These concepts then form the cornerstone for the generation of theories that provide an account of things and, in some sense or other, explain why things happen as they do. In the words of Strauss and Corbin (1990: 19): 'Concepts are the basis of analysis in grounded theory research. All grounded theory procedures are aimed at identifying, developing, and relating concepts.'

Good practice: Use a computer to help with the data analysis

There are a number of commercially available software programs that can help researchers with the analysis of qualitative data. It is good practice to store the data in a suitable program – such as NVivo – right from the beginning of the data collection. Such programs are designed to help researchers to code their qualitative data and to develop categories and concepts based on these codes.

Link up with Computer-assisted qualitative data analysis, p. 309.

The constant comparative method

The grounded theory approach uses the constant comparative method as a means of analysing the data. This entails a commitment to comparing and contrasting new codes, categories and concepts as they emerge – constantly seeking to check them against existing versions. By comparing each coded instance with others that have been similarly coded, by contrasting instances with those in different categories, even using hypothetical possibilities, the researcher is able to refine and improve the explanatory power of the concepts and theories generated from the data. Such comparison helps the researcher to refine the codes, categories and concepts by doing the following:

* highlighting the similarities and differences that exist (promoting better categories and descriptions);
* allowing researchers to integrate categories and codes under common headings (facilitating the reduction of complex phenomena to simpler elements);
* allowing researchers to check out their developing theories as they emerge (incorporating a way to verify them or refute them at the stage of production rather than after the event).

By using the constant comparative method the researcher can never lose sight of the data, or move the analysis too far away from what is happening on the ground. It ensures that any theory developed by the research remains closely in touch with its origins in the data – that it remains 'grounded' in empirical reality. This is of vital importance to the whole approach.

Key point: Data analysis using the constant comparative method

Analysis should always involve:

- *coding* and categorizing the raw data (e.g. interview tapes);
- constantly *comparing* the emerging codes and categories with the data;
- *checking* them against new data specifically collected for the purpose;
- generating *concepts* and theories that are thoroughly grounded in the data.

Displaying the process of analysis

The process of analysing the data needs to be explained to those who read reports about grounded theory research. The logic and reasoning used to move from open coding to the eventual concepts and theory should be described along with some justification for the coding decisions made by the researcher. The process of analysis, in other words, needs to be transparent. It is not sufficient to describe the process of collecting the data and then move on to 'these are my findings' or 'this is my interpretation of the data'. This leaves a gap in the account of the research.

The process of analysis cannot be depicted in every minute detail. Necessarily, any account can only capture the key points of what is likely to be a complex, iterative process of making sense of the data. It is, none the less, vital that some information is provided to the reader about the logic used by the researcher when deciding on how to interpret and re-interpret the data. This information allows readers to decide for themselves whether the decisions of the researcher seem reasonable: they do not simply have to 'take the researcher's word for it' that the concepts and theory really do derive from the data.

Link up with Audit trail, p. 327.

Good practice: Displaying the analytic process

When software like NVivo is used to aid the coding process, it becomes possible to display aspects of the analytic process visually using diagrams showing the link between categories, codes and concepts.

Theories and grounded research

The grounded theory approach, when it was originally conceived by Glaser and Strauss, was a reaction against the kind of 'grand' theories produced through the *logico-deductive method* of science that Glaser and Strauss encountered during the late 1950s and early 1960s. As Layder (1993: 42) points out:

> Such theories are generally 'speculative' in nature because they have not grown directly out of research, and thus remain ungrounded. As a consequence, these theories very often lack validity because they do not 'fit' the real world and thereby remain irrelevant to the people concerned.

Glaser and Strauss were dissatisfied with this approach and argued that a theory developed through the grounded theory approach would have distinct advantages over those derived from the more traditional 'scientific' methods.

First, it is unlikely that new data will be found that serve to refute the theory. Since the theory has been built upon substantive data extracted from field-work, the theory should already take account of all the crucial aspects of the situation it explains so that there should be no 'nasty surprises' waiting to be uncovered that will point to a major weakness in the theory. This contrasts with theories that have been logically deduced and that are then subjected to test by seeing if they work in practice. The 'scientific' approach certainly is susceptible to such nasty surprises and radical rethinks about the theory when findings do not support the theory. In grounded theory the testing is conducted as an integral part of the development of the theory – as an ongoing process – not as a separate process conducted after the theory has been put together in an abstract form.

Second, the theory has more credibility. Because the theory emerges from the data, there ought to be a comfortable fit between the facts of the situation and the theory used to explain them. Put simply, the theory is shaped by the facts and therefore there should be a good fit. On this basis there can be no allegations that researchers are in any sense *forcing* a fit between the data and the theory. By contrast, the process of testing theories can involve a search, more or less consciously, for facts that fit the theory. They can end up being selective about what they 'see' and what they find, managing to corroborate their theory by a process of selective perception in which facts that do not fit the theory get subtly edited out of the picture as irrelevant or non-existent.

Substantive theory and formal theory

There are two kinds of theory that can be generated using the grounded theory approach. The first is linked closely to the empirical situation that has been the subject of study. It is a fairly localized kind of theory and is known as *substantive theory*. This is by far the most common kind of theory associated with the approach. The other kind of theory is more conceptual, with more general coverage and application to circumstances beyond particular settings. This is known as *formal theory*. Ultimately, the aim is to move from a growing body of good, grounded substantive theories towards the integration of these in higher-level formal theories.

Developments in grounded theory

Since the notion of a grounded theory approach was first conceived subsequent works by the originators have moved in slightly different directions. This divergence reflects two potential stances that coexist within the original grounded theory approach. On the one hand, there is Glaser's version (Glaser 1978, 1995, 1999, 2003). As Charmaz (2000: 510) argues, 'Glaser's position often comes close to traditional positivism, with its assumptions of an objective, external reality [and] a neutral observer who discovers data'. It rests on the belief that the meaning of the data will emerge inductively from the data if studied using a suitably neutral methodology. Put simply, the meaning exists in the data and the grounded theory approach allows the researcher to extract the meaning and develop it into a more abstract theory. By looking closely at the data, concepts will occur to the researcher and these concepts can be developed and refined by continually comparing them and checking them with the original data and with new data collected specifically to verify the concepts.

Contrasting with this there is Strauss's version (Strauss 1987; Strauss and Corbin 1990, 1998), which moves towards a more *post-positivist* stance. This stance sees the researcher as inevitably imposing some shape and sense on to the data. It accepts that researchers cannot be entirely neutral and that the meaning attached to any data involves some kind of *interpretation* by the researcher. The meaning will not, cannot, simply emerge inductively from the data. In practice, the researcher needs to *make* sense of the data; that is, to interpret the data in a systematic way. To this end there is extensive guidance offered by Strauss and Corbin (1990, 1998) on how researchers should proceed with their analysis, turning the spotlight away from the data and more towards the procedures for analysing the (qualitative) data. Glaser, for his part, has expressed strong reservations about this trend, arguing that there is a potential to 'force' the data to fit researchers' categories rather than let the data speak for themselves (Glaser 2003).

Some writers have wanted still greater emphasis on the role of the researcher as interpreter rather than discoverer of reality. In line with this, Charmaz (2014) has advocated a *constructivist* grounded theory, Clarke (2005) has adapted grounded theory to *postmodernism* in what she calls 'situational analysis', and Corbin (Corbin and Strauss 2015) has developed her earlier Straussian position to reflect the postmodernist critique with its emphasis on the existence of alternative perspectives and constructions of realities.

The researcher who wants to use the grounded theory approach needs to be aware that such debates and developments exist under the umbrella term 'grounded theory'. They might even need to delve into the schisms and controversies in order to defend their research as being in line with a particular version of grounded theory (see Bryant and Charmaz 2010). Professional researchers and those using grounded theory as a core feature of a PhD would fall into this category. Project researchers, however, are less likely to need to pursue the methodology to this depth. They should be justified in saying that they have adopted a grounded theory provided their research:

- uses theoretical sampling as the basis for an emergent research design;
- develops codes and concepts through an iterative process involving constant reference to fieldwork data;
- includes some account of how the codes and concepts were developed;
- aims to produce 'theory', at least in the form of modest localized explanations based on the immediate evidence.

 Caution: The use and misuse of the term 'grounded theory'

The term 'grounded theory' is often used in a rather loose way to refer to approaches that accept some of the basic premises but do not adopt the methodological rigour espoused by the originators of the term. All too frequently Glaser and Strauss are cited by way of justification for methodologies that actually bear few of the hallmarks of the strict conception of 'grounded theory'. Worse than this, there is a very real danger that the term 'grounded theory' can be hijacked and cited as justification for what is, in reality, sloppy research. Taken out of context, 'grounded theory' can be misused as a rationale for approaching research:

- without too clear an idea of the topic of research;
- without a clear basis in mind for selecting the sample;
- with a general 'jump in at the deep end', 'try it and see', 'find out as we go' approach.

This is certainly not in tune with the spirit of grounded theory and its clear concern with rigour in the analysis of qualitative data.

Advantages of the grounded theory approach

Suited to small-scale research

From a project researcher's point of view, use of the grounded theory approach can be appealing because it lends itself to being conducted by lone researchers working on a limited budget.

Suitable for exploratory research

The approach permits a degree of flexibility in both the selection of instances for inclusion in the sample and the analysis of the data – both of which are well suited to the exploration of new topics and new ideas.

Explanations are grounded in reality

Concepts and theories are developed with constant reference to the empirical data and this means that, unlike speculative, abstract theory, they are built on a sound foundation of evidence. This ensures that grounded theories are kept in touch with reality.

Recognized rationale for qualitative research

The notion of grounded theory has currency in the research community and it has become a recognized rationale for qualitative research. Grounded theory provides a standard justification that can fend off potential criticism from those who might otherwise question the rigour of small-scale qualitative research.

Adaptable

The approach is fairly adaptable, lending itself to use with a variety of qualitative data collection methods (e.g. interviews, observation, documents) and forms of data (interview transcripts, fieldwork, texts).

Systematic way of analysing qualitative data

Especially as developed by Strauss, this can be helpful to the newcomer who might wonder how on earth he/she can make sense of the data and how he/she can move towards developing concepts and ultimately theories.

Theory development

The approach includes the means for developing theoretical propositions from data, and should boost project researchers' confidence in the realms of theorizing. All researchers – not just the venerable experts – are encouraged to arrive at modest theories on the basis of the data that they have collected.

Disadvantages of the grounded theory approach

Planning

The approach does not lend itself to precise planning. The use of 'theoretical sampling' means that it is not possible to predict precisely in advance the nature of the sample that will be used. And the need to achieve 'theoretical saturation' makes it impossible to state at the outset the eventual size of the sample. The voyage of discovery comes with a price and that price is the ability to plan all aspects of the research in advance and anticipate when the research will be completed.

Context

By focusing research on specific instances of behaviour in particular settings, there is a tendency to divorce the explanation of the situation being studied from broader contextual factors. In particular, there is the danger that the theory generated from the data might ignore the influence of social, economic and political factors (e.g. power, globalization, migration, social class, gender and race inequalities) and the historical background to events, which might be vital to any full and valid theory explaining the phenomenon.

Open-mindedness

An 'open-minded' approach to the data is something that can operate at a variety of levels. The need to approach things with an 'open mind' is a fundamental principle of the grounded theory approach but, in practice, it raises some awkward questions. Researchers are inevitably influenced by prior conceptions based on their own culture and personal experience. The question is, how far can these be put to one side for the purposes of analysing the data? There is also the controversial point about how far previous concepts and theories should be allowed to influence matters. Should grounded theory researchers avoid undertaking a literature review in order to avoid having their minds 'contaminated' by existing concepts and theories? And, if so, does this invite the possibility of 'reinventing the wheel' or failing to learn from what has been researched in the past? Within the grounded theory approach different researchers adopt different positions on such issues.

Complexity

The systematic way of analysing data developed by Strauss and Corbin can be daunting in terms of the complexity of the process. Indeed, Strauss's development of 'guidance' for the analysis of qualitative data actually incensed his former collaborator, Barney Glaser, who saw the template and framework for analysis as unnecessary and going against the spirit of grounded theory by 'forcing' categories and codes on to the data, rather than letting them 'emerge' naturally.

Positivism

Interpretivists will be unhappy with any suggestion that substantive theories provide the one correct explanation of things. Yet in the writings of Glaser (rather than Strauss) there are occasions when this position is taken. There is a positivistic strand of thought in which the 'grounding' of theory means that it is not liable to be refuted by the later discovery of facts that do not fit the theory. If the theory emerges from the data and is meaningful to the participants, then it is a good theory that stands in its own right – not open to alternative interpretation.

Empiricism

The approach can be criticized as being 'empiricist'. By looking to fieldwork data as the source of its theories, and by setting itself against the use of general theories, it opens itself to the criticism that it relies too heavily on the empirical data – expecting an explanation to exist within the accumulated data, waiting to be 'discovered' by the researcher. This inductive approach is rather naive about the complex relationship between theory and data collection and the way it calls for researchers to approach the data without the use of prior theories and concepts.

Generalizations

Generalizing from the findings can be misunderstood. It is important for those using the grounded theory approach to be clear that any generalizations derived from the research are *theoretical* generalizations. They are 'abstractions' from the data that are conceptual and which are used to construct theories. They are not generalizations in the sense that many people might think of them, and grounded theory researchers need to be careful to avoid any impression that they are attempting to identify patterns of behaviour in the population on the basis of the small, purposively selected sample that they have studied. The purpose of grounded theory is not to make generalizations from the sample to a wider population as a survey approach might do.

Further reading

Birks, M. and Mills, J. (2015) *Grounded Theory: A Practical Guide*, 2nd edn. London: Sage.

Bryant, A. (2017) *Grounded Theory and Grounded Theorizing: Pragmatism in Research Practice*. New York: Oxford University Press.

Charmaz, K. (2014) *Constructing Grounded Theory*, 2nd edn. Thousand Oaks, CA: Sage.

Corbin, J. and Strauss, A. (2015) *Basics of Qualitative Research: Techniques and Procedures for Developing Grounded Theory*, 4th edn. Thousand Oaks, CA: Sage.

Holton, J.A. and Walsh, I. (2017) *Classic Grounded Theory: Applications with Qualitative and Quantitative Data*. Thousand Oaks, CA: Sage.

Oktay, J. (2012) *Grounded Theory*. Oxford: Oxford University Press.

Checklist for using the grounded theory approach

When undertaking grounded theory research you should feel confident about answering 'yes' to the following questions: ☑

1 Does empirical data form the foundation for generating concepts and theories? ☐

2 Does the data analysis involve a systematic process of coding and categorization (open coding, etc.)? ☐

3 Are the codes, categories and concepts developed with constant reference to the fieldwork data (constant comparative method)? ☐

4 Does (or will) any report of the research include a section that demonstrates how the codes and concepts have been developed? ☐

5 Is the aim of the research to generate concepts and theory geared to 'localized' explanations (substantive theory)? ☐

6 Is there an open-minded approach to the meaning of the data? ☐

7 Is there, or will there be, an explicit justification for the choice of the initial site for fieldwork in terms of its relevance to the area of research? ☐

8 Have subsequent sites been selected on the basis of theoretical sampling? ☐

9 Did, or will, the research continue until it has reached a point of theoretical saturation? ☐

10 Will the research produce explanations that are recognizable to the subjects of research? ☐

8 Action research

What is action research? • *Practical research* • *Practitioner involvement* • *Change* • *Professional self-development* • *A cyclical process of research* • *Participation and partnership in the research process* • *Emancipatory action research* • *Doing action research* • *Generalizability and action research* • *Insider knowledge and reflexivity* • *Advantages of action research* • *Disadvantages of action research* • *Further reading* • *Checklist for using action research*

Action research is a *strategy* for social research, not a method. It is concerned with the aims of research and the design of the research, but does not specify any constraints when it comes to the means for data collection that might be adopted by the action researcher.

What is action research?

Action research is normally associated with 'hands-on', small-scale research projects. Its origins can be traced back to the work of social scientists in the late 1940s on both sides of the Atlantic who advocated closer ties between social theory and the solving of immediate social problems. More recently, action research has been used in a variety of settings in the social sciences but its growing popularity as a research approach perhaps owes most to its use in areas such as education, organizational development, health and social care. In these areas it has a particular niche among professionals who want to use research to improve their effectiveness as practitioners.

Action research, from the start, has been involved with practical issues – the type of issues and problems, concerns and needs that arose as a routine part of activity 'in the real world'. This specifically practical orientation has remained a defining characteristic of action research. Early on, action research was also seen as research specifically geared to changing matters, and this too has remained a core feature of the notion of action research. The thinking here is that research should not only be used to gain a better understanding of the problems which arise in everyday practice, but actually set out to alter things – to do so as part and parcel of the research process rather than tag it on as an afterthought which follows the conclusion of the research. This points towards a third defining characteristic of action research: its commitment to a process of research in which the application of findings and an evaluation of their impact on practice become part of a cycle of research. This process, further, has become associated with a trend towards involving those affected by the research in the design and implementation of the research – to encourage them to participate as collaborators in the research rather than being subjects of it.

Together, these provide the four defining characteristics of action research:

- *Practical nature.* It is aimed at dealing with real-world problems and issues, typically at work and in organizational settings.
- *Change.* Both as a way of dealing with practical problems and as a means of discovering more about phenomena, change is regarded as an integral part of research.
- *Cyclical process.* Research involves a feedback loop in which initial findings generate possibilities for change which are then implemented and evaluated as a prelude to further investigation.
- *Participation.* Practitioners are the crucial people in the research process. Their participation is active, not passive.

Practical research

Action research is essentially practical and applied. It is driven by the need to solve practical, real-world problems. It operates on the premise, as Kurt Lewin put it, that 'Research that produces nothing but books will not suffice' (Lewin 1946: 35).

But being practical would not be enough to set it apart from other approaches to research. After all, many approaches can lay claim to this territory. Being 'practical' has a second sense as far as action research is concerned, and it is this which helps to give it a unique identity as a research strategy. The research needs to be undertaken *as part of practice* rather than a bolt-on addition to it. In Somekh's (1995: 340) words,

Action research [rejects] the concept of a two-stage process in which research is carried out first by researchers and then in a separate second stage the knowledge generated from the research is applied by practitioners. Instead, the two processes of research and action are integrated.

Practitioner involvement

If the processes of research and action are integrated, then action research must involve 'the practitioner' very closely. This provides a further meaning which can be added to the practical nature of action research: *practitioner research*. However, although it may be linked with the notion of practitioner research, it is important to appreciate that action research is not exactly the same thing as practitioner research. Edwards and Talbot stress this point: 'Practitioner research can only be designated action research if it is carried out by professionals who are engaged in researching . . . aspects of their own practice as they engage in that practice' (1999: 62). It is not enough for the research to be undertaken as part of the job, because this could include all kinds of data gathering and analysis, the findings from which might have no bearing on the practitioner's own activity. To accord with the spirit of action research the researcher needs to investigate his/her *own* practices with a view to altering these in a beneficial way.

Change

Action research is wedded to the idea that change is good. Initially, this is because studying change is seen as a useful *way of learning more about the way a thing works*. Change, in this sense, is regarded as a valuable enhancer of knowledge in its own right, rather than something that is undertaken after the results of the research have been obtained. However, the scale and the scope of changes introduced through action research will not be grand. The scale of the research is constrained by the need for the action researchers to focus on *aspects of their own practice as they engage in that practice*. So change as envisaged by action research is not likely to be a widespread major alteration to an organization. The element of change will not be in the order of a large-scale experiment such as changes in the bonus schemes of production workers at Ford's car assembly plants. No. Because, action research tends to be localized and small scale, it usually focuses on change at the micro level.

Professional self-development

One of the most common types of change involved in action research is at the level of *professional self-development*. This is in keeping with the notion of professional self-development that a person should want to improve practices and that this should involve a continual quest for ways in which to change practice for the better. Action research provides a way forward for the professional which, while it entails a certain degree of reflection, adds the systematic and rigorous collection of data to the resources the professional can use to achieve the improvement in practice.

It is important to recognize that reflection may be of itself insufficient to make the professional's endeavour 'action research'. The reflection needs to be systematic if it is to qualify as action *research*. Merely *thinking* about your own practice – though possibly a valuable basis for improving practice – is not the same as researching that action. Here a distinction needs to be made between the 'reflective practitioner' (Schön 1983) as someone who strives for professional self-development through a critical consideration of his/her practices, and the action researcher who, while also being a reflective practitioner, adds to this by using research techniques to enhance and systematize that reflection.

A cyclical process of research

The vision of action research as a cyclical process fits in nicely with the quest for perpetual development built into the idea of professionalism (see Figure 8.1). The purpose of research, though it might be prompted by a specific problem, is seen as part of a broader enterprise in which the aim is to improve practice through a rolling programme of research.

Figure 8.1 The cyclical process in action research

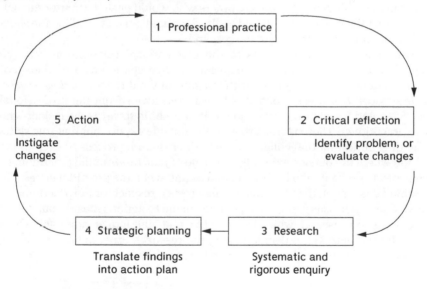

The crucial points about the cycle of enquiry in action research are (1) that *research feeds back directly into practice* and (2) that *the process is ongoing*. The critical reflection of the practitioner is not only directed to the identification of 'problems' worthy of investigation with a view to improving practice, but can also involve an evaluation of changes just instigated, which can, in their own right, prompt further research. It is fair to point out, however, that this is something of an ideal and that, in reality, action research often limits itself to discrete, one-off pieces of research.

Participation and partnership in the research process

The participatory nature of action research is one of its most distinctive features. Conventionally, research is the province of the expert, the outside authority who is a professional. This researcher more often than not initiates the process of research, sets the agenda and designs the collection and analysis of data. After the research is concluded, those involved might receive some feedback in the form of results from the research. They may, or may not, instigate changes on the basis of such findings. Broadly speaking, the act of doing research is separated from the act of making changes. Action research, by contrast, insists that practitioners must be participants, not just in the sense of taking part in the research but in the sense of being *an equal partner in the research*.

With action research it can be the practitioner, not some outside professional researcher, who wants to instigate a change and who consequently initiates the research. The research, in this sense, is practitioner-driven, with the practitioner not just an equal partner but a sponsor and director of the research process. If this sounds radical, there are others who would push the matter further, insisting that the practitioner should be the dominant partner – calling the shots at all stages and in all aspects of the research.

Even in less radical revisions to the conventional relationship between researcher and practitioners, the inclusion of participation as a fundamental feature of action research brings with it a shift in the direction of *democratizing the research process*. Control is transferred away from the professional researcher and towards the practitioner. Power shifts towards the insider who is the practitioner. There is still a role for the outside expert, but that role shifts in the direction of mutual collaboration in the research process or even to the position where the outside expert has the role of *facilitator* of the practitioner's own project, a resource to be drawn upon as and when the practitioner sees fit.

Behind this shift in the relationship there rests a respect for the practitioner's knowledge. Again, this respect may not be unique to action research but it is an aspect of action research which is distinctive and built into an approach which is broadly sympathetic to democratizing the research process by challenging the separation of expert from lay person in research.

Emancipatory action research

The participatory aspect of action research, with its 'democratization' of the research process and 'respect for practitioner knowledge', fits comfortably with a participatory worldview in which action research seeks to empower those involved (Boog 2003). Zuber-Skerritt (1996) refers to this as *emancipatory* action research. This type of action research is quite clear about the nature of the change which is brought about through action research; it is change which challenges the existing system and, in a sense, aims to 'liberate' those involved. It is change which goes beyond *technical* matters that can have a bearing on the effectiveness or efficiency of the professional's current practice. It is change which goes beyond *practical* matters that can have a bearing on the way practitioners interpret the task at hand. Emancipatory action research certainly incorporates these, but it also challenges the fundamental framework within which the practice occurs. Rather than being a stand-alone project geared to a specific localized problem, emancipatory action research forms part of a larger project with wider ambitions that include changing systems, empowering individuals and liberating groups of people from oppressive conditions.

 Key point: Three facets of action research

- *Improve practice* through the instigation of changes and evaluation of their impact.
- *Enhance understanding* through self-reflection and practical deliberation.
- *Transform practices* by challenging the boundaries to change inherent in the existing system.

Doing action research

Topic

Reprising the points already made, the choice of topic is something that should be practical and of direct relevance to the actions of a practitioner.

Methods

Action research is an approach that lends itself to a variety of research methods. It can use quantitative or qualitative data and the choice of methods will ultimately depend on the nature of the problem being investigated and the suitability of the method, or methods, for collecting accurate data. Observation and the use of documents provide methods for data collection that can be relatively unobtrusive. The use of interviews or questionnaires raises the level of visibility of the research.

Resources

The action researcher's investigation is necessarily fairly localized and relatively small-scale. None the less, the action researcher faces the difficulty of trying to combine a probably demanding workload with systematic and rigorous research. Time constraints, alone, make this hard to accomplish. Even if, as should be the case, action research is integrated with practice rather than tagged onto practice, the routine demands of the job are unlikely to be reduced by way of compensation. In the short run, prior to positive benefits emerging, the action researcher is likely to face extra work.

'Ownership' of the research

The participatory nature of action research brings with it a question mark concerning who owns the research and its outcomes. With conventional approaches to research this tends to be less complicated. To offer something of a caricature, the outsider researcher initiates the process and approaches practitioners to gain their permission for the research to be conducted (by the outsider). Having obtained authorization from relevant people, research proceeds, with the outsider 'owning' the data collected and having full rights over the analysis and publication of findings. Complications arise with various forms of sponsored research and consultancy where authorization might include certain restrictions on the rights of the two parties over the research and its findings. However, these are likely to be *explicitly* recognized as a result of negotiating access.

In the case of action research the *partnership* nature of work can make matters rather less clear-cut. Who is in charge? Who calls the shots? Who decides on appropriate action? Who owns the data? These and similar issues need to be worked out sensitively and carefully by the partners to *ensure that there are shared expectations about the nature of participation* in action research.

Ethical issues associated with action research

The distinct ethical problem for action research is that, although the research centres on the activity of the practitioner, it is almost inevitable that the activity of colleagues will also come under the microscope at some stage or other as their activity interlinks with that of the practitioner who instigates the research. Practitioners are not 'islands' – isolated from routine contact with colleagues and clients. Their practice and the changes they seek to make can hardly be put in place without some knock-on effect for others who operate close by in organizational terms.

The idea that the action researcher is exempt from the need to gain authorization, as a consequence, evaporates. Because the activity of action research almost inevitably affects others, it is important to have a clear idea of when and where the action research necessarily steps outside the bounds of collecting information which is purely personal and relates to the practitioners alone. Where it does so, the usual standards of research ethics must be observed: permissions obtained, confidentiality maintained and identities protected.

Two things follow. First, there is a case for arguing that those who engage in action research should be open about the research aspect of their practice. It should not be hidden or disguised. Second, the need for informed consent from those involved in the research should be recognized.

> **Good practice: Ethics in action research**
>
> Action researchers should respect the rights and sensitivities of colleagues and clients who become involved in the research. In practice, this means safeguarding their interests by:
>
> - being open about the existence and purpose of the research;
> - obtaining permission with regard to any data collection (such as observations or use of sensitive documents);
> - maintaining confidentiality with regard to information specifically gathered for the purposes of the research;
> - ensuring anonymity in terms of the identities of participants in any publicly available findings produced by the research.
>
> > Link up with Chapter 18, Research ethics.

Generalizability and action research

Given the constraints on the scope of action research projects, it might be argued that their findings will rarely contribute to broader insights. Located as they are in the practitioner's work-site, there are not very good prospects for the representativeness of the data in action research. The setting and constituent features are 'givens' rather than factors which can be controlled or varied, and the research is generally focused on the one site rather than spread across a range of examples. Action research, therefore, is vulnerable to the criticism that the findings relate to one instance and should not be generalized beyond this specific 'case'.

> Link up with Chapter 3, Case studies.

In one sense, this reservation needs to be acknowledged. Certainly, practice-driven research in local settings hardly lends itself to conclusions with universal application. New truths and new theories will be unlikely to find foundation in such studies alone. This caution is worth taking to heart for the action researcher: beware of making grandiose claims on the basis of action research projects. However, it can rightly be argued that action research, while practice driven and small scale, should not lose anything by way of rigour. Like any other small-scale research, it can draw on existing theories, apply and test research propositions, use suitable methods and, importantly, offer some evaluation of existing knowledge (without making unwarranted claims). It is the rigour, rather than the size of the project or its purpose, by which the research should be judged.

Insider knowledge and reflexivity

Practitioners who engage in action research have a privileged insight into the way things operate in their particular 'work-sites'. They have 'insider knowledge'.

This can be a genuine bonus for research. However, it can also pose problems. The outsider – 'the stranger' – might be better placed to see the kind of thing which, to the insider, is too mundane, too obvious, to register as an important factor. Because the practitioner cannot escape the web of meanings that the 'insider' knows, he/she is constrained by that web of meanings. The outsider 'expert' may not have the 'right' answer, but can possibly offer an alternative perspective which can help the practitioner to gain new insights into the nature of the practical problem.

Link up with
Reflexivity,
p. 89.

Advantages of action research

Participation

It involves participation in the research for practitioners. This can democratize the research process, depending on the nature of the partnership, and generally involves a greater appreciation of, and respect for, practitioner knowledge.

Professional development

It has personal benefits for the practitioner, as it contributes to professional self-development.

Practical

It addresses practical problems in a positive way, feeding the results of research directly back into practice. In the words of Somekh (1995: 340), 'It directly addresses the knotty problem of the persistent failure of research in the social sciences to make a difference in terms of bringing about actual improvements in practice.'

Continuous

It should entail a continuous cycle of development and change via on-site research in the workplace, which has benefits for the organization to the extent that it is geared to improving practice and resolving problems.

Disadvantages of action research

Scope and scale

The necessary involvement of the practitioner limits the scope and scale of research. The 'work-site' approach affects the representativeness of the findings and the extent to which generalizations can be made on the basis of the results.

Impartiality

The action researcher is unlikely to be detached and impartial in his/her approach to the research. In this respect, action research stands in marked contrast to positivistic approaches. It is clearly geared to resolving problems which confront people in their routine, everyday (work) activity, and these people therefore have a vested interest in the findings. They cannot be entirely detached or impartial in accordance with the classic image of science.

Control

The integration of research with practice limits the feasibility of exercising controls over factors of relevance to the research. The setting for the research generally does not allow for the variables to be manipulated or for controls to be put in place, because the research is conducted not alongside routine activity but actually as part of that activity.

Ownership

Ownership of the research process becomes contestable within the framework of the partnership relationship between practitioner and researcher.

Workload

Action research tends to involve an extra burden of work for the practitioners, particularly at the early stages before any benefits feed back into improved effectiveness.

Further reading

Coghlan, D. and Brannick, T. (2014) *Doing Action Research in Your Own Organization*, 4th edn. London: Sage.

Kemmis, S., McTaggart, R. and Nixon, R. (2014) *The Action Research Planner: Doing Critical Participatory Action Research*. Singapore: Springer.

McNiff, J. (2013) *Action Research: Principles and Practice*, 3rd edn. London: Routledge.

Reason, P. and Bradbury, H. (eds) (2013) *Handbook of Action Research*, 2nd edn. London: Sage.

Somekh, B. (2006) *Action Research: A Methodology for Change and Development*. Maidenhead: Open University Press.

Checklist for using action research

When undertaking action research you should feel confident about answering 'yes' to the following questions: ☑

1 Does the research project address a practical problem identified by the practitioner? ☐

2 Is there participation by the practitioner in all stages of the research project? ☐

3 Have the grounds for the partnership between practitioner and any outside expert been explicitly negotiated and agreed? ☐

4 Is the research part of a continuous cycle of development (rather than a one-off project)? ☐

5 Is there a clear view of how the research findings will feed back directly into practice? ☐

6 Does the research involve one or more of the following aims? ☐

   • Improve practice.
   • Enhance practitioner understanding.
   • Transform practices by challenging the existing system.

7 Has insider knowledge been acknowledged as having disadvantages as well as advantages for the research? ☐

8 Is the research sufficiently small scale to be combined with a routine workload? ☐

9 Does the research safeguard the identities and interests of those who contribute to the findings? ☐

© M. Denscombe, *The Good Research Guide*. Open University Press.

9 Phenomenology

What is the phenomenological approach? • Experience • The everyday world • Seeing things through the eyes of others • The social construction of reality • Multiple realities • Doing phenomenological research • Types of phenomenology: underlying essences or actual experiences • Advantages of phenomenology • Disadvantages of phenomenology • Further reading • Checklist for the use of phenomenology

What is the phenomenological approach?

As an approach to social research, phenomenology represents an alternative to positivism. Whereas positivist approaches tend to rely on measurement, statistics or other things generally associated with the scientific method (see p. 000), phenomenology entails a style of research that emphasizes:

- subjectivity (rather than objectivity);
- description (more than analysis);
- interpretation (rather than measurement);
- agency (rather than structure).

Its credentials as an alternative to positivism are further reinforced by the fact that phenomenological research generally deals with:

- people's perceptions or meanings;
- people's attitudes and beliefs;
- people's feelings and emotions.

Such a thumbnail portrait of phenomenology serves to set the scene and provide an initial view of its direction as a research strategy. It helps to explain why a phenomenological approach has proved useful for researchers in areas such as health, education and business who want to understand the thinking of patients, pupils and employees (van Manen 1990; Crotty 1996; De Chesnay 2015). And it gives a clue to why phenomenology is associated with humanistic research using qualitative methodologies – approaches that place special emphasis on the individual's views and personal experiences.

Experience

Phenomenology is concerned, first and foremost, with human experience – something denoted by the term 'phenomenology' itself. A phenomenon is something that stands in need of explanation; something of which we are aware but something that, as yet, remains known to us only in terms of how it appears to us directly through our senses. A phenomenological approach to research, following from this, concentrates its efforts on getting a clear picture of things as directly experienced by people. It is not primarily concerned with explaining the causes of things but tries, instead, to provide a description of how things are experienced first-hand by those involved.

Example 9.1

A focus on experience

The phenomenological investigation of something such as 'homelessness' would focus on the experience of being homeless. It might be interested in trying to get at the essence of what it means to be homeless. It might try to understand homelessness from the point of view of those who are themselves homeless and try to describe how they see things, how they understand the situation and how they interpret events. What it would *not* try to do is measure the extent of homelessness, or explain the causes of homelessness. Though both might be worthwhile endeavours, neither would be at the heart of phenomenological research.

The everyday world

Phenomenology is also characterized by a particular interest in the basics of social existence. This stems from a philosophical concern with the nature of 'being-in-the-world' (Heidegger 1962) and the lived experience of human beings within the 'life-world' (Husserl 1950). In practice, this translates into special importance being attached to the routine and ordinary features of social life, and to questions about how people manage to 'do' the everyday things on which social life depends. From the phenomenological perspective, the normal, routine facets of the everyday world around us are not trivial or inconsequential. Quite the opposite, they are the focus of attention.

Seeing things through the eyes of others

When dealing with the way people experience facets of their lives, phenomenology stresses the need to present matters as closely as possible to the way that those concerned understand them. The phenomenologist's task, in the first instance, is not to interpret the experiences of those concerned, not to analyse them or repackage them in some form. The task is to present the experiences in a way that is *faithful to the original*. This entails the ability to see things through the eyes of others, to understand what it feels like to be 'in their shoes' and to understand things from their point of view. This can be particularly important when dealing with things such as experiences of illness (e.g. Kugelmann 1999; Carel 2016) or experiences associated with a particular social identity or major life transition (e.g. Moustakas 1992; Charlesworth 2000; Ahmed 2006).

The social construction of reality

Phenomenology is particularly interested in how social life is constructed by those who participate in it, and it makes two points about this. First, it regards people as creative interpreters of events who, through their actions and interpretations, literally make sense of their worlds. From the perspective of the phenomenologist, people do not passively obey a set of social rules, nor do they slot into an external social structure, nor do they simply respond to their internal physiological drives or psychological dispositions. They are viewed instead as 'agents' who interpret their experiences and who actively create an order to their existence. As an approach to understanding the social world, this sets phenomenology apart from any belief that things are preordained, that there is a reality to social life that exists independently from the way people experience it or that the way we experience and understand things is structured by the way human minds are programmed to perceive things.

Second, it acknowledges that the processes of interpreting sights and sounds into meaningful events are not unique to each individual. Necessarily, they must be shared with others who live in the group or community (Berger and Luckmann 1967). If they were not, people would find it virtually impossible to interact with one another, since they could be operating on quite different understandings about what is going on. They could be living in different worlds, unable to communicate and unable to grasp the implications of other people's actions. Without some shared basis for interpreting their experiences there would be no way of knowing what others were doing or what their intentions were. There would, effectively, be no basis for social life.

 Key point

Phenomenology does not treat interpretations of the social world as totally individual things. Realities are not unique to each individual, they are shared between groups, cultures and societies.

Multiple realities

When the social world is seen as 'socially constructed' it opens up the possibility that different groups of people might 'see things differently'. There is the prospect of alternative realities – realities that vary from situation to situation, culture to culture. In this respect phenomenology stands in stark contrast to positivistic approaches to social research that are premised on the assumption of *one* reality. Whereas positivistic approaches look for explanations that fit one universal reality, phenomenological approaches tend to live with, even celebrate, the possibility of *multiple realities*. Reflecting the fact that the world as experienced by living humans is something that is created through the way they interpret and give meaning to their experiences, phenomenology rejects the notion that there is one universal reality and accepts, instead, that things can be seen in different ways by different people at different times in different circumstances, and that each alternative version needs to be recognized as being valid in its own right.

 Key point

The idea of multiple realties does not imply that there are as many social realities as there are individuals – each interpreting his/her world in their own unique way. Social realities are to some extent shared with others and phenomenology focuses on describing those shared realities and how they are constructed through interaction.

Doing phenomenological research

Description

When it comes to the matter of how phenomenologists actually do their research, a key characteristic of the approach is its emphasis on describing authentic experiences. Rather than directing their attention to explanations and analyses of experiences in an attempt to discover why they occurred, phenomenologists focus instead on trying to depict the relevant experiences in a way that is as faithful to the original as possible.

To provide a description of the *authentic* experience, phenomenological research first and foremost needs to provide a description that adequately covers the complexity of the situation. One of the crucial benefits of a phenomenological approach is that it deals with things in depth and does not try to gloss over the subtleties and complications that are essential parts of many – possibly most – aspects of human experience. The description, therefore, must be fairly detailed.

The phenomenological description should also be prepared to recognize and include aspects of the experience that appear to be self-contradictory, irrational or, even, bizarre. The researcher's role is not to act as editor for the way people explain their experiences. Nor is it to impose some artificial order on the thoughts of those being studied by trying to remedy any apparent logical inconsistencies. The social world is rarely neat and phenomenology does not involve the attempt to present life experiences as though they are entirely coherent.

Good practice: Dealing with complexities and contradictions

Phenomenological research should involve a detailed description of the experience that is being investigated – one that does not gloss over the complexities and contradictions that inhabit real life.

The suspension of common-sense beliefs

A phenomenological approach not only encourages the researcher to provide a detailed description of experiences, it also advocates the need to do so with a minimum reliance on the researcher's own beliefs, expectations and predispositions about the phenomenon under investigation.

From a phenomenological perspective, researchers are part of the social world they seek to investigate. Phenomenologists see the social world as existing only through the way it is experienced and interpreted by people – and this includes researchers as much as anyone else. Researchers, like other people, use common-sense assumptions when interpreting events, and this is where phenomenology has an important point to make for researchers. Researchers need to be *aware* of the fact that they rely on such everyday common sense, and make an effort to minimize the impact of these assumptions. They need to stand back from their ordinary, everyday beliefs and question them to see if they are blinkering the researcher's vision of what is happening. As best they can, researchers need temporarily to suspend common-sense beliefs. For the purposes of being able to provide a 'pure' description, researchers need to approach things without predispositions based on events in the past, without suppositions drawn from existing theories about the phenomenon being studied and without using their everyday common-sense assumptions. Such things need to be put to one side for the moment, 'bracketed off' so that researchers are able to describe things not through their own eyes, but through the eyes of those whose experiences are being described.

One way of 'bracketing off' presuppositions is to adopt the stance of 'the stranger' (Schutz 1962). The value of this is that it allows the researcher to see things that would otherwise be hidden from view – things that are so normal and obvious that they would not come to the attention of the researcher as something significant. A stranger is naive about how things work, and needs to figure them out from first principles before he/she can begin to operate as a competent member of the society. A 'stranger' is faced with the prospect of understanding *how* members of the society make sense of events. By adopting the stance of the stranger, then, the researcher is best able to see things for what they are, uncluttered by assumptions that form part of everyday thinking about those things.

> **Good practice: Suspending common-sense beliefs**
> Researchers who use a phenomenological approach need to be explicit about their own ways of making sense of the world and, in order to get a clear view of how others see the world, they need to suspend (or bracket off) their own beliefs temporarily for the purposes of research.

Members' accounts

Data collection by phenomenology tends to rely on tape-recorded interviews. The interviews are conducted with members of the particular group whose experiences are being investigated. These members can provide insights into the thinking of the group and, through in-depth interviews, their experiences and their reasoning can be described and explained to the researcher in a way that allows the researcher to see things from the member's point of view (Denscombe 1983).

The process of interviewing is valuable for phenomenologists for a number of reasons. First, it provides the possibility of exploring matters *in depth*. In phenomenological research, interviews tend to be relatively long (in the region of one hour, often more) so that there is plenty of time to delve deeply into issues as they arise. Second, interviews allow the interviewee to raise issues that he/she feels are important. This helps the phenomenologist's investigation by highlighting things that matter to the person being interviewed. It helps to 'see things from the member's point of view'. To encourage this, phenomenological researchers tend to use relatively 'unstructured' interviews. Rather than the interview being conducted using a series of questions devised by the researcher, unstructured interviews allow plenty of scope for interviewees to move the discussion to areas that *they* regard as significant. Third, the interview process gives an opportunity for interviewees to provide an 'account' of their experiences. It is *their* version, spoken in their own words. It allows them both to describe the situation as they see it and to provide some justification or rationale, again from their point of view. Fourth, interviews allow the researcher the opportunity to *check* that he/she is understanding the interviewee correctly. As a normal part of the interview process the researcher can take special care to make sure that what he/she is 'hearing' is really what the interviewee is trying to put across, not a partial or mistaken interpretation resulting from the researcher's common-sense assumptions or presuppositions.

> **Link up with Chapter 13, Interviews.**

Types of phenomenology: underlying essences or actual experiences

Over time, different versions of phenomenology have developed and there are sometimes disagreements among those who would call themselves 'phenomenologists' about which is the 'true' version. The social researcher who is thinking about adopting a phenomenological approach should be aware that such differences of opinion exist. Although many versions exist, it is probably most straightforward to characterize phenomenology as consisting of two main types. One version derives from the European tradition of thought and the other, the 'new phenomenology', has a North American origin.

The European version is more steeped in the discipline of philosophy and can lay claims to being the original version since it owes much to the founding father of phenomenology, Edmund Husserl. His 'transcendental phenomenology' (Husserl 1931 [2012]) approaches the study of human experience with the aim of discovering underlying, fundamental aspects of experience – features that are universal and that lie at the very heart of human experience. Though differing somewhat, the 'existential phenomenology' of Jean-Paul Sartre (1956) and the 'hermeneutic phenomenology' of Martin Heidegger (1962) draw on similar European philosophical roots and have a crucial thing in common. They share a concern with investigating *the essence of human experience.*

The kinds of experience dealt with by these writers tend to revolve around fundamental philosophical questions about 'being-in-the-world' and similar issues relating to 'the meaning of (everyday) life'. However, this form of phenomenology can operate at a more mundane level. For example, it could address something as topical and down-to-earth as bullying in schools. Based on this tradition of phenomenology the research would be interested in the experience of being bullied and, in particular, it would focus on the essential features of that experience. It would try to identify the core components of the notion of bullying by investigating the experiences of those who have found themselves the victim of bullying. It would not focus on the *extent* of bullying in schools, nor would it try to explain the *causes* of bullying. Its focus would be on the *essence of the experience of being bullied.*

Importantly, though, the European tradition of phenomenology stresses that such essences exist beyond the realms of individual, personal experiences of specific events. While such individual instances might be the starting point for investigation, the purpose is always to use them as a means for getting a clearer picture of the essential qualities of the experience that exist at a general level. In relation to the example of bullying, individual instances of bullying would be of interest only to the extent that they could be used to help the identification of the broader, essential qualities of that experience: they would be valuable as means towards an end, but would not constitute an end in themselves as far as research is concerned.

Contrasting with this tradition is the North American version of phenomenology which is more commonly linked to the disciplines of sociology, psychology, education, business studies and health studies. It emanates from the 'social phenomenology' of Alfred Schutz (1962, 1967). Schutz was primarily interested in the mental processes through which humans make sense of the many things they experience. His early work focused on the way that, in order to make sense of the social world, people interpret things through seeing them as specific instances of more general categories – a process that involves what he referred to as 'typifications'. Within the realms of phenomenology this shift in focus had important repercussions. Indeed, through his focus on interpretation of the social world, Schutz's work actually spawned a rather different kind of phenomenology. This kind of phenomenology is less concerned with revealing the essence of experience and more concerned with describing the ways in which humans give meaning to their experiences. Here lies the defining characteristic of the North American approach: *its concern with the ways people interpret social phenomena.*

This form of phenomenology retains a concern with things such as experience, an interest in everyday life and suspending common-sense assumptions in order to provide a description that is true to the way those involved experience things. However, it also incorporates elements of pragmatism and social interactionism into the approach – things that make it controversial in two ways as far as the European phenomenological tradition is concerned. First, the North American phenomenology is comfortable in describing *what* is being experienced (for example, in relation to something such as homelessness), rather than attempting to uncover the essence of what is meant by the term. Second, and linked with this, it also places some value on describing individuals' experiences for their own sake. The new phenomenology might well investigate homelessness by asking what being homeless means to those who are homeless, what events and emotions they have experienced as a consequence of being homeless and what it means to them. The experiences of the individual are taken as significant data in their own right, not something to be put to one side in order to identify the universal essence of the phenomenon.

Good practice: Clarity of purpose

In practice, it is not always easy to separate the two traditions of phenomenology. Ideas from one area are imported to the other, not always reflecting the original very faithfully. Such blurring of the boundaries complicates life for project researchers. This should not, though, deter a researcher from choosing this approach, since many aspects of social research operate in such contested domains. It does, however, highlight the need for the researcher to be very clear about his/her specific aims when investigating the phenomena of human experience.

Advantages of phenomenology

Suited to small-scale research

Phenomenological research generally relies on in-depth interviews and does not call for technologically sophisticated or expensive equipment for the purposes of data collection and analysis. Coupled with this, it is often undertaken in specific localities such as hospitals, schools or industrial plants. In both respects, it lends itself to small-scale research where the budget is low and the main resource is the researcher himself/herself.

The description of experiences can tell an interesting story

There is an inherent potential within (new) phenomenology to describe experiences in a way that is immediately accessible and interesting to a wide range of readers. By unfolding the events and laying bare the feelings experienced by people, the research is likely to attract a relatively wide readership. It deals with everyday life and people can generally relate to this.

Offers the prospect of authentic accounts of complex phenomena

The social world is complex and rarely straightforward. A phenomenological approach allows the researcher to deal with that complexity. It scratches beneath the superficial aspects of social reality. It calls for the researcher to delve into phenomena in depth and to provide descriptions that are detailed enough to reflect the complexity of the social world.

A humanistic style of research

There is a respect for people built into the phenomenological approach. It carries an aura of humanism and, in its efforts to base its enquiry on the lived experiences of people in the everyday world, it represents a style of research that is far removed from any high-minded, abstract theorizing. In effect, the researcher needs to be close to the objects of study.

Disadvantages of phenomenology

Lacks scientific rigour

The emphasis of phenomenology on subjectivity, description and interpretation contrasts with the scientific emphasis on objectivity, analysis and measurement. Although phenomenology is self-consciously non-positivist – and proud to be so – there is the danger that this can be turned against it and be treated as a weakness rather than a strength by those who do not share its stance.

Associated with description and not analysis

The importance attached to providing a detailed and accurate description of the events and experiences being studied can lead to accusations that phenomenology does nothing but provide descriptions. This might not be warranted, in particular where the phenomenologist goes on to develop explanations based on the descriptive material. There is, none the less, the danger that those who are not sympathetic to phenomenology might seize the opportunity to criticize it for its primary focus on description.

Generalizations from phenomenological studies

Phenomenological research does not normally involve large numbers of the phenomenon being studied. This will always raise questions about the representativeness of the data and how far it is justifiable to generalize from the findings. Phenomenologists, for their part, might not regard such a concern as relevant to their work, but many other kinds of researchers will be concerned with this issue.

Attention to the mundane features of life

For phenomenologists the study of routine aspects of everyday life occurs because it is fundamental for understanding the nature of the social world. For others it might be (mis)interpreted as dealing with things that are mundane, trivial and relatively unimportant compared with the big issues of the day in the spheres of social policy, international relations, economic progress, and the like.

Feasibility of suspending common sense

In principle, suspending presuppositions about the way things work might seem a reasonable way of trying to get a clearer view of them. However, it is doubtful if it is ever possible to rid ourselves entirely of such presuppositions. Socialization and the use of language make it impossible. What can be done, though, is to be reflective and self-conscious about the way perceptions are shaped by things like common sense and then to try to moderate their impact.

Further reading

Gallagher, S. (2012) *Phenomenology*. Basingstoke: Palgrave.
Kaufer, S. and Chemero, A. (2015) *Phenomenology: An Introduction*. Cambridge: Polity.
Moustakas, C. (1994) *Phenomenological Research Methods*. Thousand Oaks, CA: Sage.
Smith, J.A., Flowers, P. and Larkin, M. (2009) *Interpretative Phenomenological Analysis: Theory, Method and Research*. London: Sage.
Van Manen, M. (2016) *Phenomenology of Practice: Meaning-Giving Methods in Phenomenological Research and Writing*. London: Routledge.

Checklist for the use of phenomenology

When undertaking phenomenological research you should
feel confident about answering 'yes' to the following questions: ☑

1 Is the research concerned with one or more of the following?   ☐

   - Looking for the essential features of a phenomenon.
   - Describing the content and nature of lived experiences.
   - Investigating the everyday rules by which experience is
     structured.

2 Does the research take into consideration:

   - the social construction of reality?   ☐
   - multiple realities?   ☐

3 Have efforts been made to bracket off common-sense
   assumptions and take account of the researcher's
   presuppositions in order to provide a 'pure' description?   ☐

4 Does the research provide a description that adequately
   deals with the complexity, subtlety and contradictions of the
   phenomenon?   ☐

5 Does the description authentically represent the way things
   are seen by those whose experiences are being studied?   ☐

6 Does the research involve the suitable use of interviews and
   transcripts for checking members' meanings and intentions?   ☐

10 Systematic reviews

*What is a systematic review? · Benefits of a systematic review ·
Kinds of research problem suitable for systematic review ·
Qualitative research and systematic reviews · How to conduct
a systematic review · Issues relating to the use of systematic
reviews · Advantages of systematic reviews · Disadvantages of
systematic reviews · Further reading · Checklist for the use of
systematic reviews*

Systematic reviews are used by a range of social researchers, practitioners and policy-makers who want to get a reliable and objective overview of the evidence that is currently available on a specific topic or the impact of a new intervention. They have been applied to things such as:

- the *effectiveness* of innovations in health service delivery;
- the *dissemination* and *take up* of new practices in organizations;
- the *incidence* of illicit drug use by young people;
- the *consequences* of social policy in relation to old age pensions;
- the *success rates* of motivational interviewing for smoking cessation.

Systematic reviews tend to be associated with *evidence-based practice* – an approach that stresses the need for decisions to be based on firm evidence from good quality research – and they came to prominence in connection with medical and pharmaceutical research where they have now become well established as a method for evaluating findings from clinical trials on the effectiveness of specific drugs and particular treatments (e.g. the Cochrane Reviews).

What is a systematic review?

A systematic review is a review of the research literature whose aim is to arrive at a conclusion about the state of knowledge on a topic based on a rigorous and unbiased overview of all the research that has been undertaken on that topic. To do this, systematic reviews entail:

- a *search* for the relevant literature using explicit methods that are both rigorous and systematic;
- a *review* of the findings which compares them and evaluates them using explicit criteria;
- a *conclusion* based on an objective analysis of the existing data.

What is the difference between a systematic review and a traditional literature review?

Systematic reviews are not quite the same as a traditional literature review. There are three main areas of contrast. First, systematic reviews are a self-contained study in their own right – rather than a prelude to some empirical investigation. Second, they focus on a very specific question, usually linked to a policy or practical problem. Third, as the name indicates, they are very systematic in the process that is used to review the literature.

Link up with Chapter 20, Literature reviews.

Benefits of a systematic review

What we already know about a particular topic is not always straightforward or clear-cut. There are two main reasons for this. First, research projects investigating specific topics do not always produce the same findings on which everyone can agree. In most fields of study there are contested areas where the findings from different research projects are disputed and where people disagree about 'what is true' or 'what works best'. Second, reviews of the evidence can be based on a selection of sources which might not necessarily be the *best* sources. Indeed, there might be an emphasis on certain findings (and disregard for others) on the basis of how far the findings match the preferences of the individual doing the review rather than the quality of the research itself.

A consequence of these two difficulties is that knowledge about the available evidence can be patchy or even biased. However, this is where *systematic* reviews come into the picture. Their aim is to reduce the potential for bias by being open and honest about:

- how the search for relevant findings was conducted;
- how decisions were made about which sources to include and which to exclude;
- how judgements were arrived at about the quality of the data reported in the various published findings of research.

Key point

Systematic reviews are rigorous in the search for data and transparent in the methods of review.

Kinds of research problem suitable for systematic review

Systemic reviews are valuable when tackling specific questions on which there already exists a considerable body of evidence. They are suited to topics where previous research has established some agreement about what needs to be known and how it should be investigated, and in this respect they are more appropriately applied to findings from explanatory research than exploratory research. When the studies share some basic premises about what is to be investigated, and how this should be done, this allows a comparison of like-with-like studies whose evidence can be directly contrasted. Only when this is the case is there a reasonable prospect of using the existing research findings to arrive at some single 'objective' conclusion about what works best, what is right, where the truth lies. In practice, this means that there are five criteria that must be met in order for systematic reviews to work well:

1   The topic or problem being reviewed must be clearly defined and quite narrowly focused.
2   A substantial body of research findings must already exist on the topic.
3   The available evidence must come from studies that use similar methods.
4   The 'evidence' must lend itself to measurement, comparison and evaluation.
5   The findings are usually based on quantitative data.

Qualitative research and systematic reviews

Although the drive for systematic reviews has come predominantly from 'scientific' research where the findings are based on 'hard, quantitative data', there has also been some attention given to the use of systematic reviews with qualitative research (Dixon-Woods et al. 2006; Pawson 2006; Petticrew and Roberts 2006; Pope et al. 2007; Denyer and Tranfield 2009). The challenge facing those who want to conduct a systematic review of qualitative research is how to compare, evaluate and synthesize findings based on methodologies that do not conform to a standard model such as the randomized controlled trial (RCT). Qualitative research, after all, tends to be conducted in a variety of ways and in differing contexts – things which invariably hinder the prospect of direct comparisons between their findings. The response to this challenge, described in more detail below in relation to stage 6 in the process of conducting systematic reviews, has been to review the findings through 'narrative analysis', 'thematic analysis' and 'realist synthesis' rather than attempt to aggregate the findings from existing research (see below).

How to conduct a systematic review

There are seven key stages involved in a systematic literature review. These stages reflect both the process of actually doing a review and the requirements for writing up a systematic review. So both aspects – doing and reporting – are dealt with stage by stage in the outline that follows.

Stage 1: The scope of the study

The first task is to decide upon the specific scope of the study. It is important that the area of interest that is chosen for the review is quite specific and *narrowly focused* because this sets the boundaries in terms of the content area for the search. Systematic reviews cannot work with vague or broad topics because this would make it almost impossible to decide what research findings to search for and what evidence to consider.

When writing up the review, all significant choices made in connection with the scope of the review need to be described and justified. This is in line with the spirit of transparency which lies at the heart of systematic literature reviews. The review needs to start with a statement which pinpoints the chosen area of interest and explains why that topic warrants attention.

Stage 2: The search process

Initially this involves a careful consideration of the most accurate and appropriate 'key words' and *search terms* to be used. These should be words or short phrases that will best target the relevant research findings: they need to capture the essence of the chosen topic. Next, decisions need to be made about where these search terms will be used. Which databases, which search engines, which archives, which catalogues – what sources will be searched? This might include reference to databases such as PsychINFO, LexisLibrary, Medline (PubMed) and Web of Knowledge. Such sources need to be selected strategically in order to produce the best returns from the search. The aim here is to conduct as comprehensive a search as possible of the available literature on the topic. Ideally, it should involve not only published works but also any other relevant findings which are available, perhaps in the form of conference papers or unpublished reports, although the extent to which this is possible will depend largely on the resources that are available. Small-scale research is likely to concentrate on finding just published works.

In terms of writing up the review, and again in the spirit of transparency, there needs to be an explicit description of how the search was conducted.

As part of the 'audit trail', sufficient details about the search process need to be provided in order to allow other researchers to replicate the search should they wish to do so, and readers of the review need to be told about the reasoning behind the various choices that have been made. The account of the search process, therefore, needs to include:

- a list of the *search terms* used, and an explanation of why they were deemed to be the most appropriate ones on which to base the research;
- a list of the *databases* that were searched, along with some explanation of why these were considered to be the most relevant ones to use;
- information about the *period covered* by the search, plus a justification for focusing on those particular years;
- details about the actual *dates when the search was conducted*.

Stage 3: Evaluation of quality

The sources of information thrown up by the search process will differ in their value for the review. Some are likely to be more closely related to the topic than others, and some are likely to be of a better quality than others in terms of the research on which they are based. So decisions need to be made about which to include and which to exclude from consideration when it comes to the review. Such decisions need to be made on explicit criteria: not hunch, not convenience, not appeal nor gut reaction, but explicit and justifiable benchmarks for objective decisions. A crucial task, then, when conducting a systematic literature review is to establish a set of criteria on which to judge:

- The *relevance* of sources to the topic being considered. Findings from previous research that is close to the topic might be treated as more significant than findings that are less directly on the topic.
- The *quality* of the sources. The credibility of the findings might be gauged according to the methods used in the research, with higher significance being attached to findings produced by particular kinds of research design, for instance, or from larger samples.

These criteria need to be systematically applied to each of the studies included in the review, and that is why systematic reviews generally require the researcher to use a *data extraction form* for collecting information about the studies. The data extraction form acts as a kind of checklist with all the important items the researcher needs to record about each study listed, and space for relevant details from each study to be noted alongside each item. It is important to recognize that the specific items included in any data extraction form will be tailored to meet the specific requirements of the particular review. There is no universal form that applies on all occasions. Figure 10.1, however, provides some basic starting points for the construction of a data extraction form to be used in connection with small-scale social science projects.

Figure 10.1 Data extraction form: some basic items for inclusion

Item	Data extracted	Reviewer notes
Author(s)		
Year of publication		
Title of project		
Period when research was conducted		
Funding source/sponsors		
Location of research		
Objectives of the research		
Type of study		
Underlying tradition/philosophy of the research		
Research design		
Data collection methods		
Research population		
Number of participants		
Sampling techniques		
Factors/variables used for analysis		
Techniques for data analysis		
Quality controls: actions taken to support quality and avoid errors in the data		
Findings		
Recommendations		
Evaluation: Researcher assessment of reliability of methods and validity of findings		

As with the previous stages, when writing up the review it is vital to provide sufficient detail about the decision-making to allow other researchers to understand the reasoning and check the procedures should they wish to do so. This entails the inclusion of an open and explicit explanation for the decisions made with respect to the individual sources identified in the review. This explanation needs to cover:

- a statement of the *rationale for inclusion* or exclusion of studies;
- the specific *criteria of relevance*, and some discussion of their link with the topic of the review;
- the *criteria for quality assessment*, and some account of how these were applied;
- a copy of the *data extraction form*.

Stage 4: List of sources included in the review

A full list of the works that are to be incorporated into the review should be provided. There are two angles to this. First, it is standard practice to produce a flowchart that visually represents the process of inclusion and exclusion of studies in the review. Figure 10.2 indicates a straightforward way of doing this in the context of a small-scale social research project.

Second, there needs to be sufficient bibliographic detail to allow other researchers, should they wish to do so, to find these sources and check their contents. Normally, this is supplied in the form of a table containing the basic

Figure 10.2 Flowchart showing the inclusion and exclusion of studies from the review

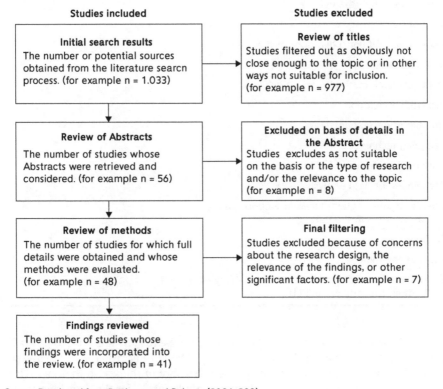

Source: Developed from Pettigrew and Roberts (2006: 300).

 Key point

When writing up the systematic review it is necessary to provide:

- a *flowchart indicating the number of studies* included and the numbers excluded at each stage of the review;
- a *table listing basic information* about each of the studies whose findings have been reviewed.

information about those studies actually included in the review subsequent to the review of Abstracts stage.

Stage 5: Descriptive summary

Having listed the research findings that will be used, the next stage in a systematic review is to produce a descriptive summary of the works – something that tells the reader about when the research projects were done, where they were done, how they were done (methods) and by whom. This entails categorizing the various studies according to a set of explicit criteria that cover the origins of the work, and counting the numbers that fall into the various categories. Such information is useful because it provides the reader with an overview of the *origins of the information* that will be included in the review.

Writing up this part of a systematic review partly involves stating how many works fall into specific categories, and partly involves a written 'narrative' that describes the nature of the research that is to be included in the review. Combined, these two aspects of the descriptive summary should capture the key dimensions of the overall body of work that has been selected for review. They should provide the reader with important signposts about the available, relevant, good quality research in terms of things like:

- how *recent* the work is;
- *what groups of people* have shown the most interest in conducting the research;
- who has *funded* or sponsored the research;
- which *regions* or *countries* are most commonly represented in the work that has been done;
- which research *methods* have been used in the studies.

Stage 6: Analysis

Meta-analysis

At the heart of the systematic review lies the analysis. What does this involve? Well, for some people the ideal thing to do would be to conduct a *meta-analysis*. For those involved in reviews of health, medical and pharmaceutical research this is often the ultimate goal. As Goldacre (2012: 14) describes it:

> When you've got all the trial data in one place, you can conduct something called a meta-analysis, where you bring all the results together in one giant spreadsheet, pool all the data and get one single, summary figure, the most accurate summary of all the data on one clinical question.

To aggregate the data in this way, however, the findings need to be based on research that shares a similar methodology. In systematic reviews of health, medical and pharmaceutical research, 'clinical trials' are the shared methodology which allows the possibility of pooling all the data together and arriving at the overall result. In the social sciences, however, there is far less prospect of aggregating findings in this way from a variety of research projects on a given topic. In the social sciences the methods used by researchers tend to be more varied and the findings less amenable to being amalgamated in the way that meta-analysis requires. For this reason, systematic reviews of research findings in the social sciences are much more likely to be based on some form of narrative analysis.

Narrative analysis

A *narrative analysis* provides an account of the findings based on the use of words (rather than figures). It involves an attempt to 'tell the story' behind the findings of the various works that have been reviewed (Tranfield et al. 2003; Denyer and Tranfield 2009). Now, in the traditional literature review the choice of the works to be reviewed, the order in which they are introduced and the emphasis that is placed on individual pieces of research are things which depend on the literary skills of the reviewer and the story he/she wishes to tell. A good literature review guides the reader; it takes them on a journey of discovery which ends with a persuasive case being made for the reviewer's conclusion about what the available evidence suggests.

In a *systematic* review, however, any narrative account needs to be based on *all* the research findings that meet explicit quality standards. Also, in a systematic review the persuasiveness of the narrative should stem from the findings themselves rather than the literary skills of the reviewer or any preferences he/she might have in relation to the conclusion to be drawn from the review. The nature of the review, in fact, needs to be more transparent, explicit and structured than would normally be associated with a traditional literature review. Whether identifying themes running through the various research findings (a *thematic* synthesis) or focusing on the reasoning used by the researchers to explain their findings (a *realist* synthesis) the narrative analysis must always endeavour to be highly systematic and objective.

Thematic synthesis: organize findings; look for themes; identify patterns

Thematic synthesis, as the name suggests, depends on identifying themes that emerge in the existing research. At one level, this involves the search for some consensus across the studies being reviewed. Is there agreement about things? Is there a shared opinion emerging from the research about the situation and its causes? Does existing research produce findings that are consistent and which point to causes and consequences upon which there is general agreement? If so, then it becomes quite easy to draw a definitive conclusion about the 'truth' of the situation or what 'works best'. If not (which in the social sciences is quite likely), then the thematic review needs to establish what the disagreements are and what issues underlie these 'contested areas'. Is it a matter of researchers approaching a topic using a similar approach and methods but arriving at different findings and alternative conclusions? Or, perhaps, it might be a matter of researchers adopting markedly different approaches to a topic which produce findings that disagree. Does the source of funding or sponsorship align with the kind of findings emerging from the research, or do findings differ according to the location in which the research took place? Whatever, the role of the thematic review is to establish where the division lines are and explain what lies behind the differences of opinion.

 Key point

A thematic synthesis focuses on the substance of the findings and any recommendations arising from the studies included in the review.

Realist synthesis: look for the underlying causes

The analysis does not necessarily have to be based on a review of the *findings* from various studies. Sometimes, it is not so much the findings as the *reasons* for the findings which are the basis for the analysis. From a critical realist perspective the quest for themes running through the literature can be directed at the factors that researchers see as explaining their findings – the *underlying causes*. As Pawson (2006, 2013) argues, a 'realist synthesis' looks across the range of relevant studies to see which underlying factors or mechanisms are being used to explain the findings. The various pieces of research included in the review can be 'regarded as case studies whose purpose is to test, revise and refine the preliminary theory' (Pawson 2006: 74). The aim is to draw on these various explanations to arrive at a conclusion which takes the form of a general proposition or theory. Using existing work, for example evaluating the effectiveness of particular social policies or interventions, the realist synthesis allows conclusions to be drawn about what will work (or not work) for whom under what circumstances.

 Key point

A realist synthesis focuses on explanations for the findings reported by the studies included in the review, and it is concerned with developing theories.

Stage 7: Conclusion

The review provides the platform for a synthesis of the distinct elements of the findings into something new – *an objective, overarching conclusion based on the various findings from all the published research that is available on a specific topic.*

The importance of the conclusions reflects the point that systematic reviews are intended to have a practical value. They are, as has been noted, associated with 'evidence-based practice' where policy-makers and others look to the systematic review for guidance. What these people want from a systematic review is some definitive statement about the 'state of things', something quite specific and clear-cut, which they can use as the basis for planning a course of action. Conclusions that involve hedging bets, sitting on the fence, or a series of either/or options are not so useful in this respect.

> **Good practice**
> Systematic reviews should aim to arrive at clear-cut conclusions.

Issues relating to the use of systematic reviews

There are three main issues relating to the use of systematic literature reviews which need to be borne in mind. The first of these is the general point that such reviews are based on findings that have been published or which, through some other means, are publicly available. As Goldacre (2012) stresses, though, not all findings from research get published. Referring in particular to the development of pharmaceutical drugs, he shows that research producing negative results are simply less likely to see the light of day. Either researchers do not bother to publish findings about things that don't work (preferring to concentrate on things that do) or there can be a more conscious pressure for commercial reasons to suppress negative results – they might prevent the further development of the drug. Commercial reasons to suppress certain research findings may not apply in the same way to social science research but the underlying point still holds – systematic literature reviews are based on *published* findings, and cannot cover findings from research which, for whatever reason, have not been made publicly available.

The second issue concerns the premise that a fairly large body of relevant published findings on a specific topic have already been published. This is more likely to be the case when it comes to trials of specific drugs or medicines, underlining the emergence of systematic literature reviews in that area. It may be less the case in relation to the social sciences. In the social sciences there will always be existing research which *relates* to a given topic, but there is less likely to be instances of previous research which is on exactly the same topic and which allows for the direct comparison of the findings. The nature of social science topics means that there is less prospect of comparing and evaluating data from different studies in a direct fashion.

The third issue continues this theme that systematic literature reviews are more easily applied to (medical) science rather than social science. Evaluating the quality of data from findings and arriving at 'objective' conclusions are things that sit more comfortably with quantitative data produced through research designs such as experiments and randomized controlled trials (Tranfield et al. 2003). Indeed, reflecting this point, it is perhaps not surprising that randomized controlled trials are considered to provide the best kind of evidence when it comes to evaluating the findings from research in the medical world (Higgins and Green 2011). But what about other kinds of research designs? Can the methods of systematic review be applied to alternative research designs such as case studies, action research, grounded theory, ethnography and phenomenology? In particular, can they work with studies that have produced qualitative data? Well, as we have seen, the answer is a qualified 'yes'. Instead of trying to combine the data from different research projects (as in 'meta-analysis') we can use some kind of 'narrative analysis' (as outlined above).

Advantages of systematic reviews

Systematic reviews have credibility

They aim to provide an impartial review of existing research and, to this end, they adopt a rigorous and transparent approach to the selection and analysis of suitable evidence. This bolsters the credibility of the findings and enhances the scientific standing of the conclusions that are drawn.

Systematic reviews have practical value – they provide answers to questions

Specifically, they address questions such as 'what works best?' and produce answers that are of direct value to policy-makers and practitioners who need some guidance about 'the truth of the matter' in the midst of large amounts of scientific evidence.

Disadvantages of systematic reviews

Reliance on existing body of knowledge

Systematic reviews work best in areas that have already attracted a lot of attention from researchers. They draw on a body of existing research findings – but for areas where there is little work that has already been done, it is not really possible to conduct a systematic review.

Resources

Systematic reviews can require a level of resourcing and teamwork not normally associated with small-scale social research projects.

Further reading

Bettany-Saltikov, J. (2012) *How to do a Systematic Literature Review in Nursing: A Step-by-step Guide*. Maidenhead: Open University Press.

Boland, A., Cherry, M.G. and Dickson, R. (eds) (2014) *Doing a Systematic Review: A Student's Guide*. London: Sage.

Gough, D., Oliver, S. and Thomas, J. (2012) *An Introduction to Systematic Reviews*. London: Sage.

Higgins, J. and Green, S. (eds) (2011) *Cochrane Handbook for Systematic Reviews of Interventions*, version 5.1.0 (updated March 2011). The Cochrane Collaboration. Available at: www.cochrane-handbook.org.

Petticrew, M. and Roberts, H. (2006) *Systematic Reviews in the Social Sciences: A Practical Guide*. Oxford: Blackwell.

Checklist for the use of systematic reviews

When undertaking a systematic review you should feel confident about answering 'yes' to the following questions: ☑

1 Has a literature *search* been undertaken that confirms there is not already a systematic review available on the topic? ☐

2 Do you have *access to the software* for logging and analysing the numerous studies and their findings? ☐

3 Is the *scope of the review* sufficiently narrow and well defined? ☐

4 Are the *criteria for inclusion* of studies in the review clear and explicit? ☐

5 Will the *methods* of the review be described in sufficient detail for readers to understand the rationale of the researcher's decisions? ☐

6 Has a *data extraction form* been produced to systematize the data collection? ☐

7 Will a *descriptive summary* of the works be included in the review? ☐

8 Will the *type of analysis* match the nature of the research findings being reviewed (meta-analysis, narrative analysis, thematic analysis, realist synthesis)? ☐

9 Is there, or will there be, a clear-cut *conclusion* resulting from the review? ☐

10 Will any limitations to the review be openly acknowledged? ☐

© M. Denscombe, *The Good Research Guide*. Open University Press.

11 Mixed methods

What is the mixed methods approach? • Benefits of using a mixed methods approach • Design of mixed methods projects • Triangulation in mixed methods research • Non-corroboration of data • Pragmatism and mixed methods • A new research approach? • Advantages of the mixed methods approach • Disadvantages of the mixed methods approach • Further reading • Checklist for the use of a mixed methods approach

A number of different names have been given to mixed methods strategies. 'Mixed research', 'mixed methodology', 'multiple research approaches', 'multi-strategy research', 'integrated methods', 'multi-method research' and 'combined methods' research are just some of the alternatives. The names bear testimony to the variety of ways in which research can be mixed and the many aspects of the research process that can be involved. A 'mixed methods' approach can be based on the mixing of research *designs*, research *strategies* and modes of *analysis*. The most common form of mix, however, involves a mix of methods and, in particular, the combination of qualitative and quantitative methods within a single research project. It is this type of mixed methods approach which is the focus of this chapter.

What is the mixed methods approach?

The mixed methods approach has three characteristic features that set it apart from other strategies for social research. These are:

1 *The combination of different types of research within a single project.* There is a willingness to combine methods from different 'paradigms' – from different traditions of research. In most cases this means mixing 'qualitative' and 'quantitative' components, with researchers variously writing about using qualitative and quantitative *methods*, qualitative and quantitative *data* or qualitative and quantitative *research*.

2 *A preference for viewing research problems from a variety of perspectives.* At the heart of the approach there is a commitment to viewing things from different angles. Rather than rely on findings from a single method or a single approach, the mixed methods approach regards the use of multiple sources as beneficial in terms of the quality and fullness of data it produces. For this reason, the idea of *triangulation* plays a major role in mixed methods research.

3 *The choice of methods based on 'what works best' for tackling a specific problem.* The approach is problem driven, and the research problem is always considered to be the most important thing when it comes to the choice of methods. It is not a matter of particular methods being intrinsically 'good' or 'bad'; it is a matter of how useful they are in terms of the specific issue that is being investigated. This primacy of the research problem, coupled with the mixing of methods from different paradigms, explains why the mixed methods approach tends to be associated with *pragmatism*.

Benefits of using a mixed methods approach

Accuracy of findings

Researchers can improve their confidence in the accuracy of findings through the use of different methods to investigate the same subject. In line with the principles of triangulation, the mixed methods approach provides the researcher with the opportunity to check the findings from one method against the findings from a different method. Where different methods produce data that are more or less the same, the researcher can feel more confident in assuming that the findings are accurate.

A more complete picture

The use of more than one method can enhance the findings of research by providing a fuller and more complete picture of the thing that is being studied. The benefit of the mixed methods approach in this instance is that the data produced by the different methods can be complementary. They can provide alternative perspectives that, when combined, go further towards an all-embracing vision of the subject than could be produced using a mono-method approach. In terms of the mixed methods approach, this tends to involve the use of both qualitative and quantitative methods as a means of seeing things from alternative perspectives and, thereby, getting a more complete overview of the subject.

Developing the analysis

Within a mixed methods strategy contrasting methods can be used as a means of moving the analysis forward, with one method being used to inform another.

In this sense, methods are introduced sequentially as a way of developing the findings obtained from a previous phase of the research.

This can be useful as a means of developing research instruments. For example, researchers who are designing a survey questionnaire can start by conducting focus groups or interviews and use these to discover what types of issues are most important to include in the subsequent survey questionnaire. In this way the quantitative data collected using the survey questionnaire are developed *from* the qualitative data that were collected through interviews or focus groups.

Mixed methods can also be used to develop *on* the findings from other parts of a research project. In this case, a new method is introduced specifically to address a research issue arising through findings produced by a previous method.

 Key point: The main benefits of using a mixed methods approach

- Check accuracy of findings.
- Provide a more complete picture.
- Help to develop the analysis.

Design of mixed methods projects

A lot of attention is given to the *design* of mixed methods projects. This is because the research design explains the rationale for mixing the various components: it indicates which methods are considered to be appropriate for the research question being investigated and it shows how the various methods can be interlinked to best advantage (Morgan 2014; Creswell 2015).

A large number of design possibilities have been suggested, and there have been numerous typologies produced which catalogue alternative designs for mixed methods research. However, the first thing to note about the various typologies for mixed methods research is the way they tend to be based on a clear distinction between qualitative and quantitative forms of enquiry. Reflecting this, the design of mixed methods research tends to follow a conventional notation in which:

- QUAL stands for qualitative data in the form of text or pictures that provide the basis for interpretations of the meaning they convey;
- QUAN stands for quantitative data in the form of numbers that provide objective measurements of observed events.

The labels QUAL and QUAN actually represent a simplified view of a complex reality. In practice, the dividing line between qualitative and quantitative approaches is not always clear-cut or simple. However, the labels QUAL and QUAN are easy to understand and they provide a convenient short-hand notation that signals the amount of *emphasis* specific methods put on interpretation (QUAL) or measurement (QUAN). For this reason, if no other, the distinction between QUAL and QUAN remains in widespread use in relation to mixed methods research designs.

The second point to note about the many mixed methods typologies is that they really boil down to some fairly simple and straightforward issues (Guest 2013). In fact, the basic things a mixed methods researcher needs to explain about his/her research design can be reduced to just three things:

- the *sequence* of the QUAL and QUAN components;
- the relative *importance* attached to the QUAL and QUAN components;
- the *purpose* of linking the QUAL and QUAN components.

Sequence

When a research design involves the use of methods or strategies drawn from different paradigms, the order in which the methods/strategies are used is significant. Given that they are used as part of the same investigation of the same research question, the sequencing reflects the researcher's beliefs about how the combination of methods and strategies works best.

For some purposes it might be better to have QUAN followed by QUAL. This is known as an *explanatory sequential design* where the qualitative research is used to help explain the results from the quantitative phase. For other purposes the opposite might be true. In an *exploratory sequential design* the qualitative phase comes first as a means of exploring a problem or developing a research tool, with the quantitative phase coming afterwards, making use of the qualitative results. The sequence in this case is QUAL/QUAN. There might also be occasions when the research is best served by conducting the QUAL and QUAN phases simultaneously. The results from both phases can then be merged subsequently at the stage of data analysis. This is known as a *convergent design*. These basic design options relating to sequence and timing are shown, using the conventional notation, in Figure 11.1.

Figure 11.1 Sequence in mixed methods research designs

Sequential studies	QUAN → QUAL	(explanatory sequential design)
	QUAL → QUAN	(exploratory sequential design)
	QUAN → QUAL → QUAN	(multiphase designs)
Simultaneous studies	QUAN ⎱ QUAL ⎰	(convergent design)

Relative importance

Research designs that incorporate aspects of both QUAL and QUAN need not necessarily attach equal weight to the two. Indeed, there is a strong likelihood that researchers will tend to regard one as the 'main' and the other as the 'subsidiary' counterbalance or check. For example, the researchers might start by collecting and analysing a relatively small amount of qualitative data as an exploratory phase of the investigation. They might use interviews or focus groups to get a feel for the relevant issues and to explore the way things are perceived. Armed with this knowledge, the researchers can then produce a questionnaire (or other quantitative research instrument) that can build on information obtained in advance. Some psychology and marketing research adopts this approach, using the QUAL as a preliminary checking device to ensure the validity of a QUAN research instrument. In this approach, it is the QUAN data that are treated as the most important material for the investigation.

In contrast to this, the design might treat QUAL as dominant, perhaps preceding the QUAN subsidiary. An example of this would be the use of a detailed case study that is followed up with a small-scale questionnaire survey to check the case study findings. The research design, in this instance, centres on the collection and analysis of qualitative data. It might, for example, consist of interview data collected from employees within a particular business. From these interviews the researchers might reach certain conclusions. At this point, they might choose to conduct a survey of other businesses to check if these conclusions tend to be borne out in other situations. The key points might be included in a questionnaire distributed to a representative sample of businesses nationwide, with the hope that the responses they receive will corroborate the conclusions based on the detailed case study. The main thrust of the investigation, in this example, is the QUAL (interviews) with the QUAN (questionnaire survey) being used in a supporting role.

In a simplified depiction of the range of possibilities, the sequencing and dominance of methods from different research paradigms might take one of several forms (Figure 11.2).

Figure 11.2 Relative importance of components in mixed methods research designs

Equivalent status	e.g. QUAL $\rightarrow$ QUAN
	QUAN $\rightarrow$ QUAL $\rightarrow$ QUAN
Dominant/less dominant status*	e.g. qual $\rightarrow$ QUAN
	QUAL $\rightarrow$ quan

* *Note*: Use of lower-case letters to denote less importance.

Purpose of the link

Mixed methods research involves more than simply having bits of QUAL and QUAN research coexisting within a project. The key to good mixed methods research is to link these components in a way that is beneficial for the research and what it is trying to achieve. And as Creswell (2015: 111) warns:

> On the reverse side, we also know what mixed methods is not – and the most apparent problem today is that researchers collect both quantitative

and qualitative data, do not integrate the two databases, and call it mixed methods. Mixed methods actually involves the integration of the two databases, which is a key element of conducting this form of research.

So, one of the crucial things that needs to be addressed within any mixed methods research design is the matter of what each component contributes to the others. Some key possibilities here are:

- *Comparison of findings.* The link might involve comparing and contrasting the findings from various (QUAL and QUAN) components as a means of cross-checking the results and confirming the accuracy of the findings.
- *Building up findings.* The link involves one component adding to the findings of another in order to provide a fuller picture. Each extra bit of the research provides a new dimension to what is known about the topic, adding an alternative perspective and producing different kinds of information.
- *Developing on the findings.* This can involve specific parts of the research being used to shape the issues looked at by subsequent components and to *inform the direction* the research should take. Or the link can be based upon the use of findings from particular components to explain findings from another part of the research. The point in this case is to *take the analysis further*.

These three options map closely onto the three main benefits associated with mixed methods research. When taken together with the options for sequencing and the relative importance attributed to the components, these provide a basic list of ten mixed methods design options for the project researcher. These design options are outlined in Figure 11.3.

Triangulation in mixed methods research

One of the defining characteristics of mixed methods research, as noted at the beginning of the chapter, is a preference for viewing research problems from a variety of perspectives. As we have seen, this can be achieved by combining different components of a research project in different ways. What each of the design options share, however, is the aim of getting a better 'fix' on the thing that is being investigated by using more than one method to see it from more than one angle. The rationale for this owes much to the notion of 'triangulation' and in the sphere of mixed methods research triangulation has assumed a particular significance as a foundation for the premise that a research topic can be better understood if it is viewed from more than one perspective.

The idea of triangulation derives from trigonometry and the geometric laws associated with triangles. These laws make it possible to find the exact location

Figure 11.3 Ten basic design options for mixed methods research

Benefit	Link	Notation	Description
Improved accuracy	Comparison of findings	QUAL + QUANT	*Convergent findings* Alternative methods address the same question and are given equal status in terms of cross-validating the findings. The findings from each method are used as a check on the accuracy of findings from the other(s).
More complete picture	Build up findings	QUAL + QUANT Qual + QUANT QUAL + quant	*Additional coverage* Different methods are used to investigate separate components of the overall question. When brought together these add new dimensions to what is known about the topic.
Developing the analysis	Inform the direction Explain the findings	QUAL → QUAN QUAN → QUAL qual → QUAN quan → QUAL QUAL → quan QUAN → qual	*Sequential contributions* Findings from one method are used to inform research in the next phase within the project. There is a clear development that plays to the strengths of different methods. Emphasis can be placed on one component rather than treating them equally.

of an item if it is viewed from two other known positions (provided there is information about the angles and distances from these two other positions). In practice, triangulation is used by geologists, surveyors, navigators and others to measure exact locations of things in the physical world.

Social researchers have adapted and developed triangulation for use in the social world. Usually drawing on Denzin's (1970) early work in this area, they point to five distinct ways in which triangulation can be used in the social sciences. These are:

1 *Methodological triangulation (between-methods)*. This is the most common form of triangulation adopted by mixed methods researchers. The use of alternative methods allows the findings from one method to be contrasted with the findings from another. The key to this form of triangulation is the use of approaches that are markedly different and which allow the researcher to see things from as *widely different perspectives* as possible.

2 *Methodological triangulation (within-methods)*. Comparisons can be made using *similar kinds of methods* rather than ones that are markedly different. This is the form of triangulation used by Campbell and Fiske

(1959) and Webb et al. (1966) in their pioneering work on triangulation. The reasoning here is that if similar methods produce the same results, it would seem reasonable to conclude that the findings are accurate and that they are authentic (rather than being some artificial by-product of the methods used).

3 *Data triangulation (use of contrasting sources of information).* The validity of findings can be checked by using different *sources of information.* This can mean comparing data from different informants (informant triangulation) or using data collected at different times (time triangulation). The notion also incorporates the idea of space triangulation (the use of more than one cultural, social or geographical context).

4 *Investigator triangulation (use of different researchers).* As a check against bias arising from the influence of any specific *researcher*, the findings from different investigators can be compared for consistency. Do the researchers 'see' things in the same way? Do they interpret events similarly? Do they attach the same codes to the same source of data (e.g. interview transcript, observed event)? To the extent that they do, the findings can be accepted with more confidence.

5 *Theory triangulation.* This involves the use of more than one *theoretical position* in relation to the data. Different theories can shape the kind of data that are collected and the way the data are interpreted. These different perspectives can be based on the approaches of different disciplines. So, for example, researchers might choose to contrast a sociological with a psychological approach to the particular topic being investigated.

 Key point: Mixed methods and triangulation: the benefits

The use of methods, data, etc. that are contrasting and relatively *dissimilar* helps to provide a fuller and more complete picture through:

- production of *complementary data* (different but related);
- production of *further data* (developing out of previous findings).

The use of methods, data, etc. that are relatively *similar* can be used to gain improved accuracy through:

- *validation of findings* in terms of their accuracy and authenticity;
- *checking for bias* in research methods;
- *development of research instruments.*

Example 11.1 The use of triangulation in mixed methods research

The use of triangulation in mixed methods research can be illustrated through a research project on classroom control (Denscombe 2012a). This research primarily made use of between-methods triangulation and information triangulation. The starting point for the research was the problem of disruptive behaviour by students in secondary school classrooms. Such behaviour has a serious impact on lessons. The circumstances giving rise to such behaviour, and the techniques used by teachers to control it are, therefore, of practical concern and typical of the kind of *research problem* that can be tackled using a mixed methods approach.

The first phase of the study involved classroom *observation*. The researcher began by sitting in classrooms making field notes about events and focusing on incidents of disruptive behaviour. This use of observation as the initial data collection method produced both quantitative data relating to the frequency of such behaviour and qualitative data relating to the circumstances surrounding the events.

These data were useful in their own right. However, when used as part of a mixed methods research design there was more to be gained from them. As part of a mixed methods study they could provide:

- *insights* about the problem and suggested further avenues of enquiry to be pursued in connection with disruptive behaviour;
- a particular *perspective* on disruptive behaviour (based on classroom observation);
- *information* that could subsequently be checked in terms of (a) accuracy and (b) interpretation against findings from alternative sources of information and different research methods.

Such benefits, though, required the data from classroom observation to be used alongside other methods and other sources of information about disruptive behaviour. To exploit the benefits of between-methods triangulation these other methods needed to be quite different from observation, allowing disruptive behaviour to be viewed from a distinctly different angle. So the research went on to include a series of one-to-one interviews. In these interviews teachers and students were asked to reflect back on actual incidents of disruptive behaviour observed by the researcher during lessons. Used in this way, the interviews served two purposes. First, they added background information helping to explain why the events occurred. Second, they produced depth information shedding light on the meaning of the events for those involved and how the situations were negotiated.

To add yet another perspective the research also made use of written, documentary sources of data on disruptive behaviour. This involved an element of data triangulation. School records and school rules provided an 'official' standpoint on the matter, which offered an interesting contrast to the findings emerging from observation and interviews. Finally, a questionnaire survey of teachers and students was used as a means of verifying the analysis and seeing how far the findings could be applied more generally to a wider population.

The research, then, used different types of methods and alternative sources of information to look at disruptive behaviour in classrooms from different angles. In an effort to get a better overall understanding of the phenomenon, it used between-methods triangulation and data triangulation. There were, though, two aspects to this better understanding. As Figure 11.4 illustrates, triangulation was used to check the accuracy of the findings (e.g. about the frequency of disruptive behaviour), and it was used to provide a fuller picture (e.g. of the significance of disruptive behaviour in terms of its meaning for teachers and students).

Figure 11.4 Mixed methods and triangulation

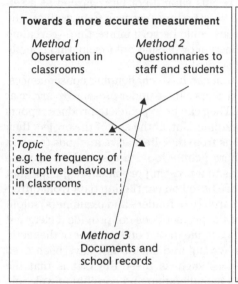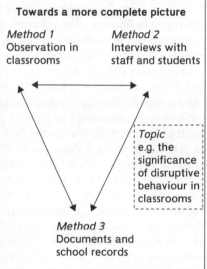

Towards a more accurate measurement

Method 1
Observation in classrooms

Method 2
Questionnaries to staff and students

Topic
e.g. the frequency of disruptive behaviour in classrooms

Method 3
Documents and school records

Towards a more complete picture

Method 1
Observation in classrooms

Method 2
Interviews with staff and students

Topic
e.g. the significance of disruptive behaviour in classrooms

Method 3
Documents and school records

 Caution: The use of triangulation in social science

The social world is different from the physical world and social researchers are not usually able to make use of fixed/objective positions, universally agreed, from which to make their observations. The use of triangulation by social researchers, therefore, is not literal. It is not the same as that used by geologists, surveyors or navigators. It generally refers more loosely to the broader underlying principle that viewing something from more than one viewpoint allows you to get more worthwhile findings from the research.

Note than in the case of accurate measurement it should not be inferred that the use of triangulation will pinpoint a precise, correct 'truth' about the situation (see Figure 11.4). It will not 'prove' that the researcher 'has got it right'. It can only help to corroborate findings and give the researcher more confidence about the conclusions. Likewise with the use of triangulation to get a more complete picture, it should never be suggested that the use of triangulation will have covered all the angles and allowed the researcher to say all there is to say on a topic. What it can do, more modestly, is help to provide a fuller understanding and produce alternative kinds of information which move things *towards* the complete picture.

Non-corroboration of data

The mixed methods approach tends to operate on the *assumption* that findings will coincide or be complementary and that this will be a positive contribution to the research project. There is, however, an inherent risk that the findings from the various components might not point in the same direction.

In principle, the non-alignment of results should not be regarded as a setback or failure of some kind. It should spur further research to investigate the difference in findings. The contradictions could be very interesting – revealing limitations to the methods of data collection or teasing out fascinating complications within the phenomenon being studied.

In practice, though, non-corroboration can have challenging consequences. Project researchers and contract researchers can be under pressure to arrive at conclusions within a given time frame. They can be expected to produce reports that have to be delivered by a given deadline. But, at the end of the project they could be left with contradictory findings from the alternative methods (or data sources) and no firm conclusion. Where people look to research to provide concrete findings or practical solutions to a pressing problem, they might not be very receptive to conclusions that are based on conflicting data from different methods. The audience for the research (e.g. funders and examiners) might feel dissatisfied that the completion of the project does not provide a clear-cut finding. They might even interpret things to mean that one or other of the methods (or data sources) employed was 'wrong' and should not have been used within the project. Under circumstances such as these the fact is that the non-corroboration of data can become a challenging and possibly unwelcome occurrence for the mixed methods researcher.

Pragmatism and mixed methods

Pragmatism is generally regarded as the philosophical partner of the mixed methods approach. This means that there is some broad agreement among mixed methods researchers that social research should not be judged by how neatly it fits with the quantitative paradigm (positivism) or with the premises of the competing camp – the qualitative paradigm (interpretivism). Decisions about which methods to use should, instead, be based on how *useful* the methods are for addressing a particular question, issue or problem that is being investigated. The crucial consideration is how well the research tools *work* rather than how well they fit within a specific research philosophy.

In the context of research, pragmatism tends to revolve around the following core ideas:

• Knowledge is based on practical outcomes and 'what works'. The key criterion for judging knowledge is how useful it is perceived to be and how well it works when applied to some practical problem.
• Research should test what works through empirical enquiry.

- There is no single, best 'scientific' method that can lead the way to indisputable knowledge.
- Knowledge is provisional. What we understand as truth today may not be seen as such in the future. Knowledge is seen as a product of our times. It can never be absolute or perfect because it is inevitably a product of the historical era and the cultural context within which it is produced. The quest for absolute 'Truth' is consequently seen as a hopeless cause.

Traditional dualisms in the field of philosophy and science are regarded as not helpful. In particular, there is a rejection of distinctions like facts/values, objectivism/subjectivism and rationalism/empiricism.

 Caution: The term 'pragmatism' is open to misinterpretation

There is a common-sense use of the word 'pragmatism' which implies expediency and a certain lack of principles underlying a course of action. There is the danger, then, that the mixed methods approach is associated with this understanding of the word and thus becomes regarded as an approach in which 'anything goes'. It should be stressed that this is not the philosophical meaning of pragmatism and it is not a meaning that should be associated with the mixed methods approach.

Mixed methods as an alternative option

The link between pragmatism and mixed methods research can be interpreted in more than one way. For some mixed methods researchers the tenets of pragmatism leave the door open for the use of purely quantitative research or purely qualitative research – providing the use of either in isolation can produce the kind of findings that work sufficiently well to answer a research problem. Pragmatism leads them to regard the use of mixed methods as a third *alternative* – another option open to social researchers if they decide that neither quantitative nor qualitative research alone will provide adequate findings for the particular piece of research they have in mind. Rather than see positivism and interpretivism as having become obsolete, these researchers regard the mixed methods approach as simply an alternative research strategy that can be used *if necessary*.

Mixed methods as a better option

There are others who see pragmatism as representing an advance in thinking about social research – the basis for a new research paradigm that should replace the earlier paradigms based on positivism and interpretivism (e.g. Tashakkori and Teddlie 1998, 2003; Johnson and Onwuegbuzie 2004; Teddlie and Tashakkori 2009; Creswell and Plano Clarke 2011). This paves the way for a subtly different stance in which the combination of quantitative and qualitative research is seen as a good thing in its own right. From this position it is not only allowable to mix methods from alternative and incompatible paradigms of research but it is also *desirable* to do so in order to provide answers that work – or, at least, that work better than those based on the use of just quantitative or just qualitative research.

A new research approach?

The image of mixed methods as a new paradigm has been useful for promoting it as the new breakthrough approach that cuts through the stand-off between two old-style narrow-visioned paradigms. It creates an identity for the approach and it literally 'makes sense' of a complex area in a way that is particularly useful for newcomers to social research who will find it easy to understand. It is useful, therefore, to *introduce* the approach along lines forged by the 'mixed methods movement' (as has been done in this chapter).

It would be wrong, however, to suggest that the use of mixed methods is entirely new to social research. The idea of combining different kinds of research methods within a single research project has been around for a long time (Teddlie and Johnson 2009; Johnson and Gray 2010; Maxwell 2016; Ramlo 2016). Numerous classic studies have brought together methods and data from contrasting paradigms using different underlying philosophies. What *is* relatively new is the identification of something called the *mixed methods approach*. As an approach, with a recognized name and research credibility, it has only come to the fore in recent years championed by writers such as Tashakkori and Teddlie (1998, 2003), Johnson and Onwuegbuzie (2004), Greene (2007), Teddlie and Tashakkori (2009), Creswell and Plano Clark (2011), Creswell (2015) and Morgan (2014).

It would also be wrong to infer that pragmatism is the only research philosophy that can be linked with the use of mixed methods. Researchers from other philosophical positions have argued for the benefits of using mixed methods. Notably, mixed methods has been linked with critical realism (Layder 1993, 1998; Pawson and Tilley 1997; Lipscomb 2008; Harrits 2011), constructivism (Denzin 2012) and transformative/emancipatory styles of research (Mertens 2009; Onwuegbuzie and Frels 2013). The use of mixed methods, then, is not *exclusively* tied to pragmatism.

Example 11.2

A classic study that used mixed methods
Between 1924 and 1933 research was conducted at the Western Electric company's Hawthorne Plant in Chicago. The aim of these *Hawthorne studies* was to discover which factors affected worker productivity. Initially,

management at the plant conducted a sequence of quasi-experiments in which they altered the level of lighting to see if this was linked with productivity. Subsequently, researchers from the Harvard Business School joined the investigation and conducted a further series of studies designed to investigate the link between fatigue, monotony and worker productivity (Mayo [1933] 2003; Roethlisberger and Dickson [1939] 2003). All these controlled, quasi-experimental studies produced rather puzzling and inconclusive results, and this prompted the researchers to introduce an alternative approach. Instead of trying to *measure* the factors that affected productivity they decided to *ask* the workers what motivated them. The researchers embarked on a huge programme of interviews with the workforce. What they found out about workers' motivation through the interviews helped the researchers to make sense of the findings from the initial experimental approaches used for the research. The interviews revealed that the workers were motivated by factors other than just money; there were personal and social rewards from work that affected their productivity as well. Once the researchers understood this, they could make sense of the results from the earlier phase. Finally, to confirm their findings from the interview phase the researchers embarked on a third phase of research which involved *observing* the informal group behaviour of workers. In this way they progressively developed the analysis of the factors influencing the productivity of the workers at the plant.

Advantages of the mixed methods approach

A better understanding of the thing that is being studied

Using a form of triangulation the mixed methods approach can be used: (1) to validate findings and improve accuracy or (2) to produce a more comprehensive account of the thing being researched.

A practical, problem-driven approach to research

As a movement, the mixed methods approach is problem driven rather than theory driven. Its underlying philosophy is that of pragmatism. As such, it gives voice to the general practice of a large proportion of social researchers who have, for years, used methods from different research paradigms because it has been practical to do so.

Clearer links between different methods and the different kinds of data

The mixed methods approach places emphasis on the integration of alternative approaches and encourages the researcher to provide an explicit account of how and why the different methods and data complement each other. Good mixed methods research avoids an arbitrary 'mix-and-match' approach.

Compensating strengths and weaknesses

Research strategies and methods each have their own strengths and their own weaknesses and a shrewd combination of strategies and methods allows the researcher to exploit the strengths of a particular method without leaving himself/herself vulnerable to criticism in connection with that method's weakness.

Disadvantages of the mixed methods approach

The time and costs of the research project can increase

The research design with its combination of phases can extend the overall time frame for research design and data collection.

The researcher needs to develop skills in more than one method

The researcher needs to develop and exercise skills covering both qualitative and quantitative approaches. Data analysis involves the need to compare, contrast and integrate the findings in a way that is likely to be more challenging than sticking with just one method. This places an additional burden on the researcher and opens up the possibility of 'missing the mark' for experts in either camp.

Findings from different methods might not corroborate one another

If findings from the different methods do not corroborate one another, the researcher can be faced with the need to extend the research to unravel the reasons for this.

The QUAL/QUAN distinction tends to oversimplify matters

When making the QUAL/QUAN distinction mixed methods researchers need to be aware that the clarity and simplicity of the terms mask a more complicated reality.

Further reading

Cresswell, J.W. (2015) *A Concise Introduction to Mixed Methods Research*. Thousand Oaks, CA: Sage.

Creswell, J.W. and Plano Clark, V. (2017) *Designing and Conducting Mixed Methods Research*, 3nd edn. Thousand Oaks, CA: Sage.

Morgan, D.L. (2014) *Integrating Qualitative and Quantitative Methods: A Pragmatic Approach*. Thousand Oaks, CA: Sage.

Teddlie, C. and Tashakkori, A. (2009) *Foundations of Mixed Methods Research*. Thousand Oaks, CA: Sage.

Watkins, D. and Giola, D. (2015) *Mixed Methods Research*. Oxford: Oxford University Press.

Checklist for the use of a mixed methods approach

When undertaking mixed methods research you should feel confident about answering 'yes' to the following questions: ☑

1 Does the research project do one or more of the following things? ☐
   • Make use of more than one research method.
   • Combine more than one kind of research data.
   • Ask questions based on different models (exploratory/explanatory).

2 Has a clear statement been made about the *benefits* of using a mixed methods strategy compared with using just one method? ☐

3 Is the *justification* for using a mixed methods strategy based on one or more of the following criteria? ☐
   • The needs of the particular research question.
   • Checking the accuracy of findings.
   • Providing a more complete picture.
   • Developing the analysis.
   • A means of compensating the strengths and weaknesses of particular methods.

4 Does the research have a clear *design* showing the sequence, dominance, and link between the QUAL and QUAN parts? ☐

5 Are details provided about how *triangulation* is used in relation to:
   • the different methods of data collection? ☐
   • the use of qualitative and quantitative data? ☐
   • the kinds of data analysis? ☐

6 Has consideration been given to the additional *skills and resources* that might be required in order to conduct mixed methods research? ☐

© M. Denscombe, *The Good Research Guide*. Open University Press.

Part 2

Methods of data collection

There are four main methods of data collection that social researchers can use: questionnaires, interviews, observation and documents. In many ways these are the social scientist's equivalent of the microscope, the scales and the micrometer that natural scientists might use in relation to material objects in the physical world. They are tools that help the researcher to gain:

- a clearer picture of things;
- an accurate measurement of things;
- facts and evidence about the subject matter.

Selecting methods: a matter of 'horses for courses'

In the following chapters there is guidance about the key features of each method. However, before choosing and using any of them it is important to consider four things. First, research methods are often associated with specific research strategies. Questionnaires tend to be linked with surveys, for example, while participant observation tends to be used with ethnography. There are some sound theoretical reasons that explain the tendency of particular methods to be linked to particular strategies. The linkage, however, is not watertight and it is important for the project researcher to recognize that there is likely to be some *element of choice* when selecting which method to use.

Second, each of the methods has its particular strengths and weaknesses. These are listed at the end of each chapter. Bearing this in mind, rather than trying to look for a method that is superior to all others in any absolute sense, it is better to look for a method that works best in practice for the specific purposes of the investigation. That is, when it comes to choosing a method, researchers should base their decision on the criterion of 'usefulness'. Researchers should ask themselves which method is best suited to the task at hand and operate on the premise that, when *choosing a method for the collection of data, it is a matter of 'horses for courses'.*

Third, research methods do not need to be seen as mutually exclusive. If no method is intrinsically better than others, and if methods are to be chosen pragmatically, then this opens up the possibility of combining methods and using a *mixed methods approach* (see Chapter 11).

Fourth, in practice there is no simple demarcation line between 'quantitative methods' and 'qualitative methods'. While some methods might seem better suited to the collection of quantitative data, others to qualitative data, it is important to recognize that methods can lend themselves to the collection of both quantitative data and qualitative data (see Table 16.1 on p. 266 and Table 17.1 on p. 306). The quantitative/qualitative distinction actually relates to the data that are collected, not the methods of collection *per se.*

Authorization for the research

Having selected the most appropriate method(s) there might be a strong temptation to get things started and forge ahead with the data collection. However, before any data collection occurs it is essential that the planned research has been given the green light to go ahead. This involves two things: ethics approval and authorization.

- *Ethics approval* is required for the vast majority of social research projects. It involves making an application to a Research Ethics Committee or its equivalent. Ethics approval must be obtained *before* embarking on data collection – this is absolutely essential. See Chapter 18, Research ethics, for further guidance on this point.
- *Authorization* is required from those in positions of power who control access to the people and settings involved in the research. This might mean getting written approval, for example, from senior managers within an organization or from 'guardians' who have responsibility for protecting the interests of vulnerable people. Again, it is vital that such authorization is obtained *before* the data collection begins.

Good practice: Approval before data collection

Always get approval in advance. Never start data collection without having already had the proposed research formally approved.

Pilot study

The method should always be tested out in advance to check how well it works in practice. No matter how much time and effort a researcher puts into devising a good data collection tool, there is no real substitute for trying it out 'in the field' with real participants. If all goes well the researcher can feel reassured that there should be no nasty surprises when the data collection proper begins. If the pilot study reveals areas for improvement, then these can be incorporated before the research goes 'live' – avoiding what might otherwise have been damaging problems for the research.

12 | Questionnaires

What is a questionnaire?

There are many types of questionnaires. They can vary enormously in terms of their purpose, their size and their appearance. To qualify as a research questionnaire, however, they should meet the following three criteria.

First, they should be designed to *collect information which can be used subsequently as data for analysis*. As a research tool, questionnaires do not set out to change people's attitudes or provide them with information. Although questionnaires are sometimes used for this purpose – for instance, as a way of marketing a product – it is not strictly in keeping with the spirit of a *research* questionnaire, whose purpose is to discover things.

Second, they should consist of *a written list of questions*. The important point here is that each person who answers the particular questionnaire reads an identical set of questions. This allows for consistency and precision in terms of the wording of the questions, and makes the processing of the answers easier. (Occasionally, pictures might be used instead of written questions.)

Third, they should *gather information by asking people directly* about the points concerned with the research. Questionnaires work on the premise that if you want to find out something about people and their attitudes, you simply go and ask them what it is you want to know, and get the information 'straight from the horse's mouth'.

When is it appropriate to use a questionnaire?

Different methods are suited to different circumstances, and questionnaires are no exception. Although they can be used, perhaps ingeniously, across a wide spectrum of research situations, questionnaires are at their most productive when:

- the information required tends to be fairly *straightforward information* – relatively brief and uncontroversial;
- there is a need for *standardized data* from identical questions – without requiring personal, face-to-face interaction;
- the respondents are *able to read and understand the questions* – the implications of age, intellect, language, and eyesight need to be considered;
- the *social climate is open* enough to allow full and honest answers.

Self-completion questionnaires

The main focus of this chapter is on *self-completion* questionnaires. Self-completion questionnaires rely on respondents working independently from the researcher, providing written answers at their own pace, in their own time. The researcher, even if present when the respondent completes the questionnaire, does not get involved with the process of filling in the answers. When researchers do have some direct involvement, however, things are a bit different. When questionnaires are delivered over the phone, or when a researcher stops someone in the street and asks them to complete a questionnaire that is read to them from a clipboard or mobile device, then it is more like using a 'structured interview'. The direct interaction between the researcher and the respondent brings into play a range of additional issues linked with the 'interviewer effect'. These issues are covered in Chapter 13 on interviews.

Successful questionnaires

The success of a research questionnaire depends on three things:

1 Response rate *(how many are returned)*
2 Completion rate *(how fully completed)*
3 Validity of responses *(how honest and accurate)*

Unless questionnaires are completed and returned to the researcher, they have no value at all. It does not matter how technically correct they might be or how beautifully designed they are, the simple fact is that research questionnaires are worthless unless and until those who receive them bother to provide answers and deliver the completed questionnaire to the researcher. Returned questionnaires that have lots of questions left unanswered, of course, are not likely to be of much use: if questionnaires are to be of any value, they must also have a sufficient proportion of questions filled in. And, of course, the value of any questionnaire will depend on the extent to which respondents provide answers that are 'real' in the sense that the information is both honest and accurate. Bogus answers or mistaken answers are perhaps worse than no answers at all. The challenge facing the researcher is how to produce a questionnaire that will achieve a good response rate, with most items in the questionnaire filled in, and where there are reasonable grounds for supposing that the answers are honest and accurate (see Table 12.1).

Table 12.1 Criteria for a good research questionnaire

Criterion	Good practice
Response rate Have a sufficient proportion of questionnaires been returned?	Inclusion of relevant information and guidance Motivation of respondents (topic and incentives) Questions tailored to capabilities of respondents
Completion rate Have all parts of the questionnaire been completed?	Minimization of response burden Avoidance of questionnaire fatigue Good questionnaire design and ease of use Inclusion of progress indicators
Validity of responses Have respondents been able to answer questions honestly and accurately?	Clear, unambiguous questions asked in the right order Sensitivity to personal feelings of respondents Assurances of anonymity and confidentiality Relevance of questions to respondents

Response rates

To bolster the chances of getting a decent response rate researchers need to take two things into consideration:

Capabilities of respondents. Different target groups might have different capabilities depending on their age, health and intellect. Where people are not able to answer, or find it hard to complete a questionnaire, the response rate will suffer. Factors to be taken into account here are things like:

- literacy (reading ability, proficiency with the language);
- sight capacity (blindness, vision disorders, age);

- vulnerability (young people, the elderly, learning disabilities);
- memory (ability of recall, amount of detail, time since event).

Respondent motivation. Getting people to take part in the research and agree to answer the questionnaire is a challenge in its own right. Increasingly, people are weary of requests for help and wary about giving away personal information. So researchers need to think carefully about what they can do to motivate people. They need to think about:

Link up with Response rates, p. 19.

- the level of interest, enthusiasm and goodwill respondents are likely to have with regards to the research project.

Completion rates

When it comes to completion rates the key concern is that respondents do not abandon their efforts part way through. The prospects of respondents proceeding to answer all parts of the questionnaire are enhanced when the time and effort it takes for the respondent to complete the questionnaire is kept to a minimum. The factor to be borne in mind here is the:

Response burden. As a rule of thumb a good questionnaire should minimize the response burden in order to bolster the prospects of a good completion rate. Two crucial factors affecting the response burden, both of which are elaborated below, are:

- the length of the questionnaire and the amount of time needed to complete the questionnaire;
- questionnaire fatigue and the effort of answering questions.

Validity of responses

This criterion of success exists primarily because self-completion questionnaires rely on information that people are prepared to divulge, and there are certain kinds of information which respondents might feel hesitant to give. When using a questionnaire to collect data, researchers need to be alert to ways in which the openness and honesty of responses might be affected by the:

Sensitivity of the topic. Certain topics can be awkward for respondents and, for this reason, the answers they give might not be completely accurate. (Or they might simply not provide any answer at all to any questions they find intrusive or embarrassing.) The implications of this are that researchers need to take into account the potential effect of asking about sensitive or embarrassing subjects which might make respondents feel uncomfortable. This would apply, for instance, if the questionnaire asked about things like personal health issues, amount of income, or any criminal record.

Relevance of questions. When constructing the questions, the researcher needs to think about not only whether the respondent will *want to* answer the kind of questions that are being asked: it is also a matter of whether they *can.* The questions must be ones on which respondents actually *have some information, knowledge, experience* or *opinions.* It is no good constructing questions where the responses are likely to be a series of 'don't knows' or 'not applicable'.

Context of the research. A willingness to divulge information for the purposes of research depends in large part on a climate of trust in which it is presumed that the personal information collected through the questionnaire will not be passed on to a third party who could exploit it for commercial gain or political repression. Even in ordinary work settings, people might feel reticent to be totally open and honest in their responses if they harbour any fear about the consequences should their bosses or colleagues become aware of the views that have been expressed. If the research takes place in a context where respondents have any fear of reprisal the validity of responses will be affected.

The length of the questionnaire

There is no hard and fast rule about the number of questions that can be included in a questionnaire. This will depend on factors such as the topic under investigation, how complex the questions are, the nature of the respondents who have been targeted and the time it takes to complete the questionnaire. Decisions about the size of a questionnaire are ultimately a matter of judgement: the researcher needs to gauge how many questions can be included before the respondent is likely to run out of patience and consign the questionnaire to the waste bin.

Every effort should be made to keep the questionnaire as brief as possible by avoiding any superfluous detail or non-essential topics. The shrewd researcher realizes that it is counter-productive to include everything that might *feasibly* have some relevance to the research issues. When designing a questionnaire, then, the researcher has to walk a tightrope between ensuring coverage of all the vital issues and ensuring the questionnaire is brief enough to encourage people to bother answering it. To accomplish this balancing act there are certain rules to bear in mind.

- *Only ask those questions which are absolutely vital for the research.* The better the research is planned, the easier it will be to identify the absolutely crucial questions and discard the 'just in case I need this information later' questions.
- *Be rigorous in weeding out any duplication of questions.* For example, if a questionnaire contains as separate questions, 'What is your date of birth?' and 'How old are you?' we need to ask just how vital it is that both are included.
- *Pilot the questionnaire to see how long it takes to answer* and then consider whether it is reasonable to expect the specific target group to spare this amount of time supplying the answers.

> **Good practice: Keep questionnaires as short as possible**
> There is, perhaps, no more effective deterrent to answering a question-naire than its sheer size.

Questionnaire fatigue

Answering a survey questionnaire takes *mental effort*. Even though someone has agreed to complete a questionnaire, they can lose enthusiasm as they progress through the answers. One obvious result of this is that the respondent will 'drop out' and not complete the questionnaire. Another consequence is that they might not complete all of the questions. A third consequence is that their effort tails off during the process of answering the questionnaire. They don't withdraw (which of course they are perfectly entitled to do) but their answers are progressively based on *minimizing the effort* taken to provide an answer. As Krosnick (1991) points out, the mental burden of answering the questionnaire can lead to 'satisficing' answers. These are answers which might appear to the researcher to be genuine but which are actually based on the respondent going through the routine of ticking boxes but doing so with minimum effort and not a lot of regard for the truth of the matter. This can involve taking the 'easy option' (e.g. agreeing with all statements), opting for 'don't know' answers, sticking to the same point on scale (following a pattern) or even resorting to random answers simply to put something in the box. The danger here is that the questionnaire will appear to have been completed, and the various questions within the questionnaire will have answers recorded against them, but those answers might not be the most accurate or most thought-through responses. At worst, they could simply be anything the respondent can find to fill the box.

The question is, 'How can this danger be minimized?' What can be done to offset the prospect of questionnaire fatigue and encourage respondents to complete questionnaires thoughtfully and honestly? There are a number of things that help when it comes to the way the researcher designs and delivers the questionnaire, the main ones being:

- *Make the task of answering questions as straightforward and easy as possible.* Everything should be clear and succinct in terms of what is being asked of the respondent, and the layout of the questionnaire should enable respondents to work their way through the questions without difficulty. They should not need to fathom what is expected of them – it should be obvious.
- *Let respondents know the extent of the burden they are facing.* At the beginning of the questionnaire the respondents should be given an honest indication of how long it will take to complete the questionnaire and how many questions are involved. With web-based questionnaires the inclusion of a 'progress indicator' is really helpful in this respect, allowing respondents to see how far they have gone and how much remains to be done.

- *Don't make unrealistic demands in terms of the questions that are asked.* Respondents are likely to become demoralized and frustrated if they are confronted with questions that are overly complex or hard to answer. The questions should take into account the ability of respondents to recall things and make judgements about things, and recognize that hard questions take mental effort to answer.

Respondent motivation

As noted earlier, the willingness of people to complete a research questionnaire is something that should never be taken for granted. Indeed, the success of a questionnaire in terms of achieving a reasonable response rate generally depends on getting potential respondents motivated to put in the time and effort to answer the questionnaire. Two things which are particularly valuable in this respect are:

- *Subject salience.* The covering letter/statement should do what it can to point out how the topic might be of interest. If the respondent can see that the topic of the questions is interesting and relevant for them personally, then there is an increased prospect that they will complete the questionnaire and put the effort into answering all questions openly and honestly.
- *Making a difference.* To the extent that respondents believe that their answers will 'make a difference' then they are more likely to engage more fully with the questionnaire and provide thoughtful and genuine answers. Again, the covering letter/statement provides an opportunity to put across the message that respondents have some stake in the findings and that their answers could contribute to some real outcome that affects them personally.

Good practice: The mindset for success

1 Start from the assumption that people will be reluctant to complete the questionnaire, and then think how you can entice them to make the effort to fill it in.
2 Put yourself in their shoes and ask, 'Why should I bother to help the researcher?'
3 Anticipate low response rates: don't be over-optimistic on this matter.

Essential parts of a research questionnaire

The main body of a questionnaire includes the various questions on which the researcher wants information. Clearly, this section is vital, and there is guidance elsewhere in this chapter on how to design the questions themselves. In addition, however, there are components of a research questionnaire that exist more by way of giving information rather than receiving it. There are bits of information that should be included for the benefit of respondents and as general features of good design.

Background information

From both an ethical and a practical point of view the researcher needs to provide some background information about the research and the questionnaire. Each questionnaire should have information about:

- *The sponsor.* Under whose auspices is the research being undertaken? Is it individual research or does the research originate from an institution? Headed notepaper is an obvious way to indicate the nature of the institution from which the questionnaire comes.
- *The purpose.* What is the questionnaire for, and how will the information be used? It is important here to reveal sufficient information to explain the purpose of the research without going too far and 'leading' the respondent into a line of answering. A brief paragraph should suffice.
- *Return address and date.* It is vital that the questionnaire contains in it somewhere quite visibly the name and contact address (postal or email) of the person(s) to whom the completed questionnaire is to be returned.
- *Confidentiality.* Respondents should be reassured that the information they provide will not be disclosed to others (assuming that the research is operating according to a conventional code of ethics for social researchers).
- *Voluntary responses.* Respondents are under no obligation to answer the questions, and reassurances about the voluntary nature of their participation should be given.
- *Thanks.* Courtesy suggests that some word of thanks from the researcher should appear as part of the introduction or right at the end of the questionnaire.

Instructions to the respondent

A good questionnaire normally includes clear instructions on how to go about answering the questions. What seems obvious to the person designing the questionnaire might not be obvious to the respondent who is looking at the questionnaire for the first time and, therefore, it is important to minimize the possibility of mistakes by providing guidance to respondents in the form of things like:

- An *example* at the start of the questionnaire can set the respondent's mind at rest and indicate exactly what is expected of him/her.
- Specific *instructions* for each style of question used in the questionnaire.

The allocation of serial numbers

With web-based questionnaires the serial numbers are added automatically. Other forms of questionnaire might need serial numbers to be added manually. In this case, each questionnaire should be numbered so that it can be distinguished from others and located if necessary. The serial number can be used to identify the date of distribution, the place and possibly the person.

Example 12.1

Introductory statement   questionnaire number

The changing transport needs of [*name of city*]   City logo

> This survey is looking at the transport needs of [*name of city*] and its findings will be used for planning improvements to local roads and transport services. It asks questions about you and your transport needs, and we hope you will personally benefit from the changes that result from the survey.
>
> This questionnaire is available online and alternative printed versions are also available in local community languages. Please answer the questions carefully. For questions 1–11 put an 'x' in the box for the answer that comes closest to your opinion, and for questions 12–14 write your answer in your own words in the space provided. If you prefer not to answer any particular question please leave it blank and continue to the next one. Write any further comments you might have on the back of the last page.
>
> Thank you for taking the time to fill in this questionnaire: it should take less than 10 minutes to complete. The questionnaire is anonymous unless you choose to provide an email address or phone number so that we can contact you in connection with the survey. All information will be treated in the strictest confidence and no data will be passed on to any third parties.
>
> You are under no obligation to participate in the research. However, most people enjoy filling in the questionnaire, and we hope that you will too. The research is being carried out by the [*University of XXXXXX*] on behalf of the city's Department of Transport and Environment. Further information about the project is available on [URL of website]. The lead researcher is [name] who can be contacted by email [email address] or phone [phone number].
>
> Please return your completed questionnaires by (*specified date*).

Devising the questions

Direct or indirect questions

Researchers need to consider whether the information being sought from the respondent is amenable to direct questions, or whether it will need to be measured by indirect means. Where the information being sought is of an overt, factual nature, there is not normally a problem on this point. The questions will take the form of 'How many times ...?' or 'When did you last ...?' However, questionnaires are frequently geared to less straightforward matters where a direct question would be inappropriate. If, for example, the researcher wishes to know what social class the respondent comes from, it would not be wise to ask the straightforward question, 'What is your social class?' Apart from the fact that some people might find this offensive, the term 'social class' has different meanings for different people, and the question will produce inconsistent answers. In this case, the researcher needs to pinpoint exactly what he/she defines as social class and then devise questions that will supply the type of information which will allow the respondent's social class to be deduced. For this purpose, indirect questions will be used about occupation, income, education, etc.

The wording of the questions

Questions should not be irritating or annoying for the respondents to answer. The success of the questionnaire, after all, depends on the willingness of the respondents to spend their time completing the answers and they should not be deterred from this task by any sense of frustration arising from the manner in which the questions are worded. There are some specific things that researchers can do to help avoid this possibility:

- *Make sure the wording is completely unambiguous.*
- *Avoid vague questions.* The more specific and concrete the question, the easier it is to give a precise answer, and in all probability the answer will prove to be of more value to the researcher.
- *Use only the minimum amount of technical jargon.* In terms of a questionnaire, the aim is not to see how clever people are.
- *Use wording that is suited to the specific target group.* Questions geared to 14-year-olds will need to be different in terms of conceptual complexity and wording from questions aimed at, for example, members of a professional association.
- *Keep the questions as short and straightforward as possible.* This will avoid unnecessary confusion and wasted time re-reading questions or trying to decipher the meaning of the question.
- *Avoid asking the same question twice in a different fashion* (except as 'check' questions).
- *Avoid the use of 'leading' questions.* These are questions which suggest an answer or which prompt the respondent to give a particular kind of answer (e.g. Would you agree that there should be controls on the emission of carbon dioxide from cars?).
- *Be sure to include sufficient options in the answer.* If the list might prove too long, selecting the main possibilities and then tagging on the 'Other (please specify)' option is a good strategy.

- *Pay attention to the way the questions are numbered.* Obviously they should be sequential, but there are clever ways of using sub-questions (e.g. 4a, 4b and so on) which can help the respondent to map his/her way through the series of questions.
- *Avoid words or phrases which might cause offence.*

Good practice: Questions should be worded with clarity and precision
There is little room for vagueness or imprecision. This means that the researcher must have a clear vision of exactly what issues are at the heart of the research and what kind of information would enlighten those issues.

The order of the questions

The ordering of the questions in a questionnaire is important for two reasons. First and foremost, it can entice or deter the respondent from continuing with the exercise of providing answers. If the respondent is immediately faced with the most complex of the questions at the start of the questionnaire this might deter him/her from going any further. However, if the questionnaire starts with straightforward questions and then gradually moves towards such questions at a later stage, there is a greater likelihood that the respondent will persevere. This same point is true for those questions which might be perceived as more personal and on sensitive issues. There will be a greater chance of success if such questions appear later in the questionnaire than if they appear at the start.

The second way in which the ordering of questions can be important is that questions asked at an earlier point in the questionnaire can affect the answers supplied at a later stage. This is evident in many commercial 'marketing/sales questionnaires' where there is a conscious attempt to make use of this feature of questionnaires.

Good practice: The order of the questions
It is usually best to ensure that:

- the most straightforward questions come at the start;
- the least contentious questions and least sensitive issues are dealt with at the beginning of the questionnaire;
- the sequence of questions does not lead the respondents towards 'inevitable' answers, where the answers to later questions are effectively predicated on the answers to earlier ones.

Check questions

'Check questions' are questions embedded in a questionnaire whose specific purpose is to check the respondent's answers for *consistency*. A check question is not a simple duplication of a question: it is a question that appears in a differ-ent guise but whose answer should be the same as an alternatively worded question that is placed elsewhere in the questionnaire. To the extent that check questions do provide answers that match, the researcher can feel some confi-dence that the questionnaire is a reliable research instrument and that the findings are valid. Where there is not a match, then it raises questions about whether the other responses on the questionnaire can be treated as honest and accurate.

Different types of questions

'Open' questions

Open questions are those that leave the respondent to decide the wording of the answer, the length of the answer and the kind of matters to be raised in the answer. The questions tend to be short and the answers tend to be long. For example, the questionnaire might ask, 'How do you feel about the inclusion of nuclear arms as part of Britain's defence capability?' and then provide a number of empty lines which invite the respondent to enter his/her thoughts on the matter.

The advantage of 'open' questions is that the information gathered by way of the responses is more likely to reflect the full richness and complexity of the views held by the respondent. Respondents are allowed space to express themselves in their own words. Weighed against this, however, there are two disadvantages which are built into the use of open questions. First, they demand more effort on the part of the respondents (which might well reduce their willingness to take part in the research). Second, they leave the researcher with data which are quite 'raw' and require a lot of time-consuming analysis before they can be used.

'Closed' questions

Closed questions structure the answers by allowing only answers which fit into categories that have been established in advance by the researcher. The researcher, in this case, instructs the respondent to answer by selecting from a range of two or more options supplied on the questionnaire. The options can be restricted to as few as two (e.g. 'Yes' or 'No'; 'Male' or 'Female') or can include quite complex lists of alternatives from which the respondent can choose.

The advantages and disadvantages of 'closed' questions are more or less a mirror image of those connected with the open questions. Briefly, the structure imposed on the respondents' answers provides the researcher with information that lends itself nicely to being quantified and compared. The answers, in fact, provide pre-coded data that can easily be analysed. Weighed against this, how-ever, closed questions allow less scope for respondents to supply answers which reflect the exact facts or their true feelings on a topic if the facts or opin-ions happen to be complicated or do not exactly fit into the range of options supplied in the questionnaire. As a result, respondents might get frustrated by not being allowed to express their views fully in a way that accounts for any sophistication, intricacy or even inconsistencies in their views.

In practice, closed to open questions exist on a continuum. In between the extremes there are a variety of question formats which provide the respondent with a greater or lesser degree of freedom in terms of the options available to them and the possibilities of providing answers 'in their own words'. This can be seen in Example 12.2 below in which there is a development from closed to open questions in the list.

The use of variety

From the outset it is worth giving some thought to whether the overall questionnaire will benefit from using a variety of kinds of questions, or whether it is better to aim for a consistent style throughout. Variety has two potential advantages. First, it stops the respondent becoming bored. Second, it stops the respondent falling into a 'pattern' of answers where, for example, on a scale of 1–5 he/she begins to put 4 down as the answer to all questions. Aiming for a consistent style of question, for its part, has the advantage of allowing the respondent to get used to the kind of questions so that they can be answered quickly and with less likelihood of confusion or misunderstanding. There is no hard and fast rule on this point: it is down to a judgement call on the part of the researcher.

Example 12.2

Ten types of question

The following questions demonstrate ten different ways of constructing questions. To illustrate the contrast between these examples they are all based on a common theme – the relationship between the UK and Europe.

1 **An amount**
   How many times have you travelled from the UK to another European country in the past 5 years? _____

2 **A 'yes/no' answer**
   Have you travelled from the UK to another European country in the past 12 months? Yes/No

3 **Choose from a list of options**
   Which ONE of the following list of European countries do you feel has the strongest economy?

Spain	UK	Belgium	Poland
Ireland	France	Germany	Italy

4 **Rank order**
   From the following list of European countries choose the THREE which you feel have the strongest economies and put them in rank order: 1 = strongest, 2 = second strongest, 3 = third strongest.

Spain	UK	Belgium	Poland
Ireland	France	Germany	Italy

5 Agree/disagree with a statement
Would you agree or disagree with the following statement?
'European unity has political disadvantages that outweigh the economic advantages'. Agree/Disagree

6 Degree of agreement and disagreement: *the Likert Scale*
To what extent do you agree or disagree with the following statement: 'Free movement of people within the European Union is a good thing'.

Strongly agree	Agree	Neutral	Disagree	Strongly disagree

7 Rate items
How significant would you rate the following factors in affecting further European integration?

	Not significant					Very significant	
Political sovereignty	1	2	3	4	5	6	7
National identities	1	2	3	4	5	6	7
Past history	1	2	3	4	5	6	7
Religious differences	1	2	3	4	5	6	7
Language barriers	1	2	3	4	5	6	7

8 Feelings about a topic: *the semantic differential*
Progress towards European unity is:

Important	1	2	3	4	5	Unimportant
Difficult	1	2	3	4	5	Easy
Risky	1	2	3	4	5	Safe
Unlikely	1	2	3	4	5	Likely
Boring	1	2	3	4	5	Interesting

9 A list
Please list three issues you feel are most important in terms of the UK's relationship with the European Union:

1.............................
2.............................
3.............................

10 A statement
What do you think about the UK's relationship with the European Union?

_____
_____
_____

> **Top tip: Questionnaire templates.**
> There are plenty of questionnaire templates available online covering a whole range of topics such as consumer behaviour, customer satisfaction, education intentions, employee satisfaction, job satisfaction and market research. Many of these templates are offered for free and can be legitimately used and adapted by researchers for their own specific projects.

Web-based questionnaires

Web-based questionnaires are well suited to the needs of small-scale social research. Generally, such questionnaires are designed using software provided by an organization that 'hosts' the questionnaire and makes it available to respondents online. The commercial companies, such as Survey Monkey, Question Pro, Survs, and many others, are easily located by doing an online search for 'web questionnaires'.

Link up with Web-based surveys, p. 26.

There are some distinct advantages to using the design facilities provided by such organizations because, as Bhaskaran and LeClaire (2010) point out:

- *They help with good practice*: There are plenty of templates and examples that are freely available which can be used as a starting point for designing the questionnaire. No need to start from scratch – help is always at hand. Also the software, in any case, tends to have built-in assistance that guides you towards good practice when setting up the questions.
- *They encourage completion*: The options available for the design and layout of the questionnaire can be used to make it appealing. Colourful images and graphs are easy to incorporate within a web-based questionnaire and these can provide a means for sparking interest in the topic and encouraging the respondent to spend time completing the questionnaire.
- *They reduce potential errors*: The questionnaire can incorporate a range of features which reduce the possibility of errors creeping in during the process of completing the questionnaire. These features boost the prospects of getting questionnaires returned that have been completed fully and clearly, and which have a minimum amount of 'missing data'.
- *They help with data processing*: The respondents' answers are automatically transferred from the questionnaire into a data file. The software does not do the analysis for the researcher, but it does transfer the data from the questionnaires and puts them into a data file which is in a format that can be entered straight into an Excel spreadsheet or some equivalent. This automated process saves the researcher an awful lot of time but, perhaps even more importantly, it also removes an element of the survey process where human error can occur.

Design options for web-based questionnaires: what features are available?

The software for designing web-based questionnaires offers a large array of options. Some of them are available when you sign up for the basic 'trial' version; others come at a price when you upgrade from the free introductory package. Table 12.2 gives an overview of the main options available. Schonlau et al. (2002), however, warn against getting carried away with the design options. The emphasis should be on keeping things clean and simple, they argue, and it is for this reason that graphics and matrix questions should be used sparingly. They also advise that making questions *mandatory* can deter people from completing a questionnaire. Such forced answers should only be used when really necessary.

Table 12.2   Design options for web-based questionnaires

Templates	A range of established designs is normally available to copy or adapt
Appearance	Options for background colour, fonts and layout are available
Logos	Logos, images and other personalizing features can be inserted
Progress bar	To show respondent how far they are through the questionnaire
Identifier	Unique number; web address of sender; time stamp
Question types	Single option answer: radio buttons Multiple choice answer: check box/drop-down menu Matrix questions: used for rating and scaling Rank order questions Open-ended text
Order of questions	Randomize the order of questions Question branching: respondent's answer determines subsequent series of questions Skip logic: to allow certain questions to be missed Question numbering: automatic
Response options	Mandatory answer: respondents will not be able to submit their questionnaire unless they have answered these questions

Radio buttons and check boxes

When preparing questions for an online questionnaire it is important to distinguish between *radio buttons* and *check boxes*. Radio buttons are used when respondents need to select a single option from a list: they do not permit the respondent to enter more than one choice from the list. Check boxes (or tick boxes) allow respondents to make multiple choices from a list: they permit respondents to choose two or more choices from the list of possible answers provided by the researcher.

[Select one from]   Check all that apply

If the appropriate choice is not made at the design stage there will be big trouble ahead when it comes to the analysis of the data. Think: 'Do I want respondents to provide one single answer to the question I am asking, or do I want to allow them to select two or possibly more options?' If you want to allow multiple responses you need to work out in advance how you plan to analyse the data. Note that the *safer* thing to do is to stick to the radio buttons, keeping things simple and straightforward by permitting just one response to be chosen from a list of alternatives presented to respondents in the question: one answer to one question.

Advantages of questionnaires

Questionnaires are economical

They can supply a considerable amount of research data for a relatively low cost in terms of materials, money and time.

Relatively easy to arrange

Self-completion questionnaires are easier to arrange than, for example, personal interviews. Respondents are free to choose when and where they fill-in the questionnaire.

The delivery of questions is standardized

All respondents are posed exactly the same questions. And with self-completion questionnaires there is little scope for the data to be affected by *interpersonal factors* or the manner in which the questions are asked.

Data processing

The answers to web-based questionnaires can be fed directly into a data file, thus automating the process of data entry. This effectively eliminates the human error factor that inevitably arises when people need to read the responses to a paper questionnaire and then enter the data manually via the computer keyboard.

Online questionnaires facilitate 'accessibility'

They can be configured so that people with sight impairment or learning difficulties can have the same opportunity as others to respond to the questionnaire. This is very important in terms of equal opportunities.

Disadvantages of questionnaires

Pre-coded questions can be frustrating

While the respondents might find it less demanding merely to tick appropriate boxes they might, equally, find this restricting and frustrating – and it could even deter respondents from completing the questionnaire.

Pre-coded questions impose a structure on the answers

This can bias the findings towards the researcher's, rather than the respondent's, way of seeing things. Questionnaires, by their very nature, start to impose a structure on the answers and shape the nature of the responses in a way that reflects the researcher's thinking rather than the respondent's thinking. Good research practice will minimize the prospect of this, but there is always the danger that the options open to the respondent when answering the questions will channel responses away from the respondent's perception of matters to fit in with a line of thinking established by the researcher.

Checks on truthfulness

Self-completion questionnaires offer little opportunity for the researcher to check the truthfulness of the answers given by the respondents. Because the research does not take place face to face and because the answers are given 'at a distance' the researcher cannot rely on a number of clues that an interviewer might have about whether the answers are genuine or not.

Further reading

Brace, I. (2013) *Questionnaire Design*, 3rd edn. London: Kogan Page.

Bradburn, N.M., Sudman, S. and Wansink, B. (2004) *Asking Questions: The Definitive Guide to Questionnaire Design*, 2nd edn. San Francisco, CA: Jossey-Bass.

Ekinci, Y. (2015) *Designing Research Questionnaires for Business and Management Students*. London: Sage.

Gillham, B. (2007) *Developing a Questionnaire*, 2nd edn. London: Continuum.

Oppenheim, A.N. (2000) *Questionnaire Design, Interviewing and Attitude Measurement*, 2nd edn. London: Continuum.

Checklist for the use of questionnaires

When using a questionnaire for research you should feel confident about answering 'yes' to the following questions: ☑

1 Has an explanation of the purpose of the questionnaire been provided? ☐

2 Has information about the researchers (including contact details) been included? ☐

3 Are there assurances about anonymity and the confidentiality of data? ☐

4 When necessary, are instructions given on how to complete the questions? ☐

5 Have thanks been expressed to the respondents? ☐

6 Has a progress indicator been included or some alternative information about the time needed for completion of the questionnaire? ☐

7 Have the design of the questionnaire and the wording of the questions been tailored to suit the particular kind of respondents? ☐

8 Have all non-essential questions been excluded? ☐

9 Does the layout of the questionnaire make it easy to follow? ☐

10 Are the questions clear and unambiguous? ☐

11 Are the questions in a suitable order? ☐

12 Has the questionnaire been piloted? ☐

13 Interviews

What is a research interview?

Research interviews are a method of data collection that uses people's answers to researchers' questions as their source of data. In this respect they have something in common with questionnaires – the data comes from what people tell the researcher. This contrasts with observational methods (which look at what people *do*) and the use of documents (where attention is given to what has been *written and recorded*). Research interviews, for their part, focus on *self-reports* – what people say they do, what they say they believe and what opinions they say they have.

Interviews and conversations

Research interviews are different from conversations (Denscombe 1983; Silverman 1985, 2013). When someone agrees to take part in a research interview they recognize that they are taking part in a formal piece of research and, through their agreement to be interviewed, they tacitly acknowledge that:

- *They give their consent to participation in the research.* From the researcher's point of view this is particularly important in relation to research ethics.
- *Interviewees' words can be used as research data.* Unless interviewees specify to the contrary, what is said during the interview can be taken as material that is both 'on record' and 'for the record'.

- *The agenda for the discussion is set by the researcher.* Although the degree of control exercised by the researcher will vary according to the style of interviewing, there is a tacit agreement that the proceedings and the agenda for the discussion will be controlled by the researcher.

Good practice: Consent to be interviewed

Although agreeing to be interviewed carries an *implicit* understanding about what the interview situation entails, it is generally good practice to put these things in writing, for example as part of the 'consent form'.

Link up with Chapter 18, Research ethics.

When is it appropriate to use interviews?

In the context of low-budget, small-scale research, the time and expense of conducting interviews is best rewarded when the research wants to explore complex and subtle phenomena – things such as:

- *opinions, feelings, emotions and experiences,* where the aim of the research is to understand them in depth rather than report them in a simple word or two;
- *complex issues,* where the research focuses on complicated matters that call for a detailed understanding of how things work, how factors are interconnected or how systems operate;
- *privileged information,* where the opportunity arises to speak with key players in the field who can give particularly valuable insights and wisdom based on their experience or position.

The structure of interviews

The extent to which the sequence of questions and answers in an interview stick rigidly to an agenda can vary and it is conventional to classify interviews as being 'structured', 'semi-structured' or 'unstructured' to signify how much flexibility there is in the format of the meeting.

- *Structured interviews* involve tight control over the format of the questions and answers. In essence, the structured interview is like a questionnaire which is administered face to face with a respondent. The researcher has a predetermined list of questions, to which the respondent is invited to offer limited-option responses. This standardizes the process of data collection, something that is particularly useful with large-scale projects involving 'computer-assisted personal interviewing' (CAPI) with many interviewers inputting responses direct into mobile devices (tablets, smart phones, laptop computers).

- With *semi-structured interviews* the interviewer still has a clear list of issues to be addressed and questions to be answered. However, the interviewer is prepared to be flexible in terms of the order in which the topics are considered, and, perhaps more significantly, to let the interviewee develop ideas and speak more widely on the issues raised by the researcher. The answers are open ended, and there is more emphasis on the interviewee elaborating points of interest.
- *Unstructured interviews* go further in the extent to which emphasis is placed on the interviewee's thoughts. The interviewer's role is to start the ball rolling by introducing a theme or topic, but then to be as non-directive as possible. The idea is to let interviewees develop their own ideas and pursue their own train of thought rather than have the discussion shaped by questions which the researcher already has in mind.

With semi-structured and unstructured interviews it is possible for the interview to develop and change through the course of the project – to be used *developmentally*. Rather than keeping each interview the same, the questions asked can change from one interview to the next as a result of information given in previous interviews and a desire to follow up new lines of enquiry. Such interviews take place consecutively and are normally associated with qualitative research and approaches such as grounded theory (see Chapter 7).

> **Good practice**
> It is crucial from the start to have a clear idea about whether the research project needs a standardized interview procedure (structured) or whether it needs to develop ideas through a more flexible approach (semi-structured or unstructured).

One-to-one interviews

The most common form of interview is the one-to-one variety which involves a meeting between one researcher and one informant. One reason for its popularity is that it is relatively easy to arrange. Only two people's diaries need to coincide. Another advantage is that the opinions and views expressed throughout the interview stem from one source: the interviewee. This makes it fairly straightforward for the researcher to locate specific ideas with specific people. A third advantage is that the one-to-one interview is relatively easy to control. The researcher only has one person's ideas to grasp and interrogate, and one person to guide through the interview agenda. A fourth advantage of conducting one-to-one interviews becomes evident when the researcher embarks on transcribing the interview tape: it is far easier to transcribe a recorded interview when the talk involves just one interviewee. There is only one voice to recognize and only one person talking at a time.

Group interviews

A disadvantage of the one-to-one interview is that it limits the number of views and opinions available to the researcher. Listening to one person at a time effectively restricts the number of voices that can be heard and the range of views that can be included within a research project. Group interviews, however, provide a practical solution to this. By interviewing more than one person at a time the researcher is able to dramatically increase the number and range of participants involved in the research.

Increasing the numbers involved can have benefits in terms of the representativeness of the data. The inclusion of more participants is likely to mean that a broader spectrum of people are covered by the research and that there might be a greater variety of experiences and opinions emerging from the investigation. Indeed, under certain circumstances researchers can deliberately select participants who are very different in order to gather widely differing views and experiences on the topic of the interview.

A group interview can be conducted very much like a one-to-one interview in the sense that the interviewer remains the focal point of the interaction that takes place. The questions and answers are channelled through the interviewer. The difference is that instead of each question prompting a response from just one interviewee, the researcher can get perhaps four responses from four people during the interview.

An alternative vision of the group interview stresses the 'group' characteristics of the interaction during an interview. It sees the group interview as distinctive in the way that it can get the participants to respond as part of a group, rather than as individuals. The researcher's incentive for using a group interview, in this case, is not a quantitative one concerned with increased numbers and improved representativeness. It is, instead, a qualitative incentive concerned with the way that group discussions can be more illuminating. The group discussion allows participants to listen to alternative points of view. It allows members to express support for certain views and to challenge views with which they disagree. The group interview, in this sense, trades on group dynamics. It uses the social and psychological aspects of group behaviour to foster the ability of participants to get involved, speak their minds and reflect on the views of others.

Focus groups

Focus groups consist of small groups of people who are brought together by a 'moderator' (the researcher) to explore attitudes and perceptions, feelings and ideas about a specific topic. Typically, they last for $1\frac{1}{2}$ to 2 hours and are useful for gauging the extent to which there are shared views among a group of people in relation to a specific topic. Ideally, focus groups have six to nine people in them. This is a large enough number to allow a range of views and opinions to be present among the group but not too large as to be unmanageable in terms of the discussion. In small-scale research projects the numbers are often smaller. The reason for this is that focus groups can be costly and time-consuming to arrange. It is not easy to organize a venue for the meeting and get six or more people to turn up on time. And it can prove to be expensive if the researcher needs to fund participants' travel and pay for the room.

Focus groups have three distinctive features which mark them out as different from other kinds of interview:

- there is a *focus* to the session, with the group discussion being based on an item or experience about which all participants have similar knowledge;
- the moderator's role is to *facilitate* the group interaction rather than lead the discussion;
- particular emphasis is placed on *group dynamics* and interaction within the group as means of eliciting information.

During a focus group session participants are encouraged to discuss the topic among themselves. This interaction helps the researcher to understand the reasoning behind the views and opinions that are expressed by group members. It provides the researcher with a method of investigating the participants' reasoning and a means for exploring underlying factors that might explain why people hold the opinions and feelings they do. As Morgan (2006: 121) puts it:

> [Focus group members] share their experiences and thoughts, while also comparing their own contributions to what others have said. This process of sharing and comparing is especially useful for hearing and understanding a range of responses on a research topic. The best focus groups thus not only provide data on *what* the participants think but also *why* they think the way they do.

Such sharing and comparing of personally held points of view can lead in either of two directions – both of which can be of value to the researcher. The group discussion can lead to some consensus with members of the group largely agreeing and arriving at some shared viewpoint. Alternatively, the group discussion might serve to expose significant differences among group members in which case the researcher is presented with data about a range of opinions and feelings relating to the topic. Either way, the benefit of the discussion and interaction, questioning and reflection, is that it reveals the reasoning and underlying logic used by participants. It thus gives the researcher an insight into not only what people think, but also *why* they hold those views.

The success of a focus group, however, depends on establishing a climate of trust within the group, and it is a key part of the role of the moderator to foster a situation in which participants feel at ease and sufficiently comfortable in the company of the other group members to express themselves freely. A crucial factor here is *confidentiality*. Group members need to feel assured that if they express a personal feeling or reveal some aspect of their personal life during the discussion that such information will be treated as confidential by the group. What is said by individuals during the focus group session ought to remain private and not be disclosed publicly by other members of the group.

Expert opinion: the Delphi technique

Interviews with experts are valuable when researchers want to get 'state of the art' information on a particular topic. However, many topics involve a degree of judgement and interpretation and experts do not always agree. This is where the Delphi technique comes in. It provides a way of using the opinions of various individual experts to move towards an agreed collective position – some consensus.

 Key point

The Delphi technique provides a way of shepherding the views of independent experts towards some workable, shared conclusion about a topic.

The technique was originally developed during the 1950s in response to the needs of the US military. The technique has been adapted and used in a variety of ways since this time but, in essence, it continues to have the following core characteristics. It is based on:

- collecting *opinions* (through a series of interviews);
- from *experts* (identified in terms of their specialist knowledge or their particular experience);
- *separately* and *anonymously* (to avoid a 'group effect' that could encourage conformity with the views of others or allow dominant personalities to have undue influence on the opinions of others);
- using an *iterative process* (that involves a sequence of questions and feedback);
- with the purpose of moving towards a *consensus* (with some shared view or areas of agreement);
- that is valuable in relation to (1) *decision-making*, (2) developing a *policy* or (3) *forecasting* a future situation.

The Delphi technique is now used across a range of social science disciplines and is particularly popular in areas such as nursing studies, public policy, social work and public health.

Web-based Delphi techniques

Recent adaptions of the Delphi technique have used the Internet to make contact with a panel of experts. This has two benefits. First, it enables the number of experts to be increased without vastly increasing the costs of research. Second, it paves the way for Delphi *conferences*. These conferences use computing and web-based technologies to replace the conventional rounds of questions and feedback with a continuous process of iteration. In this process experts can respond at any time to constantly evolving 'feedback' provided in real time. It is almost as though the separate experts were developing ideas in unison.

> The Delphi technique was named with reference to the oracle of Delphi. In ancient Greek mythology the oracle was a priestess who, acting as the voice of the god Apollo, had the power to see into the future. The oracle's forecasts were, not surprisingly, treated with extreme reverence. Subsequently, the term 'oracle' has been used broadly to refer to a person who has the special ability to see into the future and who can offer wise advice on the basis of what they see.

The Delphi technique and small-scale research

The Delphi technique was developed in the context of quasi-government research projects that were large scale, quite expensive and time-consuming. The principles can be retained, however, for use with small-scale projects, with just two main adaptations. First, the number of rounds of questioning can be reduced. The Delphi technique, in its classic form, consists of three or four consecutive rounds of questioning. Realistically, within the resource constraints of small-scale research the use of two rounds might be more feasible. It is worth bearing in mind, though, that this will inevitably limit the *iterative* aspect of the technique and the likelihood of arriving at a complete consensus of views. Second, the experts to be included in the panel need not be world leaders in the area of the research. It is possible to set the sights a little lower. A suitable 'expert' might be someone who has specialist knowledge or experience in the area of the research who is much closer to home and far more accessible.

Guidelines for using the Delphi technique in small-scale research

Step 1: *Define the problem.* Remember, the aim is to arrive at some more or less agreed view (forecast, policy, decision) based on expert opinion (using their knowledge, experience, insight). The research problem must be clear and suitable for this purpose.

Step 2: *Tailor the research design to the resources available.* The amount of time and money available for conducting the research puts practical constraints on (1) how many experts will be included and (2) how many rounds of enquiry will be used.

Step 3: *Establish contact with suitable experts.* The criteria of expertise need to be established. Note that 'expert' can sometimes be used to refer to people with 'relevant' knowledge and experience. Remember, too, that experts can be contacted and interviewed via the Internet as well face to face. For small-scale research it is likely that the number of experts will be small (fewer than 10) and that they will be selected through a purposive sampling technique (e.g. snowballing).

Step 4: *First round of questions*. At this stage the questions should be fairly general, with the aim of getting some broad understanding of how experts perceive the situation and which facts they perceive to be significant when thinking about the likelihood of specific future events or the impact of particular policies.

Step 5: *Initial analysis and feedback*. The facilitator's task at this point is to collate and summarize the experts' responses to the first round of questions. The review can cover:

* areas where opinion is shared;
* the reasoning used in each expert's initial reply;
* key factors noted by the experts and the perceived significance of these key factors;
* things on which experts say they would like more information.

Step 6: *Subsequent rounds of questions and feedback*. Each round should progressively narrow the focus of the questions and look to eliminate areas that emerge as less important. In this way the rounds of feedback and questions can facilitate an iterative process that helps achieve a consensus among the experts.

Step 7: *Final report*. The final report should aim to arrive at a definite conclusion in relation to the specific forecast, policy or decision under consideration. If a reasonable consensus cannot be achieved, though, the report should acknowledge any persisting divergence of opinion among the experts

The interviewer effect

Personal identity

People respond differently depending on how they perceive the person asking the questions. In particular, the *sex*, the *age* and the *ethnic origins* of the interviewer have a bearing on the amount of information people are willing to divulge and their honesty about what they reveal. On sensitive issues or on matters regarded as rather personal, the interviewer's identity assumes particular importance. If interviewees feel awkward or defensive there is the possibility that they might supply answers which they feel fit in with what the researcher expects from them – fulfilling the perceived expectations of the researcher. Or the answers might tend to be tailored to match what the interviewee suspects is the researcher's point of view, keeping the researcher happy.

Either way, the quality of the data suffers. Bearing this point in mind, social researchers should consider the following questions:

• What are the social status, educational qualifications and professional expertise of the people to be interviewed, and how do these compare with my own? Is this likely to affect the interviewer–interviewee relationship in a positive or negative manner?
• Is there likely to be an age gap between myself and the interviewee(s) and, if so, how might this affect the interview?
• In relation to the topic being researched, will interviewing someone of the opposite sex or a different ethnic group have an impact on their willingness to answer questions openly and honestly?

Self-presentation

Conventional advice to researchers has been geared to minimizing the impact of researchers on the outcome of the research by having them adopt a passive and neutral stance. The idea is that the researcher:

• presents himself/herself in a light which is designed not to antagonize or upset the interviewee (conventional clothes, courtesy, etc.);
• remains neutral and non-committal on the statements made during the interview by the interviewee.

The researcher's 'self', adopting this approach, is kept firmly hidden beneath a cloak of cordiality and receptiveness to the words of the interviewee. To a certain degree, this is sound advice. The researcher, after all, is there to listen and learn, not to preach. The point is to get the interviewee to open up, not to provoke hostility or put the interviewee on the defensive.

Personal involvement

One line of reasoning argues that a cold and calculating style of interviewing reinforces a gulf between the researcher and the informant, and does little to help or empower the informant. Now, if the aims of the research are specifically to help or empower the people being researched, rather than dispassionately learn from them, then the approach of the interviewer will need to alter accordingly (Oakley 1981). Under these circumstances, the researcher will be inclined to show emotion, to respond with feeling and to engage in a true dialogue with the interviewee. The researcher will become fully involved as a person with feelings, with experiences and with knowledge that can be shared with the interviewee. A word of warning, though. This style of interviewing remains 'unconventional', and the researcher needs to be confident and committed to make it work. The researcher also needs to feel sure that his or her audience understand and share the underlying logic of the approach rather than expecting the researcher to adopt the cool and dispassionate stance.

Skills for face-to-face interviewing

A good research interview is not simply a casual conversation. This point has already been made. Unlike casual conversations, research interviews require a good deal of concentrated effort if they are to be successful. The researcher needs to think about how to get the best response from the interviewee and how to make the interview as productive as possible in terms of the aims of the research. This is particularly the case with face-to-face interviews. In this context:

- *The good interviewer needs to be attentive.* This may sound obvious, but it is all too easy to lose the thread of the discussion because the researcher needs to be monitoring a few other things while listening closely to what the informant has to say: writing the field notes, looking for relevant non-verbal communication, checking that the recorder is working.

- *The good interviewer is sensitive to the feelings of the informant.* This is not just a matter of social courtesy, though that is certainly a worthy aspect of it. It is also a skill which is necessary for getting the best out of an interview. Where interviewers are able to empathize with the informant and to gauge the feelings of the informant, they will be in a better position to coax out the most relevant information.

- *The good interviewer is able to tolerate silences* during the talk, and knows when to shut up and say nothing. Anxiety is the main danger. Fearing that the interview might be on the verge of breaking down, the researcher can feel the need to say something quickly to kick-start the discussion. Feeling uncomfortable when the conversation lapses into silence, the interviewer can be all too quick to say something when a more experienced interviewer would know that the silence can be used as a wonderful resource during interviews.

- *The good interviewer is adept at using prompts.* Although silences can be productive, there might be times during an interview when the researcher judges that it is necessary to spur the informant to speak. But research interviews are not police interviews. Researchers cannot *demand* that the informant answers the questions. Instead, they need to nudge the informant using suitably subtle prompts.

- *The good interviewer is adept at using probes.* There are occasions during an interview when the researcher might want to delve deeper into a topic rather than let the discussion flow on to the next point. An informant might make a point in passing which the researcher thinks should be explored in more detail. Some explanation might be called for, or some justification for a comment. Some apparent inconsistency in the informant's line of reasoning might be detected, an inconsistency which needs unravelling. Without being aggressive the good interviewer knows how to probe points further when it is required.

- *The good interviewer is adept at using checks.* One of the major advantages of interviews is that they offer the researcher the opportunity to check that he/she has understood the informant correctly. As an ongoing part of the normal talk during interviews, the researcher can present a summary of what they think the informant has said, which the informant can then confirm as an accurate understanding, or can correct if it is felt to be a misunderstanding of what has been said. Such checks can be used at strategic points during the interview as a way of concluding discussion on one aspect of the topic.

- *The good interviewer is non-judgemental.* As far as possible interviewers should suspend personal values and *adopt a non-judgemental stance* in relation to the topics covered during the interview. This means not only biting your lip on occasion, but also taking care not to reveal disgust, surprise or pleasure through facial gestures. The good interviewer must also *respect the rights of the interviewee.* This means accepting if a person simply does not wish to tell you something and knowing when to back off if the discussion is beginning to cause the interviewee particular embarrassment or stress. This is a point of personal sensitivity and research ethics.
- *With group interviews and focus groups, the good interviewer/facilitator manages to let everyone have a say.* It is vital to avoid the situation where a dominant personality hogs the discussion and bullies others in the group to agree with his or her opinion.

Good practice: Tactics for interviews – prompts, probes and checks

Prompts: Offer some examples (to help with answering the question).
Repeat the last few words spoken by the interviewee (to invite them to continue).
Repeat the question (to clarify and allow more time for a response).
Remain silent (to allow a pause that encourages them to pursue their thoughts).

Probes: Ask for an example.
Ask for clarification.
Ask for more details.

Check: Summarize their thoughts, e.g. So, if I understand you correctly . . .
What this means, then, is that . . .

Conducting a face-to-face interview

Planning the interview

In the case of face-to-face interviews, securing an agreement to be interviewed is normally easier if the prospective interviewee is *contacted in advance.* This allows both parties to arrange a mutually convenient time for the interview. At this point, of course, the researcher will probably be asked how long the interview will take, and should therefore be in a position to respond. It is most unlikely that busy people will feel comfortable with a suggestion that the interview will 'take as long as it takes'. The researcher needs to make a bid for an *agreed length of time* whether it be 15 minutes, half an hour, 45 minutes or an hour.

Where a face-to-face interview takes place 'on site', events are sometimes beyond the control of the researcher. This means there is an added danger that things can go wrong. Through whatever means, though, the researcher needs to try to get a *location for the interview* which will not be disturbed, which offers privacy, which has fairly good acoustics and which is reasonably quiet. This can prove to be a pretty tall order in places such as busy organizations, schools and hospitals, but at least the desirability of such a venue should be conveyed to the person arranging the interview room.

Within the interview room, it is important to be able to set up the *seating arrangements* in a way that allows comfortable interaction between the researcher and the interviewee(s). In a one-to-one interview the researcher should try to arrange seating so that the two parties are at a 90-degree angle to each other. This allows for eye contact without the confrontational feeling arising from sitting directly opposite the other person. With group interviews, it is important to arrange the seating to allow contact between all parties without hiding individuals at the back of the group or outside the group.

Introduction and formalities

At the beginning of a research interview there should be the opportunity to say 'Hello', to do some introductions, to talk about the aims of the research and to say something about the origins of the researcher's own interest in the topic. During the initial phase, there should also be confirmation that you have permission to record the discussion and reassurances about the confidentiality of comments made during the interview. The aim is to set the tone for the rest of the interview – normally a relaxed atmosphere in which the interviewee feels free to open up on the topic under consideration. *Trust* and *rapport* are the keywords.

During the pre-interview phase, the interviewer should do two other things:

- prepare the recording equipment;
- as far as possible, arrange the seating positions to best advantage.

Starting the interview

The first question takes on a particular significance for the interview. It should offer the interviewee the chance to settle down and relax. For this reason it is normally good practice to *kick off with an 'easy' question*: something on which the interviewee might be expected to have well-formulated views and something that is quite near the forefront of their mind. Two tactics might help here.

- Ask respondents, in a general way, about themselves and their role as it relates to the overall area of the interview. This allows the researcher to collect valuable *background information about informants* while, at the same time, letting informants start off by covering familiar territory.

- *Use some 'trigger' or 'stimulus' material,* so that the discussion can relate to something concrete, rather than launch straight into abstract ideas.

Monitoring progress

During the interview the researcher should keep a discreet eye on the time. The good researcher needs to wind things up within the allotted time and will have covered most of the key issues during that time. While doing this the good interviewer also needs to attend to the following things during the progress of the interview itself:

- *Identify the main points being stated by the interviewee* and the priorities as expressed by the interviewee. With focus groups, what consensus is emerging about the key points?
- Look for the underlying logic of what is being said by the informant. *The interviewer needs to 'read between the lines'* to decipher the rationale lying beneath the surface of what is being said. The interviewer should ask 'What are they really telling me here?' and, perhaps more significantly, 'What are they *not* mentioning?'
- *Look for inconsistencies* in the position being outlined by the interviewee. If such inconsistencies exist, this does not invalidate their position. Most people have inconsistencies in their opinions and feelings on many topics. However, such inconsistencies will be worth probing as the interview progresses to see what they reveal.
- Pick up clues about whether the informant's answers involve an element of *boasting* or are answers intended to *please the interviewer.*
- Be constantly on the look-out for the kind of answer that is *a 'fob-off'.*
- *Get a feel for the context* in which the discussion is taking place. The priorities expressed by the interviewee might reflect events immediately prior to the interview, or things about to happen in the near future. They might be 'issues of the moment', which would not assume such importance were the interview to be conducted a few weeks later. The researcher needs to be sensitive to this possibility and find out from the interviewee if there are events which are influencing priorities in this way.
- Keep a suitable level of eye contact throughout the interview and *make a note of non-verbal communication* which might help a later interpretation of the interview talk.

Finishing the interview

Having kept an eye on the time, and having ensured that most of the required areas for discussion have been covered, the interviewer should draw events to a close making sure that:

- the interviewee is invited to raise any points that they think still need to be covered and have not been covered so far;

- the interviewee is thanked for having given up the time to participate in the interview.

Recording the interview

Memory is a rather unreliable way of capturing the discussion that happens during a face-to-face interview. As psychologists tell us, human memory is prone to partial recall, bias and error. Interviewers, instead, should rely on other more permanent records of what was said.

Audio and video recordings

In practice, most face-to-face interviewers rely on *audio recordings*. Initially, interviewees can feel rather inhibited by the process of recording but most participants become more relaxed after a short while. When used sensitively, audio recording does not pose too much of a disturbance to interview situations, and it has certain clear benefits. Audio recordings offer a *permanent record* and is fairly complete in terms of the speech that occurs. They also lend themselves to being checked by other researchers. However, the downside is that they capture only speech, and miss non-verbal communication and other contextual factors. Video recordings, for their part, capture non-verbal as well as verbal communications and offer a more complete record of events during the interview. And as with audio recordings, they provide a permanent record that can be checked by other researchers. The use of video recordings, however, tends to be the exception rather than the rule. It is not the cost factor that explains this, because video equipment is not particularly expensive. Generally, it is the intrusiveness of video recordings that deters researchers from using them. For practical purposes most interviewers would consider that audio recordings provide data that are good enough for the purpose of the research, and that the benefits gained through the video recording of an interview are outweighed by the extra disruption that video recording brings to the setting.

Link up with Transcribing audio recordings of interviews, p. 307.

Good practice: Recording equipment

Use equipment that is good enough to supply adequate sound (or visual) reproduction.

- Be certain that the equipment is functioning well before the interview.
- Have a reliable power source plus back-up in case of emergency.
- Choose storage devices that have enough memory to cover the planned duration of the interview.

Field notes

Under certain circumstances interviewers will need to rely on field notes. Most commonly this occurs when interviewees decline to be recorded. When this happens it raises the prospect of there being no record of the actual discussion that takes place. This means that the words spoken during the interview will always remain a matter of recollection and interpretation. Of course, where the discussion touches on sensitive issues, commercially, politically or even personally, this might well suit the needs of certain interviewees. Field notes, however, offer a compromise in such situations. Provided that they are written during the interview or, if this is not feasible, as soon afterwards as possible while events remain fresh in the mind, they provide the interviewer with some permanent record of the event which can be referred to at various later stages in the research in order to refresh the memory about what was said.

Field notes, however, can play another role in relation to interviews: they can be used as a *complement to audio recording*. They can be used to fill in some of the relevant information that a recording alone might miss. Field notes can cover information relating to the context of the location, the climate and atmosphere under which the interview was conducted, clues about the intent behind the statements and comments on aspects of non-verbal communication as they were deemed relevant to the interview.

> **Good practice: Write field notes as a complement to audio recordings**
> When conducting face-to-face interviews it is valuable to combine the use of audio recording with field notes to provide important supplementary information.

Online interviews

Online interviews can be conducted with anyone who has access to a computer and the Internet. The costs are negligible and this mode of conducting interviews allows the researcher to interview people across the world without worrying about the time and costs of travel. This is obviously an attractive proposition.

Real time with visual contact

Online interviews can take place in real time and include visual contact between the interviewer and the interviewee. Using a webcam and communication software such as Skype the interview can be conducted very much like a face-to-face interview – only at a distance. Such online interviews share the benefits and drawbacks associated with personal interaction involved in face-to-face interviews but avoid the costs and inconvenience associated with travel.

Without direct visual contact

Online interviews can be conducted in ways that do not include real-time visual interaction between the interviewer and the interviewee. An online interview can be based on straightforward email correspondence with a sequence of written questions prompting follow-up answers from the respondents. Or it can take place using social networking sites, discussion forums or even SMS text messaging. Basically, interviews can be conducted online using any of the available communication platforms. Like face-to-face interviews these kinds of interview retain a basic question and answer sequence. There are, however, some significant differences that need to be taken into account, and these are outlined below.

Recording online data

When online interviews are based on emails, social networking sites or SMS text messages the responses are provided in *written format*. There is, therefore, no need to transcribe verbal statements which, in turn, means there are no transcription errors, nor are there any indecipherable parts of the interview which are unusable. Added to that, the responses are already in a digital format that can be downloaded directly into a word processor or qualitative data analysis software (e.g. NVivo).

Private contact with interviewees

The use of social networking sites, discussion forums and, indeed, any online technology for interviews depends crucially on one thing: it must allow *private exchanges* between the interviewer and the interviewees. When conducting one-to-one interviews online it is essential that the exchanges are private and that care is taken to avoid the messages getting distributed to other users. With group interviews and focus groups online the same proviso operates: the communication must be restricted to just those people directly involved.

 Caution: Online interviews

Care needs to be taken to ensure that questions and especially the answers are not broadcast to everyone using the network or forum.

Remoteness

In contrast with face-to-face interviews there is *no direct visual contact* involved. The effect of this is that the respondent is more 'remote' and distant not just in a physical sense but in a psychological sense as well. This can have some interesting consequences. On the downside, it means that the researcher has less opportunity to confirm the identity of the interviewee or verify the information given by that person. It can be difficult to know for certain who the respondent is or that their answers are genuine and honest.

Weighed against this, the remoteness can have its benefits. The most significant of these is that it can reduce the 'interviewer effect' through the way it does the following:

- *Reduces the culture and gender effects of interaction.* The absence of visual clues means that what is stated by the interviewees is less likely to be affected by status factors linked to the respective age, sex, ethnicity, accent and social class of the interviewer and the interviewee. It acts as an 'equalizer' in terms of the communication.
- *Overcomes embarrassment on some topics.* The lack of face-to-face contact can help to reduce any sense of discomfort when responding to questions on sensitive topics. The contact, being less 'personal', is less likely to cause embarrassment because there is no direct interaction with the researcher. There is no need to feel awkward in the presence of a researcher whose age, sex, social class or ethnic origin could inhibit the interviewee from giving a candid and honest answer.

Time delay

Another difference from conventional face-to-face interviews is that, depending on the particular online platform being used, there can be a time delay between the questions and answers. Again, this can have an impact on the information provided by the respondent. Specifically, it allows interviewees *time to reflect on the question* and provide a response that they have had time to think about carefully. Now this could be a good thing from the researcher's point of view, or it might not be if the researcher is hoping to get a fast reaction to the question rather than a cautiously considered answer.

Written responses to interview questions

An important thing to bear in mind here is that there can be a significant difference in the way people express themselves verbally compared with the way they express themselves in writing. At one level this could affect the *style* of language. In the context of an online interview people might use the kind of informal 'text talk' and abbreviations associated with online media and social networks, whereas in the context of a face-to-face interview a more formal style might be adopted. At another level it can affect the *quantity* of data gathered through the interview. A likely consequence of needing to write answers is that interviewees will use fewer words than they would have done if they were talking to an interviewer face-to-face. As is so often the case with social research methods, however, there is not a hard and fast rule on this. With interviewing, a lot depends on how confident and articulate the person is in face-to-face situations. Someone who is shy could well prefer to write a response and perhaps go into greater depth and detail using a keyboard than talking directly to a researcher in a face-to-face interviewer situation.

Key point: Online interviews

If the online interview does not make use of software such as Skype to conduct the equivalent of a face-to-face interview, then researchers need to weigh up the likely consequences of collecting interview data in terms of:

- the remoteness and loss of visual contact;
- the time-delay between interactions;
- the reliance on written answers rather than spoken words.

How do you know the informant is telling the truth?

This is a crucial question facing research interviews. When the interview is concerned with gathering information of a factual nature the researcher can make some checks to see if the information is broadly corroborated by other people and other sources. When the interview concerns matters such as the emotions, feelings and experiences of the interviewee, it is a lot more difficult to make such checks. Ultimately, there is no absolute way of verifying what someone tells you about their thoughts and feelings. Researchers are not 'mind readers'. But there are still some practical checks researchers can make to gauge the credibility of what they have been told. It should be stressed, though, that these are not watertight methods of detecting false statements given during interviews. They are practical ways of helping the researcher to avoid being a gullible dupe who accepts all that he/she is told at face value. They help the researcher to 'smell a rat'. By the same token, if the following checks are used, the researcher can have greater confidence in the interview data, knowing that some effort has been made to ensure the validity of the data.

Check the data with other sources

The researcher should make efforts to corroborate the interview data with other sources of information on the topic. *Triangulation* should be used. Documents and observations can provide some back-up for the content of the interview, or can cast some doubt on how seriously the interview data should be taken. Interview content can even be checked against other interviews to see if there is some level of consistency. The point is that interview data should not be taken at face value if it is at all possible to confirm or dispute the statements using alternative sources.

Link up with Triangulation, p. 167.

Check the plausibility of the data

Some people are interviewed specifically because they are in a position to know about the things that interest the researcher. The 'key players' are picked out precisely because they are specialists, experts, highly experienced – and their testimony carries with it a high degree of credibility. This is not necessarily the case with those chosen for interview on some other grounds. When assessing the credibility of information contained in an interview, the researcher needs to gauge how far an informant might be expected to be in possession of the facts and to know about the topic being discussed. The researcher should ask if it is reasonable to suppose that such a person would be in a position to comment authoritatively on the topic – or is there a chance that they are talking about something of which they have little knowledge?

Look for themes

Where possible, interview research should avoid basing its findings on one interview. It is safer to look for themes emerging from a number of interviews. Where themes emerge across a number of interviews, the researcher does not have to rely on any one person's statements as the sole source of what is 'real' or 'correct'. A recurrent theme in interviews indicates that the idea/issue is something that is shared among a wider group, and therefore the researcher can refer to it with rather more confidence than any idea/issue that stems from the words of one individual.

> **Link up with Chapter 17, Qualitative data.**

Advantages of interviews

Depth of information

Interviews are particularly good at producing data that deal with topics in depth and in detail. Subjects can be probed, issues pursued and lines of investigation followed over a relatively lengthy period.

Insights

The researcher is likely to gain valuable insights based on the depth of the information gathered and the wisdom of 'key informants'.

Equipment

Interviews require only simple equipment (digital recorder, computer, online connection).

Informants' priorities

Interviews are a good method for producing data based on informants' priorities, opinions and ideas. Informants have the opportunity to expand their ideas, explain their views and identify what *they* regard as the crucial factors.

Flexibility

With semi-structured and unstructured interviews adjustments to the lines of enquiry can be made during the interview itself. Interviewing allows for a developing line of enquiry.

High response rate

Interviews are generally prearranged and scheduled for a convenient time and location. This ensures a relatively high response rate.

Validity of the data

In the case of face-to-face interviews, direct contact at the point of the interview means that data can be checked for accuracy and relevance as they are collected. In the case of online interviews there is also the elimination of errors at the data entry stage. The researcher is no longer faced with passages in an audio-recorded interview where voices cannot be heard clearly and where there is consequently some doubt about what was actually said.

Therapeutic

Interviews can be a rewarding experience for the informant. Compared with questionnaires, observation and experiments, there is a more personal element to the method, and people tend to enjoy the rather rare chance to talk about their ideas at length to a person whose purpose is to listen and note the ideas without being critical.

Disadvantages of interviews

Validity of the data

The data from interviews are based on what people say rather than what they do. The two may not tally. What people say they do, what they say they prefer and what they say they think cannot automatically be assumed to reflect the truth.

Interviewer effect

Interviewee statements can be affected by the identity of the researcher. However, online interviews can go a long way towards avoiding this problem.

Reliability

With semi-structured and unstructured interviews consistency is hard to achieve. The data collected are, to an extent, affected by the specific context and the specific individuals involved.

Time-consuming

Semi-structured and unstructured interviews produce data that are not pre-coded and have a relatively open format. This means that data preparation and analysis are generally 'end-loaded'. The transcribing and coding of interview data are a major task for the researcher which occurs *after* the data have been collected.

Resources

With face-to-face interviews the costs of the interviewer's time and travel can be relatively high, particularly if the informants are geographically dispersed.

Inhibitions

In the case of face-to-face interviews, the audio recorder (or video recorder) can inhibit the informant. Although the impact of the recording device tends to wear off quite quickly, this is not always the case. Online interviews, of course, do not have this problem.

Invasion of privacy

Tactless interviewing can be an invasion of privacy and/or upsetting for the informant. While interviews can be enjoyable, the other side of the coin is that the personal element of being interviewed carries its own kinds of dangers as well.

Further reading

Brinkmann, S. and Kvale, S. (2015) *InterViews: Learning the Craft of Qualitative Research Interviewing*, 3rd edn. Thousand Oaks, CA: Sage.

Cassell, C. (2015) *Conducting Research Interviews*. London: Sage.

Diamante, T. (2013) *Effective Interviewing and Information Gathering: Proven Tactics to Increase the Power of Your Questioning Skills*. New York: McGraw-Hill/Business Expert Press.

Gillham, B. (2005) *Research Interviewing: The Range of Techniques*. Maidenhead: Open University Press.

Kamberelis, G. and Dimitriadis, G. (2013) *Focus Groups: From Structured Interviews to Collective Conversations*. London: Routledge.

Keats, D.M. (2000) *Interviewing: A Practical Guide for Students and Professionals*. Maidenhead: Open University Press.

Mann, S. (2016) *The Research Interview: Reflective Practice and Reflexivity in Research Processes*. Basingstoke: Palgrave Macmillan.

Checklist for the use of interviews

When conducting research interviews you should feel confident about answering 'yes' to the following questions: ☑

1   Is it clear which type of interview is being used and why (one-to-one, group, online, focus group)? ☐

2   Does the format of the interview match the aims of the research in terms of the kind of data that are required (structured, semi-structured, unstructured)? ☐

3   Have field notes been written to provide supplementary information about the interaction during the interview? ☐

4   Have relevant details been collected about the context within which the interviews took place (location, prior events, ambience, etc.)? ☐

5   Has consideration been given to the effect of the recording equipment on the openness with which informants replied? ☐

6   Where possible, have attempts been made to check the accuracy and honesty of statements made by interviewees (plausibility, themes, triangulation)? ☐

7   With semi-structured and unstructured interviews have prompts, probes and checks been used to gain worthwhile, detailed insights? ☐

8   Has consideration been given to the interviewer effect and the way the researcher's self-identity might affect:
   • the interaction during the interview? ☐
   • the interpretation of the data? ☐

9   With online interviews has consideration been given to the effects of:
   • the loss of visual clues during the interaction? ☐
   • the use of non-real-time communication? ☐

14 Observation

What is observational research? • Perception and memory •
Systematic observation • Observation schedules • Sampling and
observation • Retaining the naturalness of the setting • Example of
an observation schedule • Advantages of systematic observation •
Disadvantages of systematic observation • Further reading on
systematic observation • Checklist for the use of systematic
observation • Participant observation • Types of participation •
Example: participation in the normal setting • Fieldwork • Research
ethics • Self, identity and participant observation • Dangers of
fieldwork • Advantages of participant observation • Disadvantages
of participant observation • Further reading on participant
observation • Checklist for the use of participant observation

What is observational research?

There are essentially two kinds of observational research used in the social
sciences. The first of these is *systematic observation* (also known as 'structured
observation'). Systematic observation has its origins in social psychology – in
particular, the study of interaction in settings such as school classrooms. It is
normally linked with the production of quantitative data and the use of
statistical analysis. The second is *participant observation*. This is mainly
associated with sociology and anthropology, and is used by researchers to
investigate the lifestyles, cultures and beliefs of particular social groups. It is
normally associated with qualitative data and ethnographic approaches to
research.

These two methods might seem poles apart in terms of their origins and their
use in current social research, but they share some vital characteristics:

- *Direct observation.* They both rely on direct evidence of the eye to witness
  events at first hand. In this respect they stand together, in contrast to methods such as questionnaires and interviews, which base their data on what

informants tell the researcher, and in contrast to documents where the researcher tends to be one step removed from the action.

- *Fieldwork in natural settings*. They both rely on collecting data in real-life situations, out there 'in the field'. Fieldwork observation occurs in situations which would have occurred whether or not the research had taken place. The whole point is to observe things as they normally happen, rather than as they happen under artificially created conditions such as laboratory experiments. There is a major concern to avoid disrupting the *naturalness of the setting* when undertaking the research. In this approach to social research, it becomes very important to minimize the extent to which the presence of the researcher might alter the situation being researched.

- *The issue of perception*. Systematic observation and participant observation both recognize that the process of observing is far from straightforward. Both are acutely sensitive to the possibility that researchers' perceptions of situations might be influenced by personal factors and that the data collected could thus be unreliable. They offer very different ways of overcoming this, but both see it as a problem that needs to be addressed.

Perception and memory

It might seem reasonable to assume that two researchers looking at the same event will see the same things and make identical records of what took place. However, in practice there is a reasonable chance that the two researchers could produce different records of the thing they jointly witnessed. Why should this be the case? The competence of each individual researcher is a factor which has to be taken into consideration. The powers of observation, the powers of recall and the level of commitment of individual researchers will vary, and this will have an effect on the observational data that are produced. However, the variation in records also reflects more general psychological factors connected to memory and perception, and there are three things which are particularly important that emerge from the work of psychologists in this area.

First, psychologists point to the frailties of human memory and the way that we cannot possibly remember each and every detail of the events and situations we observe. We forget most of what we see, but what we forget and what we recall are not decided at random. There is a pattern to the way the mind manages to recall certain things and forget others. There is *selective recall*.

Second, they point to the way the mind filters the information it receives through the senses. It not only acts to reduce the amount of information, it also operates certain 'filters' which let some kinds of information through to be experienced as 'what happened', while simultaneously putting up barriers to many others. There is *selective perception*.

Third, they point to experiments which show how these filters not only let in some information while excluding the rest, but also boost our sensitivity to certain signals depending on our emotional and physical state, and our past experiences. What we experience can be influenced to some extent by whether we are, for instance, very hungry, angry, anxious, frustrated, prejudiced, etc. What we experience is shaped by our feelings at that moment and by the emotional baggage we carry around with us as a result of significant things that have happened to us during our lifetime. These things account for *accentuated perception*.

Without delving too deeply into the psychology of perception, it is easy to appreciate that, as human beings, researchers do not simply observe and record the events they witness in some mechanical and straightforward fashion. In practice, there is *an element of interpretation* with the mind acting as an intermediary between 'the world out there' and the way it is experienced by the individual.

Systematic observation

The possibility that different observers might produce different records of the situation is rather worrying when it comes to the use of observation as a method for collecting data. It suggests that the data could vary depending on the particular observer rather than the event being researched. But it is precisely this problem which is addressed by *systematic* observation. Systematic observation, as the name suggests, is a research method that introduces a system to the process of observation, a system that aims to produce data that are consistent between observers – eliminating variations arising from the psychological factors that influence individual researchers' perceptions of events and situations.

Observation schedules

To achieve this aim, systematic observation makes use of *observation schedules*. These schedules contain a list of items that act much like a checklist. All observers involved with a project use identical schedules and thus have their attention directed to the same things. This helps to make the record of the events consistent between researchers because *what* is being observed is dictated by the items contained in the schedule.

Observation schedules not only specify *what* is to be observed, they also specify *how* those things are to be measured. This is important. The data collected by different observers are hardly likely to be consistent and standardized simply by directing attention to key items of interest and then leaving it up to individual observers to decide how they record the item. Individuals could choose different terms to describe what they see and produce collections of data that, while focused on the same event or behaviour, might vary widely in format and detail. To be *systematic* the observation needs to include some way of ensuring that that the events or behaviour are recorded in an objective and consistent manner. This is done by collecting *quantitative* data based on counts, amounts and frequencies relating to the item of interest. Rather than portray the events or behaviour in words, the purpose of the observation schedule is to produce data using things like:

- the *frequency of events*: making a numerical count of the frequency with which the items on the observation schedule occur;
- the *duration of events*: quantifying the amount of time covered by an event or taken by a specific behaviour. When instances of the item occur they are timed, start to finish, so that the researcher gets information on the total time for each item and the points at which it occurred during the overall time-block for the period of observation.

When researchers are properly trained and experienced there should be a good *inter-observer reliability* with different researchers producing almost identical data when observing the same social setting. The influence of the individual researcher and factors affecting his/her perception and memory should be minimal.

Good practice

Observation schedules should:

- ensure that all researchers are alert to the same activities and looking out for the same things;
- get researchers to record data systematically and in a standardized fashion.

Selection of specific items for inclusion in the observation schedule

Events and behaviour that occur within social settings tend to be complex and multifaceted. This creates a challenge for researchers wishing to use systematic observation. In settings where they might want to use an observation schedule it is likely that there will be many things going on at the same time – so many, indeed, that it would be impossible for any observation schedule to cover every aspect of what happens in the setting. Inevitably, then, researchers need to exercise some *selectivity* in terms of the items they include in the schedule and the ones they leave off the list.

When selecting which events or behaviours to include in the observation schedule, there are four basic things that need to be taken into consideration. First and foremost, the items to be included should be valid indicators of the topic that is being investigated. Obviously, the findings from an observation schedule will only be of value if the items listed in the schedule are the most *relevant* for the purposes of the investigation. Precise records of something that is irrelevant will not advance the research at all. Previous research and previous theories provide the key to deciding what things warrant attention and, initially, a *literature review* should be used to identify significant things to be included in the observation schedule.

Second, the items that are included should cover all possibilities: they should be *complete*. Care needs to be taken to ensure, as far as is possible, that the categories on the observation schedule cover the full range of possibilities and that there are not gaps which will become glaringly evident once the observation schedule is used in the field.

Third, the items should be *clear-cut and self-evident*. Observers should not need to decipher the action or wonder whether an action fits one or another category – it should be fairly obvious. This means that items on the schedule should only include *overt behaviours and events* that are observable in a direct manner. Things like attitudes and thoughts that need to be inferred by the researcher are not suitable because they are not visible in a direct manner. It also means that the items need to be *precise*. There should be no ambiguity and no overlap between the items on the observation schedule.

Last, but not least, the choice of items for inclusion needs to take account of the *frequency and sequencing* of events to be observed. On the one hand, the items should occur with *sufficient regularity* for the observer to be able to collect a reasonable amount of data. If the event is something that occurs infrequently it will prove frustrating and wasteful of time to have a researcher poised – waiting, waiting, waiting for something to happen. On the other hand, if the actions or events are too frequent it might be impossible for the observer to keep up to speed. If the events are bunched and all come at once the observer might well find it impossible to log all instances.

 Key point: Suitability of events or behaviour for observation

The events or behaviour selected for inclusion in an observation schedule should be:

- relevant – the best indicators of the thing being investigated;
- complete – include the full range of possibilities for the item;
- overt – observable and measurable in a direct manner;
- obvious – require a minimum of interpretation by the researcher;
- precise – there should be no ambiguity about the categories;
- easy to record – occur with sufficient regularity and sequence for the observer to be able to log the occurrences accurately.

Sampling and observation

Researchers using systematic observation generally organize their research around set time-blocks of observation in the field. For example, these might be one-hour chunks of time *in situ*. These time-blocks themselves need to be chosen so as to avoid any bias and to incorporate a representative sample of the thing in question. So, if the research were to involve observations of interaction in school classrooms the researcher would need to ensure that the research occurred across the full school week, the full school day and a cross-section of subjects. To confine observations to Friday afternoons, or to one subject such as history, would not provide an accurate picture across the board.

The same applies to the selection of people or events for inclusion in the study. To get a representative picture of the situation, systematic observation can involve a deliberate selection of people or events to be observed so that the data cover a cross-section of the whole research population. This can take the form of:

- *Time-sampling* to ensure a sequence of snap-shot observations at set intervals. Every 30 seconds, for instance, the observer could record the relevant events or behaviour that are happening at that instant.
- *Tracking the activities of specific individuals one after another*. Individuals can be observed for predetermined periods of time, after which the observer's attention is switched to another person in a rota designed eventually to produce a reasonable profile covering all those involved.

> Link up with Chapter 2, Sampling.

Good practice: Use field notes to complement systematic observation data

Quantitative data produced by systematic observation schedules should be complemented by field notes (qualitative data) in which the researcher (1) describes the *context* and (2) records his/her impressions about the *circumstances* surrounding the events or behaviour being observed. Such background information helps to explain the events that are observed and should be logged with the schedule results to help the observer understand the data he/she has collected.

Retaining the naturalness of the setting

The presence of a researcher is likely to be noticed by the people being observed. They will be aware that there is a person on site who is not normally around and that this person is using some equipment (such as a laptop, tablet or clipboard). Curiosity will be raised, and inevitably there will be some disruption to normality. The challenge for the researcher is to ensure that such disruption is relatively short-lived and that soon things will settle down and people will cease to pay much attention to the observer. The aim for the researcher is to 'fade into the background' and be ignored by those whose behaviour is being observed so that the naturalness of the setting can be resumed. There are three things that help with this:

- *Positioning*. Unobtrusive positioning is vital. But the researcher still needs to be able to view the whole arena of action.
- *Avoiding interaction*. The advice here is to be 'socially invisible', not engaging with the participants in the setting if at all possible.

> **Link up with the Observer effect, p. 72.**

- *Time on site*. The longer systematic observers are 'on site' the more their presence is taken for granted and the less they have any significant effect on proceedings.

Example of an observation schedule

Art classes in a primary school could be studied using systematic observation. This could involve the use of an observation schedule specifically designed to collect data about pupils' activity during the lessons. The motive for doing the research might be to provide quantitative, objective data in support of the art teacher's bid for resources to have a second sink installed in the art classroom, and to do so by measuring the amount of lesson time wasted by students queuing to clean their paintbrushes in the one sink that is currently available in the classroom. A simple observation schedule that could be used for this purpose might be as shown in Figure 14.1.

Figure 14.1 Observation schedule

Location: School A.   Teacher: Chris Jones   Art lesson
Observation #4
Date: 28 April
Time: 11 a.m. to 12 noon

Name	Time starts queuing	Time arrives at sink	Queuing time
Asha	11.15	11.15	0
Sami	11.15	11.18	3
Douglas	11.15	11.20	5
Olivia	11.16	11.23	7
Jack	11.17	11.24	7
Jing	11.19	11.26	7
Max	11.22	11.28	6
Olga	11.23		

In the example in Figure 14.1, a decision has been made to record the amount of time spent queuing. It would have been possible to record the number of occasions that students in the class queued, or to have noted at intervals of, say, 30 seconds over a one-hour period how many students were queuing at that moment. These would have provided three slightly different kinds of results. If we were concerned with how queuing interrupted the concentration of students on a task it would have been more appropriate to record the *frequency*. Had the aim been to look at bottlenecks in the queuing, then *time sampling* would have allowed the ebb and flow of students to the sink to be shown quite clearly. In this example, however, the aim is to support the claim that students' time is wasted in queues for the sink and it is therefore appropriate to record the *amount* of time spent in the queue.

The item to be observed in this example is suitably straightforward. It is reasonable to presume that standing in line is an obvious and observable form of behaviour and that, despite some occasions when students might not be solely concerned with getting their paintbrushes clean when they join the queue (they might be socializing or wasting time deliberately), standing in line offers a fairly valid indicator of the thing that is of interest to the researcher: time wasted queuing.

Advantages of systematic observation

Direct data collection

It directly records what people do, as distinct from what they *say* they do.

Objective, factual, quantitative data

It produces *objective* observations. The use of an observation schedule provides an answer to the problems associated with the selective perception of observers to the extent that the schedule effectively eliminates any bias from the current emotions or personal background of the observer. The factual, quantitative data can be very persuasive in terms of policy and management decisions.

Efficient

It provides a means for collecting substantial amounts of data in a relatively short time-span.

Pre-coded data

It produces quantitative data which are pre-coded and ready for analysis.

Reliability

When properly established it should achieve high levels of inter-observer reliability in the sense that two or more observers using a schedule should record very similar data.

Disadvantages of systematic observation

Behaviour, not intentions

This method of data collection focuses on overt behaviour and manifest events. It therefore describes what happens, but not *why* it happens. It does not deal with the intentions that motivated the behaviour or factors that caused the events.

Oversimplifies

Systematic observation assumes that overt behaviours can be measured in terms of categories that are fairly straightforward and unproblematic. This is premised on the idea that the observer and the observed share an understanding of the overt behaviour, and that the behaviour has no double meaning, hidden meaning or confusion associated with it. As such, systematic observation has the inbuilt potential to oversimplify; to ignore or distort the subtleties of the situation.

Contextual information

Observation schedules, by themselves, tend to miss contextual information which has a bearing on the behaviours recorded.

Naturalness of the setting

Although researchers who use systematic observation express confidence that their presence does not actually disrupt the naturalness of the setting to any significant extent, some question mark must surely remain about the observer's ability to fade into the background. Can a researcher using an observation schedule really avoid disrupting the naturalness of the setting?

Further reading on systematic observation

Bakeman, R. and Gottman, J.M. (1997) *Observing Interaction: An Introduction to Sequential Analysis*, 2nd edn. Cambridge: Cambridge University Press.
Croll, P. (1986) *Systematic Classroom Observation*. London: Falmer Press.
Gillham, B. (2008) *Observation Techniques: Structured and Unstructured Approaches*. London: Continuum.
O'Leary, M. (2014) *Classroom Observation*. London: Routledge.
Yoder, P. and Symons, F. (2010) *Observational Measurement of Behavior*. New York: Springer.

Checklist for the use of systematic observation

When conducting systematic observation you should feel
confident about answering 'yes' to the following questions: ☑

1   Are the events/behaviour to be observed:
    • sufficiently clear-cut and unambiguous to allow reliable coding? ☐
    • the most relevant indicators for the purposes of the research? ☐

2   Is the observation schedule complete (incorporating all
    likely categories of events/behaviour)? ☐

3   Do the events/behaviour occur regularly enough to provide
    sufficient data? ☐

4   Does the observation schedule avoid multiple simultaneous
    occurrences of the event/behaviour which might prevent
    accurate coding? ☐

5   Is the kind of sampling (event/point/time) the most appropriate? ☐

6   Do the planned periods for observation provide a represen-
    tative sample (time, place, context)? ☐

7   Have efforts been made to minimize any disturbance to the
    naturalness of the setting caused by the presence of the
    observer? ☐

8   Is there provision for the collection of contextual informa-
    tion to accompany the observation schedule data? ☐

Participant observation

Participant observation is an unobtrusive method of data collection that allows the researcher to gather information about lifestyles, cultures and beliefs. In contrast to systematic observation it tends to produce qualitative data and it focuses on the meanings behind actions rather than overt aspects of behaviour. Perhaps most significantly, though, it calls for the researcher to participate in the situation rather than observe from the touchline. As Becker and Geer (1957: 28) make the point in their classic definition:

> By participant observation we mean the method in which the observer participates in the daily life of the people under study, either openly in the role of researcher or covertly in some disguised role, observing things that happen, listening to what is said, and questioning people, over some length of time.

It is a method that places particular emphasis on:

Link up with
Chapter 9,
Phenomenology.

Link up with
Chapter 5,
Ethnography.

Link up with
the Observer
effect, p. 72.

- *Getting an insider's perspective*: The experience of participating in everyday life situations can help researchers to get a 'feel' for the situation which can generate insights into particular lifestyles, cultures or beliefs. These insights come specifically from being able to see things from the perspective of an insider.

- *Providing depth and detail*: Lifestyles, cultures and beliefs can be very intricate and complex things – difficult to understand and hard to explain. There is more likelihood of producing a good account of such things using a method that puts the researcher 'on site' and in the thick of the action for a reasonable period of time.

- *Retaining the naturalness of the setting*: There is a concern for seeing things 'as they really are' without disturbing the normality of life. This makes preserving the naturalness of the setting a key priority.

Types of participation

Participation can take a number of forms. These vary in the extent to which the researcher's role is made explicit to those being observed. At one extreme the researcher's role might be kept completely hidden. At the other extreme those being observed might be made fully aware of the presence of the researcher and his/her intentions to collect data. The range of possibilities, however, generally boils down to three basic alternatives:

- *Total participation*, where the researcher's role is kept secret. The researcher assumes the role of someone who normally participates in the setting. Consent cannot be gained for the research, which poses ethical problems.

- *Participation in the normal setting*, where the researcher's role may be known to certain 'gatekeepers', but may be hidden from most of those in the setting. The role adopted in this type of participant observation is chosen deliberately to permit observation without affecting the naturalness of the setting, but it also allows the researcher to keep a distance from the key group under study. This distance might be warranted on the grounds of propriety, or the researcher lacks the personal credentials to take on the role in question.
- *Participation as observer*, where the researcher's identity as a researcher is openly recognized – thus having the advantage of gaining informed consent from those involved – and takes the form of 'shadowing' a person or group through normal life, witnessing at first hand and in intimate detail the culture/events of interest. It involves 'hanging out' with the people being studied.

Example: Participation in the normal setting

There are settings where researchers might be reluctant to engage in total participation. For example, in Humphreys' (1975) study of impersonal sexual encounters in public toilets, he adopted a 'lookout' role which allowed him to be accepted as part of the general scene without actually taking part in the sexual encounters. And when O'Connell Davidson (1995) was studying the working practices of Madame Desirée – a prosperous independent prostitute – she occasionally posed as Madame Desirée's receptionist working from a desk outside the rooms used by clients. This allowed her to be part of the normal scene but also allowed her a judicious distance from the heart of the action. In this instance the researcher's role was not totally secret. Madame Desirée knew that O'Connell Davidson was a researcher, but the clients did not.

Fieldwork

The researcher enters the field to learn about the situation. The longer the researcher is able to spend 'on site' the better because the longer he/she is part of the action, the more can be learnt about the situation. Good participant observation demands that the researcher devotes considerable time to the fieldwork. This is not a hit-and-run research method. Time on site is needed to gain trust, to establish rapport and foster insights, insights that are the trademark of participant observation as a research method.

What to observe

Participant observers usually start out being fairly non-selective in terms of what they observe. Before anything else they aim to get an 'overall feel' for the situation, and to do this they tend to begin by engaging in what can be termed 'holistic observation'. This is valuable as a background scene-setting device but, in practice, getting a general feel for the setting normally acts as a prelude to more *focused observations*. As things emerge which appear to have particular significance or interest, observation will shift from the broad canvas of activity in the setting towards specific areas. Things which emerge as important, strange or unusual invite closer scrutiny. Following from focused observations the researcher might be able to undertake special observations which concentrate on aspects of the setting in which there appear to be things which are unexpected or contradictory. Attention can be focused upon things that, according to the observer's common sense, ought not to happen. Finally, observations can try to *identify issues and problems* which participants themselves regard as crucial. The point is to observe instances which indicate how members of the setting see things – their views, beliefs and experiences.

Making field notes

The fieldwork researcher needs to translate the observations into some permanent record at the very earliest opportunity. This might be 'field notes' in the form of written records or tape-recorded memos. Whatever the form, the researcher doing fieldwork needs to develop a strategy for writing up field notes as soon as possible after the observation.

The need to do so stems from two things. First, the human memory is not only selective, but also frail. It is so easy to forget things, particularly the minor incidents and passing thoughts, if field notes are delayed for a matter of days, let alone weeks. *Field notes are urgent business.* The researcher needs to build into the research some provision to make the field notes on a regular and prompt basis. The second factor involved here is the general need to take field notes outside the arena of action. To take field notes while engaging in the action as a participant, to state the obvious, would be (1) to disrupt the naturalness of the setting, and (2) to disclose the researcher's role as observer. As a general rule, then, participant observers need to establish occasions during fieldwork, or very soon afterwards, when they can make field notes in private and unknown to those being observed. The simplest strategy is to write up the field notes as soon as you get home – assuming that home is separate from the field being studied.

> **Good practice: Making field notes with participant observation**
> Detailed field notes should be made to accompany participant observation. These notes should be made as soon as possible following each episode of observation.

Research ethics

Participant observation can pose particular ethical problems for the researcher. If 'total' participation is used, then those being studied will not be aware of the research or their role in it. They can hardly give 'informed consent'. The justification for such covert research cannot depend on consent, but draws instead on two other arguments. First, if it can be demonstrated that none of those who were studied suffered as a result of being observed, the researcher can argue that certain ethical standards were maintained. Second, and linked, if the researcher can show that the identities of those involved were never disclosed, again there is a reasonable case for saying that the participant observation was conducted in an ethical manner.

Whichever variant of participant observation is used there is the possibility that confidential material might 'fall into the hands' of the researcher. Now, while this is true of most research methods its prospects are exacerbated with the use of participant observation owing to the closeness and intimacy of the researcher's role *vis-à-vis* those being researched. Confidential material might be disclosed inadvertently by someone who does not know the research interest of the participant. Or, possibly even more problematic, things might get revealed as a result of the trust and rapport developed between the researcher and those being observed. This could be true for any of the variants of participant observation. The ethical problem is whether to use such material and how to use it. And here the guidelines are quite clear: (1) any use of the material should ensure that no one suffers as a result; and (2) any use of the material should avoid disclosing the identities of those involved. Any departure from these guidelines would need very special consideration and justification.

> **Link up with Chapter 18, Research ethics.**

Self, identity and participant observation

Equipment for research: the 'self'

One of the attractions of participant observation is that it hinges on the researcher's 'self', and does not call on much in the way of technical back-up in the form of gadgets or software. Nor does it tend to produce data that call for statistical analysis. *The key instrument of participant observation methods is the researcher as a person.*

This suggests that there is little in the way of 'entry costs' to act as a deterrent. Equipment costs are very low. There might appear to be no need for training (though this, of course, would be a fallacy). The researcher, it might seem, can jump right into the fieldwork and get on with it. However, as we see in the next sections, this dependence on the 'self' is not altogether a straightforward advantage.

Access to settings

From the participant observer's point of view gaining access to a setting might involve something more than getting approval from relevant authorities or getting a 'gatekeeper' to help open doors to the necessary contacts and settings.

When engaging in the total version of participant observation there is a further issue affecting access. If the researcher is to adopt a role in the setting then he or she needs to have the *necessary credentials*.

To operate 'under cover' in a setting it is obvious that the researcher should not stand out like a sore thumb. Depending on the situation this can effectively exclude many researchers from many roles. The age factor will bar most (all?) researchers from using participant observation to investigate student cultures in schools. Observing the setting as a teacher is a more likely prospect. Sex will offer other barriers. Male researchers will be hard pushed to use total participant observation for the study of, for example, cocktail waitresses. Observing as a barman in the setting is a more likely prospect. Black researchers will find it exceptionally difficult to infiltrate the Ku Klux Klan. The biological factors place severe constraints on access to situations. Skills and qualifications provide another barrier. To participate in the sense of adopting a role it is necessary to have the necessary skills and qualifications associated with that group. As Polsky (2006) points out, his study of pool hall hustling was only possible as a participant observer because – through a 'misspent youth' – he was already something of an accomplished pool player himself. The would-be researcher, however, might be reluctant or unable to achieve such a skill specifically for the purpose of a piece of research. Following the logic here, there are many, many roles which the researcher will be unable to adopt – from brain surgeon to tree surgeon – because of a lack of personal credentials.

Selecting a topic

In view of the constraints on access as a full participant, there are two things which emerge that have a direct bearing on the selection of a topic.

- To a large extent researchers who do participant observation have their topic selected for them on the basis of their pre-existing personal attributes. The 'choice' is rarely much of a free choice. The researcher's self – age, sex, ethnicity, qualifications, skills, social background and lifestyle – tends to direct the possibilities and provide *major constraints on the roles that can be adopted* and the *groups who can be observed*.

- While it is arguably the most revealing and sensitive of research methods in the social sciences, it is also very demanding. *It is not a soft option.* The level of commitment needed for full participant observation can be far more than that demanded by other methods – commitment in terms of researcher's time and the degree to which the act of research invades the routine life of the researcher.

It is not surprising, then, that many of the fascinating studies emerge as 'one-offs' in which researchers have explored an area of social life for which they are uniquely qualified to participate through their own past experience. It is far more unusual to find examples where researchers have been deliberately employed to infiltrate a group (e.g. Festinger et al. 1956) or where researchers have consciously adopted a role which is alien to them and which involves danger and discomfort (e.g. Griffin 1962).

Another consequence of the restrictions to full participation is the decision of many social researchers to opt for the version of participant observation which is not 'total participation'. Participation in the setting and participation as observer offer approaches which side-step some of the dangers of total participation and offer a more palatable experience for the researcher on many occasions (e.g. Whyte [1943] 1993; Humphreys 1975; O'Connell Davidson 1995).

 Key point: Choosing a topic to suit your 'self'

Researchers using participant observation generally choose a topic about which they have some insider knowledge and personal experience. The setting is normally one where the researcher can fit in easily and comfortably without disturbing the naturalness of the setting. In both senses, then, the choice of topic tends to suit the researcher's 'self'.

Dangers of fieldwork

Doing participant observation can be dangerous. First, there is *physical danger*. As Lee (1995) points out, being physically injured while doing fieldwork is fairly unlikely but, depending on the circumstances, cannot be ignored as a possibility. It is a potential built into some forms of fieldwork. Danger lurks for anthropologists who travel in remote regions with inhospitable climates and treacherous terrains. In the early years of the century, evidently, there were instances where anthropologists were actually killed by the people they were studying (Howell 1990). Danger lurks for political scientists who operate in unstable societies where the rule of law is tenuous and civilians can get caught up in factional disputes. Danger lurks for sociologists and ethnographers when they make contact with groups whose activities are on the margins of, or even outside, the law (e.g. Garrett 2013). As they tap into the underworlds of drugs, prostitution, football hooligans, bikers, religious sects and the like, they are taking a risk. This is not just a reference to the prospect of getting mugged or assaulted, or of retribution if the cover is blown at some stage. There is also the danger posed by the lifestyle itself and the impact on health of a changed diet and changed accommodation. Changing lifestyle carries its own hazards. Of course, if the researcher were to become dependent on the use of hard drugs, the health consequences could be far more dramatic.

The fieldwork could involve a second danger: *legal prosecution*. Being 'part of the scene' when hard drugs are around immediately puts the researcher at risk of prosecution. There are no special immunities afforded to social researchers.

The researcher who chooses to engage in such fieldwork might also jeopardize his/her social well-being. The 'other' life he/she is called upon to live for the purposes of the research can have an adverse effect on domestic life, on relationships with others and on commitments to do with work and leisure which make up the 'normal' life of the researcher. *The researcher, in effect, needs to sustain two lifestyles,* and these may not be compatible. Being away from home, being out late and doing fieldwork at 'unsocial' hours can tax the patience of the nearest and dearest. And then there is the psychological danger resulting from the dual existence demanded of fieldwork such as this. The lifestyle, at its worst, can have something of a traumatic effect on the researcher, or can have a lasting or permanent effect on the researcher's personality.

Going native

When it requires some form of 'dual existence' the success of participant observation depends on the researcher being able to draw a line between the two roles. There is a danger, though, that researchers might become unable to draw a clear distinction between themselves as researchers and themselves as participants. At its most extreme it can involve *joining the group that you set out to study.* If the researcher's 'self' gets lost in this way this is rather like an anthropologist forgetting all about the research and settling down to live out their days as a member of the 'tribe' that they had originally set out to study. This is known as 'going native'.

> ### Good practice: Avoid dangerous fieldwork
> A risk assessment of the fieldwork setting should be conducted and potential dangers identified. Although experienced researchers might venture into dangerous contexts to conduct their participant observation, this should not be done by project researchers.

Advantages of participant observation

Basic equipment

Participant observation uses the researcher's 'self' as the main instrument of research, and therefore requires little by way of technical/statistical support.

Non-interference

It stands a better chance of retaining the naturalness of the setting than other social research methods.

Subjects' points of view

As a method of social research, participant observation is good for getting at actors' meanings as they see them.

Insights

It provides a good platform for gaining rich insights into social processes and is suited to dealing with complex realities.

Context

The data produced by participant observation have the potential to be particularly context-sensitive and 'ecologically valid'.

Disadvantages of participant observation

Access

There are limited options open to the researcher about which roles to adopt or settings to participate in.

Commitment

Participant observation can be a very demanding method in terms of personal commitment and personal resources.

Danger

Participant observation can be potentially hazardous for the researcher; physically, legally, socially and psychologically risky.

Deception

When researchers opt to conduct full participation, keeping their true identity and purpose secret from others in the setting, there are ethical problems arising from the absence of consent on the part of those being observed, and of deception by the researcher.

Reliability

Dependence on the 'self' of the researcher and on the use of field notes as data leads to a lack of verifiable data. Reliability is open to doubt. Because participant observation relies so crucially on the researcher's 'self' as the instrument of research, it becomes exceedingly difficult to repeat a study to check for reliability. The dependence on field notes for data, constructed (soon) after fieldwork and based on the researcher's recollections of events, does little to encourage those who would want to apply conventional criteria for reliability to this method.

Representativeness of the data

There are problems of generalizing from the research. The focal role of the researcher's 'self' and the emphasis on detailed research of the particular setting open participant observation to the criticism that it is difficult to generalize from the findings. In one sense, this might hold water as a valid criticism. After all, the situations for research using participant observation are not selected on the grounds of being representative. As we have seen, they tend to be chosen on the basis of a mixture of availability and convenience. However, it might be argued that it is inappropriate to apply standard criteria of reliability and generalizability to this method.

Further reading on participant observation

DeWalt, K.M. and DeWalt, B.R. (2011) *Participant Observation: A Guide for Fieldworkers*, 2nd edn. Lanham, MD: AltaMira Press.

Garson, D.G. (2014) *Participant Observation*. Asheboro, NC: Statistical Publishing Associates.

Gillham, B. (2008) *Observation Techniques: Structured and Unstructured Approaches*. London: Continuum.

Jorgensen, D.L. (1989) *Participant Observation: A Methodology for Human Studies*. Thousand Oaks, CA: Sage.

Checklist for the use of participant observation

When undertaking participant observation you should feel confident about answering 'yes' to the following questions: ☑

1 Does the participant observation research allow insights to events, cultures and lifestyles that would not be possible using other methods? ☐

2 Are there good grounds for believing that participant observation will not, or did not, disturb the naturalness of the setting? ☐

3 Is it clear which type of participant observation will be, or has been, used (total participation, participation in normal setting, participation as observer)? ☐

4 Has consideration been given to the ethics of the fieldwork (secrecy, consent, confidentiality)? ☐

5 Has the influence of the researcher's self-identity been examined in terms of:
   • the choice of fieldwork situation? ☐
   • access to the setting? ☐
   • the perception of events and cultures? ☐

6 Has sufficient time been spent in the field:
   • to allow trust and rapport to develop? ☐
   • to allow detailed observations and an in-depth understanding of the situation (detail, context, interconnections)? ☐

7 Have field notes been made at the time or soon after participating in the field? ☐

8 Has a risk assessment been conducted which shows that there are no specific dangers linked with the fieldwork? ☐

© M. Denscombe, *The Good Research Guide*. Open University Press.

15 Documents

What is documentary research? • Sources of documentary data •
Access to documentary sources • The credibility of documentary
sources • Image-based research • The use of 'created' images •
The use of 'found' images • Advantages of documentary research •
Disadvantages of documentary research • Further reading •
Checklist for the use of documents (text and visual images)

What is documentary research?

Documentary research, as the name implies, is a kind of social enquiry that uses documents as its source of data. More specifically, it treats documents as a source of *primary* data and, in this respect, it contrasts with the use of questionnaires, interviews or observation in social research. Documents can exist as:

- *written text* (e.g. books, articles, reports);
- *digital communication* (e.g. web pages, SMS texts, blogs, social network sites);
- *visual sources* (e.g. pictures, video, artefacts).

Whatever form they take, documents have two features that are useful when it comes to social research. First, they contain information that can be *used as evidence* of something. Built into the concept of a 'document' is the idea that the information it contains is of value beyond its literal contents. It stands for something and it conveys something that is significant and useful. This feature is obvious in documents such as contracts, charters, deeds, registers, reports, forms and certificates. For social researchers, though, this suggests that documents can serve as a source of data that can be used to reveal things that are not immediately apparent. Rather than take the contents at face value there are things to be learnt from a deeper reading of the document. Documentary research, for this reason, generally goes beyond

Link up with
Chapter 17,
Qualitative
data.

the straightforward collection of facts from documents: it tends to involve *interpreting* the document as well, looking for hidden meanings or structures in the work.

Second, the notion of a document carries with it the idea of a *permanent record*. Documents provide some record whose existence, if not permanent for all of time, does at least persist in a stable form well beyond the moment in which it was produced. The information documents contain is neither fleeting nor transitory: it is captured in some format or other, and saved. This feature, again, is useful in the context of social research.

Sources of documentary data

Government publications and official statistics

Government publications and official statistics would appear to provide a documentary source of information that is:

- *Authoritative.* Since the data have been produced by the state, employing large resources and expert professionals, they tend to have *credibility*.
- *Objective.* Since the data have been produced by officials, they might be regarded as *impartial*.
- *Factual.* In the case of the statistics, they take the form of numbers that are amenable to computer storage/analysis, and constitute 'hard facts' over which there can be no ambiguity.

It is not surprising, then, that in the Western world government publications and official statistics have come to provide a key source of documentary information for social scientists. However, the extent to which such documents can live up to the image of being authoritative, objective and factual depends very much on the data they contain (see below).

Newspapers and magazines

The 'Press' provides a potentially valuable source of information for research purposes. One reason for this is that newspapers and magazines can supply good, up-to-date information. In this case, the value of the newspaper or magazine for the research will stem from one or a combination of:

- the expertise of the journalists;
- the specialism of the publication;
- the insider information which the correspondents can uncover.

So, for example, in the UK, business researchers might use *The Economist* or the *Financial Times* for these reasons. Of course, the discerning researcher will also realize that there are plenty of newspapers and magazines whose contents should *not* be relied upon to reflect anything approaching an objective account of real events!

Records of meetings

The bureaucratization of industrial society has created a wealth of documentation in relation to administration, policy, management, finance and commerce. These provide an abundant source of data for social researchers in whatever field they operate.

The purpose of most such documentation is to enhance accountability. The records kept of meetings (minutes), the records kept of transactions, the records kept of finances, etc. are kept in principle so that people and institutions can be held accountable for their actions. This means that the records need to have two qualities, both of which happen to be of particular value for research:

- *Systematic picture of things that have happened.* These might be decisions of a committee or transfers of money between accounts. Whatever the records, though, the principle behind them is that they provide a detailed and accurate picture of what took place. They have got to make events sufficiently transparent for the readers to comprehend what took place and why.
- *Publicly available.* The records only serve the function of accountability to the extent that they are made available to relevant people to scrutinize.

Letters and memos

Private correspondence between people can be used for research purposes. This can take the form of memos sent between people at work or even personal letters exchanged between people. The more private the correspondence, of course, the more difficult it is for the researcher to gain access to the documents. These are really at the other end of the spectrum from the publicly available reports, and pose far more of a challenge for the researcher when it comes to getting hold of such documents and, especially, when it comes to getting permission to use them as research data.

Letters and memos also differ from reports in terms of the extent to which there is any formal obligation on the writer to give a full and accurate portrayal of events. Because they are written to specific people, rather than for a broader public, their contents are likely to rely far more on assumptions about what the other person already knows or what that person feels. They are more likely to 'fill in the bits' rather than paint the whole picture. They can be expected to be from a personal point of view rather than be impartial. When contemplating the use of letters or memos as data for research, then, you need to recognize that they are not very reliable as accounts which depict objective reality, but they are extremely valuable as a source which reveals the writer's own perceptions and views of events.

Diaries

As a source of documentary data, diaries are written by people whose thoughts and behaviour the researcher wishes to study. For research purposes such diaries are important in terms of recording things that have already happened. We are not talking about the kind of diaries which act as a planner, noting commitments in the future that need to be scheduled. For research purposes, the diary is normally a retrospective account of things that have happened.

There are three crucial elements to this kind of diary – three elements which, incidentally, are shared with the literary diary and the statesman's diary:

- *factual data*: a log of things that happened, decisions made and people involved;
- *significant incidents*: the identification of things seen as particularly important and a description of the diary-writer's priorities;
- *personal interpretation*: a personal reflection and interpretation of happenings, plus an account of the personal feelings and emotions surrounding the events described.

Each of these three things has the potential to provide a rich source of data for the researcher. However, the accounts they provide should not be used by the researcher as a statement of objective fact. That would be very naive. As a retrospective account, diaries must always be seen as a *version* of things as seen by the writer, filtered through the writer's past experiences, own identity, own aspirations and own personality.

It is also worth noting that diaries, as a form of documentary data, lend themselves to being analysed in a variety of ways. As a method of data collection they do not prescribe such matters and, as Alaszewski (2006) argues, they can be analysed using approaches as widely different as content analysis, grounded theory and discourse analysis.

> **Link up with Chapter 17, Qualitative data.**

Website pages and the Internet

Documents, as a form of data, include material obtained via the Internet. In a sense, the medium through which the document is obtained is not the issue. We can read newspapers in their original paper form, or we can read them on microfiche or via a CD-ROM. Equally, we can obtain documents through website pages, apps on mobile devices or email, and this does not, of itself, have a bearing on the use of the output as a document for research. Websites, though, can be treated as documents in their own right. Home pages, etc. can be treated as a form of document, and their content analysed in terms of the text and images they contain. In effect, they can be treated like *online documents*.

Access to documentary sources

Probably the greatest attraction of using documentary sources is their accessibility. To get hold of the material the researcher needs only to visit the library or go online via a computer. The Internet provides the researcher with access to a host of government sites that provide a wide range of information on social and economic factors. In the UK a list of government websites can be found at https://www.gov.uk, and in the USA there are sites such as http://www.gpo.gov that offer entry points to search for official data and government publications. This means that vast amounts of information are conveniently available without much cost, without much delay, without prior appointment, without the need for authorization and without any likelihood of ethical problems.

However, as Table 15.1 indicates, while access to documents in the public domain is certainly straightforward, there are times researchers might need to use materials whose availability is deliberately restricted. One obvious reason for restricting access is to make money. Those who hold the information do so for commercial reasons and, when this is the case, researchers need to pay for access to the data. Many academic articles and market research data, for example, will only be accessible on condition of payment of money.

Table 15.1 Access to documents for research

Availability	Types of document	Access via	Typical use
Public domain	Books, journals, official statistics, some company records	Internet, libraries	Academic research and consultancy
Commercial	Market research data, archive material	Payment	Academic research and consultancy
Restricted access	Medical records, police files, internal memos, personal papers/diaries, some tax accounts	Negotiations with gatekeepers, sponsors	Academic research and consultancy
Secret	Military plans, Cabinet minutes, corporate plans, records of illegal trade	Insider knowledge, participation, deception	Investigative journalism, fraud detection, undercover work

Access will be restricted, as well, when the documents contain sensitive information. When researchers want access to such documents it is likely that they will need to enter into negotiations with those who hold the data in order to persuade them to allow the researcher the privilege of access to the material. Documents such as police files and medical records, and certain kinds of company reports and memos, might rightly be considered sensitive and confidential by those who 'own' them, and they are only likely to grant access when they are convinced that the researcher will honour the confidentiality of the material and use it in a way that will not harm the interests of anyone concerned.

Good practice: Gaining access to documentary sources of data

Researchers should check in advance whether their access to documentary data sources will need authorization or require payment. The feasibility of using documentary research should then be assessed bearing in mind any restrictions these factors might impose on full access to the documents.

Access to information on the Internet can be controlled by the actions of certain strategic 'gatekeepers' who can influence what information is made available and who is allowed access to that information. Internet researchers need to be sensitive to the role of 'moderators' and 'webmasters' in filtering the information. Some sites, but by no means all, are controlled by people whose role it is to monitor the content of the site and the conduct of those who use it. Moderators (mailing lists, chat rooms) and webmasters (email servers) acting in this capacity are effectively 'gatekeepers'. They have the power to deny access to the site and might need to be persuaded of the relevance and worthiness of a proposed piece of research before they will grant access.

Then, of course, there are documents to which researchers will be denied access – documents considered to be secret. Companies may have secret strategic plans regarded as too sensitive for even a bona fide researcher. The government wishes to keep many documents secret 'in the national interest'. Records of illegal activities, whether a drug smuggler's diary or a second set of books for VAT returns, are extremely unlikely to be opened to the researcher. To get access to such secret documents requires the approach of investigative journalism or participant observation with a degree of deception and covert infiltration being used.

The credibility of documentary sources

For the purposes of research, documentary sources should never be accepted at face value. Their validity is something that needs to be established and it is important that any documents used as sources of data are evaluated in relation to four basic criteria:

Authenticity. Is it the genuine article? Is it the real thing? Can we be satisfied that the document is what it purports to be – not a fake or a forgery?

Representativeness. Is the document typical of its type? Does it represent a typical instance of the thing it portrays? Is the document complete? Has it been edited? Is the extract treated 'in context'?

Meaning. Is the meaning of the words clear and unambiguous? Are there hidden meanings? Does the document contain argot and subtle codes? Are there meanings which involve 'what's left unsaid' or 'reading between the lines'?
Validity. Is it accurate? Is it free from bias and errors?

Official statistics and government publications

Official statistics and government publications provide an enticing source of documentary data for social researchers. This is because they tend to be free and can be accessed readily via the Internet. Added to this, their status as 'official' documents would suggest that they can be treated as credible sources of information: objective, complete and up to date. Social researchers, however, need to exercise a bit of caution on this matter. Although it might be reasonable to use official statistics and government publications with a degree of confidence, it would be naive in research terms to simply accept information from such sources as self-evidently true and beyond the need for scrutiny.

A lot depends on *the extent to which the event or thing being measured is clear-cut and straightforward*. The more clear-cut the event, the more confidence we can have in the data. Official statistics on things such as births, deaths, marriages and divorce, therefore, are things which can be treated as pretty accurate and complete. Whether or not someone is born or dies, whether a marriage or divorce occurs, these are events that happen or don't happen, with little scope for 'creative accounting' or biased interpretation.

Things like unemployment, homelessness and ill health, though, are far less clear-cut. There are a number of ways of defining these things and this opens up the possibility of disputes about whether the statistics depict real levels of unemployment, etc., or whether they offer a picture biased by the nature of the definition that has been used. In this instance, a lot depends on *whether there are vested interests behind the statistics that are produced*. When those who produce the statistics stand to gain or lose on the basis of what the figures reveal, the astute researcher should treat them with some caution. Trade figures, hospital waiting lists, sales figures, all have consequences for people who want or need the statistics to reveal a particular trend. And official statistics are not immune to the point. Governments can have a vested interest in a variety of statistics, from trade to inflation, from unemployment to health.

A third factor that can affect the credibility of official documents is *the extent to which the statistics are the outcome of a series of decisions and judgements made by people*. The more the statistics are the end-product of a series of choices made by people – choices that involve judgement and discretion – the more the data can be regarded as a 'social construction' rather than a detached, impartial picture of the real world.

Example: the social construction of crime statistics

Crime statistics are based on those crimes that people decide to report to the police. A large proportion of crimes, however, never gets reported. Petty crimes may go unreported. Theft is frequently not reported, particularly when people see no chance of recovering their property and when the property is not insured. (If a claim is to be made through insurance, a 'crime number' is needed from the police and this motivates people to report the crime.) Many crimes are not discovered and so do not get reported (e.g. embezzlement). There are 'crimes with no victims' where, unless someone is caught by the police no record of the offence will ever appear (e.g. recreational drug use). In the case of some crimes there may be an unwillingness of the victim to complain because of the accruing stigma (e.g. rape) or fear of retribution.

Even when a crime is reported to the police there is a level of discretion open to them about how they interpret things and whether to formalize the matter. A lot of 'crime' is sorted out informally, without ever entering the system as a recorded crime. Even when it is in the system, the nature of the offence is open to some degree of interpretation. From the police officer receiving the report onwards, there is some scope for leeway and interpretation about (1) whether to prosecute; (2) what kind of offence gets noted; (3) whether a caution is given; (4) whether the matter proceeds to court; and (5) whether the prosecution is successful or not. At each stage, people are taking decisions, using discretion and making judgements. Overall, these can have a marked impact on the end-product – the official statistics. It means that there will be a huge difference (in the case of crime) between the real level of crime in society and the figures that get published by the government as 'the crime rate'. It is estimated that recorded crime may be as little as one-fifth of 'actual' crime.

Records of meetings

Records of meetings, whether publicly available or on restricted access, purport to depict things that have happened in a full and accurate manner. However, there is ample evidence that such records tend to be partial – in both senses of the word. They will tend to be selective in terms of what they report, emphasizing some things and ignoring others, and thus recording only part of the overall event. They will also tend to reflect a particular interpretation of what happened, recording events from a particular angle. We should remember that when such records are produced as part of public accountability there will be a tendency to be cautious about what is recorded. Things might have been said 'off the record' or following 'Don't minute this but ... '. The records, in other words, may be subtly edited to exclude things which might render people vulnerable to criticism when the record is published. *The researcher, therefore, needs to be cautious about accepting such records at face value.* Publicly available records reflect upon matters in a way that is publicly acceptable at a given time and in a given social sphere. They tend to offer a version of reality massaged to meet public expectations.

Documents on the Internet

The credibility of documents available on the Internet poses a particular problem for researchers, not least because there are few restrictions on what is placed on the Internet. This calls for particular vigilance on the part of researchers to ensure that any documents from the Internet used for research are evaluated carefully in terms of their credibility. As well as the checks that relate to all documents, additional scrutiny should be given to the websites hosting the documents, in particular:

- The *authoritativeness* of the site. A university or government site might add some credibility to the source, whereas a private web page might need to be viewed with caution.
- The *trustworthiness* of the site. Does the site convey a sense of serious and legitimate purpose? Does it contain suitable disclaimers and explicit statements about its purpose?
- How *up to date* the site is. Attention should be given to how regularly the pages are updated. Is the date of last updating visible and, crucially, is it recent?
- The *popularity* of the site. The extent of interest in a website and the size of its audience can suggest something about the site's recognition and popularity. These can be gauged by the number of times people have logged on to that site – the number of 'hits' on the site.

Good practice: Always assess the credibility of documentary sources

Before being used in research, documents should always be checked in terms of their credibility. Researchers should evaluate documents asking:

- What purpose was the document written for?
- Who produced the document? What was the status of the author and did he or she have a particular belief or persuasion that would colour the version of things?
- If it reports on events, was it a first-hand report directly witnessed by the author? How long after the event was the document written?
- When was the document produced? In what social context and climate?

Image-based research

The documents referred to so far have been text based. There are, however, alternative kinds of documentary data available to social researchers. Visual images can be used as data in their own right – distinct from text, numbers or sounds as a potential source of research information. Just like other documents, visual images can prove to be valuable for the purposes of the research in terms of:

- the factual information they contain;
- how they represent things (the symbolism and hidden meanings communicated through the document or image).

Types of image

For practical reasons there has been a tendency to concentrate on two-dimensional 'still' images, such as photographs, as the source of image-based data. Photographs are relatively inexpensive. They also lend themselves to analysis and reproduction alongside more conventional text-based research, e.g. in printed journals or academic dissertations. Potentially, though, there are a wide variety of visual images that could be used. There have been adventurous attempts on occasion to explore the possibilities of moving images and even three-dimensional objects (Banks 2007; Emmison et al. 2012; Banks and Zeitlyn 2015; Rose 2016) (Table 15.2).

Table 15.2   Potential sources of image-based documentary data

Still	Movie	Object
Photographs, drawings, advertisements, graffiti	Video recording, archive film	Cultural artefacts, clothing and fashion items, built environment and places, body signs/language

The use of 'created' images

Researchers can generate images specifically for the purposes of their investigation – so-called *created* images. The visual images, in this sense, provide primary source data. These images can be valuable as a means of recording things. Researchers can make records of events, people, cultures, and so on by photographing, filming or drawing them. Such visual records provide an alternative to tape recordings (*sound*), an alternative to the use of written documents such as field notes, diaries or minutes (*text*) and an alternative to the use of quantitative data such as figures from questionnaires or statistics based on systematic observation (*numbers*).

> **Link up with** Analysis of image-based data, p. 321.

In order to create images for research, it is important to use equipment that will produce material of sufficiently high quality for the purposes of data analysis. Cameras/phones for photographs and camcorders for videos come in a range of technical specifications and prices and the researcher needs to have the resources to use equipment that is good enough to do the job.

There are also a range of social and cultural issues that need to be considered. For example, filming objects such as buildings, transport facilities and artefacts would appear to be fairly unproblematic as a means of data collection. There are circumstances, however, where filming and photography are not allowed. Some countries might regard it as a security threat, depending on the location. There are issues of privacy to be considered, and in galleries and museums there are often restrictions on photography and filming of the artefacts. Forethought needs to be given to the legal and cultural context within which data collection is to take place in order to minimize the risk that the filming or photography of specific objects will be regarded as an offence or as offensive.

When the image-based research involves people, there is all the more need for sensitivity to the social and cultural context. As Prosser and Schwartz (1998: 119) point out, researchers need to appreciate that 'making pictures can be a threatening act (amply demonstrated by the metaphors photography invokes: we "load", "aim" and "shoot").' The act of being 'captured' on film can be perceived as threatening even if the researcher's intention is benign, and this likelihood has two important repercussions for the process of data collection:

| Link up with
| The observer
| effect, p. 72. |

- It can *limit access* to research sites. If people feel threatened, if they feel that there is an invasion of privacy, they might well refuse to cooperate with the research.
- It can cause people to *become self-conscious* and to act in a way that they would not do normally.

Bearing this in mind, researchers need to be conscious of the way their actions will be perceived. Consideration needs to be given to the impact of things like:

- *The equipment*. Flash photography will be more evident than daylight photography, and a discreet small digital camera will be less visible than bulky, professional camcorder equipment.
- *The situation*. Certain events involve film records more normally than others. Ceremonial events, for instance, might allow the use of created images by the researcher in a way that would not be the case in more personal, intimate circumstances.
- *The people involved*. People who live 'in the public eye', those with high-profile jobs and people like media celebrities, will probably be fairly comfortable in the knowledge that they are being filmed or photographed because it is a routine part of their working lives. They might, however, reserve the right to privacy on occasions when they are 'off duty', regarding this as their personal and private life.
- *Personalities*. Extroverts and publicity seekers will be likely to adore the attention of the camera in a way that more introverted and camera-shy people will not.

These factors come into play, of course, only when people are aware that they are being photographed or filmed. This need not always be the case. The researcher might choose to undertake covert research, in which the process of filming is kept secret from those who are being studied. There are particular ethical issues that arise in this case and to gain approval from any relevant authorizing body (e.g. an ethics committee) a strong case will need to be made for *not* seeking informed consent from those being studied. This pertains to a range of social research methods but the fullness of the data captured on film can make people all the more defensive and reticent to co-operate – more than would be the case if the research relied on things like interviews or questionnaire data.

Link up with Chapter 18, Research ethics.

The use of 'found' images

Documentary research can be based on images that already exist rather than ones produced by the researcher for the specific purposes of the research. They can use *found* images that have been produced by other people for reasons not directly connected with the researcher's investigation.

The kind of images used depends largely on the subject discipline of the researcher. Media studies and marketing often use advertisements and newspaper photographs. Anthropologists, historians and sociologists will use images of groups and cultural events portrayed using film, photographs, paintings, graffiti or artefacts. Such items contain a visual record that can be used to provide factual information about groups or events, or the images can be interpreted to provide some better understanding of the ideas and lifestyles that generated the images.

As a source of data, 'found' images sidestep a number of problems associated with the data-gathering process for 'created' images. Technical issues about equipment and practical issues of access to locations, for instance, no longer arise since the image already exists. Immediately, this suggests that the use of found images is an attractive proposition for the social researcher because it requires less skill to produce and may well prove less expensive if it saves fieldwork, travel and production costs. Equally attractively, it overcomes the ethical concerns of getting informed consent in those cases where the image involves living people. Added to this, the Internet offers a huge stock of downloadable images that social researchers can potentially use. No fieldwork and no travel are required.

However, the ease with which found images can be obtained should not seduce the researcher into opting for their use without recognizing that there are also some specific issues that need to be weighed against the ease and cost factors – issues surrounding the authenticity of the images and copyright protection.

Authenticity

As with other documentary data, the social researcher who uses visual images will want to feel certain about the authenticity of the image. This is particularly the case with 'found' images that are to be used as a source of factual information. The researcher needs to be wary about whether the image has been tampered with, changed or edited from the original. Computer software makes this increasingly simple to do. Photographic images, in particular, are relatively easy to alter and the researcher should not take it as a matter of trust that the image is genuine. As Loizos (2000: 95) warns:

> One fallacy is implied by the phrase 'the camera cannot lie'. Humans, the agents who wield cameras, can and do lie: ... they can distort the evidential recording capacity of visual data just as readily as they can distort written words.

Copyright

Ownership of an image is an important issue particularly if the image is to be reproduced and made publicly available through the process of research. Where the image has been created by the researcher there is generally not too much of a problem. The image is usually owned by the researcher. However, this may not always be the case. In some cases ownership of the image might be claimed on behalf of the person or event portrayed. However, as Banks and Zeitlyn (2015: 168) note, this issue is 'relevant largely to representations of celebrities, those deemed likely to have a financial interest in the use of their representations'.

If the image already exists, there is a good chance that it 'belongs' to some person, company or institution, in which case it is necessary to obtain permission to use the image. At one extreme this might be a fairly informal thing. If, for example, the image to be used is a personal photograph from a family album the necessary permission could involve little more than getting approval (preferably in writing) from the owner for the use of the image for research purposes. At the other extreme, images based on advertisements, or works of art, or drawn from news media, entertainment magazines or the Internet, are the kind of thing that will probably require a very formal request to the copyright holder for permission to reproduce the image. If the copyright holder agrees to this, it might be conditional on the payment of a fee. The fee can be prohibitively large and it is important to make it clear when requesting permission that the image is to be used for the purposes of small-scale, private research from which there will be no monetary gain. Fees might be waived or reduced under these circumstances, though this will depend on the nature of the image and the policies of the particular copyright holder.

If the image to be used has an obscure origin and the copyright holder cannot be traced there is a standard solution to the problem which consists of making a clear statement at the start of any report or dissertation along the lines that 'Efforts have been made to obtain permission from copyright holders of the (photographic images) used. Where the copyright owners have not been traced the author invites further information from anyone concerned and will seek to remedy the situation.' This does presume, of course, that rigorous efforts have indeed been made and the statement should not be used as a way to avoid the work of tracing copyright holders.

Key point: Copyright and visual images

Special care should be taken to ensure that the use of visual images for research purposes, especially those downloaded from the Internet, do not infringe copyright laws.

 Caution: The use of image-based data

Despite claims that contemporary society has become more of a 'visual culture' than in the past, and despite some signs of a growing interest in visual research, the use of image-based data remains relatively uncommon in the social sciences. Part of the reason for this is that film, video and three-dimensional images do not readily fit the medium within which research data and analyses are normally presented. They may not fit in dissertations, journals or computer documents that favour a two-dimensional, text-based format. Although digital technology now makes it easy to incorporate pictures and video data within such documents it is clear that image-based research remains somewhat marginalized and, as yet, struggles to achieve a parity of status in the social sciences with research whose data take the form of numbers or words. The project researcher undertaking small-scale research might do well to bear this in mind.

Advantages of documentary research

Access to data

Vast amounts of information are held in documents. Depending on the nature of the documents, most researchers will find access to the sources relatively easy and inexpensive.

Cost-effective

Documentary research provides a cost-effective method of getting data, particularly large-scale data such as those provided by official statistics.

Permanence of data

Documents and images generally provide a source of data which is permanent and available in a form that can be checked by others. The data are open to public scrutiny.

Disadvantages of documentary research

Credibility of the source

Researchers need to be discerning about the information they use. They need to evaluate the authority of the source and the procedures used to produce the original data in order to gauge the credibility of the documents or images. This is not always easy. Internet documents, in particular, need special scrutiny. Information found on the Internet can be up-to-date and good quality stuff. However, just as easily, it can be out-of-date, poor quality material because there is little control over what is placed on the Internet.

Secondary data

When researchers use documents as a source of data, they generally rely on something which has been produced for other purposes and not for the specific aims of the investigation.

Social constructions

Documents and images can sometimes owe more to the interpretations of those who produce them than to an objective picture of reality.

Further reading

Banks, M. and Zeitlyn, D. (2015) *Visual Methods in Social Research,* 2nd edn. London: Sage.

Plummer, K. (2001) *Documents of Life 2: An Invitation to a Critical Humanism,* 2nd edn. London: Sage.

Prior, L. (2003) *Using Documents in Social Research.* London: Sage.

Rose, G. (2016) *Visual Methodologies: An Introduction to Researching with Visual Materials,* 4th edn. London: Sage.

Scott, J. (1990) *A Matter of Record: Documentary Sources in Social Research.* Cambridge: Polity.

Spencer, S. (2011) *Visual Research Methods in the Social Sciences: Awakening Visions.* London: Routledge.

Checklist for the use of documents (text and visual images)

When undertaking documentary research you should feel confident about answering 'yes' to the following questions: ☑

1 Am I satisfied that the documents/images are genuine in terms of what they purport to be (not drafts, forgeries, misleading second versions, etc.)? ☐

2 Have I considered the credibility of the documents or images in terms of:

- their source (published book, journal article, official statistics)? ☐
- their author or creator (status, role, in a position to know)? ☐
- their sponsorship (organization, funding, pressure group)? ☐
- the accessibility of the information they use (public domain, restricted, secret)? ☐

3 Have website sources been evaluated in terms of their accuracy and how recently they have been updated (where applicable)? ☐

4 Am I satisfied that I have taken account of possible bias in the document or image arising from:

- its purpose (description, theory, persuasion)? ☐
- how representative it is (typical, extreme)? ☐
- the editing and selection of extracts used in it? ☐
- its interpretation of facts or theories? ☐
- sensitivity to the information or image it contains? ☐

5 Have I provided full details of the sources of the texts or images used? ☐

6 Has the research avoided contravening copyright laws? ☐

Part **3**

Data analysis

The purpose of analysing something is to gain a better understanding of it. Through a detailed examination of the thing that is being studied the analysis aims to do the following:

- *describe* its constituent elements; or
- *explain* how it works; or
- *interpret* what it means.

Description

A description can provide the basis for research in its own right. There are types of social research such as ethnography and phenomenology where the researcher's aim is to portray particular cultures or experiences in depth and in detail, allowing the texture and subtlety of the situation to become visible to the reader. In this case the description is valuable in its own right through the way it allows new insights to be gained. On other occasions descriptions are used as a starting point for research – a platform for a subsequent analysis based on explanation or interpretation. The logic here is that there needs to be a clear vision of what the thing entails before it is possible to give an accurate explanation or interpretation of how it works. Either way, whether the description is to be used in its own right or as a prelude to further investigation, the emphasis is on providing details about:

- *What* the thing looks like: measurements, components, appearance, duration, etc.
- *When* it happened: dates, context of other events, etc.
- *Who* was involved: the individuals, the demographics of the sample/population, etc.
- *How often* it happens: frequency, duration, etc.

Explanation

An explanation looks for rules and regularities that underlie the occurrence of particular social phenomena. The aim is to find out how things work by looking for evidence of cause–effect relationships in the data. Once the researcher has discovered the causes of specific behaviour, events or interactions there is the possibility of predicting how and when things might happen in the future – a prospect which has proved very enticing for disciplines such as economics and psychology but which has also been relished by many researchers in areas of health, education and business studies. What these researchers are trying to discover is:

- *How* things are connected: associations and correlations, etc.
- *Why* things happen: underlying mechanisms, causes, etc.
- *When* things will happen: probability of recurrence, projections for the future, etc.

Interpretation

Interpretation, like explanation, is interested in patterns and regularities that lie behind the occurrence of social phenomena. The difference is that interpretive researchers see their analysis as a matter of providing an understanding rather than providing something that is an objective, universal truth. Interpretivists are still interested in gaining knowledge about how and why things happen, but they are sceptical about the prospects of being able to provide explanations that can ever be purely objective. They argue that, to a greater or lesser extent, theories must inevitably reflect the cultural and historical context within which the research takes place and be shaped by the personal values and experiences of the researcher. Any theories that are produced, it follows, will be 'value laden' rather than objective. The consequence of such reasoning is that for interpretivists the aim of analysis is to produce a viable account of how things work (rather than discover regularities that exist objectively in the social world). Bearing this in mind, they tend to focus on things like:

- *How* and *why* things happen: in terms of possible mechanisms, potential causes, plausible theories, etc.
- *Who* undertook the research: researcher biography, identity and experiences.
- *When and where* the study took place: cultural and historical context, social values.
- *What* alternative explanations exist: comparisons with competing theories.

The process of data analysis

The analysis of research data tends to follow a process involving five stages. The stages can be seen in relation to both quantitative and qualitative data, as Table P3.1 shows. However, it also shows that there are differences between quantitative and qualitative data analysis, with quantitative approaches tending to shape their data more consciously and more explicitly in the earlier stages of the process compared with qualitative approaches. More details on the specific approaches to data analysis are provided in Chapters 16 and 17.

Table P3.1   Five stages of data analysis

		Quantitative data	Qualitative data
1	Data preparation	Coding (which normally takes place before data collection) Categorizing the data Checking the numbers	Cataloguing the text or visual data Transcribing the text Preparation of data and loading to software (if applicable)
2	Initial exploration of the data	Look for obvious trends or correlations	Look for obvious recurrent themes or issues Add notes to the data. Write memos to capture ideas
3	Analysis of the data	Use of statistical tests (e.g. descriptive statistics, factor analysis, cluster analysis) Link to research questions or hypotheses	Code the data Group the codes into categories or themes Comparison of categories and themes Look for concepts (or fewer, more abstract categories) that encapsulate the categories
4	Presentation and display of the data	Tables Figures Written interpretation of the statistical findings	Written interpretation of the findings Illustration of points by quotes and pictures Use of visual models, figures and tables
5	Validation of the data	External benchmarks Internal consistency Comparison with alternative explanations	Data and method triangulation Member validation Comparison with alternative explanations

Source: Adapted from Creswell and Plano Clarke (2007: 129, table 7.1).

16 | Quantitative data

*The use of quantitative data · Sources of quantitative data ·
Types of quantitative data: nominal, ordinal, interval, ratio ·
How much data? · Analysing one variable · Likert scales ·
Analysing two variables · Presenting the data using tables and
charts · Tables and charts: which ones to choose? · The quality
of the data: validity and reliability · Advantages of using
quantitative data · Disadvantages of using quantitative data ·
Further reading · Checklist for the analysis of quantitative data*

The analysis of quantitative data need not require the use of advanced mathematics or complicated statistical tests. For most practical purposes project researchers can rely on basic mathematics and simple 'descriptive' statistics in order to:

- summarize the profile of the data (frequencies, mid-points, spread);
- explore connections between parts of the data (correlations and associations);
- present the data and portray the findings (charts, graphs, tables).

For this reason, there is no attempt in this chapter to cover more advanced statistical procedures that use quantitative data for testing hypotheses or forecasting outcomes. For those who want to study the statistical analysis of quantitative data in more depth there are many textbooks and online resources that are readily available, and reference should be made to such sources.

The use of quantitative data

There is strength in numbers and quantitative data can provide a powerful and persuasive foundation for social research. This is because quantitative data are based on precise measurements that can be used to address crucial questions such as:

- How many? based on a count of the number of items;
- How often? based on the frequency of items;
- How big?' based on the size of items (smallest, largest, average);
- What proportion? based on ratios, percentages or fractions;
- How does it compare? based on profiles involving the mid-point and spread of data;
- Is there an association between items? based on evidence of a correlation.

Sources of quantitative data

A variety of methods can be used to produce quantitative data. Closed questions in a questionnaire are the most likely source for project researchers engaged with small-scale social research but, as Table 16.1 indicates, quantitative data can come from particular types of interviews, observation and documents as well.

Table 16.1   Sources of quantitative data

Source of data	Research method	See pages
Answers to closed questions	Questionnaires	194–6
Content analysis of transcripts	Interviews	312–14
Measurements from experiments	} Observation	70–3
Observation schedule used with events		226–8
Content analysis of secondary source data	Documents	245–7

Types of quantitative data: nominal, ordinal, interval, ratio

From a researcher's point of view one of the main attractions of quantitative data is that the numbers provide a *precise, definite measure* of the thing being investigated. Used correctly, this can be true. However, it is possible to use quantitative data wrongly and to draw conclusions from the data that are unwarranted. Principally, this arises from the fact that *numbers can stand for different kinds of things* – a point highlighted by Stevens's (1946) distinction between nominal, ordinal, interval and ratio scales of measurement. Stevens identified a hierarchy within quantitative data in which *interval* and *ratio* data are recognized as 'real' numbers that lend themselves readily to mathematical analysis, while *ordinal* and *nominal* data need to be treated with caution because they are subject to certain restrictions in terms of the kinds of analysis that can be used.

Nominal data (also known as 'categorical' data)

There are occasions when numbers are actually nothing more than labels – the equivalent of a name. The number 14 when it appears on the door of a house, for instance, is the equivalent of a tag such as 'Rose Cottage'. Likewise, the number 31 on the front of a bus simply tells us which route it is on. In themselves such numbers are of little value in terms of measurement because they are effectively a *name* rather than a real number.

We can, however, measure such 'names' in certain ways and thus produce nominal data. Continuing the example above, the number 31 actually designates a *category* of bus – it is a label that is attributable to all those that operate on that specific route. It is quite possible to add up the number of times such 'labels' occur and to produce some valuable descriptive data about the quantity of 31 buses on a route and their frequency – data that can be compared with other bus routes.

In social research typical examples of nominal data occur when quantitative data are collected on groups of people who share a specific quality or identity, such as an occupation (e.g. nurse, teacher, bricklayer), marital status (e.g. single, married, widowed, divorced), illness (e.g. diabetes, lung cancer, dementia) or ethnic group (e.g. White, South Asian, African-Caribbean). Nominal data also includes quantitative data generated through questions where people choose between two options (e.g. yes/no, smoker/non-smoker, male/female). This is known as *dichotomous data*. In either case nominal data does not measure the thing itself. It measures the frequency with which things 'of that type' occur. It measures categories of things, and this is why such data are commonly referred to as *categorical* data.

When the quantitative data are 'nominal' they can be analysed in some ways but not others. They can be used to talk about amounts and frequencies of things and provide answers to questions such as 'How many?', 'How often?' and 'What proportion?' When it comes to 'averages', however, there are limitations to what can be said on the basis of this kind of data. With nominal data, for example, it makes no sense to calculate the average of a city's bus routes, or the average of different types of illness or the average of two occupations.

Ordinal data (also known as 'ranked' data)

Ordinal data measures the *rank order* of items or events relative to others. This might be the *order* in which things occur; which comes first, second, third and so on. It might represent a *preference* of choices: favourite, next favourite . . . least favourite. It could be some form of *level*: highest, middle, lowest. It could be measure of *quality*: which is the best, which second best and so on. Or it could be a measure of *magnitude*: largest, next largest and so on through to the smallest.

In research terms, ordinal data appears routinely in connection with research findings on things like examination grades (A–E) and customer satisfaction ratings and opinion surveys using 'Likert scales' (see below). As with nominal/categorical data it is possible to calculate the frequency with which items or events occur, but ordinal data adds a little more precision in the sense that the researcher can analyse the data in terms of some relevant numerical order.

> **Link up with Likert scales, p. 278.**

However, although the numbers assigned to the ranks might encourage the idea that they can be treated as ordinary numbers, it would be wrong to simply presume this because, in fact, we cannot know that the distances between the ordinal measures 1, 2, 3, 4 and 5 are equal.

Interval and ratio data (also known as 'scale' data)

With interval data the numbers reflect known amounts of difference in the thing being measured as well some measure of order or sequence. An obvious example would be data collected for the years 1977, 1987, 1997, 2007 and 2017. These dates not only differ in terms of being earlier or later than one another, they are also earlier or later by a known timespan interval. *Ratio data* exists where not only are the 'distances' between data points proportionate but also they exist on a scale that has a 'true zero'. In the physical sciences they measure properties such as length, height and weight. In the social sciences, they are quantitative measures of things like income (e.g. £ per year), productivity (e.g. units produced per month), mortality (e.g. deaths per 1000 of the population) and migration (e.g. number of people leaving a country to live elsewhere).

The distinction between interval and ratio data is a technical one that does not generally affect the data analysis significantly: they are often treated as the same thing and referred to simply as 'scale' data. They can both be considered 'real' numbers in the sense that they correspond with naturally occurring properties of the thing they are measuring. Interval and ratio data have the most potential in terms of mathematical manipulation and statistical analysis. They can be multiplied and divided, and they can be averaged in a way that can help the researcher to make sense of the data that have been collected.

Example 16.1

Types of quantitative data

Suppose we are interested in buying a second-hand car and that our budget is limited to £17,000. The decision about which car to buy is likely to include types of data that correspond with the different scales of measurement.

Measurement type		
Categorical	Nominal	Type of car (manufacturer, body type, colour).
Rank order	Ordinal	Car's condition rated as 'good', 'average' or 'poor'
Scale	Interval	Year of manufacture (e.g. 2013)
	Ratio	Running costs per year (including tax, insurance, servicing, fuel)
		Price of the car (£0 to £17,000)

 Caution: Types of measurement and the analysis of quantitative data

Although it has become conventional to warn researchers about the need to distinguish between different types of quantitative data, there is some debate among statisticians about the *practical* significance of the hierarchy and the extent to which social researchers actually need to trouble themselves with the distinction between scales of measurement (Velleman and Wilkinson 1993; Gorard 2006; Walker 2010). Without getting embroiled in the finer technicalities of this debate the best general advice for project researchers using quantitative data is that they should:

- be *aware of the different types of quantitative data;*
- *think* about the kind of thing that is being measured (quantified) and what the numbers represent;
- *be cautious,* and avoid any attempt to analyse the data in a way that is not sensible or justifiable.

How much data?

In principle, quantitative analysis works better with large amounts of data, and the normal advice for researchers wanting to use quantitative data is to 'think big'. In general, it is good practice to collect as large an amount of quantitative data as possible.

Having made this point we need to recognize that small-scale research projects, by their nature, face constraints that limit the amount of data that can be collected and analysed. Whereas large-scale projects are likely to operate in the realms of 1,000 or more, small-scale projects are likely to be working with less than 100. This poses the question of whether there should be a minimum number when it comes to the use of quantitative data, an absolute amount below which the use of quantitative data should be avoided. Unfortunately, there is no simple rule on the matter. There are, however, certain guidelines to good practice that should be observed.

Good practice: There should be no attempt to exaggerate the amount of data.

When working with less than 100 items of data project researchers should be particularly careful to ensure that:

- There is no attempt to conceal the actual numbers involved. Researchers must not attempt to disguise the fact that the dataset is quite small, for example by presenting findings as percentages. Instead, it is good practice to show the findings just as numbers (e.g. 15 out of 25 respondents said . . .) or possibly using both the proportion and the actual numbers (e.g. 60 per cent, n = 15).
- Any generalizations from the data are treated cautiously, recognizing that the data might not be representative. Researchers should use good sense in terms of the nature of the claims that are made on the basis of the limited amounts of data.
- Any statistical test that is used is one that works with relatively small numbers (e.g. *chi-square* or *t-test* described later in the chapter). In terms of the use of statistical techniques some work quite well with relatively low amounts of data and in this context it is common to find reference to a minimum figure of 30.

Analysing one variable

When researchers focus their attention on a single quantitative variable they are interested in the patterns of variation the data might display. Such 'univariate' analysis explores the profile of a single variable on the premise that there is much to be gained from getting a clear picture of things like frequencies, mid-points and the dispersion of the data

Frequencies

To get a clear picture of the frequency with which events or items occur it is likely that the raw data will need to be transformed in a way that helps to make sense of the data. As Table 16.2 shows, it is rather difficult to make sense of raw data when the number of items goes above 10.

Initially, it is some help to construct an *array of the raw data*, i.e. to arrange the data in order. As Table 16.3 shows, this immediately helps in terms of getting some grasp of what the data mean.

Table 16.2   Raw data example

Days absent from work through illness during the previous year, 30 employees

1	12	0	9	4	7
5	3	6	15	10	8
4	36	3	13	3	3
3	6	3	6	0	0
10	5	8	0	10	2

Source: Human Resources Dept. Healthy Life Insurance Co.

Table 16.3   Array of raw data example

Days absent from work through illness during the previous year, 30 employees

0	2	3	5	8	10
0	3	3	6	8	12
0	3	4	6	9	13
0	3	4	6	10	15
1	3	5	7	10	36

Source: Human Resources Dept. Healthy Life Insurance Co.

A further stage in organizing the data is to make a *tally of the frequencies* (see Table 16.4). This gives a clearer picture of which items or events are the most common and is far better in terms of being able to 'read' the data. It immediately suggests certain things about the data and invites questions about why certain things might occur more often than others.

Table 16.4   Tally of frequencies example

Days absent from work through illness during the previous year, 30 employees

Days	Frequency	Days	Frequency	Days	Frequency
0	4	5	2	10	3
1	1	6	3	12	1
2	1	7	1	13	1
3	6	8	2	15	1
4	2	9	1	36	1

Source: Human Resources Dept. Healthy Life Insurance Co.

Where there are a large number of frequencies, the researcher can organize the data by grouping the frequencies (see Table 16.5). Such *grouped frequency distributions* are very valuable because they reduce the number of categories that are presented to the reader, thus simplifying the task of interpreting the information. In a sense, the findings are pre-packaged by the researcher so that the meaning of the data is easier to comprehend.

Table 16.5 Grouped frequency distribution example

Days absent from work through illness during the previous year, 30 employees

Group	Frequency
0–2 days	6
3–5 days	10
6–8 days	6
9–11 days	4
12–14 days	2
15+ days	2

Source: Human Resources Dept. Healthy Life Insurance Co.

 Caution: The effect of grouping the data

When the data are grouped they are no longer 'raw' data. Splitting the data into groups may make the data easier to understand, but the groups themselves are not generally inherent in the data. The groups are defined by the researcher. They reflect choices and decisions on the part of the researcher and alternative groupings might be possible which could provide a rather different vision of what the data mean.

Central tendency (the average, the mid-point, the most common)

A measure of central tendency adds another dimension to our understanding of the profile of the data: it tells us something about 'the middle'. There are, though, three different questions we could ask at this point: 'What is the average?', 'What is the mid-point? or 'What is most common?', and researchers need to be very clear when dealing with measures of central tendency which one they are referring to.

The mean (the arithmetic average)

This is what most people have in mind when, in common parlance, they think about 'the average'. It is a measure of central tendency based on the arithmetic average. This indicator of central tendency is useful because it is mathematically precise and because it accords with some notion of what the data suggest is 'normal'.

How to calculate the mean

Add together all the values for a particular variable. This total is then divided by the number of cases.

In the example of days absent from work through illness we can calculate from Table 16.2 that the total number of days lost is 195. Dividing this by the number of employees ($n = 30$) provides us with a mean of 6.5 days per employee over the previous year.

It is worth bearing in mind, though, that the mean can be affected by a small number of *extreme values ('outliers')* – values that might be very different from the rest of the distribution. The one employee who was absent for 36 days in the previous year effectively distorts the average. If this employee were to be 'taken out of the equation' the mean number of days absent through illness would drop substantially to 5.5 (i.e. 159 divided by 29). Two things will minimize the impact of such outliers. First, a large dataset: an outlier will have less of a distorting impact on a large sample than it will on a small sample, because the extent of its deviation from the rest will get subdivided more and more as the size of the sample gets bigger. Second, and linked to this, calculations of the mean are safest when there are relatively few outliers, and the outliers that do exist have a tendency to balance up and cancel each other out.

The median (the middle value)

The median is the mid-point of a range of values: half of all the values in the distribution lie to one side of it and half to the other. In contrast to the mean the median works well with a low number of values and it offers a quick and easy-to-grasp measure of the central point of the data.

How to calculate the median

Values in the data are placed in either ascending or descending rank order, and the point which lies in the middle of the range is the median. When there are an even numbers of values the median is the mid-point of the two central values.

Continuing the example based on days absent through illness at the Healthy Life Insurance Company the median can be calculated in the following way. There are an even number of items (30 employees) and when the number of days absent are listed from highest to lowest the median lies exactly half way, that is between the 15th and 16th in the list (see Table 16.3). Since in this example both the 15th and 16th on the list lost 5 days through absence, the median is 5.

A benefit of this measure of central tendency is that the median is not affected by extreme values, the 'outliers'. Looking at Table 16.3 it should be clear that the 36 days absent from work recorded in relation to one person, which in terms of the data is an obvious outlier, does not affect the calculation of the median. As far as the median is concerned, that value could lie anywhere between 5 and infinity because its sole significance is that it exists in the top half. Now this, of course, can cut both ways. While the median is unaffected by outliers, it is equally insensitive to the implications of any such extreme values. It effectively eliminates such data from the picture.

The mode (the most common)

When social researchers use the mode as a measure of central tendency they are looking for the value which is *most common*. Looking at Table 16.4 it is easy to see that 6 employees were absent for 3 days during the previous year and that, among the 30 employees, this was the most common period of absence. The mode, in other words, is 3.

> **How to calculate the mode**
>
> Identify the value that occurs most frequently in relation to a specific variable. This is the mode. If there is no value that occurs more frequently than others, then there is no mode.

Like the median, the mode is unaffected by outliers or extreme values. It focuses only on the most common value and ignores all others. As a measure of central tendency it has plenty of scope for use in relation to social data. For example, it makes sense to talk about the most commonly watched soap opera on television, whereas we cannot sensibly talk about the mean or median of a soap opera.

> **Key point: The difference between means, medians and modes**
>
> When describing data, social researchers need to be aware of the difference between the three measures of central tendency and decide which is most appropriate for their specific purpose.

Dispersion (the spread of data)

To describe a set of frequencies it is valuable to provide not only a measure of central tendency but also to give some idea of the way the data are spread out from that central point – *a measure of dispersion*. There are many possibilities for describing the spread of data but the primary ways are (1) to calculate the difference between the highest and lowest values in the dataset (the range), (2) to divide the dataset into portions and compare how evenly things are distributed across the range (fractiles), and (3) to provide a standardized measure which indicates how far, on average, values in the dataset are spread from the mean (the 'standard deviation').

The range

This is the simplest way of describing the spread of data. It is none the less effective, and a valuable method of giving an instant image of the dispersion of the data. Table 16.3 above tells us that in the human resources department of the company there was a range of 36 in terms of days absent from work through illness (i.e. the maximum of 36 minus the minimum of 0).

How to calculate the range

Subtract the minimum value from the maximum value

Although the range is valuable as an instant picture of how wide the data are spread it does have a rather serious limitation as a statistic. It is governed by the extreme values in any set and may consequently give a biased picture of the spread of the values in between the extremes. In the example above the range of 36 is heavily influenced by the outlier value of 36. However, looking at the dataset it is evident that 29 of the 30 in the dataset have a range of just 15. So although reference to the range of values is quick and easy it needs to be used cautiously, with attention paid to any extreme values and the way these might give a misleading impression of the spread.

Fractiles

Fractiles are based on the idea of dividing the data into separate sections (fractions), each of which contains the same number of cases. When *quartiles* are used the data are divided into four sections. *Deciles* operate on the same principle but, as the name suggests, they divide the range into tenths. Where *percentiles* are used the data are divided into 100 equal parts.

How to calculate fractiles

List the values for a variable in terms of magnitude, largest down to smallest. Divide the list into portions, each one containing the same number of data cases.

There are two uses of fractiles for social researchers. First, they can be used for the selection of cases to analyse. Researchers can use them as a way of eliminating extreme highs and lows from the data they wish to examine. For example, by focusing on those cases that come in the second and third quartiles researchers know that they are dealing with exactly half of all the cases and, more than that, they are dealing with the half that are 'in the middle'. This middle part of the range is known as the 'inter-quartile range'. With incomes, for instance, use of the inter-quartile range overcomes the possibility of some very high incomes distorting the overall picture, since these would occur in the top quartile. Likewise, by not using the bottom quartile the researchers would eliminate very low incomes from their analysis.

A second use of fractiles is for comparison. They allow comparisons to be made between those cases that occur at one end of the range and those that occur elsewhere in the range. The top quarter can be compared with the bottom quarter, or the highest 10 per cent with the lowest 10 per cent. The most prominent use of this is in comparisons of income and wealth. The top decile (the 10 per cent of all earners who earn more than the other 90 per cent of earners) can have their pay compared with the 10 per cent of all earners who earn the least. Used in such a way fractiles can be a valuable tool for the social scientist in describing the spread in a frequency distribution.

Standard deviation

To get a clear picture of the dispersion of the data it is useful to know the average amount by which the values are spread out from the middle. This is where the standard deviation (often shortened to s.d.) becomes useful. It is a measure of how far, *on average*, the values for any particular variable are spread out around the mean. The greater the spread of values, the larger the standard deviation.

How to calculate the standard deviation

Spreadsheet packages such as MS Excel have a function that calculates the standard deviation automatically for any given column of figures. This makes life easy and it is likely to be the way that most project researchers will calculate the standard deviation. (But it is important to note the Caution box below.)

Otherwise, the standard deviation can be calculated in six straightforward stages. Refer to Table 16.6 to see how these work. Stage 1, calculate the mean of the values for the variable. Stage 2, for each item subtract this mean value from the actual value. Stage 3, square each of the 'differences from the mean'. (This is necessary because otherwise the positive and the negative differences from the mean, when totalled, would always cancel each other out and the overall total of differences from the mean would inevitably equal zero.) Stage 4, add together all the 'squares of the differences from the mean'. Stage 5, divide this total by the number of cases in the dataset. (This gives us the mean of 'the sum of the squares', which in statistical jargon is known as the 'variance'.) Stage 6, calculate the square-root of this figure (the 'variance'.) This puts the units back to the same as those in the actual distribution being looked at.

Table 16.6 Standard deviation for 'days absent from work'

Values for each item on the variable (n = 30)	Stage 2 Value minus the mean	Stage 3 Square of differences from the mean	
1	–5.5	30.25	
5	–1.5	2.25	
4	–2.5	6.25	
3	–3.5	12.25	
10	3.5	12.25	
12	5.5	30.25	
3	–3.5	12.25	
36	29.5	870.25	
6	–0.5	0.25	
5	–1.5	2.25	
0	–6.5	42.25	
6	–0.5	0.25	
3	–3.5	12.25	
3	–3.5	12.25	
8	1.5	2.25	
9	2.5	6.25	
15	8.5	72.25	
13	6.5	42.25	
6	–0.5	0.25	
0	–6.5	42.25	
4	–2.5	6.25	
10	3.5	12.25	
3	–3.5	12.25	
0	–6.5	42.25	
10	3.5	12.25	
7	0.5	0.25	
8	1.5	2.25	
3	–3.5	12.25	
0	–6.5	42.25	
2	–4.5	20.25	
Stage 1 Mean	0	Stage 4 Sum of squares	Stage 5 Variance	Stage 6 Standard deviation
6.5		1373.5	45.8	6.8

In the case of the data in Table 16.6 the standard deviation works out to be 6.8. This indicates the average amount by which individuals in the human resources department varied from the mean (6.5 days) in terms of the days they were absent from work due to illness. This figure, of course, is inflated by outlying values, in this instance the value of 36 days absent from work on the part of one individual. If this outlying value is eliminated, the standard deviation becomes 4.1 days rather than 6.8 days, demonstrating the potential of outliers to skew standard deviation statistics based on relatively small datasets.

 Caution: Research population or research sample: it makes a difference

The process outlined in Table 16.6 is based on the standard deviations of *populations* (in statistics represented by the Greek letter sigma 'σ'). The data are based on a complete research population (i.e. all of the employees in the human resources department). However, computer programs generally assume that the figures are drawn from a *sample,* not a population. They provide *standard deviations of samples* (in statistics denoted by the symbol '*s*'). When the dataset is based on a *sample* there is a slight difference in the way the standard deviation is calculated. To be specific, the variance is calculated on the basis of '*n* - 1' where n is the number of items in the variable. In Table 16.6 this happens at stage 5, and entails dividing the sum of the squares by 29 rather than 30. The reason for this is that $n - 1$ provides a more accurate measure of variance when drawing data from a sample (rather than the population). The point to note is that the standard deviation will differ to some small degree depending on whether the data are deemed to be (1) based on a population or (2) drawn from a sample.

 Link up with The research population, p. 18.

Likert scales

Likert scales (or similar scales) are the most common source of quantitative data in small-scale social research. They provide a straightforward tool for gathering quantitative data that can be embedded in questionnaires, and they have become a familiar feature of customer satisfaction forms, opinion surveys and the like. With such scales people are asked to provide a response to a question by indicating their view on a scale with a fixed number of points ranging from one extreme to an opposite extreme. The Likert scale requires respondents to mark their level of agreement or disagreement with a given statement using the format shown in Figure 16.1.

Figure 16.1 Likert scale

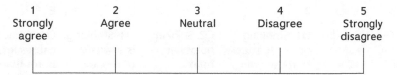

1	2	3	4	5
Strongly agree	Agree	Neutral	Disagree	Strongly disagree

Scales like this enable the researcher to measure a psychological attitude or disposition by converting it into a number: personal feelings and opinions on a topic get quantified. In the example above 'Strongly agree' is converted to '1', 'Agree' becomes '2' and so on. The data collected in such a fashion are ordinal data because the responses can be placed in rank order in terms of the extent to which they agree with a particular statement: 1 more so than 2, 2 more so than 3.

Link up with Web-based questionnaires, p. 196.

How to analyse data from Likert-type scales using MS Excel spreadsheet

1 Enter the data

Enter the data on to the spreadsheet in the format illustrated in Table 16.7.
If the data were collected using an online survey then usually they can be downloaded direct into MS Excel or similar spreadsheet.

2 Code the data

If the data appear as text – 'Strongly agree' etc. – then they need to be coded (1–5) and the text data converted to the numeric code as illustrated in Table 16.8.

3 Frequencies

The data can now be described in terms of *frequencies*: 'how many' people responded 'Strongly agree', how many answered 'Agree' and so on with respect to each question. To obtain these figures we can use the COUNTIF function. Before doing so, be sure to move the cursor to a position outside the columns of data. From the AutoSum drop-down menu on the top right-hand side of the screen locate the COUNTIF function. Then indicate the range of cells to be included, and then the specific value to be counted. The formula takes the format:

=COUNTIF(B2:B87,4)

In the example above this would show the number of respondents (B2:B87) who answered 'Agree' (4) to Q1.

Table 16.7 Likert data downloaded to a spreadsheet

	A	B	C	D	E
1	Questionnaire no.	Q1. Smoking gives pleasure to those who smoke.	Q2. Smoking helps people relax.	Q3. Smoking is a waste of money.	Q4. Tobacco causes less harm than alcohol.
2	JD/101	Disagree	Agree	Strongly agree	Strongly Disagree
3	LF/101	Agree	Strongly agree	Strongly disagree	Neutral
4	CR1/101	Disagree	Disagree	Strongly agree	Agree
⬇	⬇	⬇	⬇	⬇	⬇
85	PW/112	Neutral	Agree	Strongly agree	Disagree
86	MH/112	Strongly agree	Strongly agree	Neutral	Neutral
87	CR2/112	Neutral	Neutral	Strongly agree	Disagree

Table 16.8 Likert data coded a spreadsheet

	A	B	C	D	E
1	Questionnaire no.	Q1. Smoking gives pleasure to those who smoke.	Q2. Smoking helps people relax.	Q3. Smoking is a waste of money.	Q4. Tobacco causes less harm than alcohol.
2	JD/101	2	4	5	1
3	LF/101	4	5	1	3
4	CR1/101	2	2	5	4
⬇	⬇	⬇	⬇	⬇	⬇
85	PW/112	3	4	5	2
86	MH/112	5	5	3	3
87	CR2/112	3	3	5	2

4 Proportions and percentages

The data can be looked at in terms of the *proportion* of people responding in a particular way to each question. To do this we can use the results of the COUNTIF function to make statements such as '64 out of 87 respondents agreed . . .' or 'only 26 out of the 83 respondents who responded to this question disagreed with the statement that . . .'.

When the number of respondents is large enough it becomes appropriate to describe things in terms of *percentages*. To do this, for each question we divide the number who answered 'Strongly agree' by the total number of respondents, and then express the figure as a percentage. This process is then repeated for the other four possible responses.

> **Link up with**
> How much
> data, p. 269.

Caution: Missing values

When analysing the data it is vital that the figure used in relation to the number of respondents is the actual number who provided an answer to that question, rather than the overall total of people in the survey. *Missing values* must be eliminated from the calculation. In MS Excel, cells that are left blank (because there was no response on this item) are automatically treated as missing values and excluded from the calculations.

---

5 Means and standard deviations

When the responses have been coded into numbers it is easy to calculate the mean and standard deviation for the responses to each question. As always it is important to be sure the cursor is positioned away from the columns of data before starting. From the AutoSum menu on the Home tab select AVERAGE, and then mark out the column of cells relating to a specific question. The spreadsheet automatically calculates the arithmetic mean. A similar procedure can be used to calculate the standard deviation using the STDEV function. The two formulae take the following formats:

=AVERAGE(D2:D87)
=STDEV(D2:D87)

Caution: Likert-type scales: treating ordinal data as if they were interval/ratio data

There is some controversy about how data from Likert-type scales can be analysed. Likert-type scales produce ordinal data and it might be presumed, at first glance, that such data would be subject to the general limitations associated with ordinal data; i.e. that they cannot be analysed using the arithmetic mean or the standard deviation to depict the mid-point or the spread of the data. In practice, however, many social researchers go ahead to calculate means and standard deviations on the basis of data from Likert-type scales. It is common to find the responses to a rating scale averaged to a figure of, say, 1.35 or 3.66. Some experts regard this use of ordinal data as statistically unsound and something to be avoided. Others, including Likert (1932) himself, argue that there are technical and practical justifications that allow data from Likert-type scales to be used as though they were interval/ratio data. Project researchers need to be aware of this controversy if they choose to analyse their Likert-type data using means and standard deviations.

Analysing two variables

The analysis of a quantitative dataset can go beyond a focus on a single variable. Moving beyond this, it can look at two variables and, using *bivariate* analysis, it can investigate the nature of any apparent correlations and patterns of association between the two variables. When doing this, there are three basic questions researchers need to consider:

- *Are the results statistically significant?* How confident can I be that any apparent association between variables has not occurred simply by chance?
- *Is there some cause and effect relationship* between particular variables or do the variables simply co-vary? Can I identify which is the *independent variable* that causes a change in the *dependent variable*?
- *How strong is the relationship* between the variables, and how closely do changes in one variable match changes in another?

A dataset can contain a number of variables and there are statistical techniques that can help the researcher to find out which variables are linked to which others and which variables have the most powerful influence. Such *multivariate analysis*, however, tends to involve more advanced statistics and, in the context of small-scale social research, the likelihood is that the search for patterns and relationships in the data will be restricted to just two variables at a time. For this reason, this chapter focuses on *bivariate* analysis dealing with associations between two variables.

Statistical significance

Good researchers are very cautious in their approach to the search for patterns and relationships in the data. They approach things with a sceptical mindset and start from the premise that any pattern they might detect in the data could actually be the outcome of nothing more than sheer chance. As an expression of this cautious approach researchers using statistics start with a *null hypothesis*. They approach their findings with the presumption that there is no real pattern or no real relationship between sets of data, and they will only be persuaded to reject this position if there is 'overwhelming' statistical evidence to the contrary. Statistical tests can prove extremely useful in this respect. They can:

- provide an estimate of the probability that any association we find between variables is the product of sheer chance;
- provide a benchmark for researchers, indicating whether to proceed on the assumption that the apparent connection can be treated as 'real' or whether it should be ignored because it is unreliable evidence.

In the social sciences there is a convention that researchers will not accept that observed patterns or relationships are worthy of being considered 'real' unless the probability of them arising by chance is less than 1 in 20. In technical terms this involves a *significance level of $p < 0.05$*. Only if the patterns or relationships are shown to have a 'probability of less than 5 per cent' of being due to chance (shown as $p < 0.05$) will the good researcher be persuaded to reject the null hypothesis. Like members of a jury the researcher needs to be persuaded *beyond reasonable doubt* and this happens where the findings are likely to be true at least 19 times out of 20.

 Key point: A cautious approach and the null hypothesis

Social researchers should start from the premise that there is no real pattern or no real relationship between sets of data and only be persuaded to reject this position if the statistics point to a probability of less than 1 in 20 ($p < 0.05$) that the results arose by chance.

Dependent and independent variables: cause and effect

Research findings that point to an association between two variables only establish that they co-vary. Of themselves the findings say nothing about whether changes in one variable are directly caused by changes in another. There are statistical techniques that can be used to establish whether there is a causal relationship between variables and, if so, which variable(s) cause the changes. However, these tend to be used with multivariate analysis and rely on more advanced statistics.

For the purposes of project research using bivariate analysis it is generally possible to identify both the existence of a causal relationship and its direction on the basis of good sense using existing knowledge or established theory. Drawing on such background knowledge, variables can generally be identified as being either 'independent variables' (which *cause* changes) or 'dependent variables' (which change as a consequence of changes in the independent variable). So, for example, it is reasonable to assume that variables such as sex, age and ethnic group can be treated as independent variables without needing to statistically prove the point. If data collected by the Human Resources Department of the Healthy Life Insurance Company happened to reveal an association between 'days absent from work' and the sex of the employee, no one could reasonably contest the assumption that 'days absent from work' is the dependent variable and that 'sex' is the independent variable. Having made this point, good researchers do not *assume* that cause and effect in relationships are obvious. They are wary of using 'common sense' and do not jump to conclusions without giving careful thought to the possibility of alternatives.

Good practice: Dependent and independent variables

The analysis of an association between variables should include some explicit reasoning about the nature of the link and the basis for treating particular variables as 'dependent' or independent' in relation to one another.

Correlations and scatter plots (two numerical variables with interval or ratio data)

Correlation statistics are concerned with the *strength of the relationship* between variables. They use a *correlation coefficient* to indicate how much the change in one variable matches changes in the other variable. Correlation coefficients range from +1 to −1. A plus value indicates a positive correlation where an increase in one variable is accompanied by an increase in the other. A minus value indicates a situation where an increase in one variable is accompanied by a decrease in the other. In the middle, a value of zero indicates no evidence of the two variables being correlated (see Figure 16.2).

Figure 16.2 Correlation coefficients

+1 ◀───────────────	0	───────────────▶ −1
perfect	no	perfect
positive correlation	relationship	negative correlation
(one goes up, other goes up)		(one goes up, other goes down)

There are two commonly used types of correlation statistic. The main one is Pearson's correlation (or Pearson's product moment correlation, to give it its full name) which works with interval and ratio data. An alternative which works with ordinal data is Spearman's rank correlation. As the name suggests, this looks for a correlation between two sets of data that are ranked.

How to calculate the correlation coefficient of two variables

For Pearson's *r*, the two variables to be correlated should consist of (1) numerical data (interval or ratio) and (2) have an equal number of items. When the data are entered into a statistics packages like IBM SPSS or spreadsheet like MS Excel the calculation of Pearson's *r* can be accomplished using straightforward menu options. In MS Excel, for instance, the procedure follows just three steps:

1   Enter the data for the variables in two vertical columns, one for each variable.
2   Click the AutoSum pull-down menu from the top right-hand side of the screen, click the 'More functions' option, and then in the 'search for a function box' type in Pearson.
3   Select the Pearson function that is offered, and then specify the array of cells in which the data for each of the two variables are located. This automatically provides you with the correlation coefficient for the two variables

Scatter plots are often used in conjunction with correlations because they provide a visual picture of the closeness of fit between the two variables. Where there is a perfect fit between the two sets of data they will fall on to a straight line within a scatter plot, as illustrated by Figure 16.3. This is known as a 'perfect correlation' and will have a coefficient of +1 if it is positive and −1 if it is negative.

Link up with Scatter plots, p. 297.

Figure 16.3 Perfect correlation

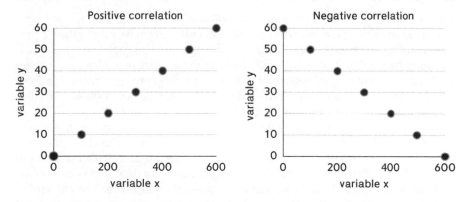

In practice, however, variables in the social sciences are rarely, if ever, perfectly correlated. The main reason this is that the relationship between variables does not occur in isolation. There are generally a host of other factors that also have an influence on the variables and, in the real world, it is virtually impossible to put these out of the way in order to measure the correlation 'all things being equal'. So, with correlations the right question to ask is 'how strong is the relationship' without ever supposing that there would be a perfect one-to-one correspondence between any two variables. Bearing this in mind, correlation coefficients in the range from 0.5 to 1.0 (+ or –) are generally considered to signify a large effect and, in practice, any correlation in the region of 0.7 can be considered to indicate a strong correlation (Figure 16.4). If the coefficient is between 0.3 and 0.5 it can be taken as an indication of some correlation between the two variables, but not a very strong one.

Figure 16.4 Strong correlation

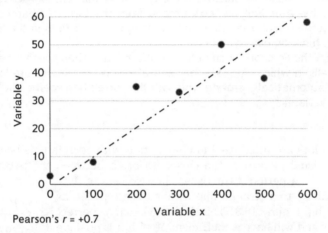

Pearson's r = +0.7

The chi-square test and contingency tables (two variables with either categorical or ordinal data)

The chi-square test is mainly used with *categorical data* and can be used with variables such as sex, ethnic group and occupation. This feature makes it particularly useful for analysing the kind of data collected by social researchers. It can also be used with ordinal data. The chi-square test provides researchers with a convenient way of determining if two variables are associated. It allows them to gauge whether any apparent link in the data between these variables can be deemed statistically significant.

The chi-square test is usually used in tandem with a 'contingency table' (see Table 16.9 and Table 16.12). When used in connection with the chi-square test there are two components to the table. One specifies the data that were actually *observed*. The other specifies the distribution of the data that might be *expected* if there was absolutely no association between the variables. The chi-square test estimates whether the difference between what was actually observed and what might have been expected (all things being equal) is large enough to be 'statistically significant', i.e. warrant the conclusion that any association that had been observed was not due to chance, not a fluke.

To illustrate this, Table 16.9 *cross-tabulates* some 'observed' data from employees in the Human Resources Department. It relates two categories of absence from work (above the mean and below the mean) with the sex of the employees.

Table 16.9 Observed and expected values in the chi-square test

Observed values				Expected values			
	Above the mean	Below the mean	Total		Above the mean	Below the mean	Total
Female	8	10	18	Female	6.6	11.4	18
Male	3	9	12	Male	4.4	7.6	12
Total	11	19	30	Total	11	19	30

It is not easy to discern from the observed data whether there is a clear relationship between sex of employee and level of absenteeism, and still less clear just by looking at the data whether any apparent association between the variables can be considered significant (in a statistical sense). This is where the chi-square test provides a useful tool for allowing such judgements to be made. It starts from the premise that if there were no association between the variables then the amounts in each of the cells of the contingency table would be in exact proportion to the total numbers in each category. These amounts can be calculated by multiplying the totals for each category and then dividing this number by the overall total of employees. So, the cell for females who are 'above the mean' is calculated thus: 18 (total female) ×11 (above the mean) which is then divided by 30 (grand total of employees) which leads to an expected value of 6.6.

For this data, the chi-square test indicates a probability of 0.27894. This is greater than $p < 0.05$ meaning that the 'null hypothesis' stands. The difference between males and females in terms of absence from work is *not* statistically significant.

How to look for associations using chi-square

Statistics packages (e.g. IBM SPSS) will generally calculate the expected values automatically once the observed/actual values have been entered, and then proceed automatically to calculate the probability of any apparent association being due to chance.

In a spreadsheet like MS Excel this probability can be obtained using the following routine.

1 Enter the observed data into a block of cells (which acts as a contingency table).
2 Calculate the expected data as explained above, and enter these into a separate block of cells.
3 On the Home tab at the top of the spreadsheet page click on AutoSum (top right) and select CHISQ.TST from the drop-down list.
4 In the next dialogue box that opens enter the location of the data cells for both the observed amounts and for the expected amounts.

> The figure that results indicates (on the basis of the chi-square test) the probability that the difference between the observed data and the expected data could be due to chance.

The main restriction on the use of the chi-square test is that there needs to be a sufficiently large dataset and/or a sufficiently even distribution among the various categories in order to get a minimum number of five units in each cell. Where cells in the contingency table have fewer than five in them it threatens the accuracy of the statistical test. There is, however, a statistical 'fix' which can be used should it become a problem (e.g. the Yates correction factor) and most statistics packages will put this into operation automatically.

The *t*-test (one variable with categorical data, the other variable with interval or ratio data)

The *t*-test is useful when researchers wish to compare two sets of data to see if there is a significant difference between them. The *t*-test has two notable strengths which are of particular benefit for small-scale research. First, it works well with small sample sizes (less than 30). Second, the groups do not have to be exactly the same size. A data set of 20 items can be compared with a data set of 15, for example.

A typical use of the *t*-test would be to compare test scores for students from two different classes who have taken the same test at about the same time. The classes are a categorical variable; the scores are interval/ratio data. The results might look like those contained in Table 16.10.

Using the *t*-test we find that $p = 0.25$. Because this is well above the conventional threshold of $p = 0.05$ it means that the difference of 5 per cent in the mean scores is not actually significant in a statistical sense and that the data should not be taken as firm evidence of a difference between the scores.

The *t*-test uses the means of the two sets of data and their standard deviations to arrive at a figure that tells the researcher the specific likelihood that any differences between the two sets of data are due to chance. The way it does this is to compare the difference in mean scores *between* two groups with the difference in the scores *within* each group. The basic logic is that when considering the difference in mean scores for any two groups we need to take into account the spread of the scores for each group. Where scores are widely spread then an observed difference in the means might not be as indicative of a real difference compared with that same amount of difference when the scores within the groups are narrowly spread.

In this example it would be appropriate to use the *independent samples* *t*-test. This is because the scores come from different sets of students. Had the teacher wished to compare the results obtained from one class on two consecutive occasions the comparison would have been between results from the same set of students and, for this reason, it would be appropriate to use the *paired samples t*-test.

Table 16.10   Typical *t*-test data

Class A (%)	Class B (%)
70	55
60	35
45	70
80	75
55	50
65	55
64	40
50	60
80	74
55	50
65	55
63	40
50	54
25	70
78	55
45	42
75	55
70	
55	
50	
mean = 60	mean = 55
p = 0.25	

How to calculate the *t*-test statistic

Statistics packages and spreadsheets generally have a *t*-test function that is quite straightforward to use. The procedure for using the *t*-test in an MS Excel spreadsheet illustrates this:

1 Open a spreadsheet page and enter the two columns of data.
2 Place the cursor on a cell which is outside these two columns.
3 Select the AutoSum tab from the top right-hand side of the screen.
4 Click 'More functions' and search for *t*-test.

5 Select the T.TEST function and enter the array of cells for each column of data in the appropriate boxes.
6 In the 'Tails' box enter the number 2 (using a two-tailed distribution).
7 In the 'Type' box enter the number 2 (for comparison of independent samples).

The resulting figure is the *probability* that any observed difference between the means of the two columns could have arisen by chance

There are other statistical tests which compare the results from two sets of data that will work with ordinal data rather than scale (interval/ratio) data. For example, the *Mann–Whitney U test* is a well-known test that works by using the rank-ordering of cases in each group. This is why it can work with ordinal data such as examination *grades* (A, B, etc.) if actual percentage scores are not available. The Mann–Whitney U test works by producing one overall ranking which is made from both groups being investigated. The positions of members of each group on this combined ranking are then used as the basis for calculating whether there is a statistically significant difference between the two groups.

How do I see if three or more groups or categories are significantly related?

This question is likely to be moving beyond the scope of interest for project researchers. It suggests a fairly large data set with more than two variables potentially connected and worthy of statistical test. It calls for a basic *factor analysis* such as one-way *ANOVA* (analysis of variance). This test analyses the variation within and between groups or categories of data using a comparison of means.

Example 16.2

Analysing the data using the mean, standard deviation, chi-square and *t*-test

The following example draws on a piece of research comparing the use of online questionnaires and paper questionnaires (Payne and Barnfather 2012). The focus was on whether certain kinds of people were more likely than others to choose one or other of the two kinds of questionnaire. The respondents were given the option as to which version of the questionnaire they chose to complete. When describing the participants the authors used the mean and the standard deviation (SD) in order to portray the age distribution of those taking part in the research.

The sample consisted of 597 students from the University of the Witwatersrand in the 2010 academic year. The sample was composed of both undergraduate and postgraduate students but was primarily from undergraduate years of study (87.5%). The mean age of the sample was 19.88 (SD = 2.02) (...). The majority of the sample (75.2%) chose to complete the paper-based version of the questionnaire. (Payne and Barnfather 2012: 392)

When analysing the results the authors wanted to know which kinds of people in the (convenience) sample of students were more likely than others to complete the online version of the questionnaire. The data they collected on the participants included both interval/ratio data and categorical data. They used the t-test in connection with those (dependent) variables that were based on interval/ratio data. They were looking for evidence that any apparent association between these variables and a preference for the use of online questionnaires was unlikely to be due to chance. In this respect they were looking for a probability of less than one in twenty (i.e. $p < 0.05$).

Independent sample t-tests revealed that the online sample was significantly older, $t(172.92) = 12.56$, $p < .0001$, spent more time on the Internet, $t(552) = 7.41$, $p < .0001$ and on Facebook per day, $t(548) = 3.02$, $p < .0014$, had more Facebook friends, $t(302.06) = 3.18$, $p = .0016$, and had had a Facebook account for a longer period of time, $t(275.31) = 8.66$, $p < .0001$. (Payne and Barnfather 2012: 392)

When analysing potential associations between variables based on *categorical* data the authors used the *chi-square test*. They used the chi-square test as a way of checking the evidence to see how likely it was that any apparent associations might be due to chance rather than anything else, again using $p < 0.05$ as the benchmark.

Chi squared tests of association revealed that females (chi-square = 4.10, $p = 0.0430$), those with lower levels of paternal education (chi-square = 4.33, $p = 0.0375$) and Caucasian respondents (chi-square = 103.29, $p < .0001$) chose online completion more often. Contrastingly Black-African respondents chose online completion less often (chi-square=81.37, $p < .0001$). (Payne and Barnfather 2012: 393)

Presenting the data using tables and charts

Tables and charts provide a succinct and effective way of organizing quantitative data and communicating the findings to others. Statistical packages and spreadsheets generally contain a table-making and a chart-making facility. So 'drawing' the tables and charts does not generally pose much of a problem for project researchers. The skill of producing good tables and charts tends to revolve far more around 'design' issues and the researcher's ability to do the following:

- present enough information without 'drowning' the reader with information overload;
- help the reader to interpret the table or chart through visual clues and appropriate presentation;
- use an appropriate type of table or chart for the purpose at hand.

Vital information

There are certain pieces of information which must always be included. If these are absent then the table or chart ceases to have much value as far as the reader is concerned. The table or chart must always have:

- a *title*;
- *information about the units being represented* in the columns of the table or on the axes of the chart (sometimes this is placed by the axes, sometimes by the bars or lines, sometimes in a *legend*);
- the *source* of the data, if they were originally produced elsewhere.

Added to this, in most cases – though not all:

- the horizontal axis is the 'x axis' and is used for the independent variable (the cause);
- the vertical axis is the 'y axis' and is used for the dependent variable (the effect).

There are exceptions to this rule and there are certain kinds of chart where the x axis becomes the vertical one and the y axis the horizontal one (e.g. a horizontal bar chart). In the absence of any other considerations, however, when constructing a chart or table the independent variable (the 'cause') generally goes on the horizontal axis and the dependent variable (the 'effect') goes on the vertical axis.

If the researcher pays attention to these points the remaining dangers to the success of the table or chart generally come from trying to be too ambitious and putting in too much detail. Simplicity is a virtue that is hard to overstress in relation to the production of tables and charts. If too much data are supplied in a table, it becomes almost impossible for the reader to decipher the meaning of the data. If too many frequencies are presented in a chart, it becomes difficult to grasp the key points. Too many patterns, too many words, too many figures, and the impact of the table or chart is lost.

 Key point

Simplicity is a virtue when it comes to the presentation of tables and charts

---

Tables

One of the main virtues of tables is their flexibility. They can be used with just about all types of numerical data. Computer software offers a variety of templates for tables, which aid the presentation of data in a visually attractive fashion.

The degree of complexity of the table depends on two things: the audience being addressed and the restrictions imposed by the format of the document in which the table appears. For the purposes of most project researchers it is likely that tables will remain fairly simple in structure. If the table *does* need to involve a considerable number of rows, the researcher should be prepared to insert horizontal and vertical 'breaks' or blank lines to ease reading and to avoid the eye slipping to the wrong line of data (see Table 16.11).

Table 16.11   Example of a basic table

Days absent from work through illness during the previous year, 30 employees

Days	Frequency	Days	Frequency	Days	Frequency
0	4	5	2	10	3
1	1	6	3	12	1
2	1	7	1	13	1
3	6	8	2	15	1
4	2	9	1	36	1

Source: Human Resources Dept. Healthy Life Insurance Co.

One particularly common use of tables is to present a comparison of sets of nominal or categorical data. Such tables are known as *contingency tables* (see Table 16.12). They allow a visual comparison of the data and also act as the basis for statistical tests of association, such as the *chi-square test*.

Table 16.12   Example of a contingency table

Days absent from work through illness during the previous year, 30 employees

Days lost	Male (n = 12)	Female (n = 18)
0–5 days	21	18
6 or more days	67	89

Source: Human Resources Dept. Healthy Life Insurance Co.

Bar charts

Bar charts are an effective way of presenting frequencies, and they are very common in reports of small-scale research. The principle behind them is that the bars should be of equal width, with the height of the bars representing the frequency or the amount for each separate category. Conventionally, there is a space between each bar. Their strength is that they are visually striking and simple to read – provided, that is, that not too many categories are used. The fewer the categories (bars) the more striking the impact. Beyond ten categories, bar charts tend to become too crowded and confusing to read. Figure 16.5 shows a simple bar chart.

There are many variations on the standard bar chart. The *pictogram* embellishes the basic idea by using symbols or images instead of the standard bar. It does not tell you anything more, but it catches the eye more readily.

Figure 16.5 Example of a simple bar chart

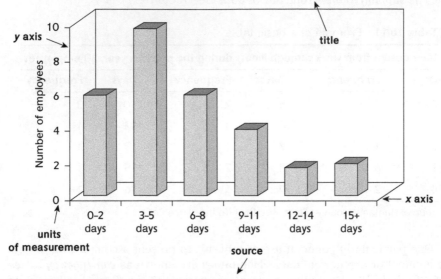

Days absent from work through illness during the previous year, 30 employees

Source: Human Resources Dept. Healthy Life Insurance Co.

Bar charts are sometimes turned on their sides to make it easier to label the categories (see Figure 16.6). In such *horizontal bar charts*, the vertical axis becomes the x axis – as an exception to the convention.

Figure 16.6 Example of a horizontal bar chart

Days absent from work through illness during the previous year, 30 employees

Source: Human Resources Dept. Healthy Life Insurance Co.

Sometimes each bar incorporates the component elements of the total for a category. This is known as a *stacked bar chart* (see Figure 16.7). A number of stacked bars can be incorporated into the same chart, allowing a more direct visual contrast than could be achieved by placing a similar number of pie charts together.

Figure 16.7 Example of a stacked bar chart

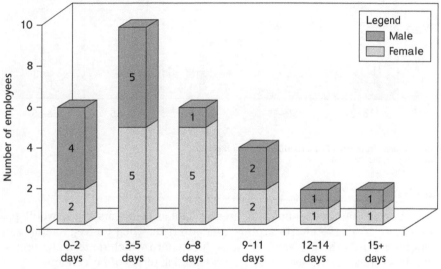

Days absent from work through illness during the previous year, 30 employees

Source: Human Resources Dept. Healthy Life Insurance Co.

Histograms

A histogram, like a bar chart, is a valuable aid to presenting data on frequencies or amounts (see Figure 16.8). Like a bar chart, the bars are normally of equal width and where they *are* of equal width, the height of the bar is used to depict variations in the frequencies or amounts. But whereas a bar chart is based on 'discrete' data or nominal data that take the form of categories of things (see examples above), a histogram is used in conjunction with *continuous* data. As the name suggests, continuous data exist on a continuum. In a histogram, the horizontal axis consists of a single variable that naturally occurs in a form of something that can be measured on a sliding-scale. This can be a variable such as age (younger to older), size (smaller to larger), length (shorter to longer), weight (lighter to heavier), temperature (colder to hotter) or time (past to present). In terms of presentation, a histogram contrasts with a bar chart to the extent that:

• there are no gaps between the bars;
• the data 'flow' along the x axis, rather than being distinct and separate items.

Figure 16.8 Example of a histogram

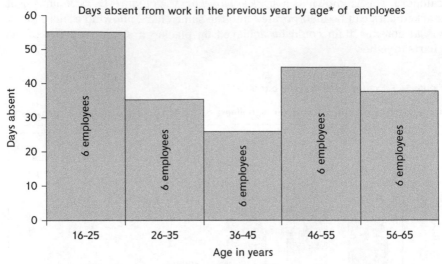

Source: Human Resources Dept. Healthy Life Insurance Co.
Note: *Age at last birthday.

Pie charts

Pie charts, as their name suggests, present data as segments of the whole pie (see Figure 16.9). Pie charts are visually powerful. They convey simply and straightforwardly the *proportions* of each category which go to make up the total. In most cases, the segments are presented in terms of percentages.

Figure 16.9 Example of a pie chart

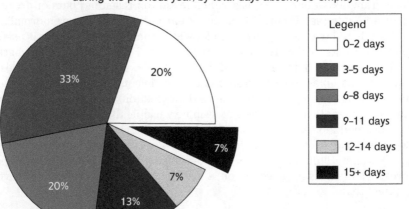

Source: Human Resources Dept. Healthy Life Insurance Co.

To enhance their impact pie charts that wish to draw attention to one particular component have that segment extracted from the rest of the pie. On other
occasions, all segments are pulled away from the core in what is known as an
exploded pie chart.

Weighed against their visual strength, pie charts can only be used with one
data set. Their impact is also dependent on not having too many segments. As
a rule of thumb, a pie chart should have no more than seven segments and have
no segment which accounts for less than 2 per cent of the total.

As a form of chart they tend to take up quite a lot of space on a page. The
labels need to be kept horizontal, and this spreads the chart out across the
page. As good practice, incidentally, the proportions should be shown as a
figure, where possible *within the segments.*

Scatter plots

A scatter plot is used to display the *extent of a relationship* between two variables (see Figure 16.10). The data are represented by unconnected points on a
grid, and the clustering or spread of such points is the basis for detecting a close
co-variation between two variables, or a not so close co-variation. The closer
the points align, the closer the relationship between the variables on the x axis
and the y axis. The more scattered the points are, the less closely the variables
are connected. The extent of the relationship is made nicely visible.

Figure 16.10 Example of a scatter plot

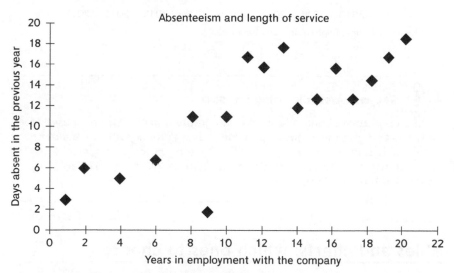

Source: Human Resources Dept. Healthy Life Insurance Co.

Line graphs

A line graph is used for depicting development or progression in a sequence of
data (see Figure 16.11). It is good for showing *trends in data.* The most common

use of the line graph is with dates. A time sequence is plotted left to right on the *x* axis. The line varies in height according to the frequency or the amount of the units. Line graphs work better with large data sets and big variations. A bar chart can be used to do the same thing, and sometimes bars and lines are combined within the same chart.

Figure 16.11 Example of a line graph

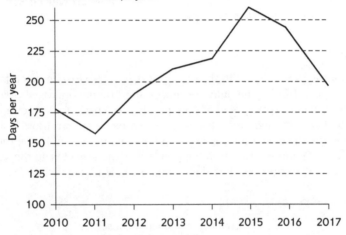

Total days absent from work through illness per year
(2010–2017), all 30 employees

Source: Human Resources Dept. Healthy Life Insurance Co.

 Caution: Avoid distorting the data

The presentation of quantitative data in graphs and charts can be used to mislead and give the wrong impression. Playing around with the scales on the *x* axis and the *y* axis can artificially exaggerate or underplay the appearance of differences in the data. Care needs to be taken to avoid distorting the data in this way.

Tables and charts: which ones to choose?

When it comes to choosing which kind of chart or table to use, researchers are faced with a range of possibilities. There is, however, no hierarchy with particular kinds of tables and charts being inherently better or worse than others. As Table 16.13 indicates when it comes to the presentation of quantitative data it is a matter of choosing the table or chart that works best. And this, in turn, depends on the kind of data being used and the particular features of the data the researcher wishes to portray.

Table 16.13 The use of suitable charts or tables

Purpose	Suitable chart or table
Amounts or Frequencies	Tables Bar charts Histograms
Proportions of a total	Pie charts Stacked bar charts
Extent of a relationship	Scatter plots Contingency tables
Covering a span of time	Line graphs

The quality of the data: validity and reliability

Good research relies on the use of good quality data. It is fairly obvious that if there are doubts about the quality of the data generated by the research then there will be doubts about the credibility of the findings. When it comes to ensuring the quality of data, however, it is important to recognize two points. First, the ways of achieving acceptable levels of quality will depend to some extent on the nature of the research being conducted. In particular, there are some differences between quantitative and qualitative research on this point.

Link up with The quality of the data: validity and reliability, p. 326.

The second point is that the quality of data is not something that 'speaks for itself': it is something that needs to be *claimed* by the researcher. This means that researchers need to be clear about the grounds on which they can argue that they have generated good quality data, and be prepared to persuade the audience for their research on this point.

When it comes to making the case for the quality of quantitative data there are generally two basic criteria that are used: validity and reliability. There are a variety of terms used in relation to validity and reliability, many of which stem from experimental research and measurement procedures in laboratory settings and some of which are not always used in a consistent manner. Project researchers, however, can avoid confusion by focusing attention on the underlying issues and by addressing two straightforward questions:

- What grounds are there for arguing that the data are relevant, accurate and precise? (The issue of validity).
- What are the grounds for arguing that the methods produce data in a consistent fashion? (The issue of reliability).

Validity

Validity refers to the relevance, accuracy and precision of the data, and it is generally discussed in relation to 'internal' and 'external' factors. In terms of internal validity the first factor to be considered is whether the research has been *asking the right questions* and looking at the right things. The data need to be directly relevant to the issues being investigated. They need to provide a relevant indicator that, when analysed, will shed some light on the research question. For example, a research project investigating 'stress at work' might count the number of days each employee takes off work for illness as an indicator of stress. When assessing the validity of the data collected the researcher will need to defend this as a good proxy for stress levels at work by making the case that there is a direct link between the two factors and that it offers a good indicator. To do this, researchers can rely on *face validity* in which they justify the relevance of the indicator on the basis of good sense and what appears to be obvious and reasonable. Or, preferably, they can use a form of *construct validity* making use of evidence from previous research in the field and draw on existing theories and knowledge on the topic to show the relevance of the data.

The validity of data, then, depends on asking the right questions. But it also depends on getting the right answers: right in the sense that are free from any errors arising during the data collection phase of the research. If respondents provide answers that, intentionally or otherwise, are wrong then the data are going to be less accurate and precise. *Piloting* the research instrument (e.g. questionnaire) is a basic way of addressing this matter and there are other measures that researchers can use such as *'check questions'* within a questionnaire to see whether people's responses are the same to a very similar question. The data, once collected, can also be checked to see if there is any evidence of systematic bias that might indicate the existence of poor questions and faulty answers. A statistical check can be made for consistency in the profile of answers within the dataset, based on the assumption that similar respondents should provide the same kind of answers to similar questions. Reference to any such *measures designed to eliminate inaccurate answers* can help the researcher's argument that the data are valid.

A third aspect of internal validity concerns the management of the data and whether the data have been organized in a suitably meticulous fashion to avoid administrative errors creeping in and affecting the quality of the data. On this score, the researcher can explain what checks were made to ensure that there were no errors arising from data entry. Where the data files have been entered via a manual process, with inputs from one source to another, there is the prospect of errors. It is the duty of the researcher to inspect the data files and check them against the sources.

The data can also be judged according to 'external' validity. In this case the validity of the data is gauged by the fit with other examples of the phenomenon and how far the findings from the particular piece of research can be *generalized*. This can operate in either of two ways. First, it can relate to the extent to which the data from the research matches what has been found in other similar phenomena at a general level. Other established research findings act as a benchmark for the accuracy of the data. To the extent that a consistency exists there is some assurance that the data can be regarded as reasonably accurate, relevant and precise. The second facet of external validity concerns the ability of the data to *explain* similar phenomena at a general level. In this case the fit is a theoretical one. If the findings suggest a theory that can be applied to situations more generally then there are grounds for believing that the data that have been collected are valid.

Reliability

Reliability refers to whether a research instrument is neutral in its effect and consistent across multiple occasions of its use. This is frequently translated as the question 'Would the research instrument produce the same results on different occasions (all other things being equal)?

There are a variety of ways researchers can check on reliability. They can, for example:

- Use the research instrument on a later occasion and then compare the results. The *test–retest* approach should produce results that are very similar.
- Split the dataset in half and compare one half with the other in terms of the findings they contain. Again, there should be a good level of consistency using this *split-half* approach.
- For data based on observations efforts can be made to find out whether different researchers would arrive at similar conclusions when looking at the same event. The level of *inter-observer reliability* should be high.

Advantages of using quantitative data

Hard data

Quantitative data are based on measurements that can be precise and objective. The findings that are produced consequently appear to be factual and not linked to the values of the researcher or his/her subjective interpretations. They present firm, definite facts that are regarded as *hard data*.

Scientific research

Quantitative data lend themselves to techniques of analysis that are consistent, repeatable and which can be checked by others. In numeric form, they are the kind of data associated with scientific research.

Statistical techniques

Statistical techniques can be used to help interpret quantitative data. The use of statistical tests of significance can provide researchers with additional credibility in terms of the confidence they have in their analysis.

Concise presentation of data

The presentation of quantitative data using graphs and tables can be a very effective way of communicating research findings. Widely available computer software takes most of the hard labour out of the design of tables and charts.

Computer-aided analysis

Spreadsheets and statistics software packages offer powerful and relatively easy-to-use tools for the analysis of quantitative data.

Disadvantages of using quantitative data

Numbers can have different properties

Researchers need to be clear about the type of numerical data they are using (nominal, ordinal, interval, ratio). Any confusion on this matter could have damaging consequences for their analysis and the conclusions that are drawn.

Quality of data

The validity of data and the reliability of methods are vital ingredients of good quantitative research. However, they are not things that are self-evident nor are they things which can be simply 'proved'. They are features of the research that need to be discussed and explained.

Data overload

Large volumes of data can be a strength of quantitative analysis but, without care, it can start to overload the researcher. Too many cases, too many variables, too many factors to consider – the analysis can be driven towards too much complexity. The researcher can get swamped.

Quantitative analysis might not be as scientifically objective as it might seem on the surface

Although the analysis of quantitative data might seem to be technical and scientific, in reality the researcher still has the ability to influence the findings in subtle ways. Researchers have an element of discretion and choice when conducting their data analysis, just as they do with qualitative data. And their decisions can influence the findings.

Further reading

Field, A. (2013) *Discovering Statistics Using IBM SPSS Statistics*, 4th edn. London: Sage.
Fielding, J.L. and Gilbert, G.N. (2006) *Understanding Social Statistics*. London: Sage.

Gorard, S. (2006) *Using Everyday Numbers Effectively in Research*. London: Continuum.
Kent, R.A. (2015) *Analysing Quantitative Data: Variable-Based and Case-Based Approaches to Non-Experimental Datasets*. London: Sage.
O'Dwyer, L. and Bernauer, J.A. (2014) *Quantitative Research for the Qualitative Researcher*. Thousand Oaks, CA: Sage.
Walker, I. (2010) *Research Methods and Statistics*. Basingstoke: Palgrave-Macmillan.

Checklist for the analysis of quantitative data

When analysing quantitative data you should feel confident about answering 'yes' to the following questions: ☑

1 Has the profile of the data been described in terms of:

   • frequencies? ☐
   • central tendency (mean, median, or mode)? ☐
   • dispersion (range, fractiles, or standard deviation)? ☐

2 Have suitable charts and tables been used to present the data? ☐

3 Are the tables or charts clear and thoughtfully designed? Has the relevant and vital information been included with any table and charts? ☐

4 Has a case been made in support of the quality of the data (i.e. that the data are valid and the methods are reliable)? ☐

5 Is the dataset sufficiently large to justify the technique of analysis applied to it? ☐

6 Is it clear which type of quantitative measure is being used (nominal, ordinal, interval, ratio) and has care been taken to avoid analysing nominal or ordinal data in a way that is unwarranted? ☐

7 If using data from a Likert-type scale does the analysis treat the data as interval/ratio data and, if so, has this decision been defended? ☐

8 Have any apparent associations between variables been checked statistically (e.g. chi-square, t-test, correlation)? ☐

9 Have statistical tests achieved a satisfactorily low probability ($p < 0.05$) to suggest the findings were not due to chance? ☐

17 Qualitative data

Types of qualitative data (words and images) · Sources of
qualitative data · Preparing qualitative data for analysis ·
Transcribing audio recordings of interviews · Computer-assisted
qualitative data analysis · The analysis of talk and text · Content
analysis · Grounded theory · Discourse analysis · Conversation
analysis · Narrative analysis · Analysis of image-based data ·
Presenting the data · The quality of the data: validity and reliability ·
Advantages of qualitative data analysis · Disadvantages of
qualitative data analysis · Further reading · Checklist for the
analysis of qualitative data

Types of qualitative data (words and images)

In the social sciences, qualitative research has focused predominantly on collecting data in the form of words. Words, however, can originate in two forms. They can be written words, as in the case of reports and documented records of meetings and events, or they can be spoken words, as in the case of interview talk. Spoken words, in order to be used as data, need to be 'captured' and given some permanence, and so the spoken words are normally recorded in some way and converted into a more amenable written format (such as a transcript) that lends itself to the researcher's needs. As a result, the data used in qualitative research tend to take the form of the *written* word.

But this is not the whole picture. Qualitative research can also be based on *visual images and artefacts*. Data can take the form of things like photographs, designs, iconic images, sculptures, clothes, etc. – things can tell a visual story of interest to the qualitative researcher. Such visual data have a content that, like words, can be analysed in terms of the meanings they hold. And though the use of such visual forms of data is not as mainstream as the use of textual data, the digital format of research publications and academic theses now provides increasing opportunities for the use of such visual data in social research.

Sources of qualitative data

Qualitative data are normally associated with strategies of research such as case studies, grounded theory, ethnography and phenomenology, and with research methods such as interviews, documents and observation. Qualitative data, however, can come from a wide variety of sources, as Table 17.1 indicates. The use of open-ended questions as part of a survey questionnaire, for example, can produce answers in the form of written words that can be analysed as qualitative data.

Table 17.1   Sources of qualitative data

Source of data	Research method	See pages
Answers to open questions	Questionnaires	194–6
Interview transcripts	Interviews	215–19
Visual recordings of events or interactions between people	Observation	252–7
Images, artefacts, symbols, cultural objects (e.g. paintings, advertisements)		
Written reports, diaries, minutes of meetings, scripts (e.g. for political speeches or media programmes)	Documents	245–7

Preparing qualitative data for analysis

The *original data should be protected*. Because qualitative data tend to be irreplaceable, it is good practice to make a duplicate of any recordings, to make copies of computer files and to photocopy any visual images or documents such as field notes or transcripts. These back copies are the ones that should be used during the process of data analysis so that the originals can be preserved and protected against any unintentional corruption or damage.

The data should also be *catalogued and indexed*. Each piece of 'raw data' should be identified with a unique serial number for reference purposes. The importance of this is that when analysing the data it is vital that the researcher is able to return to points in the data which are of particular interest. Without an adequate reference system it will be virtually impossible for the researcher to navigate back and forth through the data or to record which bits of data are significant. There are various ways of doing this but, to illustrate one possibility, when indexing page 10 of a transcript of an interview that took place with Ms Hallam at Dovedale High School, Ms Hallam might be allocated T07 (the seventh teacher interviewed, perhaps), Dovedale High School might be allocated the code 13 (as school number 13), so that the actual code added to the transcript would be anonymized as [T07:13: p.10].

Transcribing audio recordings of interviews

Audio recordings normally need to be transcribed and annotated. Transcriptions help with detailed searches and comparisons of the data. They are also necessary when using qualitative data software (see below). The amount of the raw data that needs to be transcribed will depend on the use to which the data are being put. If the contents of an interview are being used for the factual information they provide, then the researcher can be quite selective; transcription might only be needed for the purposes of small extracts that can be used as 'quotes' to illustrate particular points when writing up the findings. If the researcher is looking for the underlying structure of the talk or the implied meanings of a discussion, the audio recordings will need to be transcribed quite extensively – possibly in their entirety.

> **Link up with Chapter 13 Interviews.**

Transcribing audio recordings is very time-consuming. For every hour of talk on an audio recording it will take several more to transcribe it. The actual time will depend on the clarity of the recording itself, the availability of transcription equipment and the typing speed of the researcher. When you are planning interview research it is important to bear this in mind. From the point of view of the project researcher the process of transcribing needs to be recognized as a substantial part of the method of interviewing and not to be treated as some trivial chore to be tagged on once the real business of interviewing has been completed.

Transcription might be laborious but it is also a very valuable part of the research because it brings the researcher 'close to the data'. The process brings the talk to life again and is a real asset when it comes to using interviews for qualitative data. Also the end-product of the process provides the researcher with a form of data that is far easier to analyse than the audio recording in its original state.

> **Good practice**
> Allow sufficient time for the transcription of audio recordings. The transcription of audio recordings is a time-consuming activity. For every one hour of interview recording it can easily take three hours or more of work to transcribe the talk into text.

Annotations

When transcribing an audio recording, the researcher should put informal notes and comments alongside the interviewee's words. These annotations can draw on field notes taken during the interview or notes made soon afterwards about the interview. They should include observations about the ambience of the interview and things like gestures, outside interferences, uncomfortable silences or other feelings that give a richer meaning to the words that were spoken. These annotations should be placed in a special column on the page.

Line numbering and coding

To locate different parts of the transcript and to help navigate through to particular points in it, each line in the transcript should ideally have a unique line number by which to identify it. Qualitative data analysis software always includes a facility to do this but it is also easily accomplished using basic word processing software such as MS Word. The page layout for the transcript should include a reasonable amount of clear space on which to write notes and there should be a wide margin on the side of the page that can be used later for coding and classifying the data and for writing notes. Qualitative data analysis software allows this automatically.

Problems of transcription

The transcription of audio recordings is rarely a straightforward mechanical exercise in which the researcher simply writes down the words that are spoken by research participants. In practice, it can be quite challenging, and there are three main reasons for this:

- *The recorded talk is not always easy to hear.* Especially with group interviews, but also with one-to-one versions, there can be occasions when more than one person speaks at the same time, where outside noises interfere or where poor audio quality itself makes transcribing the words very difficult.
- *People do not always speak in nice finite sentences.* Normally, the researcher needs to add punctuation and a sentence structure to the talk so that a reader can understand the sequence of words. The talk, in a sense, needs to be reconstructed so that it makes sense in a written form. This process takes time – and it also means that the raw data get cleaned up a little by the researcher so that they can be intelligible to a readership who were not present at the time of the recording.
- *Intonation, emphasis and accents used in speech are hard to depict in a transcript.* There are established conventions which allow these to be added to a written transcript but the project researcher is unlikely to be able to devote the necessary time to learn these conventions. The result is that transcripts in small-scale research are generally based on the words and the words alone, with little attempt to show intonation, emphasis and accents. Nor are pauses and silences always reported on a transcript. The consequence is that, in practice, the data are stripped of some of their meaning.

Key point

Transcription is not always simple and straightforward. Transcription is not a mechanical process of putting audio-recorded talk into written sentences. The talk needs to be 'tidied up' and edited a little to put it in a format on the written page that is understandable to the reader. Inevitably, it loses some authenticity through this process.

Example 17.1

Interview transcripts

The following extract is part of the transcript of a group interview conducted with 15- and 16-year-olds about peer pressure and alcohol consumption. The names have been changed. Notice how, typical of a group interview, more than one person is trying to talk at once. Elise cuts across James, and then gets interrupted in turn by Gordon, who manages to hold the spotlight for a moment or two.

Line of the transcript		Code for the content	Notes
46	*Interviewer:* Do you feel under pressure to		
47	drink when you go out with your mates		
48	because they are drinking?		
49			
50	*James:* Yeh, but it's not always . . .		James looked
51	(untranscribable)		annoyed as Elise
52	*Elise:* . . . it's worse with the lads, I think,		and Gordon
53	because . . .		talked over him
54	*Gordon:* . . . I was on holiday, and I don't like		
55	beer, and all my friends were drinking. I was		
56	drinking half a glass and I thought I can stick	08	
57	that out because I don't like it at all. I was		
58	drinking it and thinking this is horrible, just		Gordon says later
59	to look like one of the crowd, because I felt a		that he drinks
60	bit left out. My brother came up to me in		beer regularly
61	front of the crowd and said 'Gordon you don't	15	now.
62	like lager!' So all my friends found out, and		
63	they said 'Look, we understand if you don't		
64	like it' – and some of the people there		
65	were just like me, they didn't like it.		

Computer-assisted qualitative data analysis

A number of computer software packages have been developed specifically to help with the analysis of qualitative data. These are generally known as CAQDAS, which stands for *computer-assisted qualitative data analysis software*.

Some of these are more popular than others and some are more expensive than others. The best-known is *NVivo*, but there are many others that can be used and there are some valuable sites online which review the many alternatives. There are also a number of books that provide detailed guidance on the use of software like NVivo (e.g. Di Gregorio and Davidson 2008; Bazeley and Jackson 2013; Silver and Lewins 2014).

It is advisable for the project researcher to use one of these computer software packages because, apart from anything else, they are designed to ensure that qualitative data are organized and stored in an appropriate fashion. In effect, using one of the packages obliges the researcher to prepare the data suitably and to take advantage of the computer's abilities to manage:

- *The storage of data.* Interview transcripts, field notes and documents can be kept in text files. Copies are quick and easy to make.
- *The coding of data.* The data can be easily coded – in the sense of both *indexing* the data (serial codes) and *categorizing* chunks of the data as a preliminary part of the analysis.
- *The retrieval of data.* The search facilities of the software make it easy to locate data once it has been coded and to pluck it out for further scrutiny.

Good practice

Use computer software for qualitative data analysis. Qualitative researchers should make use of CAQDAS packages because they help with the preparation, organization and storage of qualitative data.

CAQDAS packages, however, should not be regarded as a quick and easy fix for the task of analysing qualitative data. For one thing, *they do not actually do the analysis* – the researcher still needs to decide the codes and look for the connections within the data. The software helps with this – but there is no automatic processing of the data comparable with the way that statistics packages analyse quantitative data. And, of course, the use of computer software, no matter how straightforward, involves some start-up time. For the first-time user, there is the time taken in getting to know the package and understand its potential. There is also the time taken to input the data.

The analysis of talk and text

There are five main approaches to the analysis of talk and text: content analysis, grounded theory, discourse analysis, conversation analysis and narrative analysis. Table 17.2 summarizes the different purposes of the approaches and how these are reflected in their treatment of data.

Table 17.2 Analysis of text and talk: a comparison of five approaches

	Content analysis	Grounded theory	Discourse analysis	Conversation analysis	Narrative analysis
Purpose of analysis	Look for hidden message	Develop concepts or theory	Show how power is exercised through language	Reveal underlying rules and structure of talk and interaction	Depict constructions of personal identity and social worlds
Data	Text and talk	Text and talk	Text and talk	Text and talk	Text and talk
Work done by words	Denote things	Imply things	Presume things	Produce things	Construct things
Significance of data	Frequency of occurrence	Derived meaning	Implied meaning	Displayed meaning	Implied meaning
Focus of attention	Surface content	Meaning of content	Content in context	Structure of content	Structure or meaning of content
Units of analysis	Words and phrases	Sentences and paragraphs	Paragraphs and whole documents	Blocks of text or talk	Whole story or text
Treatment of data	Measured (based on frequency and position)	Coded (using constant comparative method)	Related (to wider social structures and processes)	Deconstructed (to display underlying rules)	Deciphered (to find symbolic significance of story)
Data analysis	Quantification of text	Interpretation of text	Implication of text	Sequence and structure of talk	Structure or social implications of the text

© M. Denscombe, *The Good Research Guide.* Open University Press.

In some instances, words are taken at face value. The text and talk are treated at a surface level for the facts and information they contain, and the analysis focuses simply on what the words describe. In others, the analysis is based on the premise that words do a lot more than simply describe something, and these approaches focus on the *work done by words*. Words are analysed in terms of what they imply and what they presume, with attention being given to the background assumptions needed to interpret the words. Or words are analysed in terms of how they produce meanings and construct social life, with attention in this case being devoted to how words underlie social structure and interaction. Such approaches analyse the text data by 'reading between the lines' to see what lies beneath the surface. In this way, the researcher can interpret the hidden meanings contained in the talk and text, or can see how things like speeches or conversations are structured in a particular fashion.

There are also *different levels of contextualization* to be found in the approaches. The unit of analysis can sometimes be individual words, sometimes sentences or paragraphs, other times the whole text, and the difference here revolves around how far the different approaches tend to isolate bits of text from (1) the words that surround them or from (2) the social context in which the words were used. For some kinds of content analysis it is not a problem to focus on instances of individual words extracted from the text. For approaches like discourse analysis and narrative analysis it is important not to separate units of the text from their wider social context. And with conversation analysis there is a particular importance given to the location of the unit of analysis within the rest of the text or talk within which it occurs.

Finally, a word on the differing philosophies of the approaches. In the case of content analysis there is a strong focus on measurement and it is interesting that although it is used in conjunction with qualitative data, it produces quantitative measurements. In this respect it might be seen as quite positivistic in its approach. Likewise with grounded theory the reliance on an inductive approach suggests an affiliation with positivism – although as we saw in Chapter 7, this is mainly the case with a specific branch of grounded theory. Discourse analysis, conversation analysis and narrative analysis, however, have little to do with positivism. Their assumptions about social reality and their preferences in terms of how the data should be treated are based, instead, on elements of critical realism, pragmatism and postmodernism. Broadly speaking, they are approaches to the analysis of qualitative data that are based on *interpretations*.

Content analysis

Content analysis can be used with any 'text' whether it is in the form of writing or visual images. It is used as a way of *quantifying* the contents of that text. Political scientists might use it to study the transcripts of speeches, educationists to study the content of children's books, and historians to study statesmen's correspondence. Whatever its specific application, content analysis generally follows a logical and relatively straightforward procedure:

Step 1: *Choose an appropriate sample of texts or images.* The criterion for the choice of such a sample should be explicit. If the choice involves sampling, then there needs to be a justification for the kind of sampling technique used (see Chapter 2).

Step 2: *Break the text down into smaller component units.* The unit for analysis can be each and every word. Alternatively, the analysis can use complete sentences as the unit, whole paragraphs or things like headlines. It can also be based on visual images or the content of pictures.

Step 3: *Develop relevant categories for analysing the data.* The researcher needs to have a clear idea of the kinds of categories, issues and ideas that he or she is concerned with and how these might appear in the text. This might take the form of 'key words' associated with the theme. So, for example, a search for sex bias in children's stories might look for instances of boys' names and girls' names – the names being treated as indicative of the nature of the content. The researcher might also wish to code the text in terms of the kinds of names, rather than just how many times such names occur.

Step 4: *Code the units in line with the categories.* Meticulous attention to the text is needed to code all the relevant words, sentences, etc. These codes are either written on the text and subsequently referred to, or entered via a computer program specially designed for the purpose.

Step 5: *Count the frequency with which these units occur.* The first part of analysis is normally a tally of the times when various units occur.

Step 6: *Analyse the text in terms of the frequency of the units* and their relationship with other units that occur in the text. Once the units have been coded, a more sophisticated analysis is possible which links the units and attempts to explain when and why they occur in the way they do.

Content analysis has the potential to disclose many 'hidden' aspects of what is being communicated through the written text (Table 17.3). The idea is that, quite independent of what the writer had consciously intended, the text carries some clues about a deeper-rooted and possibly unintentional message that is actually being communicated. You do not have to base the analysis on what the author *thought* he/she was saying

> **Link up with Chapter 15, Documents.**

Table 17.3 Content analysis

Content analysis reveals . . .	By measuring . . .
What the text establishes as relevant	What is contained (e.g. particular relevant words, ideas)
The priorities portrayed through the text	How frequently it occurs; in what order it occurs
The values conveyed in the text	Positive and negative views on things
How ideas are related	Proximity of ideas within the text, logical association

when the text contains more tangible evidence about its message (Gerbner et al. 1969; Krippendorf 2013).

The main strength of content analysis is that it provides a means of quantifying the contents of a text, and it does so by using a method that is clear and, in principle, repeatable by other researchers. Its main limitation is that it has an in-built tendency to dislocate the units and their meaning from the context in which they were made, and even the intentions of the writer. And it is difficult for content analysis to deal with the meaning of the text in terms of its *implied* meanings, how the meaning draws on what has just been said, what follows or even what is left unsaid. In many ways it is a rather crude instrument for dealing with the subtle and intricate ways in which a text conveys meaning. In practice, therefore, content analysis is at its best when dealing with aspects of communication which tend to be more straightforward, obvious and simple. The more the text relies on subtle and intricate meanings conveyed by the writer or inferred by the reader, the less valuable content analysis becomes in revealing the meaning of the text.

Grounded theory

> **Link up with Chapter 7, Grounded theory.**

The grounded theory approach is primarily associated with the analysis of interview transcripts (although it can be used with a variety of types of qualitative data). The analysis requires a detailed scrutiny of the text and involves a gradual process of coding and categorizing the data. Broadly speaking the process involves the following eight steps.

Step 1: *Explore the data.* The first task for the researcher is to become thoroughly familiar with the data. This means reading and re-reading the transcripts. It entails getting a feel for the data and becoming immersed in the minute details of what was said, what was done, what was observed and what is portrayed through the data. To start with the researcher can take a fairly superficial look at the text (or images). Because some time might have elapsed since the data were collected, and because there is likely to be a considerable amount of data to work on, the aim should be to refresh the researcher's memory about the content of the data and to remind him/her about the broad scope of the material that is available. Returning to the data for further inspection, the researcher should begin to cross-reference the material with field notes to enable a better understanding of the data *in context.* Subsequent re-readings of the data should allow the researcher to identify *themes* in the data.

Step 2: *Write memos.* As the analysis progresses new things will emerge as relevant or new interpretations might spring to mind. As new insights come to the researcher, the ideas need to be noted. Brief thoughts can be appended to the data but more detailed insights are easier kept as *memos.* These memos are of practical value as a means for logging new thoughts and exploring new possibilities in relation to the analysis of the data. Such memos, in addition, are valuable in the way they provide a documented record of the analytic thinking of the researcher as they refine the codes and categories. In this sense memos are a notepad on which the researcher records how and why decisions were taken in relation to the emerging analysis of the data. In effect, they render the process of analysis explicit and accountable, and can form part of the 'audit trail' (see below).

Step 3: *Code the data.* Codes are tags or labels that are attached to the 'raw' data. They can take the form of names, initials or numbers; it does not matter as long as the code is succinct and is used systematically to link bits of the data to an idea that relates to the analysis. The use of codes in connection with the interpretation of data is quite distinct from the process of putting a *reference* code on the various pieces of data so that the parts can be identified and stored in an organized manner. During the interpretation of the data the researcher engages in *analytic* coding.

Whatever the form of the data – interview transcripts, field notes, documents, photographs or video recordings – the first thing the researcher needs to do is decide on the *units* that will be used for coding the data. This process is sometimes known as 'unitizing' the data. With text data the units could be as small as individual words, they could be lines in the text, complete sentences or they could be paragraphs. Whichever, a decision needs to be made on what chunks of the data are to have codes attached to them.

Next, a decision needs to be made about the kind of thing that will be coded. Obviously, this will be guided to a considerable extent by the nature of the research problem but, to give an indication of the coding decision involved at this point, the researcher could base his/her coding on things like:

- a kind of event;
- a type of action;
- a shade of opinion;
- an instance of the use of a particular word or expression;
- an implied meaning or sentiment.

Finally, a decision needs to be made on the choice of initial codes that might usefully be applied to the data. The researcher can use respondent categories for this purpose; that is, base the initial codes on something that springs from the contents of the data. Or, the initial codes can be based on personal/professional hunches about what will prove useful for the analysis. The choice is not crucial at the initial phase of analysis because the codes are subject to a continual process of refinement during the research, so if the initial codes are 'incorrect', later versions will be refined and improved.

Step 4: *Categorize the codes.* The next task is to identify ways in which the codes can be grouped into categories. The categories act as an umbrella term under which a number of individual codes can be placed. The terms 'taxonomy' and 'typology' are sometimes applied to this stage in the analysis, reflecting the general idea of classifying the various components of the data under key headings. The task for the researcher is to 'make the link'.

Step 5: *Reduce the number of codes and categories.* At the beginning there are likely to be a large number of codes and categories – too many to be useful for any meaningful analysis. Part of the analysis, then, is to identify where there is sufficient congruence between them to allow some to be merged and others to be brought together within a broader category. Each of the codes brought together within the category will have some feature that is shared with the others and, of course, this feature will be particularly relevant for the emerging analysis. At this point some decisions also need to be made about which parts of the data are more important than others. Attention has to be focused on these parts, with other parts of the data being relegated to the side lines. The importance of such parts of the data, it should be stressed, is determined solely by their significance for the emerging analysis.

Step 6: *Develop a hierarchy of codes and categories.* Making sense of the data will involve differentiating among higher level and lower level codes. The higher level codes will be broader and more inclusive. Crucially, though, the task for the researcher is to develop hierarchical pyramids of codes by subsuming some (lower level) codes under other broader (higher level) codes. The categories will necessarily operate at a higher level of generality which will allow them to cover a number of lower-level, more specific codes (see Figure 17.1).

Figure 17.1 The grounded theory approach to the analysis of qualitative data

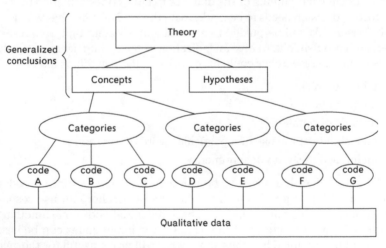

Step 7: *Check the emerging codes, categories and concepts with the data.* The steps towards refining the categories and concepts form part of an iterative process. They are steps in the 'data analysis spiral' which means that each task is likely to be revisited on more than one occasion as the codes, categories and concepts are developed and refined.

Step 8: *Move towards key concepts.* In principle, grounded theory analysis aims to use the higher level codes and categories as the basis for identifying key concepts. The development of these concepts is the main purpose of the analysis because the concepts provide some new understanding of the data and constitute the foundations for any theory or general conclusions to emerge from the research.

Good practice: Check the emerging analysis against competing theories and alternative explanations

Researchers should review their analysis in the light of other explanations of similar data. Competing theories should be considered, and the analysis should be evaluated in relation to the alternatives. Particular attention should be paid to any instances within the researcher's own data that might appear to contradict the emerging analysis.

Discourse analysis

Discourse analysis approaches qualitative data with the view that they should never be taken 'at face value'. Instead, they should be 'deconstructed' to reveal the hidden messages that they contain. It is an approach to the analysis of qualitative data that focuses on the *implied meaning* of the text rather than its explicit content. It is concerned with what is accomplished through the use of words – what words 'do' rather than what they literally represent – and draws on the philosophical influence of people like Wittgenstein (1968) and Austin (1962). Discourse analysis has been developed by postmodernists such as Foucault and Derrida and is familiar within the fields of social psychology, sociology and linguistics. It is used in relation to a wide range of social research areas including cultural studies, marketing (especially advertising), education and feminist studies.

In line with other approaches to qualitative data analysis, discourse analysis likes to keep *close to the data*. The task of the researcher is to interrogate the data with the aim of showing just how the discourse can be discerned through the particular data being studied. Discourse analysis, in this sense, does not differ from the kind of qualitative data analysis outlined elsewhere in this chapter to the extent that it relies on:

* a close scrutiny of the text/image;
* a firm grounding of conclusions within the data.

However, discourse analysis differs from approaches like content analysis and grounded theory in the way its analysis goes beyond the 'evidence' to be found within the text, talk or images being used as data. This is almost inevitable because discourse analysis, in its attempt to reveal the cultural assumptions that need to come into play in order to understand the data, looks at what is *absent* from the text or image as well as what is contained. It looks at what is *implied* as much as what is explicit. The question arises: 'How would you know what was missing if you did not have some idea of what should be expected to "fill the gaps" and "speak the unspoken"?' The answer to this is that researchers who undertake discourse analysis need to bring into play 'outside' factors in order to complete the picture and read between the lines. They must use existing knowledge about society, culture, politics, etc. and incorporate more general, background knowledge to decipher the significance of the message contained in the data.

Critical discourse analysis tends to add a political bite to the approach. It explores the ways the hidden, background meanings that are used to make sense of a text or image serve the interests of some groups more than others. In fact, this approach explores how power in society is achieved through discourse and how this is evident in particular instances of text or images. In doing so, it relies quite heavily on the use of political, economic and social ideologies as its frame of reference for understanding the meanings embodied in the data.

One limitation of using discourse analysis is that it does not lend itself to the kind of *audit trail* (see below) that might be needed to satisfy conventional evaluations of the research. It is not easy to verify its methods and findings. This is because the approach places particularly heavy reliance on the insights and intuition of the researcher for interpreting the data. Some discourse analysts eschew the idea that their research can, or should, be subject to any process of verification. They argue, in effect, that the findings stand as just 'the researcher's interpretation' – no better and no worse than anybody else's. No more scientific; no more credible. This is a controversial stance and it is one that could prove unwise for a project researcher to adopt. But, unless the researcher is prepared to risk taking this 'postmodernist' position, they need to be aware of the difficulties of verification inherent in the approach. With this in mind, what practical guidance can be given in relation to discourse analysis?

Be clear about which aspects of discourse are being studied

The researcher needs to specify whether the particular talk, text or image is being used in relation to:

- the shared background meanings and cultural assumptions necessary to make sense of the data themselves (micro);
- the wider ideology and cultural relations that are created and reinforced through the data (macro).

Be clear about which aspects of deconstruction are best applied

There is no hard and fast process involved in discourse analysis, but the researcher who embarks on deconstructing the data needs to have a clear vision of the things he/she is looking for and the way these link with the micro and macro aspects of discourse. A number of relevant questions to be asked include:

- Is there evidence of a wider ideology being communicated via the talk, text or images?
- Do the data reflect particular social, political or historical conditions in which they were produced?
- In what way does the talk, text or image stem from other sources ('intertexuality')?
- How is power or influence being exerted through the talk, text or image?
- Whose version of reality is being portrayed through this talk, text or image?
- How are people, processes and objects categorized and defined through the talk, text or image?
- Are there people, processes or objects that are notably absent or excluded?
- Are there contradictions within the talk, text or image? How are these coped with?
- What things are missing from the talk, text or image?
- Are there views that appear to be suppressed?
- Are there things that are not said that might have been expected to be stated?
- What rhetorical or linguistic devices are being used to argue the point?
- What version of things is being portrayed as normal/abnormal, legitimate/illegitimate, moral/immoral, natural/unnatural, etc.?
- Would alternative interpretations of the talk, text or image be possible or likely depending on the particular audience?

Conversation analysis

Conversation analysis focuses on the structure and sequencing of everyday talk. It is often considered to be a variant of discourse analysis because it focuses attention on how things get done through language use. In this instance researchers look at naturally occurring talk and the way that routine aspects of everyday life get accomplished through language (Clift 2016; Hutchby and Wooffitt 2008; Sidnell 2010). There have been studies of things like taking turns in everyday conversation, greeting people, starting a school lesson – apparently mundane and minute parts of social life but ones that advocates of *ethnomethodology* stress are the fundamental building blocks of social interaction – without which there would be no such thing as social life.

Conversation analysts are inclined to underplay the extent to which they draw on presuppositions. However, their analysis must still rely on cultural insights. Indeed, the researcher's background knowledge can be argued to be absolutely essential to the sensible interpretation of routine conversation. For any reasonable interpretation, it is vital that the researcher has appropriate background knowledge, shared with those doing the talking. Otherwise, they would literally have no way of knowing what was going on.

Narrative analysis

A narrative relates to a story. A story can be told in many forms; in writing through books and in speech through interviews, as well as a whole host of other mediums perhaps less commonly used as sources of data by social researchers such as visual images, music and drama. Treated as a narrative, though, the story needs to have certain properties (Andrews et al. 2013; Bold 2012; Elliott 2005; Riessman 2003, 2008). Normally, it would be expected to do the following:

- *Have some specific purpose.* This could be a moral message or it could be an account of personal circumstances. Whatever the subject matter of the story, it has to be leading somewhere.
- *Contain a plot line linking the past to the present.* There is normally some sense of development and change over time in which past events are recounted and linked explicitly to the present.
- *Involve people.* The theme needs to have a human element to it, referring to feelings and experiences in the context of social events and human interaction.

For qualitative research such stories can be useful in two ways. First, they can be analysed in terms of how they *construct the social world*. The point here is that stories can have a special importance in culture which can go well beyond that of entertainment. They might be parables with strong moral lessons involved. They might be contemporary news stories built on underlying beliefs about rights and wrongs in politics. Or they might be 'classics' with great symbolic significance, handed down from generation to generation as part of the transmission of culture, telling of how things were and why things happened and serving to bolster the beliefs and values that bind a society together. Second, they can be analysed in terms of how they *construct a personal world*. This aspect of narrative analysis links quite closely with research on life histories and oral histories. It is concerned with the way that stories are used by people as ways of representing themselves and their lives to others. The stories are used, consciously or not, as a device through which people describe and explain themselves and the circumstances surrounding their existence.

Narrative analysis applied to any such stories is not overly concerned with whether the content of the story is built on truth or myth; the focus is more on how those stories *work*. The stories are analysed to reveal the way the story constructs and interprets the social world, and the focus of attention is on:

- the meanings and ideology the story conveys;
- the techniques and communicative devices the story-teller uses;
- how the story links with the cultural and historical context within which it is told.

Analysis of image-based data

The kind of analysis used for image-based data depends on the purposes for which the data were collected. Broadly, images are used for either, or both, of two reasons:

- for the factual information they contain;
- for the cultural significance and symbolic meaning that lie behind their content.

There are various strands to the analysis of visual images. Without becoming embroiled in the detail of the differences it is perhaps possible to identify three elements to the analysis of image-based data:

- *the image itself:* contents, genre, styles;
- *the producer:* intentions and context (by whom, when, under what circumstances, why, the intention of the creator);
- *the viewer:* interpretation and context.

The image itself can be valuable as a source of *factual information*. There is a case to be made that images provide a relatively reliable source of data – preferable, at least, argues Collier (2001: 59) to the 'deceptive world of words'. Objectively frozen in time, the image contains evidence of things with a clarity that words could never hope to match. Photographs from archives, film from distant fieldwork settings, snapshots from a family album, each contains a firm record of events that can be subsequently analysed by the researcher. 'Such images are produced to serve as records of reality, as documentary evidence of the people, places, things, actions and events they depict. Their analysis is a matter of extracting just that kind of information from them' (van Leeuwen and Jewitt 2001: 4).

> **Link up with** Image-based research, p. 252.

Content analysis

To help get to grips with the information contained in large collections of images researchers can use *content analysis*, and it is quite possible to produce quantitative data as part of the analysis of images (see Bell 2000, for a detailed account of this). In practice, however, image-based research has largely favoured a qualitative approach. The key reason for this is that social researchers in recent years have become reluctant to take the content of images entirely 'at face value'. Rather than accepting images as neutral depictions of reality (along with the positivistic connotations this has), most social researchers in the twenty-first century would acknowledge, as Rose (2016) argues, that images do not contain 'one right meaning'. What they depict is open to interpretation and it would be rather naïve to presume that the contents of visual images are self-explanatory. Without entirely abandoning the use of images in terms of their ostensive content (the 'facts' they portray), researchers have become more inclined to treat the contents as something that needs to be interpreted. The meaning of the image is the thing of value for the researcher, the meaning as given within a particular culture, within a given time, within a social context within which it was produced.

Cultural artefact

Another way of interpreting an image is as a *cultural artefact*. As a cultural artefact the focus moves away from just the content of the image and what this can tell the researcher to incorporate, also, questions about the context in which the image was produced. What purpose did/does it serve? Why was it produced? As a source of evidence the value of the image is in what lies behind the surface appearance. To give an illustration, a photograph might appear to show a family on a seaside beach. At one level the researcher could use the image to get factual information about the style of beachwear worn at the time the photograph was taken. Provided the photograph was authentic, the image acts as a source of factual data. However, that same image might be interpreted as a cultural artefact by asking questions about how and why it was produced. Who took the photograph? Why was it taken? What importance is attached to it that might explain why it has been kept over a long period of time? What equipment was used to take the photograph? Such lines of enquiry could help researchers to understand the significance of family holidays, the role of photograph albums and the nature of leisure activity in their cultural context. That is, the meaning of the photograph goes beyond the superficial content depicting two adults and two children at the seaside.

Symbolic representation

The analysis of images can also interpret them in terms of what they denote. This approach probes the image as a *symbolic representation* whose interest lies not so much in the 'facts' contained in the image as in the significance attached to the contents by those who view it. Images, used in this way, provide a source for uncovering ideologies and cultural codes. Drawing on the field of 'semiotics' the researcher first considers the various aspects of the content to see what they denote. Taken at face value, what do they 'say'? Next the researcher considers the connotations of the key elements in the image. What associations spring to mind when looking at those elements? Then, in the final stage of analysis, semiotics moves towards drawing contrasts and similarities with other signs in a way that helps us to understand the symbolism of the image. (See Penn 2000, for further information on the semiotic analysis of still images.)

It is important to note that reading the message is not entirely an individual, personal thing in which each viewer interprets things differently. While there is certainly some scope for variation, semiotics and cultural studies operate on the premise that there is a degree of consensus among viewers about the meaning of an image. People who come from a similar cultural background, who are members of the same society or who have been brought up within a particular ideological tradition (e.g. democracy, Christianity), might be expected to make sense of images in roughly the same way. As members of social groups they will have been *socialized* into ways of seeing what is meant by visual images – learning from others since their early years how to make sense of visual clues contained in things like signs, advertisements, portraits and music videos.

Caution: Context is important

When using images for research purposes there is always the danger that they might be 'taken out of context'. Events prior and subsequent to the moment captured by the image might have a crucial bearing on the meaning that can be attributed to it.

Presenting the data

An explanation of statistical techniques and data manipulation always accompanies the use of quantitative data in research yet, all too often, an account of the comparable processes is missing or very scant when it comes to reports that have used qualitative data. The process that leads from the data to the researcher's conclusions gets ignored, with the reader of the research report being given little or no indication of how the data were actually analysed. The quality of qualitative research is increasingly coming under the microscope in this respect and, quite rightly, those who use qualitative data are now expected to include in their accounts of research a description of the processes they used to move from the raw data to their findings.

Key point

Researchers need to be explicit about the analytic procedures they have used. It is not acceptable to say 'this is how I collected the data' (methods) and 'these are my results' (findings) without giving an account of *how* the data were analysed.

Qualitative researchers, however, face a special challenge when it comes to depicting the process involved in the analysis of their data (Woods 2006). Partly, this is because qualitative data analysis is 'a messy, ambiguous, time-consuming, creative, and fascinating process. It does not proceed in a linear fashion: it is not neat' (Marshall and Rossman 2011: 207). Partly, it is because the data are not as amenable to being presented in a concise fashion as is the case with quantitative data. Quantitative data can be represented using statistics and tables. These provide a succinct and well-established means enabling researchers to encapsulate the findings from large volumes of data and provide the reader with explicit information about the techniques used for data analysis. The challenge for qualitative researchers is to depict their kind of data analysis within the confines of a relatively few pages when dealing with:

- a fairly complicated and messy process of data analysis;
- a relatively large volume of data based on words or images.

To deal with this challenge, qualitative researchers need to come to terms very quickly with the fact that it is not feasible for them to present all of their data. They need to be selective in what they present and acknowledge that they have to act as an editor – identifying key parts of the data/analysis and prioritizing certain parts over others.

Next, and linked with the editorial role, it needs to be recognized that the data chosen for inclusion within a report does not constitute evidence that proves a point. It is more likely to be introduced as an illustration of a point that is being made. Because the reader of the report does not normally have access to all the data, they have no way of knowing whether the selection was a fair reflection of the data or not. Further discussion of this point can be found in relation to the use of extracts from interview transcripts.

Finally, the representation of qualitative data/analysis involves an element of 'rhetoric'. That is, the credibility of the research owes something to the skill of the researcher in managing to produce a persuasive account of the research that 'touches the right buttons' and conveys a sense of authority and authenticity. There are some different styles of writing that qualitative researchers can employ to achieve this (van Maanen 1995; Woods 2006). Without delving into the rhetorical devices themselves, the point to note is that the credibility of qualitative research, although it still depends on providing relevant factual details relating to the research procedures, also relies on the literary skills of the researcher to write a convincing account.

Link up with Chapter 19, Research reports.

Good practice: The use of diagrams

In reports based on qualitative research it is particularly useful to include diagrams that show the link between the concepts that are developed. This provides the reader with a visual picture of what can often be complex links. It also gives some transparency to the process of data analysis.

The use of interview extracts in research reports

Extracts from transcripts play an important role in qualitative research. They can be interesting in their own right, giving the reader a flavour of the data and letting the reader 'hear' the points as stated by the informants. Or they can be used as a piece of evidence supporting the argument that is being constructed in the report by the researcher. What an extract is very unlikely to do, however, is provide proof of a point. There are two reasons for this:

- *The significance of extracts from transcripts is always limited by the fact that they are, to some extent, presented out of context.* Extracts, as the very word itself suggests, are pieces of the data that are plucked from their context within the rest of the recorded interview. This opens up the possibility that the quote could be taken 'out of context'. Everyone knows the danger of being quoted out of context. The meaning of the words is changed by the fact that they are not linked to what came before and what was said after. The shrewd researcher will try to explain to the reader the context within which the extract arose but, inevitably, there is limited opportunity to do this in research reports.
- *The process of selecting extracts involves a level of judgement and discretion on the part of the researcher.* The selection of which parts of the transcript to include is entirely at the discretion of the researcher, and this inevitably limits the significance which can be attached to any one extract. It is an editorial decision which reflects the needs of the particular research report. How does the reader know that it was a fair selection, representative of the overall picture?

As a result, in the vast majority of reports produced by project researchers, extracts will serve as illustrations of a point and supporting evidence for an argument – nothing more and nothing less. It is important that the project researcher is aware of this when using extracts and avoids the temptation to present quotes from interviewees as though they stand in their own right as unequivocal proof of the point being discussed.

Having made this point, there are some things the researcher can do to get the best out of the extracts that are selected.

- Use quotes and extracts verbatim. Despite the points above about the difficulty of transcribing recordings, the researcher should be as literal as possible when quoting people. Use the exact words.
- Change the names to ensure anonymity (unless you have their explicit permission to reveal the person's identity).
- Provide some details about the person you are quoting, without endangering their anonymity. The general best advice here is to provide sufficient detail to distinguish informants from one another and to provide the reader with some idea of relevant background factors associated with the person, but to protect the identity of the person you quote by restricting how much information is given (e.g. teacher A, female, school 4, geography, mid-career).
- Try to give some indication of the context in which the quotation arose. Within the confines of a research report, try to provide some indication of the context of the extract so that the meaning *as intended* comes through. As far as it is feasible, the researcher should address the inevitable problem of taking the extract 'out of context' by giving the reader some guidance on the background within which the statement arose.

The quality of the data: validity and reliability

The credibility of qualitative research is not easily judged using the criteria conventionally used for quantitative research. It is not feasible, for instance, to check the quality of research and its findings by replicating the research in the same way that scientists might repeat an experiment. The first reason for this is that it is virtually impossible to replicate a social setting. Time inevitably changes things and the prospects of assembling equivalent people in similar settings in a social environment that has not changed are, to say the least, slim. The second reason is that the researcher tends to be intimately involved in the collection and analysis of qualitative data, so closely involved that the prospects of some other researcher being able to produce identical data and arrive at identical conclusions are equally slim.

Link up with
The quality
of the data:
validity and
reliability,
p. 299.

Recognizing such difficulties, some qualitative researchers have suggested abandoning any commitment to these conventional ways of judging the quality of research. The majority, though, have been rather more reticent to abandon the conventional criteria used by the positivistic research. They make the point that, although the nature of qualitative research means that it will never be possible to be verified in the same way as quantitative research, there is still a need to address the need for verification (e.g. Kirk and Miller 1986; Seale 1999; Gibbs 2007; Silverman 2011; Miles et al. 2014). Such qualitative researchers have adopted a more pragmatic or 'subtle' realist perspective 'that does not give up on scientific aims as conventionally conceived, but also draws on the insights of post-scientific conceptions of social research' (Seale 1999: x). The discussion and guidance that follow are rooted in this point of view.

Credibility (validity)

The issue here is the extent to which qualitative researchers can demonstrate that their data are accurate and appropriate. Lincoln and Guba (1985) make the point that it is not possible for qualitative researchers to prove in any absolute way that they have 'got it right'. (As a consequence, they prefer to use the term 'credibility' in relation to this aspect of the verification of research.) There are, though, steps to be taken that can help with the task of persuading readers of the research that the data are *reasonably likely* to be accurate and appropriate. These steps provide no guarantee, because none are available. They offer, instead, reassurances that the qualitative data have been produced and checked in accord with good practice. It is on this basis that judgements can be made about the credibility of the data. To address the matters of accuracy and appropriateness of data qualitative researchers can use:

- *Respondent validation.* The researcher can return to the participants with the data and findings as a means of checking the validity of the findings. This allows a check on factual accuracy and allows the researcher's understandings to be confirmed (or amended) by those whose opinions, views or experiences are being studied.

- *Grounded data*. One of the key benefits of qualitative research is that the findings will have been grounded extensively in fieldwork and empirical data. Qualitative research tends to involve relatively long times spent 'on location' conducting the fieldwork and it builds on a detailed scrutiny of the text or visual images involved. This provides a solid foundation for the conclusions based on the data and adds to the credibility of the research.

- *Triangulation*. Avoiding any naïve use of triangulation, the researcher can use contrasting data sources to bolster confidence that the data are 'on the right lines'.

> **Link up with** Triangulation, p. 167.

Dependability (reliability)

With qualitative research the researcher's 'self' tends to be very closely bound up with the research instrument – sometimes an integral part of it. As a participant observer or interviewer, for example, the researcher becomes almost an integral part of the data collecting technique. As a result, the question of reliability translates from 'Would the research instrument produce the same results when used by different researchers (all other things being equal)?' to 'If someone else did the research, would he or she have got the same results and arrived at the same conclusions?' In an absolute sense there is probably no way of knowing this for certain. Yet there are ways of dealing with this issue in qualitative research – ways that accord broadly with what Lincoln and Guba (1985) call 'dependability'. Principally, these revolve around the demonstration that their research reflects procedures and decisions that other researchers can 'see' and evaluate in terms of how far they constitute *reputable procedures and reasonable decisions*. This acts as a proxy for being able to replicate research. Only if such information is supplied is it possible to reach conclusions about how far another researcher would have come up with comparable findings. As a check on reliability, this calls for an explicit account of the methods, analysis and decision-making and 'the provision of a fully reflexive account of procedures and methods, showing the readers in as much detail as possible the lines of enquiry that led to particular conclusions' (Seale 1999: 157). In effect, the research process must be open for audit.

Good practice: An audit trail

An audit trail should be constructed and mapped out for the reader – allowing them to follow the path and key decisions taken by the researcher from conception of the research through to the findings and conclusions derived from the research. But, as Lincoln and Guba (1985: 319) stress, 'An inquiry audit cannot be conducted without a residue of records stemming from the inquiry, just as a fiscal audit cannot be conducted without a residue of records from the business transactions involved.' This is why it is good practice to keep a fairly detailed record of the process of the research decisions. The principle behind the audit trail is that research procedures and decision-making could be checked by other researchers who would be in a position to confirm the existence of the data and evaluate the decisions made in relation to the data collection and analysis.

Transferability (generalizability)

Qualitative research tends to be based on the intensive study of a relatively small number of cases. Inevitably, this raises questions about how representative those cases are and how likely it is that what was found in the few cases will be found elsewhere in similar cases. The thorny issue is often raised through the question, 'How can you generalize on the basis of such a small number?' Statistically speaking, this is a reasonable question. It is one that is difficult to dodge.

Some qualitative researchers try to side-step the issue by asserting that it is not their business to make such generalizations. They argue that the findings from things like case studies are worthwhile in their own right simply as a depiction of the specific, possibly unique, situation. This, however, is a minority position. The majority of qualitative researchers accept that the issue is relevant but argue that it needs to be approached in a different way when being used in relation to qualitative research. They point out that generalizability is based on the statistical probability of some aspect of the data recurring elsewhere, and it is a probability that relies on a large sample that is representative of the wider population. Research based on small numbers and qualitative data needs an alternative way of addressing the issue. This alternative way is what Lincoln and Guba (1985) have called 'transferability'. This is an imaginative process in which the reader of the research uses information about the particular instance that has been studied to arrive at a judgement about how far it would apply to other comparable instances. The question becomes 'To what extent *could* the findings be transferred to other instances?' rather than 'To what extent *are* the findings likely to exist in other instances?'

Good practice: Transferability of findings

The researcher needs to supply information enabling others to infer the *relevance and applicability of the findings* (to other people, settings, case studies, organizations, etc.). In other words, to gauge how far the findings are transferable, the reader needs to be presented with relevant details on which to base a comparison. If, for example, the research is on the eating habits of young people and it is based on interviews with 55 students in one school, the findings might not be generalizable to the population of students in all schools. However, armed with appropriate information about the age/sex/ethnicity of the students and the social context of the school, it becomes possible to think about how the findings might apply to similar students in similar schools. Armed with the appropriate information, the reader can consider the transferability of the findings.

Confirmability (objectivity)

This issue of objectivity concerns the extent to which qualitative research can produce findings that are free from the influence of the researcher(s) who conducted the enquiry. At a fundamental level it needs to be recognized straight away that no research is ever free from the influence of those who conduct it. Qualitative data, whether text or images, are always the product of a process of interpretation. The data do not exist 'out there' waiting to be discovered (as might be assumed if a positivistic approach were adopted) but are produced by the way they are interpreted and used by researchers. This has consequences for the prospects of objectivity. First, it raises questions about the involvement of the researcher's 'self' in the interpretation of the data and, second, it raises questions about the prospects of keeping an open mind and being willing to consider alternative and competing explanations of the data.

The researcher's 'self'

The researcher's identity, values and beliefs cannot be entirely eliminated from the process of analysing qualitative data. There are, though, two ways in which qualitative researchers can deal with this involvement of the self. On the one hand, they can deal with it by saying:

> The researcher's identity, values and beliefs play a role in the production and analysis of qualitative data and therefore researchers should be on their guard to distance themselves from their normal, everyday beliefs and to suspend judgements on social issues for the duration of their research.

At this end of the scale researchers know that their self is intertwined with their research activity but proceed on the basis that they can exercise sufficient control over their normal attitudes to allow them to operate in a detached manner, so that their investigation is not clouded by personal prejudices. In this case the researcher needs to suspend personal values and beliefs for the purposes of the production and analysis of the data.

On the other hand, qualitative researchers could take the position that:

> The researcher's identity, values and beliefs play a role in the production and analysis of qualitative data and therefore researchers should come clean about the way their research agenda has been shaped by personal experiences and social backgrounds.

At the extreme, this approach can take the form of celebrating the extent to which the self is intertwined with the research process. There are those who argue that their self gives them a privileged insight into social issues, so that the researcher's self should not be regarded as a limitation to the research but as a crucial resource. Some feminist researchers and some researchers in the field of 'race' make the case that their identity, values and beliefs actually *enable* the research and should be exploited to the full to get at areas that will remain barred to researchers with a different self. So some feminists argue that only a woman can truly grasp the significance of factors concerned with the subordination of women in society. Some black researchers would make a similar point in relation to 'race' inequality.

Between the two positions outlined above lie a variety of shades of opinion about the degree to which the researcher's self can and should be acknowledged as affecting the production and analysis of qualitative data. However, there is a general consensus on the key point: *the role of the self in qualitative research is important*. To ignore the role of the researcher's self in qualitative research, then, would be ill-advised.

A reflexive account of researcher's self

The analysis of qualitative data calls for a reflexive account by the researcher concerning the researcher's self and its impact on the research. There is a growing acceptance among those involved in qualitative data analysis that some *biographical details about the researcher warrant inclusion as part of the analysis*, thus allowing the writer to explore the ways in which he/she feels personal experiences and values might influence matters. The reader of the research, by the same token, is given valuable information on which to base a judgement about how reasonable the writer's claims are with regard to the detachment or involvement of self-identity, values and beliefs.

An open mind

Qualitative researchers, like all researchers, need to approach the analysis of the data with an open mind. If they do not, they can be accused of lacking objectivity. In practice, a way of demonstrating such openness is for the researcher to take seriously the possibility of having 'got it wrong'. This is actually a fundamental point in relation to the production of knowledge. It is linked to the argument that good research is concerned not with the verification of findings but with their 'falsification'. For the project researcher there are perhaps two aspects of this which can be addressed quite practically. Qualitative researchers should:

- *Avoid neglecting data that do not fit the analysis.* Good research should not ignore those instances within the data that might appear to disconfirm the researcher's analysis. There might be only a few such 'outliers'. There might be just the occasional bit of data that does not fit nicely or that contradicts the general trend. These should not be ignored, but should be actively investigated to see if there is an explanation for them that can be accommodated within the emerging analysis, of whether there is some genuine significance in them. Looking for, and accounting for, negative instances or deviant cases that contradict the emerging analysis are important.
- *Check rival explanations.* Alternative possible explanations need to be explored. The researcher needs to demonstrate that he or she has not simply plumped for the first explanation that fits, rather than seeing if rival theories work or whether there are hidden problems with the proposed explanation.

> **Good practice: The need to be open about the researcher's 'self'**
> Qualitative researchers should provide some biographical details about themselves and their interest in the research. They should also address the issue of objectivity by demonstrating the extent to which they have approached the research with an 'open mind'.

Advantages of qualitative data analysis

There is a richness and detail to the data

The in-depth study of relatively focused areas, the tendency towards small-scale research and the generation of 'thick descriptions' mean that qualitative research scores well in terms of the way it deals with complex social situations and the subtleties of social life.

The data and the analysis are 'grounded'

With qualitative research the findings are based upon evidence drawn from real-world settings. There is little scope for 'armchair theorizing' or 'ideas plucked out of thin air'.

There can be alternative explanations

Qualitative analysis, because it draws on the interpretive skills of the researcher, opens up the possibility of more than one explanation being valid. Rather than a presumption that there must be, in theory at least, one correct explanation, it allows for the possibility that different researchers might reach different conclusions, despite using broadly the same methods.

There is tolerance of ambiguity and contradictions

To the extent that social existence involves uncertainty, accounts of that existence ought to be able to tolerate ambiguities and contradictions, and qualitative research is better able to do this than quantitative research. This is not a reflection of a weak analysis. It is a reflection of the social reality being investigated.

Disadvantages of qualitative data analysis

Generalizability of the findings

One repercussion of qualitative research's tendency to rely on the detailed, in-depth study of a small number of instances is that it becomes more difficult to establish how far the findings may be generalized to other similar instances.

The analysis takes longer

Computer programs can assist with the management of the data and they can even help with the analysis, but nowhere near to the extent that they can with quantitative data. A key factor here is that qualitative data are generally unstructured when they are first collected in their 'raw' state (e.g. interviews, field notes, photographs) and need to be coded before they can be analysed.

Questions can be raised about the objectivity of the findings

Qualitative research recognizes more openly than does quantitative research that the researcher's own identity, background and beliefs have a role in the creation of data and the analysis of data.

There is the danger of taking the data 'out of context'

The analysis of qualitative data needs to be wary about wrenching the data from its location (1) within a sequence of data (e.g. interview talk) or (2) within surrounding circumstances. Both things have a bearing on the meaning of the text or image.

Further reading

Bazeley, P. (2013) *Qualitative Data Analysis: Practical Strategies*. London: Sage.
Bazeley, P. and Jackson, K. (2013) *Qualitative Data Analysis with NVivo*. London: Sage.
Grbich, C. (2013) *Qualitative Data Analysis: An Introduction*, 2nd edn. London: Sage.
Harding, J. (2013) *Qualitative Data Analysis from Start to Finish*. London: Sage.
Miles, M.B., Huberman, A.M. and Saldana, J.M. (2014) *Qualitative Data Analysis: A Methods Sourcebook*, 3rd edn. Thousand Oaks, CA: Sage.
Silver, C. and Lewins, A. (2014) *Using Software in Qualitative Research: A Step-by-step Guide*, 2nd edn. London: Sage.
Silverman, D. (2014) *Interpreting Qualitative Data*, 5th edn. London: Sage.

Checklist for the analysis of qualitative data

When analysing qualitative data you should feel confident about answering 'yes' to the following question: ☑

1 Does the data analysis do one or more of the following?   ☐

- Give a detailed description of the culture of specific groups.
- Describe people's experiences and the meanings they attribute to situations.
- Explain the impact of complex social processes and settings.
- Look for hidden messages – content analysis.
- Develop concepts or theories – grounded theory.
- Expose the workings of power through language – discourse analysis.
- Reveal underlying rules and structures of talk – conversation analysis.
- Give an account of the construction of self and social world – narrative analysis.
- Explain the meaning and cultural significance of images – image-based analysis.

2 Has the analysis been based on a depth scrutiny of the data?   ☐

3 Has the data analysis taken an iterative approach?   ☐

4 Does any report of the findings include an explicit account of the process of data analysis?   ☐

5 Have sufficient details been incorporated to allow an 'audit' of key decisions in the process of the research?   ☐

6 Have relevant details been supplied to permit readers to think about the transferability of the findings?   ☐

7 Has the topic been approached with an 'open mind'?   ☐

8 Are the selection criteria for people or items in the study:
- appropriate to the aims of the research?   ☐
- suitable for the form of qualitative analysis undertaken?   ☐

9 Does the research report include some reflexive account of the researcher's self and its possible impact?   ☐

10 Does the analysis address the original aims and purpose of the research?   ☐

© M. Denscombe, *The Good Research Guide*. Open University Press.

Part **4**

Context

Social research takes place within a context that shapes the possibilities of what can be done. That context is society. Society places limits on what researchers can do in the pursuit of knowledge and it has expectations about how research should be conducted.

The most obvious way in which such limits and expectations confront the researcher is through the duties and obligations associated with *research ethics*. Society sets certain standards of conduct which researchers are expected to maintain and good research must meet these standards. Its methods must be acceptable within the cultural norms of the society in which it takes place and accord with a variety of moral, legal and safety considerations. Chapter 18 outlines the expectations that operate in the western world in the twenty-first century and provides guidance on how these expectations can be met.

The context of research is also significant in terms of the accountability of researchers and the obligation this places on researchers to make their research findings available for scrutiny by a wider public. As the twenty-first century progresses, an increasing emphasis is being placed on the dissemination of findings from research and the need to make findings easily accessible to other researchers or anyone who has an interest in the outcomes from a research project. This brings into the foreground the role of the research report as the means by which researchers communicate their work. Chapter 19 outlines the general features of research reports. It also suggests ways in which project researchers can provide an account of their research to an audience with a specific interest in evaluating the quality of the research that has been under-taken. Chapter 20 introduces the key aims of literature reviews, showing how they are crucial for developing the ideas that shape the direction and design of the research. Added to this, and building on Chapter 19, they are a vital feature of research reports, providing the readers with a rationale for the research. Bearing this in mind, the chapter includes some practical guidance on how to write a good critical review of the literature.

18 Research ethics

Social researchers are expected to approach their task in an ethical manner. On moral grounds, this expectation stems from the belief that the public should be protected from researchers who might be tempted to use any means available to advance the state of knowledge on a given topic. It rests on the assumption that researchers have no privileged position in society that justifies them pursuing their interests at the expense of those they are studying – no matter how valuable they hope the findings might be.

Ethics Committee approval

The importance attached to research ethics is evident in the fact that social researchers will normally need to get prior approval for their investigation from an *Ethics Committee*. Even with small-scale research, it is increasingly the case that before the research can be conducted it will need to have been scrutinized by a committee of suitably qualified experts to ensure that the design of the research includes appropriate measures to protect the interests of the people and groups covered by the research. Those conducting investigations as part of any academic qualification will normally be required to have their plans vetted by an Ethics Committee within their university before they are allowed to start the investigation. Submissions to Ethics Committees will be judged according to the broad principles for ethical research outlined below, and might include further specific stipulations depending on the field of the research.

> **Good practice: Get ethics approval before commencing data collection**
>
> Approval from an Ethics Committee should be obtained *before* any primary data are collected from the people involved in the research. The approval process can take weeks, sometimes months, to complete and this needs to be taken into consideration when planning the data collection phase of the research.

Kinds of research that need ethical approval

Research that involves data collection from or about living individuals generally requires ethical scrutiny. This means that projects will normally need to be considered by an Ethics Committee if they plan to collect data directly from or about people using the following methods:

- questionnaires;
- interviews or focus groups;
- participant observation or systematic observation.

This scrutiny is intended to ensure that no harm is caused by the investigation. Why is this necessary? In many cases social research might seem fairly innocuous involving perhaps some market research questions about people's purchasing habits or some other kind of enquiry that would not appear to pose much of a risk to the well-being of those who take part in the research. However, the dangers of social research can be real and substantial. It is the role of an Ethics Committee to consider the potential risks entailed in carrying out a proposed piece of research and to arrive at a conclusion about whether the risks have been considered, whether effective precautions will be taken to minimize the risks, and whether the plan of work is likely to produce worthwhile results without endangering the well-being of the participants involved.

Ethics Committees will pay particular attention to any kinds of research that, in the words of the Economic and Social Research Council (ESRC), 'involve more than minimal risk' to participants. This is the kind of research that involves:

- vulnerable groups (e.g. children, people with a learning disability);
- sensitive topics (e.g. sexual, religious or illegal behaviour);
- deception or research carried out without the informed consent of participants;
- use of confidential information about identifiable individuals;
- processes that might cause psychological stress, anxiety, humiliation or cause more than minimal pain;
- intrusive interventions (e.g. administration of drugs or vigorous physical exercise that would not be part of participants' normal lives).

Exceptions to the rule

There are certain kinds of research that do not need to go through a process of formal scrutiny by an Ethics Committee. First, there can be exceptions when the investigation is regarded as part of routine and normal work, and therefore not really 'research' as such. In the National Health Service, for instance, data collection and analysis undertaken as part of the routine work and management of the organization would not normally need to be submitted to an Ethics Committee for approval (Department of Health 2005). The kind of investigations and data collection which would *not* need approval include:

- audits;
- service evaluation;
- clinical case studies;
- equipment testing;
- customer satisfaction surveys.

Second, there can be exceptions when the research draws exclusively on published secondary source material. Library-based research, archive research, historical research, the use of official statistics and economic data are the kind of research that fall into this category. If the research uses aggregated data where individuals cannot be identified, if it uses data that are already in the public domain, or if the research relates to historical or fictional characters, then it might be treated as involving little risk and therefore permissible without the need for prior approval by an Ethics Committee. The thinking here is that there are no problems that can arise in the data collection phase (because the data have already been collected on a previous occasion) and no privacy issues because the data are in the public sphere and widely available to anyone.

The risks associated with social research, however, are not limited to the harm that might potentially occur during the data collection phase. As we shall see, research ethics is also concerned with the repercussions for participants resulting from the publication of findings. These things apply whatever the kind of social research that is being conducted and, for this reason, there is an increasing tendency to require *every* social research project to go through some initial vetting, some kind of scrutiny, before it is allowed to proceed. Even if the data collection appears to be unproblematic, institutions need to feel assured that any research conducted under their auspices (for a university degree, or by an employee) equally meets the required ethical standards when it comes to the analysis of the data and the dissemination of the data.

 Caution

Be aware that research ethics applies to *all* social research, even if formal approval from an Ethics Committee is not required.

Codes of research ethics

Codes of research ethics provide guidance on the kind of actions that should be taken and the kind that must be avoided when undertaking research. Professional research associations almost always publish a code of conduct that they expect their members to abide by. Research funding bodies and government departments that commission research have similar guidelines governing acceptable practice in the context of research. There is some difference in emphasis between these codes. Market research associations approach things in a slightly different way from medical associations, reflecting the different nature of the procedures the researchers are likely to use and the potential harm that might be done to participants. Market researchers collecting data on consumer preferences are not likely to be exposing participants to the same potential risk, psychological or physical, as health researchers investigating the effectiveness of a new drug or surgical procedure.

Good practice: Abide by a specific code of research ethics

Project researchers should identify a code of ethics that represents their academic discipline or professional association. This code should be used in relation to the research and, importantly, should be explicitly referred to in any account of the methods used in the research.

Examples of relevant codes which can be obtained online are:

The British Psychological Society: *Code of Human Research Ethics*
Social Research Association: *Ethics Guidelines*
The British Sociological Association: *Statement of Ethical Practice*
The Market Research Society: *Code of Marketing Research Standards*
British Educational Research Association: *Ethical Guidelines for Educational Research*
Health Research Authority: *Research Governance Framework for Health and Social Care*

Personal responsibility

Ultimately, researchers must take personal responsibility for their actions when conducting research. Codes of research ethics establish the key principles for conducting research but, as Hammersley (2015) reminds us, principles do not necessarily provide guidelines for action that operate in a straightforward and direct manner in relation to specific situations. They establish a shared vision of what researchers should strive to achieve – a moral compass for research. But, when it comes to practical situations researchers often have to make judgements and interpret the principles.

In these situations they cannot 'hide behind the rules' and slavishly follow prescribed rules of conduct.

 Key point

Codes of ethics and Ethics Committee approval do not absolve researchers from personal responsibility for the decisions they take when conducting research.

Core principles of research ethics

There are four key principles which underlie codes of research ethics. These principles have their origins in medical research and were established initially in response to atrocities committed during the Second World War which purported to have been done in the name of science and the progress of medical knowledge. Through the Nuremberg Code (1947–49), and later the Declaration of Helsinki (1964), the international community established the foundations for research ethics and enshrined the fundamental principle that *the ends do not justify the means in the pursuit of knowledge.*

The Nuremberg Code and the Declaration of Helsinki have been developed over the years and various professional bodies, academic disciplines and government departments have adapted them for use in the context of social research as distinct from medical research. These codes of ethics for social research stick to the core principle (that in their pursuit of knowledge researchers must not ruthlessly use any means at their disposal) and they develop this along four lines. Social researchers are expected to conduct their investigations in a way that:

- protects the interests of the participants;
- ensures that participation is voluntary and based on informed consent;
- avoids deception and operates with scientific integrity;
- complies with the laws of the land.

Principle 1: Participants' interests should be protected

There is general agreement that people should not suffer as a consequence of their involvement with a piece of research. Those who contribute to research as informants or as research subjects should be no worse off at the end of their participation than they were when they started. Nor should there be longer-term repercussions stemming from their involvement that in any sense harm the participants.

In accordance with this principle, researchers have a duty to consider in advance the likely consequences of participation and to take measures that safeguard the interests of those who help with the investigation. First, they need to ensure that participants do not come to any *physical harm* as a result of the research. With some kinds of research there needs to be careful consideration of the physical safety of participants, anticipating any threats arising from the time/location of meetings, travel to such locations, or even the possibility of the participant suffering retribution from people who feel threatened by the participant's involvement in the research or the disclosure of particular information. The possibility might seem quite remote, but researchers have a responsibility to anticipate such risks and avoid any physical harm from occurring.

Second, care needs to be taken to *avoid psychological harm* resulting from research. Any investigation that is potentially going to lead to trauma, stress or other psychological harm will be considered unethical. Researchers therefore need to anticipate the likelihood that their investigation might be perceived as intrusive, touch on sensitive issues, or threaten the beliefs of the participants because these are the kinds of thing that could give rise to psychological harm.

Third, participants should suffer *no personal harm* arising from the disclosure of information collected during the research. Disclosure of personal information could be embarrassing for the participants and, depending on the type of information, it could also involve economic loss or even the prospect of legal action being taken against participants on the basis of the disclosed information if it was to come to the attention of relevant authorities (e.g. employers, Inland Revenue, social security inspectors, the police, customs officials). There is broad agreement, therefore, that researchers need to protect the interests of the participants by ensuring the confidentiality of information that is given to them. When publishing results, care needs to be taken not to disclose the personal identities of individuals who have contributed to the findings.

Fourth, the participants should stand to benefit from the outcomes from the research. This does not mean that each participant is expected to gain personally from taking part in the research but that, in principle, a person *such as them* might benefit at some point in the future as a consequence of the research. The idea is that participants are not just 'guinea pigs' whose sole value is that of providing data. Their willingness to devote time and effort, indeed their willingness to expose themselves to risks, should be done on the basis of getting something back. Not money, but some other form of benefit for people like them. This stems from the ethical principle of 'beneficence' which states that research on people should always be done 'for the good of people', never frivolously or for malicious purposes.

Fifth, and linked to this, participants should be treated *fairly and equally* in terms of the participation in the research. People should not be included in the research, nor excluded from the research, on grounds which are unfair or irrelevant. And this is not just a matter of good practice in terms of gaining a representative sample: it is an ethical point based on the idea that any benefits or risks associated with a piece of research should be shared equally among all those concerned. The reasoning is easy to see in the case of medical research. As Goldacre (2012) argues, it is unfair to trial Aids vaccines in Africa if the prime beneficiaries of any breakthrough will be residents of rich countries in the West and where the risks are taken by those who, in all likelihood, will not be able to afford any new breakthrough vaccine that results from the research. In social research, this translates as meaning that researchers need to ensure that their research design does not discriminate against the involvement of parties whose voices ought to be heard and whose interests need to be represented through their inclusion as participants in the research. For ethical reasons, that is, the research design should be sure to represent the interests of all relevant people, including the underprivileged, the weak, the vulnerable and minority groups.

Good practice: Protecting participants' interests

Researchers should:

- anticipate any threats to the *personal safety* of participants, and take steps to avoid these occurring;
- respect participants' privacy and sensitivities, and *avoid undue intrusion* when collecting data;
- treat all information disclosed to them during research as *confidential*, and not disclose it to other participants or people not connected with the research;
- guarantee the *anonymity* of individuals and organizations in any published documents arising from the research – unless participants give explicit (and written) consent to identify them by name;
- ensure that the benefits and risks associated with inclusion in the research are spread *fairly and equally* among relevant groups.

Principle 2: Participation should be voluntary and based on informed consent

People should never be forced or coerced into helping with research. Their participation must always be voluntary, and they must have sufficient information about the research to arrive at a reasoned judgement about whether or not they want to participate. These are the premises of 'informed consent'. Particularly where the kind of information collected is of a sensitive nature, there is a need to get informed consent. But, more than this, there is often a need to get that consent *in writing*. When the consent is in writing, it acts as a way of formally recording the agreement to participate and confirming that the participant has been informed about the nature of the research. This protects the researcher from any possible accusation that he or she acted improperly when recruiting people to take part in the research.

> **Good practice: Informed consent**
>
> For participants to be able to give informed consent researchers need to:
>
> - make it very clear that participation is *voluntary,* and that partici-pants can *withdraw* from the research at any time should they wish to do so;
> - provide participants with *adequate information* about the research;
> - specify what kind of *commitment* is being required of participants.
>
> A formal way to confirm that participation is on the basis of informed consent is to use a *consent form* (see the template below).

What if it is not possible to get written consent?

It may not always be possible to gain consent from all those who take part in a research project. Research on crowd behaviour at football matches or observation of the movements of visitors to art galleries are clearly instances where it would prove impossible to get everyone to complete a consent form. There are other occasions where it may not be deemed practical or, indeed, necessary to get written consent. Approaching people in the street to ask a few questions about their shopping habits, for example, might not be seen as requiring the completion of a consent form. In this case there is some tacit consent. The agreement to answer the questions clearly indicates that their participation is voluntary and, because the nature of the participants' involvement in the research is rather 'low risk', under the circumstances this 'verbal consent' might be deemed sufficient. The codes of conduct of the professional associations generally recognize this and include clauses that acknowledge that exceptions might need to be made to the general rule about written consent. Normally, the conditions under which researchers can collect data ethically without getting written consent are those where:

- the form of data collection is unlikely to involve much by way of personal risks to the informant, and
- it is not realistically possible to get such consent.

Principle 3: Researchers should operate in an open and honest manner with respect to the investigation

Researchers are expected to avoid deception or misrepresentation in their dealings with participants. They are expected to be open and explicit about what they are doing – to let people know that they are researchers and that they intend to collect data for the purposes of an investigation into a particular topic. Furthermore, they are expected to tell the truth about the nature of their investigation and the role of the participants in that research.

Good practice: Openness in the conduct of research

Researchers should:

- produce a *brief summary* of the aims of the research and the nature of the data that are to be collected. This should be no more than one page in length and written without jargon so that the purpose of the research can be clearly understood by potential participants and others who might have an interest in the research;
- where possible, develop a *website* for the project so that information about the project can be widely available to interested parties. Links from the home page can be used to provide further information about the researchers (their credentials and experience) and more details about the background to the project for those who might want to know more.

There is also an expectation that researchers operate with 'scientific integrity'. This means, in effect, that researchers are expected to uphold the highest standards of professionalism and honesty in terms of their treatment of the data and dealings with other researchers. On the first point, working ethically means doing the best possible job to collect and analyse data in an objective and honest way. Researchers should not be swayed to supply findings that suit the needs of those who fund or sponsor the research. Nor should they allow personal preferences and ideals to cloud their judgement and get in the way of providing a balanced and dispassionate interpretation of their findings. They should be 'fair' and unbiased. On the second point, there is an expectation that researchers should acknowledge the contribution of others and not 'steal' their work through plagiarism. Researchers certainly need to 'use' the work of others – either by way of building upon it or by criticizing it – but when doing so they should always explicitly acknowledge the source of the other work.

Scientific integrity covers two further obligations on the researcher. First, the researcher is expected to have the appropriate experience and *competence* to undertake the investigation. Without this there is a danger that the participants might be harmed. Thinking of medical research the point behind this is easy to see. With social research too, however, Ethics Committees will look to be reassured that researchers will restrict their investigations to those styles of research for which they are qualified and for which their experience makes them well prepared. Second, as we have already noted, there is a clear expectation that researchers should not engage in research which is frivolous or whimsical, or for which there is not a good 'scientific' reason to believe that something of value will be learnt as an outcome. Behind both these points there is the principle that participants should not be exposed to the risk of harm or inconvenience by being asked to participate in research that is not likely to be beneficial. This is the principle of 'beneficence'.

> **Good practice: Honesty and integrity in the conduct of research**
> Researchers should:
>
> - avoid deception or misrepresentation in their dealings with participants;
> - provide fair and unbiased interpretation of their findings;
> - explicitly acknowledge any sponsorship or vested interests relating to the research;
> - avoid plagiarizing other researchers' work;
> - have the necessary skills and experience to carry out the research;
> - show that real benefits are likely to emerge from the research.

What if some deception is necessary?

There are occasions when it is not feasible for the researcher to be completely open and honest with participants. To be so would automatically jeopardize any prospect of the investigation actually taking place or would cause participants to react to the research in a way that would contaminate the results. Many psychology experiments, for example, would be ruined if the subjects knew in advance what the researcher was investigating, and it has been estimated that about three-quarters of psychology experiments involve giving participants information that, in one respect or another, actually misleads them about the purpose of the experiment. Some types of ethnographic study, likewise, involve fieldwork where the researcher needs to disguise his/her true role because if people knew that research was being conducted they would act differently from normal, and the 'naturalness' of the setting would be destroyed.

When some form of deception is seen as necessary, researchers face an ethical dilemma: from the point of view of good research design, deception is regarded as essential, yet from the point of view of ethical research such deception is bad practice. The codes of conduct published by professional associations, however, generally acknowledge that, on certain occasions, some deception by researchers might be warranted as absolutely necessary for the purposes of the research. Such occasions, though, need to be treated as exceptions to the rule – ones that can be justified only on the basis of the very special circumstances surrounding the particular investigation. The conditions under which it might be acceptable generally require the researcher:

- to provide an explicit justification for why the deception is vital and why there is no suitable alternative approach that would permit full disclosure about the nature of the research;
- to use a 'debriefing' session in which, after the event, participants are put in the picture about the true nature of the enquiry and why they could not be informed about this at the beginning.

Principle 4: Research should comply with the laws of the land

Social researchers are expected to abide by the laws of the land: they do not stand above the law nor should they put themselves outside the law. Bearing this in mind, there are some laws which are of particular relevance for social researchers. First, there are those laws that set bounds to what is acceptable in terms of the topic of the research. There are areas where the nature of any research project is likely to 'cross the line' in terms of the law, and for this reason project researchers should steer well clear of such areas. Obvious examples would be the way that research involving empirical investigation into topics such as terrorism, drug trafficking, paedophilia, prostitution or pornography could all too easily, and unintentionally, end up breaking the law. Second, there are certain ways of collecting data that could fall foul of the law. There are data protection laws that need to be considered, laws against hacking into computers, laws against fraud, and copyright laws, all of which set boundaries around what can be legitimately used as a means for collecting data. The data protection laws also have a bearing on the way that researchers need to store their data and the extent to which personal data can be distributed to third parties not actually involved with the research (see below).

Link up with Data protection, p. 349.

> **Good practice: Compliance with the law**
>
> To help them stay within the law, researchers should:
>
> - avoid researching *sensitive topics* where the methods of data collection and analysis might lead them to break the law;
> - take care on matters relating to the ownership of the data, *intellectual property rights* and copyright matters;
> - take reasonable measures to ensure that *data are kept private and secure*.

Written consent form

When researchers seek informed consent on a formal basis it is standard practice to use a 'consent form'. This form does two things. First, it provides the potential participant with enough information about the research and their involvement for them to make an *informed* decision. Second, it provides the researcher with some documented evidence that the participant has agreed to take part in the research – *written consent*. The forms vary in length and detail according to the nature of the research, but generally include the following sections.

Identity of the researcher

Participants are entitled to know who is conducting the research and where they can be contacted. The consent form, therefore, should include:

- the name(s) of the researcher;
- an address and other contact details at which he or she can be contacted;
- where appropriate, the name of the organization under whose auspices the research is being conducted.

Information about the research

There needs to be a statement providing enough detail for the participant to understand, in broad terms, the aims, methods and anticipated outcomes of the research. This must be brief since participants will not normally wish to spend a lot of time reading page after page of details. Some researchers present the information on a separate sheet that can be left with the participant for future reference. At other times, the statement is limited to a few sentences on the consent form itself. Either way, participants need to be provided with a brief description of:

- what the research is investigating;
- how it is to be conducted;
- who, if anybody, is sponsoring the research;
- what benefits are likely to emerge from the investigation.

Expectations about the participant's contribution

Informed consent presumes that participants know in advance what tasks the researcher expects them to undertake and what, if any, reward they might expect for their efforts. They will need to be told whether they are expected to take part in an interview, take part in a laboratory experiment, or complete a questionnaire. And they should be given some indication of how much time this is likely to take. They might also need to know whether any expenses they incur will be paid for by the researcher, and whether they will receive some kind of payment or other incentive (such as a free copy of the final report of the research). The consent form, then, should specify:

- why they were selected for inclusion in the study;
- what tasks the participant will undertake;
- how much of their time this is likely to take;
- what general benefits or specific incentives there might be for taking part in the research.

The right to withdraw consent

Signing a consent form does not oblige participants to continue in the role if, at some subsequent stage, they no longer wish to do so. The consent form is not a contract that binds a person to the task of helping with the research – and this should be made clear on the consent form itself. Participants should be made aware that, should they wish to do so, it is their right to withdraw their consent at any time.

Confidentiality and security of data

The consent form needs to incorporate some commitment by the researcher with regard to the conduct of the research and the treatment of the data. Any agreement to take part in research ought to be made with an understanding of what code of ethics the researcher will use and what measures will be taken to safeguard the data and protect participants from any disclosure of their individual identity. Such assurances could include:

- specifying which professional association's code of ethics will be used during the course of the research;
- what security measures will be taken to ensure the confidentiality of the data;
- how anonymity of the data will be guaranteed (if appropriate).

Ownership and use of the data

It can be prudent to get participants' formal approval for the researcher to use the information they provide and the words they use for the purposes of academic research and publications arising from the project.

Signature of the participant, with date

This signature can incorporate an acknowledgement that the participant has been advised about the requirements of the research and has understood what is involved (e.g. 'I have read and understood the written details provided for me about the research, and agree to participate in the project. Signed . . .').

Counter-signature of the researcher, with date

It is good practice for the researcher, as well as the participant, to sign the consent form effectively committing the researcher to uphold his or her side of the agreement.

Data protection

Prompted by the potential of computers to store and process vast quantities of information, and given further impetus by the growth of the Internet, most societies have *data protection laws* that are designed to protect the public from the unscrupulous collection and use of personal data. In the UK, as in many other countries, Human Rights legislation and Freedom of Information laws have imposed certain controls on the misuse of data, but the main piece of relevant legislation is the Data Protection Act (1988). This law relates to 'personal data' - data that includes personal details from which living individuals can be identified – and covers data held on any 'relevant filing system'. This includes paper records as well as computer files if they are kept systematically.

The Data Protection Act says that anyone storing such data is acting as a 'data controller' and this carries with it three responsibilities. First, data controllers must 'notify' the *Information Commissioner's Office* (http://www.ico. org.uk/) about the kind of data they hold, the purpose for which it is being used, and who the data will be disclosed to. This provides the Information Commissioner's Office with a national picture of what data is being held, who holds the data, and how that data is being used. Second, data controllers assume responsibility for keeping the data *secure* and ensuring the data are *accurate* and up to date. The legislation is designed to ensure that data held about individuals is handled properly and that the organizations involved take steps to ensure that the information on their database is correct. And third, data controllers become responsible for making the data *available* if, and when, any individual applies to see the data that is held about them. From a civil liberties point of view this is the key aspect of the legislation: it allows individual citizens to find out what data is held about them and, if necessary, challenge the validity of the data.

The implications for small-scale research

At first glance it might seem that, to comply with the law, social researchers will need to go through the process of notifying the Information Commissioner's Office (or equivalent regulatory body if not in the UK) about the data they hold. In reality, though, this is unlikely to be the case – particularly for small-scale social researchers conducting research as part of a university course. There are three reasons for this.

First, the Act does not apply to anonymized or aggregated data. Provided it is not possible to identify individuals from the data that are being held, and that the process of anonymization cannot be reversed, the data are not regarded as 'personal'. Bearing this in mind, researchers might ask themselves whether they really need to have personal identifying information attached to their dataset. Is it vital to directly link personal details (name, address, telephone number and email address, etc.) to each participant's data? If not, it makes sense to ensure that the data are duly anonymized.

Second, where research is conducted under the auspices of a large organization the organization itself might have a 'notification' that already covers the activity of the individual researchers who study with, or work for, that organization. Students and staff at universities are likely to be covered in this way particularly with respect to research conducted for academic dissertations and coursework.

Third, the Act includes a number of exemptions, meaning that certain kinds of data held by certain kinds of organization do not need be 'notified' to the

Information Commissioner's Office. *'Personal data that is processed only for research, statistical or historical purposes'* is one of them.

In practice, then, individual small-scale social researchers in the UK do not normally need to go through the process of notifying the Information Commissioner's Office about the data they hold.

Data protection principles

Although small-scale researchers may not need to formally notify the Information Commissioner's Office about the data they hold, this does not mean that the legislation simply 'does not apply' or that the standards for data protection established through the Act can be ignored. It is important to recognize that the legislation identifies some fundamental principles about data protection and effectively sets a benchmark for good practice when it comes to the storage and dissemination of personal data. To meet these standards social researchers should:

- *Collect and process data in a fair and lawful manner.* There is an obligation on researchers to stick within the law in the way they collect their data and, equally, to avoid deception or subterfuge in order to get their information.
- *Use data only for the purposes originally specified.* It is not legitimate to collect data for one purpose and then use them for some other purpose that was not stated at the time the data were collected.
- *Collect only the data that are actually needed.* Researchers should not collect vast amounts of data anticipating that some of it might come in useful now or at some time in the future. The data collection should be targeted at the current and actual needs of the project.
- *Take care to ensure the data are accurate.* Researchers, like other data collectors, have a duty of care to make sure the data they hold are accurate and, where appropriate, kept up to date.
- *Keep data no longer than is necessary.* Although researchers do not need to erase data after any given time, the legislation establishes the principle that data should be kept for use rather than simply accumulated. Obviously, in research terms there is some real value in retaining data for future comparison and checking, and for large projects there is generally some stipulation that all data must be kept for a minimum period following the completion of a project (ranging from 2 years to 10 years and upwards depending on the nature of the data).
- *Keep the data secure.* Very importantly, data should be kept safe. Depending upon the sensitivity of the data, appropriate measures need to be taken to avoid the possibility of them falling into the wrong hands by being lost or stolen. With data held on computers, this entails a suitable use of passwords or encryption to prevent unauthorized access to the data. With paper documents, the data need to be kept under lock and key.

- *Control the distribution of the data.* It is legitimate for researchers to give copies of their data to other researchers for specifically research purposes but data should not be distributed to third parties who might use the data for other purposes.
- Where possible, *anonymize the data.* The researcher should consider whether it is really necessary to collect data that are linked to identifiable individuals since anonymized data are exempted from the legislation. Data that are anonymous cannot be traced to any particular individual.

Ethics and Internet research

Internet-based research involves the same principles of research ethics as all other research. However, it brings with it some issues that warrant particular attention and a considerable amount of attention has been paid to the new kinds of challenge faced by Internet research in terms of things like informed consent, privacy and deception, confidentiality and legislation (McKee and Porter 2009; Heider and Massanari 2012; Farrimond 2013; Ess 2014).

Informed consent and 'Internet surveys'

When Internet research takes the form of *surveys, questionnaires or interviews*, then the issues of consent and anonymity follow the lines of traditional research in the sense that the role of the researcher is explicit and expectations about consent can be met in an open and relatively unproblematic fashion. An outline of the research can be emailed to prospective respondents. Alternatively, they can be asked to visit a website where the information is held. Or, again, with forums and chat rooms the information and consent details can be posted ahead of the time when it is proposed to begin the research.

Confirming that the would-be participant has read the information, and understands it, is rather more difficult. One possibility here is to ask for the email, the attachment, the posting or the web page containing the information to be sent back to the researcher as a way of confirming that it has been read and understood, and that there is agreement to participation. If sent back from email or a web page, the form could contain a tick box (yes/no) that allows the would-be participants to confirm their willingness to take part – a kind of proxy signature that, though it is not as good as a formal signature, at least signals agreement to take part in a project whose details have been made available. Alternatively, those who have been contacted could be asked to print off a copy of the downloaded form, sign it and return it to the researcher through the ordinary post. This provides a more robust kind of informed consent, but takes more effort on the part of the would-be participant and might well have the effect of deterring them from agreeing to participate.

Special care needs to be taken in the case of research that, intentionally or otherwise, includes children and young people. Permission from parents or someone with equivalent parental authority is needed according to most codes of conduct for research and this applies just as much to Internet research as it does to conventional data collection methods. Although it is difficult to be certain about the age of contacts on the Internet, researchers are still expected to:

- use their best endeavours to identify any respondents who might be aged under 16;
- where appropriate, seek parental permission (or its equivalent) on behalf of such young people;
- abide by relevant national laws relating to contact with children and young people.

Privacy and the use of 'online documents'

Internet research that involves the study of online documents can pose interesting questions in terms of privacy. Such research focuses on various forms of texts and images that have been put online – but were not produced with research in mind. The motive for putting the material online could be commercial, political, religious or personal and they might take the form of web pages, blogs, discussion forums or messages on social network sites. A crucial point, though, is that wherever they appear and whatever form they take they were not intended as things that would form the basis for research data.

The decision to seek consent for the use of the material needs to be made on the basis of how *public or private* the communication was intended to be. If the material was intended for public consumption and intended to reach a wide audience then there would not normally be a requirement to gain consent before using that material as data for a research project. It is published work in the public domain. Analysis of company websites, online journals, tweets and the like fall into this category. In the case of more private material the situation becomes more murky. Contributions to a discussion forum, for example, might be intended for a particular online community and things said on social network sites might be intended for a restricted group of 'friends'. Ethically speaking, the researcher needs to think about how far the writer *intended* the words for unrestricted public consumption and how personal the material is in terms of its content. The more personal and private the communication is, the more the researcher should be inclined to seek consent before using the material as research data.

Deception and the study of online communities

Internet research that involves participation in an online community can involve issues surrounding the use of deception by the researcher. Such issues do not occur if the researcher chooses to be explicit about the reasons for joining in with the group and openly seeking the consent of the members to his/her participation. However, the nature of online communities means that it is often possible to conduct covert research and observe the workings of a community without openly declaring a presence in the group. It allows researchers to monitor and record events secretly by hiding in the background and not declaring their presence. It enables them to enter chat rooms and observe proceedings by 'lurking' rather than joining in. Researchers can read postings to bulletin boards, again observing proceedings without disturbing the natural course of events.

The question is, does this involve a form of *deception*? Should Internet researchers be morally obliged to declare their presence and state openly the purpose for observing events? There is a position on research ethics that would say 'yes'. Others, however, would argue that the information provided through these channels has been made open and public by those who supplied it, arguably removing any need on the part of the researcher to disclose the existence of the research activity or to try to get consent from those who are to become the objects of study. On the understanding that such information is 'public', some Internet researchers (e.g. Denzin 1999) have chosen to proceed without being open about who they are and what they are doing. Under specific circumstances they argue that it is not necessary to get permission to use the postings as data for research. Any researcher contemplating such Internet research needs to be aware of the alternative views and should explicitly state their considered position on this issue.

Separate from the issue of not declaring a presence, the Internet also makes it relatively easy to adopt an alias or take on a false (online) identity for the purposes of the research. This sidesteps the need for researchers to be fully honest about who they are and why they wish to participate in the group's online interactions and it can pave the way for actively engaging with a community without destroying the naturalness of the communication between the members. But is this simply a matter of deception and can it be ethical? Well, as with any research, there can be situations where researchers argue that some degree of deception is unavoidable; when it is *not expedient* to disclose research activity because to do so would be to jeopardize the research aims. A good illustration of this is provided by Glaser et al. (2002), who collected data from chat rooms associated with white racist groups. They wanted to find out what kind of events or circumstances triggered such people into advocating physical violence against ethnic groups, and they covertly conducted semi-structured interviews with 38 participants through these chat rooms. The sensitivity of the issue meant that they did not seek informed consent. They argued that racists appear to 'express their views rather freely [on the Internet], at least when they are interacting with those they perceive to be like-minded' (Glaser et al. 2002: 181) and that revealing the researchers' identity and purpose would have been likely to deter such openness. In this specific case, under these special circumstances, they were able to gain the approval of the relevant Ethics Committee (at Yale University) on the grounds that:

- the respondents' statements were made in a public forum under conditions that were entirely normal for the chat room and so were naturally occurring data;
- the deception was absolutely necessary in order for the research to be undertaken;
- respondents' identities were carefully protected.

Confidentiality

It is difficult, arguably impossible, for researchers using the Internet to *guarantee* that respondents' contributions will be private and will not be traced back to them. Despite the efforts of individuals and organizations to protect the anonymity of sources of Internet communications, and despite the potential of encryption, the reality is that governments and security agencies have the power and the ability to trace just about any kind of Internet communication should they wish to do so. Researchers, therefore, should be wary about making promises they are not in a position to keep, and should word statements about the confidentiality of data supplied via the Internet in a way that acknowledges the point, yet also reassures the respondent that all reasonable precautions will be taken to avoid the disclosure of identities.

Legislation

The laws that need to be observed vary from country to country and are evolving to meet the repercussions of the spread of the Internet. In the face of this uncertainty, researchers are best advised to make a clear statement to participants about which country's legal jurisdiction is being applied as far as the research is concerned – normally the country in which the researcher is based. Complications arise when researchers wish to base their research in more than one country – for example, with collaboration between universities in the UK, Russia and the USA. Such complications, however, are fairly unlikely to arise in the context of a small-scale research project. Broadly, though, there are three aspects of legislation that are likely to affect Internet research and that need to be reflected in the researcher's use of the Internet for data collection:

- *Data protection*: the data should be collected, stored and used in accordance with relevant data protection legislation.
- *Copyright*: downloading text and images is simple, but the *use* of text and images needs to be in accordance with copyright conventions and legislation concerned with things like trademarks and intellectual property rights.
- *Sensitive issues*: researchers hold no special position in the eyes of the law and need to exercise particular caution when investigating topics that are politically sensitive or that involve things like pornography or terrorism.

Research ethics throughout the whole research process

Although attention in the past tended to focus on the data collection stage, there is now an awareness that researchers are expected to operate in accordance with ethical standards at all stages of the research process.

At the *planning stage* approval needs to be obtained by an Ethics Committee. Before any empirical research gets under way, the plans for the research are normally scrutinized by people with relevant experience and expertise to check that appropriate measures will be in place to enable the research to meet the required ethical standards.

During the *data collection stage* researchers need to be vigilant to ensure that no harm is caused to participants. Potential risks, possible dangers and unwanted by-products from the research should have been predicted and pre-empted through the design of the research but, none the less, as the data collection progresses there needs to be a constant monitoring of events to prevent any unforeseen circumstances from causing harm to participants.

At the *data analysis stage* there is a need to act with integrity and high professional standards. Researchers are expected to be honest in the way they analyse the data and must avoid any temptation to manipulate the data or approach things in a biased manner.

At the *dissemination stage* there is a need to prevent, as far as possible, any negative *impact* on the lives of those who contributed to the research findings. The findings, once they are made public, could do harm to personal reputations and even jeopardize well-being. Anonymity is an important way in which researchers can minimize this prospect.

Further reading

Farrimond, H. (2013) *Doing Ethical Research*. Basingstoke: Palgrave Macmillan.

Israel, M. (2015) *Research Ethics and Integrity for Social Scientists*, 2nd edn. London: Sage.

Oliver, P. (2010) *The Student's Guide to Research Ethics*, 2nd edn. Maidenhead: Open University Press.

Ransome, P. (2013) *Ethics and Values in Social Research*. Basingstoke: Palgrave Macmillan.

Checklist for research ethics

When considering the ethics of the research you should feel confident about answering 'yes' to the following questions: ☑

1 Will prior *approval* for the research be obtained, or has it already been obtained, from a relevant Ethics Committee? ☐

2 Will the research be conducted in accordance with a specific (and named) *code of research ethics*? ☐

3 Will *informed consent* be obtained from participants? If not, can this be justified in relation to the nature of the research? ☐

4 Will reasonable steps be taken to safeguard the *security of the data?* ☐

5 Will the data collection process:
   • avoid harm, stress or emotional upset to those taking part? ☐
   • respect the privacy of individuals and *avoid undue intrusion*? ☐

6 Will the interests of participants be protected through:
   • maintaining the *confidentiality* of information? ☐
   • protecting their *anonymity*? ☐

7 Does the process of selecting participants ensure that the *benefits and risks are spread fairly* and equally among relevant groups? ☐

8 Will the research *avoid the use of deception*? If not, can this be justified in relation to the nature of the research? ☐

9 Will data be collected using only *legal* and legitimate means? ☐

10 Will the research be conducted with professional integrity in an *honest*, objective and unbiased fashion? ☐

11 Will the research *respect social values and cultural norms* of the society within which it is conducted? ☐

12 Has consideration been given to the likely *impact of publishing* research findings on those who contribute to the research? ☐

© M. Denscombe, *The Good Research Guide*. Open University Press.

19 Research reports

Research is not complete until the aims, methods and findings have been written up in some form of research report (e.g. a dissertation, a thesis or an article). Such reports are vital because the purpose of research is to contribute to knowledge and this means that the findings from a research project need to be distributed, disseminated and discussed in the wider world rather than being kept private. Some military research and research on commercially sensitive topics, admittedly, might involve special efforts to keep the results secret, but these instances need to be regarded as exceptions to the general rule which is this: *research findings should be distributed and made available for scrutiny by other researchers.*

Writing a research report, though, is not a simple, mechanical process of 'writing up' what happened. It requires a degree of *writing craft* in order to present the details of the research in a fashion that is interesting and accessible to the specific *audience* for whom the report is produced. The report also needs to conform to certain *conventions* and adopt a format that is readily recognized by those who will evaluate the work. This chapter, therefore, provides some guidelines to the relevant conventions and writing styles that are associated with good research reports.

The structure of research reports

There is a conventional structure to research reports (Figure 19.1). The order in which they present material, and even the headings used, tend to conform to a familiar pattern – a pattern which is dictated largely by the need to present information in a logical order, with each new section building on information that has been provided earlier.

Figure 19.1 The structure of a research report

The preliminary part
- Title
- Abstract
- Key words
- List of contents
- List of tables and figures
- Preface
- Acknowledgements
- List of abbreviations

The main text
- Introduction
- Literature review
- Methods of investigation
- Findings
- Analysis and discussion
- Conclusions and recommendations

The end matter
- Appendices
- References

The conventional structure for reporting research divides the material into three parts: the preliminary part, the main text and the end matter. This is as true for a full-length book as it is for a PhD, for a brief journal article and for a workplace project.

The preliminary part

- *Title.* The title itself needs to indicate accurately the contents of the work. It also needs to be fairly brief. A good way of combining the two is to have a two-part title: title and subtitle. The first part acts as the main title and gives a broad indication of the area of the work. The second part adds more detail. For example, 'Ethnicity and friendship: the contrast between sociometric research and fieldwork observation in primary school classrooms'.
- *Abstract.* An abstract is a synopsis of a piece of research. Its purpose is to provide a brief summary which can be circulated widely to allow other people to see, at a glance, if the research is relevant to their needs and worth tracking down to read in full. An abstract is normally about 250–300 words in length, and is presented on a separate sheet.
- *Key words.* Researchers are often asked to identify up to five 'key words'. These words are 'identifiers' – words that capture the essence of what the report is all about. They can combine two, sometimes three, words if necessary. For example, 'employee motivation' can be used as a key word. It identifies a concept in a way that any single, individual key word does not. Key words are needed for bibliographic searches.

- *List of contents.* Depending on the context, this can range from being just a list of chapter headings and their starting page through to being an extensive list, including details of the contents within the major section of the report, for instance, based on headings and sub-headings.
- *List of tables and figures.* This should list the titles of the various tables and figures and their locations.
- *Preface.* This provides the opportunity for the researcher to give a personal statement about the origins of the research and the significance of the research for the researcher as a person. In view of the importance of the 'self' in the research process, the Preface offers a valuable place in the research report to explore, albeit briefly, how the research reflects the personal experiences and biography of the researcher.
- *Acknowledgements.* Under this heading, credit can be given to those who have helped with the research. This can include people who acted as 'gatekeepers' in relation to fieldwork, academic supervisors, and those who have commented on early drafts of the research report.
- *List of abbreviations.* If the nature of the report demands that many abbreviations are used in the text, these should be listed, usually alphabetically, under this heading, alongside the full version of what they stand for.

The main text

The main text is generally divided into sections. The sections might be chapters as in the case of a larger piece of work, or headings as in the case of shorter reports. In either case, they are normally presented in the following order.

- *Introduction.* For the purposes of writing up research there needs to be an introduction. On most occasions this will be a stand-alone section or chapter, but it might be incorporated in other ways. The important thing to recognize is that, at the beginning, the reader needs to be provided with information about:
  - the *background* to the work (in relation to significant issues, problems, ideas);
  - the *aims* of the research;
  - key *definitions* and concepts to be used;
  - optionally, in longer pieces, an *overview* of the report (mapping out its contents).
- *Literature review.* This might be presented as an integral part of the 'Introduction' or it might appear as a separate chapter or section. It is, though, essential that in the early stages of the report there is a review of the material that already exists on the topic in question. The current research should build on existing knowledge, not 'reinvent the wheel'. The literature review should demonstrate how the research being reported relates to previous research and, if possible, how it gives rise to particular issues, problems and ideas that the current research addresses.

- *Methods of investigation.* At this point, having analysed the existing state of knowledge on a topic, it is reasonable to describe the methods of investigation. See 'Research methods section' (below) for guidance on how this should be done.

- *Findings.* This is where the reader is presented with the relevant findings. The idea at this stage is to describe the findings rather than launch immediately into a discussion of what they might tell us. First things first: let's see what we have found.

- *Analysis and discussion.* In this section of the report the findings are analysed. The findings are reviewed and interrogated to see what they imply. And then this leads on to a discussion that connects the emerging ideas to the theories and ideas, issues and problems that were noted earlier in the report as providing the context in which the research was conceived. The researcher 'makes sense' of the findings by considering their implications beyond the confines of the current research.

- *Conclusions and recommendations.* Finally in the main text, the researcher needs to draw together the threads of the research to arrive at some general conclusion and, perhaps, to suggest some way forward. Rather than let the report fizzle out as it reaches the end, this part of the report should be constructive and positive. It can contain some of the following things:

  - a retrospective evaluation of the research and its contribution;
  - recommendations for improving the situation, guidelines or codes of practice;
  - identification of new directions for further research.

The end matter

- *Appendices.* This is the place for material which is too bulky for the main body of the text, or for material which, though directly relevant to the discussion, might entail too much of a sidetrack if placed in the text. Typical items that can be lodged in an appendix are:

  - extensive tables of data;
  - questionnaires used in a survey;
  - extracts from an interview transcript;
  - memos or minutes of meetings;
  - technical specifications.

- *References.* Sources cited in the body of the text are listed in this part of the report. See the guidance on referencing below.

Research methods section

Research reports normally include a description of the methods used to collect the data. In larger works this appears in a separate chapter. In shorter reports and articles it tends to be limited to a section under a 'research methods' heading or to a clearly identifiable paragraph or two. This account of the methods is vital in order for the reader to make some informed evaluation of the study. Basically, if the reader is *not* told how and why the data were collected, he or she cannot make any judgement about how good the research is and whether any credibility should be given to its findings or conclusions.

Within the confines of the space available the methods section should do three things: (1) describe how the research was conducted; (2) justify these procedures; and (3) acknowledge any limitations to the methods employed.

Describe how the research was conducted

Precise details need to be given, using specific and accurate numbers and dates. These should address basic questions about the data collection process such as:

- *what* methods were used (the technical names)?
- *when* did the research take place (month and year, duration of research)?
- *where* did the research take place (location, situation)?
- *how* was access to the data or subjects obtained?
- *who* was involved in the research (the population, sample, cases, examples)?
- *how many* were involved in the research (precise numbers)?
- *how* were they selected (sampling technique)?

Justify these procedures

An argument needs to be put forward supporting the choice of methods. The methods should be justified as being:

- *reasonable* in terms of the resources and time available;
- *reliable* and *appropriate* for collecting the necessary type of data;
- *suitable* for addressing the issues, problems or questions that underpin the research and likely to produce data that are *valid*;
- conforming with *ethical* standards.

Acknowledge any limitations to the methods employed

Good research evaluates the weaknesses as well as the strengths of its methodology. The researcher should acknowledge:

- any inherent limitations of the methodology;
- the scope of what can, and cannot, be concluded on the basis of the research that was undertaken;

- any ways in which resource constraints had a direct influence on the volume or kind of findings produced;
- any reservations about the authenticity, accuracy or honesty of answers;
- the ways in which, in retrospect, alternative methods might have proved to be more useful;
- any unexpected factors which arose during research that influenced the outcome.

Referencing

It is essential to acknowledge the original sources of the ideas, arguments and supporting evidence that are directly mentioned in a research report. These sources must be 'referenced'. Broadly speaking there are two conventions that can be used for this: the *numerical system* (e.g. the Vancouver system) or the *author-date system* (e.g. the Harvard system). The numerical system involves placing a number in the text at each point where the author wishes to refer to a specific source. The full references are then given at the end of the book or individual chapters, and these can be incorporated into endnotes. It is the other system, the author-date system, however, which is more common in social research and, for that reason, further details in this chapter will concentrate on this convention.

Citing sources

In the author-date system the sources are referenced by citing the name of the author and the date of publication of the relevant work. This is done at the appropriate point in the text – immediately connected to the idea, argument or supporting evidence that has been introduced to the discussion. To avoid cluttering the text, full details of the publication are not given at this point. They are subsequently given at the end of the report where readers who might wish to do so can see all the details of the author(s) and publication. The author-date system involves referring to authors in the text in the following ways:

- Baker (2017) argues that communism has a dubious future.
- It has been argued that communism has a dubious future (Baker 2017).
- The point has been made that 'it is not easy to see what contribution communism will make in the twenty-first century' (Baker 2017: 131).

In the References section towards the end of the research report, the full details of 'Baker 2017' are given, as they are for all the authors' works cited in the report. For Baker, it might look like this:

Baker, G. (2017) The future of communism in a globalised economy, *International Journal of Politics and Economics*, 25(1): 249–66.

Listing references

Using the author-date system the References section contains a list of the works cited in the research report. This list appears in (1) *alphabetical order* based on (2) *the surname of the authors* and includes (3) *all the sources cited*. The list is restricted to just those sources that have been referred to within the report and does not include other works that, though they might be relevant, have not actually been cited. The information supplied about the sources covers:

- *Author's name and initial(s)*. Surname followed by forename or initial. If the book is an edited volume, then (ed.) or (eds) should follow the name.
- *Date of publication*. To identify when the work was written and to distinguish different works published by the same author(s).
- *Title*. The title of a book is put in italics and uses capital letters for the first letter of the main words. Papers and article titles are not in italics and have titles in lower case.
- *Journal name* (if applicable). This usually appears in italics. The name of the journal is followed by details of the specific volume and issue number of the journal in which the article appears plus the relevant page numbers.
- *Chapter in an edited volume*. If the source is a contribution to an edited volume, then details are given about the book in which it appears (i.e. editor's name, title of edited volume).
- *Place of publication*. This is usually the city in which the publisher is located.
- *Publisher*. This is included for books but not for journals.
- *Edition*. If the work appears in a second or subsequent edition this needs to be specified.

Look at the References section towards the end of this book to see examples of how the author-date system presents information about the sources that are cited. Further guidance on referencing techniques can be found in sources such as the *Publication Manual of the American Psychological Association* and Turabian's (2013) manual for writers.

Good practice: Use referencing software

Software packages help with the organization of references and with citing sources referred to in research reports. Packages like *EndNote, Mendeley, RefWorks* and *Zotero* allow the researcher to adhere to any one of the many styles that might be required.

Guidelines on style

The conventions associated with writing research reports are rather like the rules of writing which operate for the English language. Experienced writers might occasionally break the rules, but the assumption is that they realize they are breaking the rules and are doing so consciously for a particular purpose – to achieve a specific effect. Inexperienced writers, however, are better advised to play safe and stick to the rules. The same applies in relation to research reports: unless you are experienced, it is safer to abide by the conventions.

- *Use the third person.*

This means adopting the following style: 'Research involved the distribution of 164 questionnaires . . .; A response rate of 46 per cent was achieved . . .; Findings from the research indicated that . . .'. This is particularly the case for formal reports such as dissertations and theses. This style contrasts with use of the first person which takes the form: 'I distributed 164 questionnaires . . .; I received 46 per cent back . . .; From the research I found that . . .'. Sometimes this style is to be found in qualitative research when researchers are keen to emphasize their personal involvement and the role of their personal identity in the collection and analysis of the data. Or, it might be used in the context of an informal report intended for restricted distribution. It is more conventional, however, to use the third person.

- *Use the past tense.*

For the most part this convention poses little trouble because researchers are reflecting upon events that happened in the past. It might be the recent past, but none the less the writing up refers to things that were done and events that happened.

Guidelines on presentation

For the production of dissertations and theses each university will have its own specific regulations and guidelines that stipulate the technical requirements in terms of things like the layout of the text and the referencing system, and publishers always include guidance to authors which spell out their own particular policy as far as the presentation of work is concerned. These requirements must be followed. The general advice about presentation, however, is that research reports should:

- *Ensure good standards of spelling and grammar.*

Perhaps obvious, this requirement is still worth stressing. Spell-checkers are normally built into word-processing packages and can be used to eliminate typing errors as well as helping with awkward spellings. Scrutiny of the text by the researcher is still needed, however, to avoid those text errors which cannot be picked up by the spell-checker; where 'at' has been typed instead of 'an', for example.

- *Develop logical links from one section to the next.*

A good report is one that takes the reader on a journey of discovery. The pathways of this journey should be clear, and the reader should never be left in doubt about the direction of the discussion or the crucial points that are being argued. The logic of the discussion should build point on point towards a final conclusion.

- *Use headings and sub-headings to divide the text into clear sections.*

Judicious use of headings and sub-headings can separate the text into blocks in a way that makes the reader's task of understanding the overall report far easier. They act as signposts. As with signposts, too few and the reader gets lost, too many and the reader gets confused. As with signposts, their success depends on being clear and being in the right place.

- *Be consistent in the use of the referencing style.*

Whether the *author-date* or the *numerical* style is used there should be consistency throughout the report. Use one or the other, not a mixture of the two.

- *Use care with the page layout.*

The visual element of the presentation is important and the researcher should give some consideration to things like the page layout and the use of graphs, tables and illustrations to enhance the appeal of the report.

- *Present tables and figures properly.*

Link up with Presenting quantitative data, p. 291.

Tables and figures should be presented in a consistent style that provides the reader with the necessary information to decipher the meaning of the data contained in them.

Writing for an audience

Research reports need to be tailored to meet the expectations of the audience for whom they are produced. For example, research reports produced for an academic qualification – an undergraduate project, a master's dissertation, a doctoral thesis – will be assessed by supervisors and examiners who will be focusing on detail, rigour, precision, coherence and originality as top priorities. A different audience might hold different expectations. In the case of commissioned research the audience might be more concerned with reading a report that is succinct, easy to digest and strong on practical outcomes. When writing a report, then, the researcher has to think carefully about who will read it and how best to make sure that the report is pitched at the right level. Different kinds of audience will have a bearing on:

- the style of presentation;
- the detail and length of the account;

- the amount of technical detail included;
- the terminology used.

> **Good practice: Meet the readers' expectations**
> Research reports should be tailored to meet the expectations and abilities of the audience for whom they are written.

Producing accounts of research

Finally, there is a fundamental point worth bearing in mind in relation to the nature of research reports. When writing a research report it is important to recognize that the task is not one of simply recording what happened during the project. Writing up is actually a skilful process of distilling the key events and decisions that occurred during a project and, within the confines of the space that is available, capturing and presenting these for a particular audience. A research report can never be a literal description of what took place. No matter how scrupulous the researcher might be, the end product – even if it is a dissertation or thesis – will always be an edited *account* of the research. There are four reasons for this. First, there are always limitations to the space available to provide the account of what happened, which means the researcher needs to provide an *edited version* of the totality. Decisions need to be made about what details are included and which are considered less important and can be missed out of the account.

Second, the editorial decisions taken by the researcher are likely to be shaped by the researcher's need to present the methods in their best possible light. Quite rationally, the researcher will wish to put a positive spin on events and to bring out the best in the process. Without resorting to deceit or untruths, the account of research will almost certainly entail some upbeat *positive filtering*. The point, after all, is to justify the procedures as 'good' research.

Third, although research notes will be used to anchor the description of what happened during the course of the research, the writing up is inevitably *a retrospective vision*. Situations and data are likely to have a different meaning when viewed from the end of the research process from that at the time they occurred. They will be *interpreted with the wisdom of hindsight*.

Fourth, the impact of social norms and personal values on the way we interpret events pretty well guarantees that, to a greater or lesser extent, any account of research should be regarded as a *version of the truth* rather than a literal depiction of what happened. Within the social sciences, the idea of a purely objective position is controversial, and a researcher would be naïve to presume that his or her account can stand, without careful consideration, as an 'objective' description of what really occurred.

Further reading

Denscombe, M. (2012) *Research Proposals: A Practical Guide*. Maidenhead: Open University Press.

Murray, R. (2013) *Writing for Academic Journals*, 3rd edn. Maidenhead: Open University Press.

Murray, N. and Hughes, G. (2008) *Writing Up Your University Assignments and Research Projects: A Practical Handbook*. Maidenhead: Open University Press.

Reid, M. (2012) *Report Writing*. Basingstoke: Palgrave Macmillan.

Turabian, K. (2013) *A Manual for Writers of Research Papers, Theses, and Dissertations*, 8th edn. Chicago, IL: University of Chicago Press.

Checklist for writing research reports

When writing a research report you should feel confident about answering 'yes' to the following questions: ☑

1 Is there a suitable structure and logical development to the report? ☐

2 Is the text written in a clear style, free of spelling and grammatical errors? ☐

3 Have the necessary conventions been followed in the writing up of the research? ☐

4 Does the report meet the expectations of the main audience for the research (format, style, length, detail)? ☐

5 Has an appropriately detailed and precise description of the research process been provided? ☐

6 Has the choice of method(s) been justified in relation to the type of data required and the practical circumstances surrounding the research? ☐

7 Have the limitations of the research methodology been acknowledged? ☐

8 Are the references complete and do they follow a recognized style (e.g. author-date system)? ☐

9 Are the tables, figures, illustrations and diagrams properly labelled? ☐

© M. Denscombe, *The Good Research Guide*. Open University Press.

20 Literature reviews

> *What is a literature review? • What is the purpose of a literature review? • The literature search • Critically reviewing the literature • Completing the literature review • Guidelines for good practice • Further reading • Checklist for writing a literature review*

What is a literature review?

A literature review is a component of the research process that sets the scene for the rest of the research project. It does this in two ways. First, it provides the *background* to the research, explaining the need for the research in terms of particular issues or problems. Second, it looks at the state of play in terms of research that has already been conducted in the area, attempting to draw on *existing knowledge* to give the investigation a sensible design and direction. A literature review generally starts prior to any data collection in the field. This enables researchers to build upon the knowledge that already exists and to avoid 'reinventing the wheel'.

Not only does a review of the literature set the scene for the researcher. When writing a report of the research it also sets the scene for the readers. For this reason a literature review normally occurs *towards the beginning* of any account of the research so that it can inform the reader's understanding about why the research has taken place and provide them with the basis for judgements about the suitability of the research design and methods for the particular topic being investigated. Within any reasonably substantial report there is likely to be a section specifically devoted to the literature review. In brief research reports, the essence of the literature review might be woven into the Introduction or Background sections.

> **Link up with** Chapter 19, Research reports.

What is the purpose of a literature review?

The literature review puts the research *in context*. To be more precise, it locates the research within the context of the published knowledge that already exists about the area that is being investigated. Specifically, it serves to do the following things.

Identify the intellectual origins of the work

The studies included in the literature review act like signposts telling readers which works are regarded as the most important intellectual roots of the research. This locates the research within the range of existing theories and practices and, at the same time, provides the opportunity to acknowledge the contribution of others and the way the current research has been influenced by the writings of other people.

Show familiarity with existing ideas, information and practices related to the area of interest

For research to have any credibility there is a reasonable assumption that those conducting the research will have done some background preparation and have developed some proficient awareness of what counts as good practice and theory in the area of the investigation. Without necessarily purporting to be experts, researchers can be expected to know something about the main issues and debates in the field. The literature review provides the opportunity to demonstrate such familiarity and thus enhance the credibility of the research in the eyes of those who read it and who might be influenced by its findings. This is, of course, particularly important in connection with academic dissertations and research theses.

Identify the contribution that can be made by the new research

Having reviewed the findings from existing research it should be possible to indicate how the new research might contribute to the existing research and debates. This contribution should be specified clearly and concisely as part of the conclusion to the literature review. The contribution might be in terms of something practical or it might be something theoretical. Whatever it is, the literature review ought to demonstrate the *need for the research* and convince the reader that the research addresses an area that warrants investigation. It might be a matter of *building upon* what has gone before, using the existing findings as a platform for deciding where to go and what new bits of knowledge are needed to move things forward. Alternatively, it might be a matter of identifying areas that have been overlooked so far, using the review of the literature to show that the research *fills a gap* in existing knowledge. Or the research might adopt a *critical stance*, reviewing the existing material to show its inadequacies. In this case the literature review will point to the flaws in earlier investigations and produce an argument that the current research does a better job. Whichever stance it takes, the literature review needs to argue the research project involves some element of *originality*.

Justify the research approach that has been chosen

On the basis of reviewing the theories and methods previously used to study the topic it should be possible to draw conclusions about the approach that is likely to be best suited to the investigation. These should be summarized towards the end of the literature review.

Arrive at specific research questions

Having considered the relevant debates and their particular focus of attention it should be possible to conclude that it will be valuable to conduct research into specific questions. The research questions are effectively the end-product of the literature review and should be stated explicitly at the end. They provide a platform for a discussion on how data on the specific questions will be collected and analysed (which is normally contained in the methodology section that follows on directly from the literature review).

 Caution

It is worth noting that a small minority of qualitative researchers take the view that the guidance provided by a literature review acts as an impediment to open and fresh thinking about a topic; it is regarded as an unwarranted constraint on the way the researcher approaches the topic. An element of this thinking can be found, for instance, in some grounded theory approaches (see Chapter 7). It has to be stressed, though, that for the vast majority of social researchers a literature review is seen as an essential ingredient of good research.

The literature search

The literature search tracks down the relevant sources to include in the review. There are a variety of routes for identifying the published works on a specific topic but these generally require searches using *key words*. Key words capture the essence of the topic the researcher wishes to investigate. Armed with four to six key words, preferably in some hierarchical order of importance in relation to the area of inquiry, the researcher can make the most of searches using:

- *Internet* browsers, which open up access to relevant literature on a global scale, including the latest research from a huge variety of sources;
- *bibliographies*, which offer a ready-made list of published sources on a topic, and these can be accessed quite easily through libraries.

Another useful way of identifying key sources is through the *references* in books and articles to the sources they have used. These should provide a good indication of the significant works in the field and will need to be included among the sources covered in the review.

How many sources?

The literature search is liable to reveal a large number of potential sources that could be included in the literature review, and researchers are always faced with the problem of deciding how many to include from the huge volume of material that might be available on the topic. There is no formula that can be applied to all cases on this matter. Expectations will differ according to the context. Research that has been conducted as part of a short in-house action research project might refer to just a small number of sources. At the other end of the continuum, a PhD thesis will be expected to contain a detailed and extensive literature review likely to cover more than 100 sources. In between, there are master's dissertations, journal articles and technical reports that will, as a very broad guideline, cover around 20 to 30 sources. It should be stressed, though, that such figures are not presented as concrete targets to be aimed for but as 'ball-park' figures that reflect the number of sources that researchers tend to include in their literature reviews.

> **Link up with Chapter 10, Systematic reviews.**

 Key point

All research can be linked with predecessors. Even if the idea for the research has been plucked out of thin air by the researcher in a moment of inspiration, and therefore is not obviously building upon earlier theories, by the time the idea has been translated into a research project some consideration needs to have been given to how it fits in with established paths of research. It does not matter exactly how the idea for the research was conceived; before it comes to fruition the idea for the research needs to have been contextualized in terms of existing relevant knowledge.

Critically reviewing the literature

The business of critically reviewing the literature calls for judgement and insight on the part of the researcher. To this extent, it is a creative exercise, not a mechanical chore. The point is not just to identify the literature that is relevant to the topic of investigation. Nor is it just to describe the contents of these works. The key to success lies in providing a *critical review* of the key sources.

The 'review' element of a critical review involves two things:

- A description of the *key issues and themes* running throughout the works.
- An *overview of the literature*. A review is not just about the contributions of each separate item but is about the relevant literature as a whole and what can be gleaned in terms of guiding the research.

The 'critical' element of a critical review requires:

- An *evaluation* of the ideas, information and practices contained in the various works. Providing a timid, sit-on-the-fence descriptive account of the literature is not sufficient. For the newcomer, in particular, this can seem a daunting task. It is necessary, nevertheless, for the review to compare and contrast the works and arrive at conclusions about their relative merits and failings.

 Key point

The literature review should not consist of a sequence of summaries of relevant published work. The review is more than a catalogue or inventory of items. The ultimate aim is to provide an *analysis* of the various components – not just a list of their contents.

Completing the literature review

The literature review paves the way for research. However, it is likely to continue as an activity during the rest of the research as well, and will continue through the life of the project. Newly published works need to be considered; new sources are discovered; different things become relevant as the research progresses. This is particularly the case with qualitative research. The result is that the literature review is not finally pulled together and put into shape until the writing-up phase of the research at the end of the project.

Guidelines for good practice

Regard the literature search as an essential component of the research process

It is *part* of the research process itself and, like the data collection procedures, the process should be:

- rigorous – the approach needs to be systematic and thorough;
- recorded – some details of the search should be logged for reference.

Make the connections with other work in the field early on in the planning and design of the research

Even if the research question comes 'out of thin air' in a moment of personal inspiration, the task for the researcher is to locate work that has already been done in the area: (a) to make sure the proposed investigation does not simply copy something that has already been done; and (b) to identify how the proposed research compares and contrasts with the other work in the field. Good research should always be aware of how it connects with theories, practices and problems that already exist.

Explain the context of the research in an explicit manner

The literature review should clearly demonstrate how the research is linked to the current context of policies, practical problems and theoretical issues. The links should never be taken for granted; the context should never be assumed to 'speak for itself'.

Provide a review of the literature, not a list of summaries

It is important to avoid the trap of listing a series of summaries of works. Their content may indeed be relevant, and the summaries might be accurate, informative and clear. The listing might show that the researcher has read the relevant material, however, what is required is something over and above all this. It is an analysis of the overall picture which highlights the main features and which provides insights about the strengths and weaknesses of the available knowledge on the topic. Ultimately, the review is about the totality of the works included rather than each separate piece.

Further reading

Aveyard, H. (2014) *Doing a Literature Review in Health and Social Care: A Practical Guide*, 3rd edn. Maidenhead: Open University Press.

Booth, A., Sutton, A. and Papaiaonnou, D. (2016) *Systematic Approaches to a Successful Literature Review*, 2nd edn. London: Sage.

Coughlan, M. and Cronin, P. (2017) *Doing a Literature Review in Nursing, Health and Social Care*, 2nd edn. London: Sage.

Hart, C. (1998) *Doing a Literature Review: Releasing the Social Science Research Imagination*. London: Sage.

Machi, L.A. and McEvoy, B.T. (2016) *The Literature Review: Six Steps to Success*, 3rd edn. Thousand Oaks, CA: Corwin.

Neville, C. (2016) *The Complete Guide to Referencing and Avoiding Plagiarism*, 3rd edn. London: Open University Press.

Oliver, P. (2012) *Succeeding with Your Literature Review: A Handbook for Students*. Maidenhead: Open University Press.

Ridley, D.D. (2012) *The Literature Review: A Step-By-Step Guide for Students*, 2nd edn. London: Sage.

Rumsey, S. (2008) *How to Find Information*, 2nd edn. Maidenhead: Open University Press.

Checklist for writing a literature review

When writing a literature review you should feel confident about answering 'yes' to the following questions: ☑

1 Has the potential contribution of the research been discussed in terms of one or more of the following? ☐

   • Adding to existing knowledge in a specific way.
   • Filling a gap in existing knowledge.
   • Exposing inadequacies in existing knowledge.

2 Is it clear how the literature review has shaped the design and direction of the research? ☐

3 Has the literature search been conducted in a rigorous and systematic fashion? ☐

4 Have details of the literature search process been summarized as an integral part of the literature review? ☐

5 Have key works on the topic been compared, contrasted and evaluated? ☐

6 Does the review provide some overview of what the relevant literature as a whole has to say on a topic? ☐

7 Does the literature review culminate in a sequence of clearly identified research questions? ☐

References

Ahmed, S. (2006) *Queer Phenomenology: Orientations, Objects, Others*. Durham, NC: Duke University Press.

Alaszewski, A. (2006) *Using Diaries for Social Research*. London: Sage.

Andrews, M., Squire, C. and Tamboukou, M. (2013) *Doing Narrative Research*, 2nd edn. London: Sage.

Austin, J.L. (1962) *How to Do Things with Words*. Oxford: Clarendon.

Aveyard, H. (2014) *Doing a Literature Review in Health and Social Care: A Practical Guide*, 3rd edn. Maidenhead: Open University Press.

Bakeman, R. and Gottman, J.M. (1997) *Observing Interaction: An Introduction to Sequential Analysis*, 2nd edn. Cambridge: Cambridge University Press.

Banks, M. (2007) *Using Visual Data in Qualitative Research*. London: Sage.

Banks, M. and Zeitlyn, D. (2015) *Visual Methods in Social Research*, 2nd edn. London: Sage.

Barnett, V. (2009) *Sample Survey Principles and Methods*, 3rd edn. Chichester: Wiley.

Bazeley, P. (2013) *Qualitative Data Analysis: Practical Strategies*. London: Sage.

Bazeley, P. and Jackson, K. (2013) *Qualitative Data Analysis with NVivo*, 2nd edn. London: Sage.

Becker, H. and Geer, B. (1957) Participant observation and interviewing: a comparison, *Human Organization*, 16(3): 28–35.

Bell, P. (2000) Content analysis of visual images, in T. van Leeuwen and C. Jewitt (eds) *The Handbook of Visual Analysis*. London: Sage.

Berger, P. and Luckmann, T. (1967) *The Social Construction of Reality*. London: Allen Lane.

Bettany-Saltikov, J. (2012) *How to do a Systematic Literature Review in Nursing: A Step-by-Step Guide*. Maidenhead: Open University Press.

Bhaskaran, V. and LeClaire, J. (2010) *Online Surveys for Dummies*. Hoboken, NJ: Wiley.

Birks, M. and Mills, J. (2015) *Grounded Theory: A Practical Guide*, 2nd edn. London: Sage.

Blair, J., Czaja, R.F. and Blair, E.A. (2014) *Designing Surveys: A Guide to Decisions and Procedures*, 3rd edn. Thousand Oaks, CA: Sage.

Boellstorff, T., Nardi, B., Pearce, C. and Taylor, T. (2012) *Ethnography and Virtual Worlds: A Handbook of Method*. Princeton, NJ: Princeton University Press.

Boland, A., Cherry, M.G. and Dickson, R. (eds) (2014) *Doing a Systematic Review: A Student's Guide*. London: Sage.

Bold, C. (2012) *Using Narrative in Research*. London: Sage.

Boog, B.W.M. (2003) The emancipatory character of action research, its history and the present state of the art, *Journal of Community & Applied Social Psychology*, 13(6): 426–38.

Booth, A., Sutton, A. and Papaiaonnou, D. (2016) *Systematic Approaches to a Successful Literature Review*, 2nd edn. London: Sage.

Brace, I. (2013) *Questionnaire Design*, 3rd edn. London: Kogan Page.

Bradburn, N.M., Sudman, S. and Wansink, B. (2004) *Asking Questions: The Definitive Guide to Questionnaire Design*, 2nd edn. San Francisco, CA: Jossey-Bass.

Brewer, J. (2000) *Ethnography*. Buckingham: Open University Press.

Brickman-Bhutta, C. (2012) Not by the book: Facebook as a sampling frame, *Sociological Methods and Research*, 41(1): 57–88.

Brinkmann, S. and Kvale, S. (2015) *InterViews: Learning the Craft of Qualitative Research Interviewing*, 3rd edn. Thousand Oaks, CA: Sage.

Britton, A., Ben-Shlomo, Y., Benzeval, M., Kuh, D. and Bell, S. (2015) Life course trajectories of alcohol consumption in the United Kingdom using longitudinal data from nine cohort studies, *BMC Medicine*, 13(47): 2–9.

Bryant, A. (2017) *Grounded Theory and Grounded Theorizing: Pragmatism in Research Practice*. New York: Oxford University Press.

Bryant, A. and Charmaz, K. (2010) *The Sage Handbook of Grounded Theory* (paperback edition). London: Sage.

Burgess, R.G. (1984) *In the Field: An Introduction to Field Research*. London: Allen & Unwin.

Callegaro, M., Lozar Manfreda, K. and Vehovar, V. (2015) *Web Survey Methodology*. London: Sage.

Campbell, D.T. and Fiske, D.W. (1959) Convergent and discriminant validation by the multitrait-multimethod matrix, *Psychological Bulletin*, 56(2): 81–105.

Carel, H. (2016) *Phenomenology of Illness*. Oxford: Oxford University Press.

Cassell, C. (2015) *Conducting Research Interviews*. London: Sage.

Charmaz, K. (2000) Grounded theory: objectivist and constructivist methods, in N. Denzin and Y. Lincoln (eds) *Handbook of Qualitative Research*, 2nd edn. Thousand Oaks, CA: Sage.

Charmaz, K. (2014) *Constructing Grounded Theory*, 2nd edn. London: Sage.

Charlesworth, S.J. (2000) *A Phenomenology of Working Class Experience*. Cambridge: Cambridge University Press.

Chatrakul Na Ayudhya, U., Smithson, J. and Lewis, S. (2014) Focus group methodology in a life course approach – individual accounts within a peer cohort group, *International Journal of Social Research Methodology*, 17(2): 157–71.

Clarke, A.E. (2005) *Situational Analysis: Grounded Theory after the Postmodern Turn*. Thousand Oaks, CA: Sage.

Clausen, J.A. (1986) *The Life Course: A Sociological Perspective*. Englewood Cliffs, NJ: Prentice-Hall.

Clift, R. (2016) *Conversation Analysis*. Cambridge: Cambridge University Press.

Coghlan, D. and Brannick, T. (2014) *Doing Action Research in Your Own Organization*, 4th edn. London: Sage.

Collier, M. (2001) Approaches to the analysis of visual images, in T. van Leeuwen and J. Jewitt (eds) *Handbook of Visual Analysis*. London: Sage.

Cook, T.D. and Campbell, D.T. (1979) *Quasi-Experimentation: Design and Analysis Issues for Field Settings*. Chicago, IL: Rand McNally College.

Corbin, J. and Strauss, A. (2015) *Basics of Qualitative Research: Techniques and Procedures for Developing Grounded Theory*, 4th edn. Thousand Oaks, CA: Sage.

Coughlan, M. and Cronin, P. (2017) *Doing a Literature Review in Nursing, Health and Social Care*, 2nd edn. London: Sage.

Couper, M.P. (2011) The future of modes of data collection, *Public Opinion Quarterly*, 75(5): 889–908.

Cresswell, J.W. (2015) *A Concise Introduction to Mixed Methods Research*. Thousand Oaks, CA: Sage.

Creswell, J.W. and Plano Clark, V. (2007) *Designing and Conducting Mixed Methods Research*. Thousand Oaks, CA: Sage.

Creswell, J.W. and Plano Clark, V. (2011) *Designing and Conducting Mixed Methods Research*, 2nd edn. Thousand Oaks, CA: Sage.

Creswell, J.W. and Plano Clark, V. (2017) *Designing and Conducting Mixed Methods Research*, 3nd edn. Thousand Oaks, CA: Sage.

Croll, P. (1986) *Systematic Classroom Observation*. London: Falmer Press.

Crotty, M. (1996) *Phenomenology and Nursing Research*. Melbourne: Churchill Livingstone.

Daniel, J. (2012) *Sampling Essentials: Practical Guidelines for Making Sampling Choices*. Thousand Oaks, CA: Sage.

De Chesnay, M. (ed.) (2015) *Nursing Research Using Phenomenology: Qualitative Designs and Methods in Nursing*. New York: Springer.

de Vaus, D. (2001) *Research Design in Social Research*. London: Sage.

de Vaus, D. (2014) *Surveys in Social Research*, 6th edn. London: Routledge.

Denscombe, M. (1983) Interviews, accounts and ethnographic research on teachers, in M. Hammersley (ed.) *The Ethnography of Schooling: Methodological Issues*. Driffield: Nafferton Books.

Denscombe, M. (2006) Web-based questionnaires: an assessment of the mode effect on the validity of data, *Social Science Computer Review*, 24(2): 246–54.

Denscombe, M. (2008) The length of responses to open-ended questions: a comparison of online and paper questionnaires in terms of a mode effect, *Social Science Computer Review*, 26(3): 359–68.

Denscombe, M. (2009) Item non-response rates: a comparison of online and paper questionnaires, *International Journal of Social Research Methodology*, 12(4): 281–91.

Denscombe, M. (2010) *Ground Rules for Social Research*, 2nd edn. Maidenhead: Open University Press.

Denscombe, M. (2012a) *Classroom Control: A Sociological Perspective*. London: Routledge.

Denscombe, M. (2012b) *Research Proposals: A Practical Guide*. Maidenhead: Open University Press.

Denyer, D. and Tranfield, D. (2009) Producing a systematic review, in D. Buchanan and A. Bryman (eds) *The Sage Handbook of Organizational Research Methods*. London: Sage.

Denzin, N.K. (1970) Strategies of multiple triangulation, in N.K. Denzin (ed.) *The Research Act in Sociology: A Theoretical Introduction to Sociological Method*. New York: McGraw-Hill.

Denzin, N.K. (1999) Cybertalk and the method of instances, in S. Jones (ed.) *Doing Internet Research: Critical Issues and Methods for Examining the Net*. Thousand Oaks, CA: Sage.

Denzin, N.K. (2012) Triangulation 2.0, *Journal of Mixed Methods Research*, 6(2): 80–8.

Department of Health (2005) *Research Governance Framework for Health and Social Care (England)*, 2nd edn. London: Department of Health.

DeWalt, K.M. and DeWalt, B.R. (2011) *Participant Observation: A Guide for Field-workers*, 2nd edn. Lanham, MD: AltaMira Press.

Di Gregorio, S. and Davidson, J. (2008) *Qualitative Research Design for Software Users*. Maidenhead: Open University Press.

Diamante, T. (2013) *Effective Interviewing and Information Gathering: Proven Tactics to Increase the Power of Your Questioning Skills*. New York: McGraw-Hill/Business Expert Press.

Dillman, D.A., Smyth, J.D. and Christian, L.M. (2009) *Internet, Phone, Mail, and Mixed-mode Surveys: The Tailored Design Method*, 3rd edn. Hoboken, NJ: Wiley.

Dillman, D.A., Smyth, J.D. and Christian, L.M. (2014) *Internet, Phone, Mail, and Mixed-mode Surveys: The Tailored Design Method*, 4th edn. Hoboken, NJ: Wiley.

Dixon-Woods, M., Bonas, S., Booth, A., Jones, D., et al. (2006) How can systematic reviews incorporate qualitative research? A critical perspective, *Qualitative Research*, 6(1): 27–44.

Dunning, T. (2012) *Natural Experiments in the Social Sciences: A Design-Based Approach.* Cambridge: Cambridge University Press.

Edwards, A. and Talbot, R. (1999) *The Hard-pressed Researcher: A Research Handbook for the Caring Professions,* 2nd edn. Harlow: Pearson.

Ekinci, Y. (2015) *Designing Research Questionnaires for Business and Management Students.* London: Sage.

Elder, G.H. Jr. (1974) *Children of the Great Depression: Social Change in Life Experience.* Chicago, IL: University of Chicago Press.

Elliott, J. (2005) *Using Narrative in Social Research: Qualitative and Quantitative Approaches.* London: Sage.

Emmel, N. (2013) *Sampling and Choosing Cases in Qualitative Research: A Realist Approach.* London: Sage.

Emmison, M., Smith, P. and Mayall, M. (2012) *Researching the Visual,* 2nd edn. London: Sage.

Erikson, E. (1959) *Identity and the Life Cycle.* New York: Norton.

Ess, C. (2014) *Digital Media Ethics,* 2nd edn. Cambridge: Polity Press.

Farrimond, H. (2013) *Doing Ethical Research.* Basingstoke: Palgrave Macmillan.

Festinger, L., Reicken, H. and Schachter, S. (1956) *When Prophecy Fails.* Minneapolis, MN: University of Minnesota Press (republished London: Harper & Row, 1964).

Field, A. (2013) *Discovering Statistics Using IBM SPSS Statistics,* 4th edn. London: Sage.

Fielding, J.L. and Gilbert, G.N. (2006) *Understanding Social Statistics.* London: Sage.

Fink, A. (2009) *How to Conduct Surveys: A Step by Step Guide.* Thousand Oaks, CA: Sage.

Fowler, F.J. (2014) *Survey Research Methods,* 5th edn. Thousand Oaks, CA: Sage.

Gallagher, S. (2012) *Phenomenology.* Basingstoke: Palgrave.

Gambetta, D. and Hamill, H. (2005) *Streetwise: How Taxi Drivers Establish Their Customers' Trustworthiness.* New York: The Russell Sage Foundation.

Garrett, B.L. (2013) *Explore Everything: Place-Hacking the City.* London: Verso.

Garson, D.G. (2014) *Participant Observation.* Asheboro, NC: Statistical Publishing Associates.

Geertz, C. (1973) Thick description: toward an interpretive theory of culture, in C. Geertz (ed.) *The Interpretation of Cultures.* New York: Basic Books.

Gerbner, G., Holsti, O., Krippendorf, K., et al. (eds) (1969) *The Analysis of Communication Content.* New York: Wiley.

Gibbs, G. (2007) *Analysing Qualitative Data.* London: Sage.

Giele, J.Z. and Elder, G.H. Jr. (1998) *Methods of Life Course Research: Qualitative and Quantitative Approaches.* Thousand Oaks, CA: Sage.

Gillham, B. (2005) *Research Interviewing: The Range of Techniques.* Maidenhead: Open University Press.

Gillham, B. (2007) *Developing a Questionnaire,* 2nd edn. London: Continuum.

Gillham, B. (2008) *Observation Techniques: Structured and Unstructured Approaches.* London: Continuum.

Glaser, B. (1978) *Theoretical Sensitivity.* Mill Valley, CA: Sociology Press.

Glaser, B. (ed.) (1995) *Grounded Theory, 1984–1994.* Mill Valley, CA: Sociology Press.

Glaser, B. (1999) The future of grounded theory, *Qualitative Health Research,* 9(6): 836–45.

Glaser, B. (2003) *The Grounded Theory Perspective II: Description's Remodelling of Grounded Theory Methodology.* Mill Valley, CA: Sociology Press.

Glaser, B. and Strauss, A. (1967) *The Discovery of Grounded Theory.* Chicago, IL: Aldine.

Glaser, J., Dixit, J. and Green, D. (2002) Studying hate crime with the Internet: what makes racists advocate racial violence, *Journal of Social Issues,* 58(1): 177–93.

Goldacre, B. (2012) *Bad Pharma*. London: Fourth Estate.

Gorard, S. (2006) *Using Everyday Numbers Effectively in Research*. London: Continuum.

Gough, D., Oliver, S. and Thomas, J. (2012) *An Introduction to Systematic Reviews*. London: Sage.

Grbich, C. (2013) *Qualitative Data Analysis: An Introduction*, 2nd edn. London: Sage.

Greene, J.C. (2007) *Mixed Methods in Social Inquiry*. San Francisco, CA: Jossey-Bass.

Green, L. (2010) *Understanding the Life Course: Sociological and Psychological Perspectives*. Cambridge: Polity.

Griffin, J. (1962) *Black Like Me*. London: Collins.

Guest, G. (2013) Describing mixed methods research: an alternative to typologies, *Journal of Mixed Methods Research*, 7(2): 141–51.

Hammersley, M. (1990) What's wrong with ethnography? The myth of theoretical description, *Sociology*, 24(4): 597–615.

Hammersley, M. (1992) *What's Wrong with Ethnography?* London: Routledge.

Hammersley, M. (2015) On ethical principles for social research, *International Journal of Social Research Methodology*, 18(4): 422–49.

Hammersley, M. and Atkinson, P. (2007) *Ethnography: Principles in Practice*, 3rd edn. London: Tavistock.

Harding, J. (2013) *Qualitative Data Analysis from Start to Finish*. London: Sage.

Harrits, G.S. (2011) More than method?: a discussion of paradigm differences within mixed methods research, *Journal of Mixed Methods Research*, 5(2): 150–66.

Hart, C. (1998) *Doing a Literature Review: Releasing the Social Science Research Imagination*. London: Sage.

Heidegger, M. (1962) *Being and Time*. Oxford: Basil Blackwell.

Heider, D. and Massanari, A.L. (eds) (2012) *Digital Ethics: Research and Practice*. New York: Peter Lang Publishing.

Higgins, J. and Green, S. (eds) (2011) *Cochrane Handbook for Systematic Reviews of Interventions*, version 5.1.0 (updated March 2011). The Cochrane Collaboration. Available at: www.cochrane-handbook.org.

Hine, C. (2000) *Virtual Ethnography*. London: Sage.

Ho, K. (2009) *Liquidated: An Ethnography of Wall Street*. Durham, NC: Duke University Press.

Hoinville, G., Jowell, R. and Associates (1985) *Survey Research Practice*. Aldershot: Gower.

Holton, J.A. and Walsh, I. (2017) *Classic Grounded Theory: Applications with Qualitative and Quantitative Data*. Thousand Oaks, CA: Sage.

Hoonakker, P. and Carayon, P. (2009) Questionnaire survey nonresponse: a comparison of postal mail and Internet surveys, *International Journal of Human–Computer Interaction*, 25(5): 348–73.

Howell, N. (1990) *Surviving Fieldwork: A Report of the Advisory Panel on Health and Safety in Fieldwork*. Washington, DC: American Anthropological Association.

Humphreys, L. (1975) *Tearoom Trade*. New Brunswick, NJ: Aldine Transaction.

Hunt, S.J. (2005) *The Life Course: A Sociological Introduction*. Basingstoke: Palgrave Macmillan.

Husserl, E. (1931) *Ideas: General Introduction to Pure Phenomenology*. London: George Allen & Unwin (reprinted 2012, London: Routledge).

Husserl, E. (1950) *Cartesian Meditations: An Introduction to Phenomenology*. The Hague: Martinus Nijhoff (reprinted 1999, Dordrecht: Kluwer).

Hutchby, I. and Wooffitt, R. (2008) *Conversation Analysis*. Cambridge: Polity Press.

Hutchison, E.D. (2015) *Dimensions of Human Behavior: The Changing Life Course*, 5th edn. Thousand Oaks, CA: Sage.

Israel, M. (2015) *Research Ethics and Integrity for Social Scientists*, 2nd edn. London: Sage.

Johnson, R.B. and Gray, R. (2010) A history of philosophical and theoretical issues for mixed methods research, in A. Tashakkori and C. Teddlie (eds) *Sage Handbook of Mixed Methods in Social and Behavioral Research*, 2nd edn. Thousand Oaks, CA: Sage.

Johnson, R.B. and Onwuegbuzie, A.J. (2004) Mixed methods research: a research paradigm whose time has come, *Educational Researcher*, 33(7): 14–26.

Jorgensen, D.L. (1989) *Participant Observation: A Methodology for Human Studies*. Thousand Oaks, CA: Sage.

Kamberelis, G. and Dimitriadis, G. (2013) *Focus Groups: From Structured Interviews to Collective Conversations*. London: Routledge.

Kaufer, S. and Chemero, A. (2015) *Phenomenology: An Introduction*. Cambridge: Polity.

Keats, D.M. (2000) *Interviewing: A Practical Guide for Students and Professionals*. Maidenhead: Open University Press.

Kemmis, S., McTaggart, R. and Nixon, R. (2014) *The Action Research Planner: Doing Critical Participatory Action Research*. Singapore: Springer.

Kent, R.A. (2015) *Analysing Quantitative Data: Variable-Based and Case-Based Approaches to Non-Experimental Datasets*. London: Sage.

Kirk, J. and Miller, M. (1986) *Reliability and Validity in Qualitative Research*. Beverly Hills, CA: Sage.

Kozinets, R. (2015) *Netnography: Redefined*. London: Sage.

Krippendorf, K. (2013) *Content Analysis: An Introduction to its Methodology*, 3rd edn. Thousand Oaks, CA: Sage.

Krosnick, J.A. (1991) Response strategies for coping with the cognitive demands of attitude measures in surveys, *Applied Cognitive Psychology*, 5(3): 213–36.

Kugelmann, R. (1999) Complaining about chronic pain, *Social Science and Medicine*, 49(12): 16–63.

Laslett, P. (1996) *A Fresh Map of Life: The Emergence of the Third Age*. Basingstoke: Macmillan.

Layder, D. (1993) *New Strategies in Social Research*. Cambridge: Polity Press.

Layder, D. (1998) *Sociological Practice: Linking Theory and Social Research*. London: Sage.

Lee, R. (1995) *Dangerous Fieldwork*. Thousand Oaks, CA: Sage.

Levinson, D. (1978) *Seasons of a Man's Life*. New York: Random House.

Lewin, K. (1946) Action research and minority problems, *Journal of Social Issues*, 2(4): 34–46.

Likert, R.A. (1932) A technique for the measurement of attitudes, *Archives of Psychology*, 22(140): 1–55.

Lincoln, Y. and Guba, E. (1985) *Naturalistic Enquiry*. Newbury Park, CA: Sage.

Lipscomb, M. (2008) Mixed method nursing studies: a critical realist critique, *Nursing Philosophy*, 9(1): 32–45.

Loizos, P. (2000) Video, film and photographs as research documents, in M.W. Bauer and G. Gaskell (eds) *Qualitative Researching with Text, Image and Sound*. London: Sage.

Machi, L.A. and McEvoy, B.T (2016) *The Literature Review: Six Steps to Success*, 3rd edn. Thousand Oaks, CA: Corwin.

Malinowski, B. (1922) *Argonauts of the Western Pacific*. London: Routledge & Kegan Paul.

Mann, S. (2016) *The Research Interview: Reflective Practice and Reflexivity in Research Processes*. Basingstoke: Palgrave Macmillan.

Marshall, C. and Rossman, G.B. (2011) *Designing Qualitative Research*, 5th edn. Thousand Oaks, CA: Sage.

Maxwell, J.A. (2016) Expanding the history and range of mixed methods research, *Journal of Mixed Methods Research*, 10(1): 12–27.

Mayer, K.U. (2003) The sociology of the life course and life span psychology – diverging or converging pathways, in U.M. Staudinger and U. Lindenberger (eds) *Understanding Human Development: Lifespan Psychology in Exchange with Other Disciplines*. Dordrecht: Kluwer Academic.

Mayo, E. (1933) *The Human Problems of an Industrial Civilization*. London: Routledge (reprinted 2003).

McKee, H.A. and Porter, J.E. (2009) *The Ethics of Internet Research: A Rhetorical, Case-based Process*. New York: Peter Lang.

McNiff, J. (2013) *Action Research: Principles and Practice*, 3rd edn. London: Routledge.

Mead, M. (1943) *Coming of Age in Samoa: A Study of Adolescence and Sex in Primitive Societies*. Harmondsworth: Penguin.

Mertens, D.M. (2009) *Transformative Research and Evaluation*. New York: Guilford.

Miles, M.B., Huberman, A.M. and Saldana, J.M. (2014) *Qualitative Data Analysis: A Methods Sourcebook*, 3rd edn. Thousand Oaks, CA: Sage.

Milgram, S. (1974) *Obedience to Authority: An Experimental View*. New York: Harper & Row.

Morgan, D.L. (2006) Focus groups, in V. Jupp (ed.) *The Sage Dictionary of Social Research Methods*. London: Sage.

Morgan, D.L. (2014) *Integrating Qualitative and Quantitative Methods: A Pragmatic Approach*. Thousand Oaks, CA: Sage.

Moustakas, C. (1992) Firebrand: the experience of being different, *The Human Psychologist*, 20(2/3): 175–88.

Moustakas, C. (1994) *Phenomenological Research Methods*. Thousand Oaks, CA: Sage.

Murchison, J. (2010) *Ethnography Essentials: Designing, Conducting, and Presenting Your Research*. San Francisco, CA: Jossey-Bass.

Murray, N. and Hughes, G. (2008) *Writing Up Your University Assignments and Research Projects: A Practical Handbook*. Maidenhead: Open University Press.

Murray, R. (2013) *Writing for Academic Journals*, 3rd edn. Maidenhead: Open University Press.

Neville, C. (2016) *The Complete Guide to Referencing and Avoiding Plagiarism*, 3rd edn. London: Open University Press.

Nilsen, A., Brannen, J. and Lewis, S. (eds) (2013) *Transitions to Parenthood in Europe: A Comparative Life Course Perspective*. Bristol: Policy Press.

O'Connell Davidson, J. (1995) The anatomy of 'free choice' prostitution, *Gender, Work and Organization*, 2(1): 1–10.

O'Dwyer, L. and Bernauer, J.A. (2014) *Quantitative Research for the Qualitative Researcher*. Thousand Oaks, CA: Sage.

O'Leary, M. (2014) *Classroom Observation*. London: Routledge.

O'Reilly, K. (2012) *Ethnographic Methods*, 2nd edn. London: Routledge.

Oakley, A. (1981) Interviewing women: a contradiction in terms, in H. Roberts (ed.) *Doing Feminist Research*. London: Routledge & Kegan Paul.

Oktay, J. (2012) *Grounded Theory*. Oxford: Oxford University Press.

Oliver, P. (2010) *The Student's Guide to Research Ethics*, 2nd edn. Maidenhead: Open University Press.

Oliver, P. (2012) *Succeeding with Your Literature Review: A Handbook for Students*. Maidenhead: Open University Press.

Onwuegbuzie, A.J. and Frels, R.K. (2013) Toward a new research philosophy for addressing social justice issues: critical dialectical pluralism, *International Journal of Multiple Research Approaches*, 7(1): 9–26.

Oppenheim, A.N. (2000) *Questionnaire Design, Interviewing and Attitude Measurement*, 2nd edn. London: Continuum.

Pawson, R. (2006) *Evidence-Based Policy: A Realist Perspective*. London: Sage.

Pawson, R. (2013) *The Science of Evaluation: A Realist Manifesto*. London: Sage.

Pawson, R. and Tilley, N. (1997) *Realistic Evaluation*. London: Sage.

Payne, J. and Barnfather, N. (2012) Online data collection in developing nations: an investigation into sample bias in a sample of South African university students, *Social Science Computer Review*, 30(3): 389–97.

Penn, G. (2000) Semiotic analysis of still images, in M.W. Bauer and G. Gaskell (eds) *Qualitative Researching with Text, Image, Sound*. London: Sage.

Perry, G. (2013) *Behind the Shock Machine: The Untold Story of the Notorious Milgram Psychology Experiments*. Melbourne: Scribe.

Petticrew, M. and Roberts, H. (2006) *Systematic Reviews in the Social Sciences: A Practical Guide*. Oxford: Blackwell.

Plummer, K. (2001) *Documents of Life 2: An Invitation to a Critical Humanism*, 2nd edn. London: Sage.

Polsky, N. (2006) *Hustlers, Beats and Others*. New Brunswick, NJ: Aldine Transaction.

Pope, C., Mays, N. and Popay, J. (2007) *Synthesizing Qualitative and Quantitative Health Research: A Guide to Methods*. Maidenhead: Open University Press.

Porter, S. (1993) Critical realist ethnography: the case of racism and professionalism in a medical setting, *Sociology*, 27(4): 591–601.

Prior, L. (2003) *Using Documents in Social Research*. London: Sage.

Prosser, J. and Schwartz, D. (1998) Photographs within the sociological research process, in J. Prosser (ed.) *Image-based Research: A Sourcebook for Qualitative Researchers*. London: Falmer.

Ragin, C. and Amoroso, L. (2011) *Constructing Social Research*, 2nd edn. Thousand Oaks, CA: Pine Forge Press.

Ragin, C. and Becker, H. (1992) *What Is a Case? Exploring the Foundations of Social Enquiry*. New York: Cambridge University Press.

Ramlo, S. (2016) Mixed method lessons learned from 80 years of Q methodology, *Journal of Mixed Methods Research*, 10(1): 28-45.

Ransome, P. (2013) *Ethics and Values in Social Research*. Basingstoke: Palgrave Macmillan.

Reason, P. and Bradbury, H. (eds) (2013) *Handbook of Action Research*, 2nd edn. London: Sage.

Reid, M. (2012) *Report Writing*. Basingstoke: Palgrave Macmillan.

Ridley, D.D. (2012) *The Literature Review: A Step-By-Step Guide for Students*, 2nd edn. London: Sage.

Riemer, J. (1979) *Hard Hats: The Work World of Construction Workers*. Beverly Hills, CA: Sage.

Riessman, C.K. (2003) *Narrative Analysis*. Newbury Park, CA: Sage.

Riessman, C.K. (2008) *Narrative Methods for the Human Sciences*. Thousand Oaks, CA: Sage.

Roethlisberger, F.J. and Dickson, W.J. ([1939] 2003) *Management and the Worker*. London: Routledge.

Rose, G. (2016) *Visual Methodologies: An Introduction to Researching with Visual Materials*, 4th edn. London: Sage.

Rumsey, S. (2008) *How to Find Information*, 2nd edn. Maidenhead: Open University Press.

Sartre, J.-P. (1956) *Being and Nothingness: An Essay on Phenomenological Ontology*. New York: Methuen.

Schön, D. (1983) *The Reflective Practitioner: How Professionals Think in Action*. New York: Basic Books.

Schonlau, M., Fricker, R. and Elliot, M. (2002) *Conducting Research Surveys via E-mail and the Web*. Rand Monograph MR-1480-RC. Available online at: http://www.rand.org/pubs/monograph_reports/MR1480.html.

Schutz, A. (1962) *Collected Papers*, vol. 1. The Hague: Martinus Nijhoff.

Schutz, A. (1967) *The Phenomenology of the Social World*. Evanston, IL: Northwestern University Press.

Scott, J. (1990) *A Matter of Record: Documentary Sources in Social Research*. Cambridge: Polity Press.

Seale, C. (1999) *The Quality of Qualitative Research*. London: Sage.

Settersten, R.A. (1997) The salience of age in the life course, *Human Development*, 40(5): 257–81.

Sidnell, J. (2010) *Conversation Analysis: An Introduction*. Chichester: Wiley-Blackwell.

Silver, C. and Lewins, A. (2014) *Using Software in Qualitative Research: A Step-by-Step Guide*, 2nd edn. London: Sage.

Silverman, D. (1985) *Qualitative Methodology and Sociology*. Aldershot: Gower.

Silverman, D. (2011) *Interpreting Qualitative Data: Methods for Analyzing Talk, Text and Interaction*, 4th edn. Thousand Oaks, CA: Sage.

Silverman, D. (2013) *Doing Qualitative Research: A Practical Handbook*, 4th edn. London: Sage.

Silverman, D. (2014) *Interpreting Qualitative Data*, 5th edn. London: Sage.

Simons, H. (2009) *Case Study Research in Practice*. London: Sage.

Smith, J.A., Flowers, P. and Larkin, M. (2009) *Interpretative Phenomenological Analysis: Theory, Method and Research*. London: Sage.

Smith, T.W. (2013) Survey-research paradigms old and new, *International Journal of Public Opinion Research*, 25(2): 218–29.

Somekh, B. (1995) The contribution of action research to development in social endeavours: a position paper on action research methodology, *British Educational Research Journal*, 21(3): 339–55.

Somekh, B. (2006) *Action Research: A Methodology for Change and Development*. Maidenhead: Open University Press.

Spencer, S. (2011) *Visual Research Methods in the Social Sciences: Awakening Visions*. London: Routledge.

Stake, R. (1995) *The Art of Case Study Research*. Thousand Oaks, CA: Sage.

Stevens, S.S. (1946) On the theory of scales of measurement, *Science*, 103(2684): 677–80.

Strauss, A.L. (1987) *Qualitative Analysis for Social Scientists*. Cambridge: Cambridge University Press.

Strauss, A.L. and Corbin, J. (1990) *Basics of Qualitative Research: Grounded Theory Procedures and Techniques*. London: Sage.

Strauss, A.L. and Corbin, J. (1998) *Basics of Qualitative Research: Techniques and Procedures for Developing Grounded Theory*, 2nd edn. Thousand Oaks, CA: Sage.

Sue, V.M. and Ritter, L.A. (2012) *Conducting Online Surveys*. Thousand Oaks, CA: Sage.

Swanborn, P. (2010) *Case Study Research: What, Why and How?* London: Sage.

Tashakkori, A. and Teddlie, C. (1998) *Mixed Methodology: Combining Qualitative and Quantitative Approaches*. Thousand Oaks, CA: Sage.

Tashakkori, A. and Teddlie, C. (eds) (2003) *Handbook of Mixed Methods in Social and Behavioral Research*. Thousand Oaks, CA: Sage.

Teddlie, C. and Tashakkori, A. (2009) *Foundations of Mixed Methods Research*. Thousand Oaks, CA: Sage.

Teddlie, C. and Johnson, R.B. (2009) Methodological thought since the 20th century, in C. Teddlie and A. Tashakkori (eds) *Foundations of Mixed Methods Research*. Thousand Oaks, CA: Sage.

Thomas, G. (2016) *How to Do Your Case Study: A Guide for Students and Researchers*, 2nd edn. London: Sage.

Thyer, B.A. (2012) *Quasi-Experimental Research Designs*. New York: Oxford University Press.

Tourangeau, R., Conrad, F. and Couper, M. (2013) *The Science of Web Surveys*. Oxford: Oxford University Press.

Tranfield, D., Denyer, D. and Smart, P. (2003) Towards a methodology for developing evidence-informed management knowledge by means of systematic review, *British Journal of Management*, 14(3): 207–22.

Turabian, K. (2013) *A Manual for Writers of Research Papers, Theses, and Dissertations*, 8th edn. Chicago, IL: University of Chicago Press.

Van Leeuwen, T. and Jewitt, J. (eds) (2001) *Handbook of Visual Analysis*. London: Sage.

Van Maanen, J. (ed.) (1995) *Representation in Ethnography*. Thousand Oaks, CA: Sage.

Van Manen, M. (1990) *Researching Lived Experience: Human Science for an Action Sensitive Pedagogy*. London, Ontario: Althouse.

Van Manen, M. (2016) *Phenomenology of Practice: Meaning-Giving Methods in Phenomenological Research and Writing*. London: Routledge.

Velleman, P.F. and Wilkinson, L. (1993) Nominal, ordinal, interval and ratio typologies are misleading, *American Statistician*, 47(1): 65–72.

Walker, I. (2010) *Research Methods and Statistics*. Basingstoke: Palgrave Macmillan.

Watkins, D. and Giola, D. (2015) *Mixed Methods Research*. Oxford: Oxford University Press.

Webb, E.J., Campbell, D.T., Schwartz, R.D. and Sechrest, L. (1966) *Unobtrusive Measures: Non-reactive Research in the Social Sciences*. Chicago, IL: Rand McNally.

Webster, M. and Sell, J. (2014) *Laboratory Experiments in the Social Sciences*, 2nd edn. Burlington, MA: Amsterdam Press.

Whyte, W.F. (1943) *Street Corner Society: The Social Structure of an Italian Slum*, 4th edn. Chicago, IL: University of Chicago Press (reprinted 1993.)

Wilson, R., Gosling, S.D. and Graham, L.T. (2012) A review of Facebook research in the social sciences, *Perspectives on Psychological Science*, 7(3): 203–20.

Wittgenstein, L. (1968) *Philosophical Investigations*. Oxford: Basil Blackwell.

Woods, P. (2012) *The Divided School*. London: Routledge.

Woods, P. (2006) *Successful Writing for Qualitative Researchers*, 2nd edn. London: Routledge.

Yin, R. (2014) *Case Study Research: Design and Methods*, 5th edn. Thousand Oaks, CA: Sage.

Yoder, P. and Symons, F. (2010) *Observational Measurement of Behavior*. New York: Springer.

Zuber-Skerritt, O. (ed.) (1996) *New Directions in Action Research*. London: Falmer Press.

Index